IN THE SHADOW
OF THE RED BANNER

IN THE SHADOW OF THE RED BANNER

Soviet Jews in the War against Nazi Germany

Yitzhak Arad

Yad Vashem * Jerusalem
The International Institute for Holocaust Research

Cover Design and Typesetting by S. Kim Glassman

ISBN: 978-965-229-487-6

1 3 5 7 9 8 6 4 2

Gefen Publishing House, Ltd.
6 Hatzvi Street
Jerusalem 94386, Israel
972-2-538-0247
orders@gefenpublishing.com

Gefen Books
600 Broadway
Lynbrook, NY 11563, USA
1-800-477-5257
orders@gefenpublishing.com

www.gefenpublishing.com

Printed in Israel   *Send for our free catalogue*

CONTENTS

This book is dedicated to

the half million

Soviet Jewish soldiers and partisans,

my comrades in arms,

who fought against Nazi Germany

in the Great Patriotic War.

The publication of this book was made possible
by a grant from the
Diana and Eli Zborowski Family Foundation

CHAPTER FOUR:
THE ARMED JEWISH UNDERGROUND

PREFACE

"We have often heard it said that there are no Jews at the front, that they don't fight. It is our duty to tell about how Jews did fight at the front…and to that end we must, as quickly as possible, publish a book which will convincingly tell the story about the part the Jews played in the war. Mere statistics are not enough. We need real stories, we need a book of Jews, heroes, who are fighting in the war for our country. The truth must be told, the whole truth, and that will be enough." (Ilya Ehrenburg at the plenary session of the Jewish Anti-Fascist Committee in Moscow, February 20, 1943)

This book is about the part played by the Jews of the Soviet Union in the Great Patriotic War (Velikaia Otechestvennaia *Voina*)[1] against Nazi Germany, and about their contribution to the costly victory, a story that has yet to be told in its entirety. They fought – and how they fought! – on the most arduous, blood-soaked front of the Second World War, on the front of the decisive battle in which Nazi Germany was defeated. Jews fought in the armies of all the Allies: the United States, Britain, France, Poland and others, and in every instance they contributed to victory. However, when considering the high military ranks held and the number of medals of valor won, no other Jewish soldiers can compare to the Soviet Jews who fell during the Great Patriotic War.

The Great Patriotic War began with the German invasion of the Soviet Union (code-named by Germany Operation Barbarossa) on June 22, 1941, and ended on May 9, 1945, with the German surrender. The Great Patriotic War was part of the Second World War, which was fought over the entire globe. It began on September 1, 1939, with the Nazi German invasion of Poland, and ended on September 2, 1945, with the Japanese surrender to the Allied forces.

For the Soviet Union, the Great Patriotic War was a defensive war, in which the Soviet peoples fought the invading German army. Nazi Germany's plan was to destroy the Soviet Communist state; turn its European areas over to German colonization; deny the indigenous peoples any form of independence, making them serfs of the German settlers; and murder the Jews. Most Soviet citizens bravely fought the Germans, not for the sake of Stalin and Communism but

---

1. *Otechestvo* means "homeland" in Russian, thus a literal translation of Velikaia Otechestvennaia Voina would be "the great war for the sake of the homeland," but in English it is known as the Great Patriotic War.

to protect their homes and homeland, to defend Mother Russia (Matushka Russia) from the foreign invader.

The Jews of the Soviet Union played an important role in the war. In the Soviet literature and historiography of the Second World War, there was a tendency to minimize their contribution. In 1948 members of the Jewish Anti-Fascist Committee were arrested, and in 1952 they were executed. One of the charges against them was that they had exaggerated the description of the role played by the Jews in the Soviet Union's achievements during the war, and that doing so expressed a trend of Jewish nationalism.

Jews of the Soviet Union fought on every front, from the Arctic Circle in the north to the Caucasian mountains in the south. They served in every branch of the army, on land, sea and in the air, and attained every commanding rank. There were Jews in the ranks of the partisans in the forests and among the commanders and organizers of the partisan movement; Jews were among the founders of the undergrounds in the cities in the territories occupied by the Germans. Jews played a critical role in the reestablishment and operation of the war industry evacuated from the territories occupied by the Germans and greatly contributed to the development of new weapons.

The introduction provides background information necessary for the understanding of the historical roots and cruel nature of the war. It relates to the ideological reasons Hitler and Nazi Germany attacked the Soviet Union, the place of the Jews in that ideology in general and of Soviet Jews in particular, and the strategic considerations behind the timing of the invasion. It also sheds light on Stalin's part in the outbreak of the war, based on documents only revealed in recent years. In addition, it stresses the unique nature of the fate of Soviet Jewry and their motivation to fight and sacrifice; as the first of European Jewry to face total annihilation, they were aware that this was a war for their very existence.

Chapter 1 is devoted to the Jewish soldiers and commanders who served in the Red Army and fought on its various fronts. It provides a chronology and describes the stages of the Great Patriotic War, highlighting the role the Jewish soldiers played in the war's decisive battles. Since there were no Jewish units in the Soviet army, I have related the activities and combat of individual Jews who excelled in battle and won high honors, from the lowest ranks as privates to the commanders of corps and armies.

One of the ways of locating Jewish fighters is the notation sometimes made of nationality or extraction on personal papers, in newspapers and in the various books dealing with the war. Another way of identifying Jews is through names (first or family) or the patronymic, which in Russia is customarily added as further identification. (The patronymic *Moiseevitch* would indicate a Jew whose father's name was Moses.) However, it is not always possible to identify a Soviet Jew by name. Many Jews have "Russian" names or names common among other peoples – either the result of a long process of assimilation, mixed marriages or the desire, for a variety of reasons, to hide their Jewish identity. Many changed their names during the war in fear of what might happen should they be captured by the Germans. As a result, many Jews fought and fell with non-Jewish names, and their Jewish identity will never be known. This chapter also deals with anti-Semitism in the ranks of the army and discusses whether the Jews were discriminated against regarding promotion, publicity of their deeds and the awarding of medals.

Recounting the acts of individual Jews provides an overall, if incomplete, picture of the part they played in the war against the German enemy. This chapter also provides an estimate of the number of Jewish soldiers who took part in the Great Patriotic War and the number of the fallen.

Chapter 2 deals with the role of the Jews in the war industry and weapons development. One of the main factors behind the Soviet army's victory, besides the valor and sacrifice of the soldiers at the front, was the success it had in evacuating the war industry from the territory conquered by the German army. About 80 percent of that industry was located in the territory occupied by the German army until the end of 1941 or in the vicinity of the battlefield, and it was in great part evacuated. The evacuation was carried out under terrible conditions of disorder and panic caused by the quick German advance. Nevertheless, during the hard winter months of 1941–42 and particularly during the following year, the war industry managed to compensate for the heavy losses in tanks, cannons, planes and other material sustained by the Soviet army during the first year of the war and to supply them with new, modern weapons. The Soviet war industry supplied the army with weapons that in both quantity and quality were as good as or better than those produced by the German army, which also exploited the factories of the countries it conquered throughout Europe. Among the industry's directors, engineers, foremen and workers, the contribution of the Jews was paramount. In addition, there were many Jews among the inventors and developers of all types of arms, from planes to guns and ammunition.

Chapter 3 deals with the environment and general conditions that gave birth to the Jewish resistance movement, the undergrounds and ghetto uprisings, the exodus to the forests and the partisan fighting in the occupied territories of the Soviet Union. To understand the ghetto underground's organization and goals, and the times of its appearance, this chapter describes the events of the Holocaust and its uniqueness, especially the public nature of the murders carried out by the Germans, which heightened the awareness that as Jews, they were doomed to death. Thus the first part of the chapter deals with the events of the Holocaust in the occupied territories, where the idea of fighting back was born. Another important factor, which gave the underground a direction and the hope that the ghetto uprising or escape from the ghetto had a goal that had a chance of success, was the fact that there were vast forests not far from the ghettos, and Soviet partisans were active in them. They and other armed forces, such as the Polish Armia Krajowa – AK (Home Army) or the Ukrainska Povstanska Armia – UPA (Ukrainian Insurgent Army), which were also active in the forests, and their relation to the Jews, influenced the ability of the Jews to organize and fight as partisans.

Chapter 4 deals with the establishment, goals and activities of the underground movements in the ghettos and the camps. Jewish undergrounds were organized in many ghettos, but they were not a unified organization, nor were they hierarchical. The undergrounds were specific to each ghetto and no contact existed between the various groups. Each ghetto's organization and activity were determined by its physical situation, such as proximity to the forests, as well as the unfolding of events relating to the ghetto. Therefore each underground is described individually, with the description of the individual groups providing an overall picture of the Jewish undergrounds. Important in this chapter are the dilemmas and arguments that took place in the underground regarding the decision to rebel in the ghetto or take to the forests, the relationship between the underground and the *Judenrat*, the challenge of how and where to procure weapons and relations with the non-Jewish underground groups; the ghetto uprisings are described as well. The chapter also deals with the Jews who were active in and among the leaders of the non-Jewish Soviet undergrounds, as well as with the undergrounds established by Jewish prisoners held in the mass killing sites who, by opening the pits and cremating the corpses of the victims, were forced by the Germans to engage in erasing their crimes. Underground groups were organized in some of the POW camps in Germany, with the aim of escaping, sabotaging in their workplaces, etc. Among the leaders of the groups were Jews who succeeded in concealing their identity.

Chapter 5 deals with the Jews in the forests – those who joined the partisan units or set up family camps. It examines the factors determining why Jews could find refuge in certain forests and not in others, and how topography and the attitude of the local population influenced them. The attitude of the Soviet partisans and their leadership toward the Jews, the existence of separate Jewish partisan units and examples of anti-Semitism are also examined. The situation of the Jews before the organized Soviet partisan movement took control of the "wild" units in the forests and what changed afterwards are also dealt with, as are the existence and fate of the family camps. The chapter gives an estimation of the number of Jews in the various forests and the number and stories of those who survived after the area was liberated.

Many books have been written about Soviet Jews who fought in the Soviet army, in the ghetto undergrounds and with the partisans against Nazi Germany. However, none of them recount the broad spectrum of Jewish activities during the war in their entirety: the army, the underground, the partisans, the battle waged by the prisoners of war for survival and the development and manufacture of weapons. This book and its descriptions are based on rich, varied archival sources, some of which have only been discovered in recent years, and on books and studies that have been published only lately. Most of the sources come from archives and books in Russia and the other members of the Commonwealth of Independent States that was formed when the Soviet Union fell apart. Other sources are Jewish, among them books published in both former Soviet republics and Israel, primarily in Russian and not accessible to the English speaker. In writing this book German sources were used as well.

I would like to thank the Jewish scholars Colonel Feodor Sverdlov, Aharon Rabinowitz and Gershon Shapiro, who devoted many years to the study of the role of Soviet Jews in the war against Nazi Germany. Their books, generally in Russian, were important in the research and writing of this book.

INTRODUCTION:
Background to the War –
Ideology and Geopolitical Developments:
March 1939–June 1941

1. Ideological Elements of Nazism:
Lebensraum, Race, Judaism and Marxism

The German attack on the Soviet Union, "Operation Barbarossa," was the product of Nazi ideology. The war was the realization of Germany and Adolf Hitler's aspirations to turn Germany into a world power, to achieve hegemony over Europe and to attain *Lebensraum*, "living space," for the German people in Eastern Europe, i.e., in Poland, the Soviet Union and along the eastern shore of the Baltic Sea. The immense stretches of land between Berlin and Moscow became the arena for the bloodiest battles of the Second World War. Hitler expressed his ideology in *Mein Kampf*, in which he wrote,

> Only an adequately large space on this earth assures a nation the freedom of existence.… If we speak of soil in Europe today, we can have primarily in mind only Russia and her vassal border states. Here Fate itself seems desirous of giving us a sign. By handing Russia to Bolshevism, it robbed the Russian nation of that intelligentsia.… It has been replaced by the Jew.… In Russian Bolshevism we must see the attempt undertaken by the Jews in the twentieth century to achieve world domination.…[1]

The German desire to expand eastward (*Drang nach Osten*, "the drive toward the east") had a racial dimension as well. Hitler said, "The Nordic race has the right to rule the world and we must take this racial right as the guiding star of our foreign policy."[2] His racist perception regarded the Jews as the greatest enemy. In his words, "The mightiest counterpart to the Aryan is represented

---

1.   Adolf Hitler, *Mein Kampf*, trans. Ralph Manheim, Sentry Edition (Boston: Houghton Mifflin, 1943), 643–46, 654–61.

2.   Alexander Dallin, *German Rule in Russia, 1941–1945: A Study of Occupation Policies* (London: Macmillan, 1957), 9. The comment was made in a conversation between Hitler and Otto Strasser on May 21, 1930.

by the Jew."[3] Hitler combined Nazi German ideology, based on expansion to the east, anti-Marxism and an infinite hatred for the Jews, with strategic policy directed at Eastern Europe, particularly the Soviet Union.

On January 30, 1939, Hitler gave a speech at the Reichstag in which he blamed the Jews for causing wars, saying, "If international financial Jewry inside and outside Europe should succeed in plunging the nations once more into a world war, the result would not be the Bolshevization of the earth and thereby the victory of Jewry, but the annihilation (*Vernichtung*) of the Jewish race in Europe."[4] One of Hitler's fundamental concepts was that Bolshevism and Judaism were one and the same, and the next war would bring about the destruction of both. He was of the opinion that through the war he could achieve two goals: the first, *Lebensraum* for the German people by eradicating the Soviet Union and occupying its territories in Eastern Europe; the second, getting rid of the sworn enemy, the Jewish people, starting with the Jews of the Soviet Union.

2. IDEOLOGY VS. REALPOLITIK: POLITICAL MOVES BETWEEN MARCH AND AUGUST 1939

The political conditions in Europe in the spring of 1939 had been fashioned by the Munich Agreement of September 29, 1938, and the German takeover of Czechoslovakia on March 15, 1939. Conditions were such that Hitler was convinced he could begin putting his expansionist ideology into practice in Eastern Europe. The appeasement policies of the Western powers (Britain and France) and their desertion of Czechoslovakia confirmed Hitler's opinion that the time and political conditions of Europe were ripe for continued German expansionism. The first target was Poland. In April 1939, after the German takeover of Czechoslovakia, Britain, France and the Soviet Union began fruitless discussions to create a mutual defense pact to stop German expansion. Poland and Romania, supported by the Western powers, were opposed to allowing the Red Army to enter their territory should Germany attack, fearing the Soviets would never leave. The Eastern European countries bordering on the Soviet Union viewed it as no less dangerous than Germany, and the Western powers were also distrustful of the Soviet Union's intentions.

---

3.   Hitler, *Mein Kampf*, 300–301, 305, 326.
4.   Adolf Hitler, *Reden und Proklamationen, 1932–1945*, ed. Max Domarus (Neustadt a.d. Aisch: Verlagsdruckerei Schmidt, 1962–63), 1058.

After the de facto acceptance of the German takeover of Czechoslovakia, the Soviet Union suspected the Western powers of encouraging German expansion to the east and promoting a German-Soviet war. On March 10, 1939, Stalin told the Eighteenth Congress of the Soviet Communist Party that he blamed the Western powers for intending "to provoke a conflict with Germany without visible grounds." Hinting to Germany that a dialogue was possible, he said that "Soviet policy in this situation [was] to preserve peace and carry out business relations with all countries...."[5]

Stalin was well aware that after the purges of the command staff in 1937–38, the Red Army needed some years to reorganize and train a new command cadre before it would be ready to wage a war. Under the circumstances, a Soviet-German war, without an alliance with Britain and France, should be prevented. The first signs of change in Soviet policy were in the media, which tempered their attacks against Nazi Germany. On May 3, 1939, Maxim Litvinov was dismissed as Soviet Union Peoples' Commissar of Foreign Affairs. Litvinov was a Jew who favored dialogue and a pact with the Western powers against Nazi Germany. His dismissal marked a change in Soviet foreign policy toward both sides. It was clear to Stalin that Litvinov the Jew was not suitable to discuss policy with Nazi Germany, and in his stead Stalin appointed Vyacheslav Molotov. Germany was only too happy to see the last of Litvinov and viewed it as a signal that the Soviet Union was ready for dialogue.

At the end of May 1939 the German embassy in Moscow sent out feelers to the Soviet foreign ministry concerning a possible rapprochement between Germany and the Soviet Union, with the intention of preventing the Soviets from joining the British-French coalition. In Hitler's assessment, if the Western powers were not sure they had the Soviet Union in their camp, they would not fight Germany if it declared war on Poland. On the other hand, if they did go to war, Germany would quickly force Poland to capitulate, at which point it would be able to turn its attention and forces to Western Europe without having to fight on two fronts. The lesson of the First World War, in which Germany had had to fight on two fronts and lost, had been well learned.

Negotiations regarding rapprochement between Germany and the Soviet Union were held in the spring and summer of 1939. At the same time, there

---

5.   Robert C. Tucker, *Stalin in Power: The Revolution from Above, 1928–1941* (New York: W.W. Norton, 1992), 587; Allan Bullock, *Hitler and Stalin: Parallel Lives* (New York: Vintage, 1993), 597–98.

were Soviet-Western negotiations about a collective defense pact against German aggression. The Soviet Union reserved the option to decide what would best serve its interests and with which side to reach an agreement.

After the Munich Agreement and Germany's takeover of all of Czechoslovakia, Stalin concluded that a European war in the foreseeable future was inevitable, and that the capitalist nations, headed by Britain and France, would reach a compromise with Hitler concerning his demands from Poland and enable him to turn his expansionist aims against the Soviet Union. Therefore, it was in the sake of Soviet interest that the oncoming war be fought between the European Fascist block – Germany and Italy – and the capitalist nations. Stalin's prognosis was that such a war, between two blocks hostile to the Soviet Union, would last several years and cause much bloodshed and suffering and would weaken both sides, a situation that in turn would bring about a wave of revolutions in the combatant countries, as had occurred during the First World War. That being the case, the Red Army, under the banner of offering aid to the revolutionary forces, would wash over Europe and the entire continent would fall like ripe fruit into the Communist basket. Stalin expressed this idea in a secret speech to the Politburo on August 19, 1939, four days before Ribbentrop's arrival in Moscow. The text of the speech was discovered only in recent years in the Osobii Archive in Moscow. Stalin said the following:

> The question of peace or war has reached a critical stage for us. If we sign a mutual aid pact with France and Britain, Germany will give up on Poland and seek a modus vivendi with the Western powers. War will be prevented but future events are liable to take a dangerous turn for the Soviet Union. On the other hand, if we accept the Germans' offer and sign a mutual nonaggression pact, they will naturally attack Poland, and French and British intervention will be unavoidable. A serious wave of riots and disorder will sweep over Western Europe. Under such conditions, we will have many opportunities to stand aside and hope to be able to intervene in the war when it is convenient for us to do so. The experience of the past twenty years has shown that in times of peace it is impossible for the Communist movement in Europe to be strong enough for a Bolshevik party to take over the government. The dictatorship of such a party will only be possible as the outcome of a great war. [Therefore] we must accept Germany's offer and cordially ask the Anglo-French delegation to leave....

We must deal with the results of a German defeat or victory in the war before the event. If Germany is defeated no one will be able to prevent the Sovietization of Germany and a Communist government will arise. We must not forget that a Soviet Germany will find itself in great danger if the Sovietization occurs as the result of a German defeat in a short war. In that case Britain and France will be strong enough to occupy Berlin and destroy a Soviet Germany. Our role, therefore, is to enable Germany to wage the longest possible war, exhausting Britain and France, so that they will not be able to overcome a Soviet Germany. By maintaining neutrality and waiting until the time is right, the Soviet Union will help the current German [government] and provide it with raw materials and foodstuffs....

Let us now examine a different assumption: a German victory.... If Germany is victorious, it will finish the war too drained to start an armed conflict against the Soviet Union for the next ten years.... In a defeated France, the French Communist Party will always be strong. It will be impossible to prevent a Communist revolution there and we will be able to exploit the situation to come to the aid of France and turn it into a [Soviet] ally. After that, all the nations under the aegis of a victorious Germany will [also] become our allies. We will then have a broad field of action to [work for] world revolution. Comrades! It is in the interest of the Soviet Union for a war to break out between the Reich and the Anglo-French capitalist block. We must do everything to make sure it lasts as long as possible to exhaust both sides. That is the reason we must agree to sign the treaty the Germans offer us and to work to make sure that war [takes place]... and to prepare for the time it ends...."[6]

Thus, Stalin clearly estimated that the oncoming war between the capitalist block and the Fascist block would enable the Soviet Union and Communism to take over Europe. In his assessment, signing a pact with Germany was necessary to ensure this aim.

---

6.   Yuri N. Afanasev, ed., *Drugaia Voina 1939–1945* (Moscow: Rossiiskii Gosudarst-
     vennyi Gumanitarnyi Universitet, 1996), 73–75.

3. THE RIBBENTROP-MOLOTOV PACT

Hitler and Stalin exchanged letters on August 20 and 21 and decided that the German foreign minister, Joachim Ribbentrop, would come to Moscow to sign the pact, the most important issues of which had already been agreed upon.[7] On August 23, 1939, the day after Ribbentrop arrived in Moscow, the document that came to be known as the Ribbentrop-Molotov Pact was signed. The official treaty was "an agreement for increasing mutual trade" and "a nonaggression pact," according to which "the two contracting parties undertake to refrain from any act of violence, any aggressive action and any attack on each other, either severally or jointly with other powers...."[8]

The pact also contained a secret protocol that divided Eastern Europe into spheres of influence: Poland was divided between the two sides, the border between them determined by the Vistula (Wisła), Narev and San rivers. Western Byelorussia, the western Ukraine and central Poland up to the Vistula would be turned over to the Soviet Union. In the north, Lithuania would be under German sphere of interest, while Latvia, Estonia and Finland would be under Soviet sphere of interest. The Soviets noted their interest in Bessarabia, which was part of Romania, while Germany stated it had no political interest in that region.

The pact served the interests of both sides. It freed the Soviet Union from the worry that Germany would invade it at that time, and gave the Red Army the breathing space it needed to strengthen itself after it had been weakened by Stalin's 1937 and 1938 purges of army officers.[9] It also gave the Soviet Union vast territories in eastern Poland (distancing the German army far to the west of the original border) and spheres of influence in both northeast and southeast Europe. Ideologically, a war between Germany and the capitalist countries, which would weaken both sides, served the interests of the Communist Soviet Union.

The treaty gave the Germans freedom to act against Poland, and should Britain and France intervene, the possibility of fighting a one-front war after Poland's swift defeat. The economic articles of the pact promised Germany would receive the Soviet raw materials that were important to its military industry. Germany was also presented with a common border with the Soviet

---

7.   Anthony Read and David Fisher, *The Deadly Embrace: Hitler, Stalin and the Nazi-Soviet Pact, 1939–1941* (New York and London: W.W. Norton, 1988), 227–28.
8.   Ibid., 253–55.
9.   During the purges, Stalin killed or imprisoned 80 percent of Red Army commanders holding the rank of regiment commander or higher.

Union, which, in accordance with Nazi ideology, would eventually serve as the German people's *Lebensraum*. The pact was a German tactical step and not a change in strategic plans. In the long run, the Soviet Union was its target for war, conquest and occupation. On August 22, 1939, while Ribbentrop was on his way to Moscow, Hitler announced to the generals assembled at Berghof that he had decided to attack Poland. Of the improved relations with the Soviet Union he said, "It was Litvinov's dismissal that decided me. It struck me like a cannonball that here was a sign of change in Moscow towards the Western Powers."[10] He noted the German people's need for *Lebensraum* and told the generals that the German army would have to be cruel. "Who remembers the Armenians of World War One? Our brutalities will be forgotten. They will not even be noticed, after we have won." As for the future of Eastern Europe, he said, "Poland will be depopulated and settled with Germans. The fate of Russia will be exactly the same after Stalin's death.… We will break with the Soviet Union, then there will be the dawn of German rule on earth."[11]

4. POLITICAL AND MILITARY DEVELOPMENTS: SEPTEMBER 1939–JUNE 1941

The Heightening of Soviet Union Control over Eastern Europe

On the morning of September 1, 1939, the German army invaded Poland. In response, on September 3 Britain and France declared war on Germany, and the Second World War began. On the morning of September 17, the Red Army crossed the Polish border. Within a few days and with almost no resistance from the Polish army, the Soviet Union took over western Byelorussia and the western Ukraine, including the cities of Vilnius (Vilna), Bialystok and Lvov. The official justification for the invasion was that "the Polish state and its government have in fact ceased to exist.… The Soviet government has directed the High Command of the Red Army to give the order to its troops to cross the Polish frontier and to take under their protection the life and property of the population of the Western Ukraine and Western Byelorussia."[12]

---

10. Read and Fisher, *Deadly Embrace*, 242.
11. Karl Schleunes, "The Making of War and the Final Solution," in *The Shoah and the War*, ed. Asher Cohen et al. (New York: Peter Lang, 1992), 31; *Documents on International Affairs 1939–1946*, vol. 1, *March–September 1939*, ed. Arnold J. Toynbee (London: Oxford University Press, 1951), 446.
12. Read and Fisher, *Deadly Embrace*, 336.

Ribbentrop went to Moscow again on September 27, 1939, the day Warsaw surrendered to the Germans, to discuss the border between the German- and Soviet-occupied territories in Poland. The following day an agreement was signed that altered the one of August 23. The Soviet Union waived its rights to the territory in central Poland and the border was moved eastward, from the Vistula to the Bug, and in return Lithuania was made a Soviet sphere of influence.

The signing of the Ribbentrop-Molotov pact led to an immediate change in the Soviet media's attitude toward Nazi Germany. The terms "Fascist barbarians" and "Fascist beasts" were no longer used. The entire party propaganda machine was recruited to explain the new political line and the great benefits in store for the Soviet Union. The Red Army as well changed the propaganda it had used to indoctrinate the troops. Stalin told Lev Mekhlis, who was Jewish and the head commissar of the Red Army, "not to make the Germans angry.... The *Red Star* [the Red Army newspaper] often writes about Fascism and Fascists. Stop, the situation has changed. There is no need to scream about it any more. There is a time and place for everything. There is no need for Hitler to get the impression that we are not doing anything but preparing to go to war against him."[13]

Soviet military publications gave the German version, which claimed that at dawn on September 1, 1939, the Poles had opened fire with the intention of taking over German lands.[14] In the Soviet media, neither the leaders of the Communist Party nor the public voiced opinions about the sharp turn in Soviet foreign policy and the pact with Nazi Germany. After the recent wave of purges, no one would dare say anything openly against Stalin or his policies.

In the new political and military reality created by the signing of the Ribbentrop-Molotov pact and by the division of Poland, Moscow turned to strengthening its hold on the Baltic states. Early in October 1939, Estonia, Latvia and Lithuania (which according to the pact had become Soviet spheres of influence) were forced to sign a mutual aid agreement with the Soviet Union, allowing the Red Army to establish military bases on their soil. In addition, as part of the agreement with Lithuania and in compensation, Vilnius and part of the Vilnius district passed into Lithuanian control on October 28, 1939.

---

13. Dimitrii Volkogonov, *Stalin: Politicheskii Portret*, vol. 2 (Moscow: Novosti, 1992), 135.
14. *Voyenny' Historicheski Zhurnal* 1, no. 6 (1940): 69.

Demands similar to those imposed on the Baltic states were also presented to Finland, including the transfer to the Soviet Union of certain territories close to Leningrad and the dismantling of fortifications along the border. Finland rejected the demands. On November 30, 1939, the Soviet Union attacked; the war between the two countries lasted until March 13, 1940. Despite its superior numbers and the quantity of its arms, the Red Army did not easily defeat the small Finnish army. The 1937–38 purges had severely damaged the commanding ranks of the Red Army and were the cause of its poor showing in the war. Nevertheless, its numerical and technological superiority forced the Finns to sue for peace and sign a treaty. Finland ceded the territories near Leningrad and gave in to other Soviet demands, but it did manage to preserve its independence. The war with Finland cost the Red Army heavy losses and was fraught with failure, but more importantly, it proved to Stalin that his army was not ready for a large-scale, modern war. His first step was to appoint General Semyon Timoshenko as Defense Minister. The 45-year-old Timoshenko, who had served with distinction in the war with the Finns, replaced Kliment Voroshilov, and the 43-year-old General Kiril Meretskov was appointed chief of staff of the Red Army. Generals who had commanded the Red Army since the Civil War in Russia (1918–22) were replaced by members of the younger generation. In January 1941 the commanding officers held war exercises in which the talents of General Georgy Zhukov were noticed, and Stalin appointed him chief of staff instead of Meretskov. However, the six months remaining before the Germans attacked the Soviet Union were not enough for Timoshenko and Zhukov to make the far-reaching changes needed by the army.

The military developments in Western and northern Europe worried the Soviet Union a great deal. In April 1940, Germany conquered Denmark and Norway. In May, Belgium, Holland and Luxemburg were crushed under the Nazi boot and Panzer divisions were moving toward Paris. The British forces abandoned their heavy arms and retreated by sea from Dunkirk. On June 10, Italy declared war on Britain and France, and a few days later Paris fell and France surrendered.

Soviet policy after the Ribbentrop-Molotov pact was based on the assumption that a war in Western Europe would be long, bloody and weaken both sides. However, Germany's rapid victories overturned that assumption. Not only was Germany not weakened, it was strengthened and emerged as the power clearly in control of Europe. The Soviets feared lest Britain fall as well, which would free Germany to turn its forces against the Soviet Union. The Soviet Union therefore decided to reinforce its foothold in Eastern Europe. On June 14, 1940, the Soviet Union issued an ultimatum to the governments of Lithuania, Latvia and Estonia, demanding they allow more Soviet troops to enter their countries and establish governments friendly to the Soviet Union. Without waiting for an answer, Soviet forces crossed the border and took over all three countries. On June 26, 1940, the Soviet Union issued an ultimatum to Romania, demanding the return of Bessarabia and the cession of northern Bukovina, insisting its request be met within 24 hours. The German ambassador in Bucharest advised Romania to comply and Romania was forced to yield these areas. On June 28, the Red Army entered Bessarabia and northern Bukovina and within a few days had taken over the entire region. The Soviet Socialist Republic of Moldavia was established in Bessarabia, and northern Bukovina was annexed to the Soviet Ukraine. The Soviet Union thus implemented all the expansionist plans in its spheres of influence, as defined in the Ribbentrop-Molotov pact, and moved its borders hundreds of miles to the west between the Baltic and Black seas. The annexed territories were important for Soviet defense because they distanced the German threat from the center of the country.

Hitler's Decision to Attack the Soviet Union

Hitler decided to attack the Soviet Union in July 1940, after the fall of France and the initiation of the Battle of Britain. Despite Germany's stunning victories in continental Europe and the fact that Britain battled alone, the island country still refused to come to an arrangement with Germany. In Hitler's assessment, the British refusal stemmed from the hope that a Soviet-German war was inevitable and that its own military situation would subsequently improve. At the same time, Hitler was worried by the Soviet takeover of Lithuania, Latvia, Estonia, Bessarabia and northern Bukovina, and by its strengthened position in Eastern Europe. On July 31, 1940, he announced to his commanders his decision to attack the Soviet Union. General Franz Halder, who was Chief of Staff of the Army High Command (Oberkommando des Heeres – OKH) wrote in his diary of Hitler's announcement to his officers at the Berghof that "Russia is the factor by [sic] which England sets the greatest store.... If Russia is beaten, England's last hope is gone.... Decision: as a result of this argument, Russia must be dealt with. Spring 1941."[15]

---

15. Walter Warlimont, *Inside Hitler's Headquarters, 1939–45*, trans. R.H. Barry (London: Weidenfeld and Nicolson, 1964), 113–14. General Warlimont was deputy

Hitler believed that a war against the Soviet Union would serve an additional strategic purpose. He had followed the increase in American military strength and noted the aid the United States extended to the British, and he was afraid that in a year or two America might join Britain in the war against Germany. A war against the Soviet Union would encourage Japan, which had expansionist aspirations in southeast Asia, to attack American- and British-controlled territories there without fear that the Soviet Union, with which Japan had clashed in Manchuria, would be able to wage war against it.[16]

Beyond those considerations, stemming from the desire to subdue Britain as quickly as possible, Hitler's decision to attack the Soviet Union was strategic and based on the Nazi ideology of expanding to the east and destroying the Jewish Bolshevik state. Thus the German army began preparations for the attack, moving large forces from Western Europe into occupied Poland and positioning units in Finland. On September 27, 1940, a comprehensive mutual aid pact was signed in Berlin by Germany, Italy and Japan. On October 11, with Romanian acquiescence, the German army entered the country on the pretext that it had to "defend [the Romanian] oil fields against British plots." All the moves were directed against the Soviet Union. While the scenario was being played out in Central Europe, Molotov was invited to visit Berlin on the pretext of discussing the strengthening of German-Soviet relations in light of the political and military changes in Europe, and he arrived on November 11. His visit yielded no practical results. The Germans' only aim had been to mislead the Soviet Union concerning its true intentions, and events on the ground proved it had been achieved.[17]

On December 18, 1940, the Wehrmacht's High Command issued Directive No. 21, Operation Barbarossa, the code name for the attack on the Soviet Union. As to the military aims of the attack, it said that "the German armed forces must be prepared to crush Soviet Russia in a quick campaign even before the conclusion of the war against England.... Preparations are to be completed by May 15, 1941.... The ultimate object is to establish a defense line against Asiatic Russia from a line running from the Volga River to Archangel."[18]

---

chief of operations for the Oberkommando der Wehrmacht. The OKW was the high command of all the German armed forces, including the land, air and navy. The OKH was the high command of the land forces.

16. Ian Kershaw, *Hitler, 1936–1945: Nemesis* (New York: W.W. Norton, 2001), 341.
17. Tucker, *Stalin in Power*, 616–19; Bullock, *Hitler and Stalin*, 681–82.
18. Nuremberg Documents PS-446, in Bullock, *Hitler and Stalin*, 681.

The economic exploitation of the territories of the Soviet Union was an important factor in the preparations for Operation Barbarossa. To that end, in March 1941 the Command for Economic Direction of the East (Wirschafts-fuhrungsstab Ost) was established, whose instructions were issued in a document nicknamed the Green Folder (Grune Mappe). The folder's main thesis was that "every necessary means had to be employed in the immediate exploitation of the occupied territories for the good of Germany…to unconditionally ensure supplies to the army by the drastic confiscation of all products and reserves in the occupied territories, especially agricultural produce.…"[19] It was clear that food supplies for the large German army on the eastern front would have to come from the occupied territories in the Soviet Union. Food for the occupied civilian populations was not a consideration, implying they would suffer a famine.

German Preparations for the Destruction of the Soviet Union and the Jews

Hitler was of the opinion that the war against the Soviet Union would be different from those fought so far against Poland, France, Britain and the other European countries. On March 3, 1941, he gave instructions to General Alfred Jodl, Chief of the OKW (Oberkommando der Wehrmacht) Operation Staff, to prepare an appendix to Directive No. 21 called Special Instructions for Directive No. 21, stating that "The forthcoming campaign is more than a mere armed conflict: it is a collision between two different ideologies.… This war will not be ended merely by the defeat of the enemy armed forces.… The Bolshevist-Jewish intelligentsia must be eliminated.… We must under all circumstances avoid allowing a nationalist Russia to appear in place of Bolshevist Russia."[20] It was the first document relating to Germany's preparations for attacking the Soviet Union that mentioned the destruction of the Jews. Hitler intended that part of these missions should not be assigned to the army but delegated to Himmler and the SS. Accordingly, an OKW Directive No. 21 was issued on March 13, 1941: "The Reichführer SS has been given by the Führer certain special tasks within the operation zone of the Army: these stem from the necessity finally to settle the conflict between two opposing political systems."[21]

---

19.   Norbert Müller, *Wehrmacht und Okkupation, 1941–1944* (Berlin: Deutscher Mili-tarverlag, 1971), 55–56.
20.   Warlimont, *Inside Hitler's Headquarters*, 150–151.
21.   Ibid., 153; Nuremberg Documents NOKW-2302.

The "special tasks" Himmler received were not specified in the document. However, it was clear that they included the elimination of the "Bolshevist-Jewish intelligentsia" in accordance with the directives issued by Hitler ten days previously. The document gave Himmler and the SS, with the agreement and collaboration of the army, the authority to eliminate all the elements that belonged, in their opinion, to the Soviet "political system," first and foremost the Jews. Implementation of the special tasks was put into the hands of the Main Office for Reich Security (Reichssicherheitshauptamt – RSHA), run by Reinhard Heydrich and subordinate to Himmler.

In May–June 1941, the OKW issued three Hitler-inspired directives. One, dated May 13, 1941, concerning military jurisdiction in the regions of Operation Barbarossa, stated that "there is no need to punish members of the Wehrmacht and those belonging to it for crimes committed against enemy civilians, even if, at the time, this act was a military crime...."[22] Thus in advance members of the army were granted individual carte blanche to carry out atrocities against civilian populations without being subject to punishment. On May 19, 1941, the OKW issued Special Order No. 1 to Directive No. 21 with an appendix entitled "The Behavior of German Forces in the Soviet Union," which said that "Bolshevism is a sworn enemy.... This struggle requires the use of cruel and determined means against the Bolshevist propagandists, partisans, saboteurs and Jews...."[23] The directive grouped Jews with saboteurs, and in times of war the fate of saboteurs is clearly execution. A third document was issued by the OKW on June 6, 1941. Entitled "Guidelines for the Treatment of Political Commissars," it stated that "the Political Commissars...are the real bearers of resistance.... Therefore, when they are captured in battle or in the course of resistance, they are, as a matter of principle, to be eliminated immediately with a weapon...."[24]

The orders made it quite clear that the army toed Hitler's line, i.e., the war with the Soviet Union was not merely military, it was ideological as well. It differed from all the other wars Germany had waged since September 1939, and legitimized brutal behavior toward civilian populations, prisoners of war and Jews.

---

22. Norbert Müller, *Deutsche Besatzungspolitik in der UdSSR* (Köln: Pahl-Rugenstein, 1980), 64–66.
23. Ibid., 53–54.
24. Nuremberg Documents NOKW-484.

CHAPTER ONE:
JEWS IN THE ARMY AND AT THE FRONTS IN THE GREAT PATRIOTIC WAR

1. THE STATUS OF JEWS IN THE RED ARMY: 1918–1939

Jewish Fighters in the Revolution and the Civil War

Soviet Jews were prominent in the Red Army, with significant numbers of Jews in every commanding rank and on every front of the Great Patriotic War – a phenomenon that developed over the course of the Red Army's history. Between 1827 and 1917, Jews were drafted and fought in Russia's wars but suffered from relentless anti-Semitism and discrimination, preventing them almost entirely from reaching commanding ranks. The revolution that granted the Jews full citizenship and the establishment of the Soviet state led to a change in their status in the army as well; many thousands of Jews joined the Red Army after various counter-revolutionary forces had killed tens of thousands of Jews in pogroms. Among the first organizers of the Red Guards, which brought the Communists to power in the October revolution of 1917, were Yakov Sverdlov in St. Petersburg, Anatoly Poliakov in Moscow and Semyon Oritzky in Odessa – all Jews. The man who organized the Red Army (officially founded in 1918), commanded it during the Civil War and deserved credit for many of the revolution's victories was Lev Trotsky – also Jewish.

Most of the officers in the tsar's army had joined the counter-revolutionary forces, leaving the Red Army with a severe lack of talented, experienced officers. The new commanders, many of them Jewish, were ideologically loyal to the Communist régime. Part of them joined the professional army after the Civil War. They were promoted to commanding ranks and, in the time between the two world wars, were among those who built up the Red Army.

According to the 1929 census, Jews made up 1.7 percent of the total male population of the Soviet Union. However, 2.1 percent of the army was Jewish and 4.4 percent of the officers; of the political officers, 10.3 percent were Jewish.[1]

---

1.   Dov Levin, "Facts and Estimates of the Jews in the Red Army during the Second World War" in *Masua* 19 [Hebrew], based on articles in the Yiddish Soviet newspaper *Der Emmes* (The truth), November 19, 1930; Arkady Timor, "Jews in the Red Army," in *Jewish Soldiers in the Armies of Europe* [Hebrew], eds. Yehuda

Stalin's purges, most of which took place between 1937 and 1939, removed many high- and intermediate-level Red Army officers, including Jews.[2]

Soviet Jews in the Spanish Civil War (1936–1939)

During the Spanish Civil War, Soviet soldiers and officers, many of them Jewish,[3] fought side-by-side with the Republicans. It was the first arena in which Jews fought against Nazi German soldiers, who fought for Franco's Loyalists. During 1937 and 1938, General Grigory Shtern was chief military advisor for the Spanish Republican government. General Yakov Shmushkevich (who in Spain was called General Duglas) was chief advisor to the Republican air force, composed primarily of Soviet planes and pilots, and Semyon Krivoshin commanded the Soviet tank units.[4]

Slutzky and Mordechai Kaplan (Tel Aviv: Maarakhot, 1977), 132. Timor used the 1926 census.

2.   F.D. Sverdlov, *Evrei Generaly* (Moscow, 1993), 13–14, 262–69. About 40,000 higher commanders were executed. Among the executed were the Jewish generals Yonah Yakir, who was one of the founders of the Red Army during the revolution; Grigory Shtern, who was chief of staff of the army in the Far East and distinguished himself against the Japanese; Yakov Gamarnik, who was forced to commit suicide; Air Force general Yakov Shmushkevich, who was arrested a few weeks before the German invasion of the Soviet Union and executed on October 18, 1941. The names are known of fifteen other Jewish generals who served as corps or division commanders. Hundreds of Jewish officers of various rank fell victim to the purges, some of whose names will never be known.

3.   Alan Rockman, *Jewish Participation in the International Brigade in the Spanish Civil War, 1936–1939* (Michigan, 1984). According to Rockman, of the 45,000 soldiers in the International Brigade, 7,000–10,000 were Jews. The exact number of soldiers sent by the Soviet Union is unknown, but according to Timor (133), 12 of the 30 tank instructors sent to Spain were Jewish. The number serves as an indication of the overall number of Jews in the Soviet delegation.

4.   Sverdlov, *Evrei Generaly*, 118. When Shtern and Shmushkevich returned from Spain they fought in the battles against the Japanese in the Far East in 1938.

2. The Numbers and Status of Jews in the Red Army during the War

A Numerical Estimation

On June 22, the first day of the war, all men born between 1905 and 1918 were drafted. Especially in the western Soviet Union, the draft was carried out under extremely difficult conditions of aerial bombings, confusion and hasty removal of government institutions to the east. Many of the prospective draftees were killed by the Germans on their way to mobilization centers. Nevertheless, by July 1, 5.3 million soldiers had been speedily inducted and sent to the front.[5] Estimation of the number of Jews in the Soviet armed forces during the war is based on official Soviet data relating to the overall number of men in uniform at any given time between June 22, 1941, and August 5, 1945, the day Japan surrendered and the Second World War ended.

On the eve of the Second World War, the Soviet Union changed its military service law to include 19-year-old men and 18-year-old high school graduates. On the eve of the German invasion, men born between 1919 and 1922 were in uniform, and with the officers in the standing army the number of soldiers was 4,901,852, with some 700,000 in the NKVD, including the Border Guards.[6]

During the war, all men aged 55 and younger were drafted. In May 1945, with the surrender of Nazi Germany, the total number of the Soviet Union's armed forces stood at 12,840,000, more than a million of whom had been wounded and hospitalized.[7] According to data published in the Soviet Union in 1993, 34,476,700 soldiers served in the Red Army during the war. In 1940, 194,000,000 people lived in the Soviet Union and its annexed territories (western Byelorussia, the western Ukraine, the Baltic states, Bessarabia and northern Bukovina). Thus, during 1941–45, more than 17.5 percent of the Soviet population was in uniform, but only one third of the population served in the army at the same time.[8]

---

5. *Velikaya Otechestvennaya Voina 1941–1945, Slovar-Spravochnik*, ed. M.M. Kirian et al. (Moscow: Politizdat, 1988), 12, 15.

6. G.F. Krivosheyev, et al., *Grif Secretnosti Sniat* (Moscow: Voennoye Izdatelstvo, 1993), 139.

7. *Encyklopedia Drugiey Wojny Swiatowej* (Warsaw, 1975), 780; Krivosheyev, *Grif Secretnosti*, 141.

8. Krivosheyev, *Grif Secretnosti*, 139.

According to the January 1939 census, the population of the Soviet Union was 170,467,000. With a natural increase of 2.5 percent by June 1941, the Soviet Union's total population was more than 178,000,000 within its September 1939 borders (prior to the annexation). On that basis, an attempt will be made to estimate the number of Jews serving in the Red Army during the Second World War, starting with those living within the pre-September 1939 boundaries. According to the 1939 census, there were 3,021,000 Jews, 1.78 percent of the total Soviet Union population. Demographer Yakov Leshchinski states that at least a quarter of a million Jews hid their identity, bringing the total number to at least 3,270,000. A natural increase of approximately 2 percent over a period of two years should be added, so that it can safely be assumed that in September 1939 the Jewish population of the Soviet Union was about 3,335,000.

If it can be assumed that the percentage of mobilized Jews was the same as that of the overall Soviet population, i.e., 1.78 percent, then there were more than 600,000 Jews in the Red Army. The actual number was smaller by about 120,000–140,000, since in certain areas of Byelorussia and the Ukraine, which had large Jewish populations, not everyone who was eligible for the draft was mobilized due to the speed of the German conquest and the confusion prevailing on the eve of the occupation. In addition, of the approximately one million Jews trapped in the occupied territories, the men born before 1905 who had been drafted into the Red Army were not initially mobilized. In 1943 and 1944 those territories were liberated and the draft of the local population was reinstated—but by that time the Nazis had killed virtually all the Jews there. Thus, the number of Jews who served in the Soviet armed forces who lived within the pre-September 1939 borders of the Soviet Union was between 460,000 and 480,000.

The number of men drafted into the army was much smaller in the territories annexed by the Soviet Union during 1939–40. Over two million Jews lived there and found themselves under occupation during the first days and weeks of the war. There were no soldiers in reserve duty, and thus the order issued on the first day of the German invasion, to mobilize the men born during the 14 relevant years, did not include those in the annexed territories. In 1940, in western Byelorussia and the western Ukraine, men born between 1919 and 1922 were drafted. The number of Jews inducted into the army from those areas is estimated at 15,000–20,000.[9] The number of Jews drafted from among

---

9.   In eastern Byelorussia and the eastern Ukraine there were about 1,300,000 Jews.

the refugees who fled to the heart of the Soviet Union should also be included, since most of them were of draft age. It is worthwhile noting that many of the Byelorussians and Ukrainians living in the annexed western territories deserted during the great retreat of the first months of the war. As a result, in October 1941 an order was issued stating that all enlisted men who were residents of western Byelorussia, the western Ukraine, Bessarabia and northern Bukovina would be removed from the army and transferred to the "work army" (*trudo-vaya armia*). However, many Jews managed to evade the new order, remaining in the army to fight.[10] There are no data relating to the number of refugees who were drafted into the Red Army, but 15,000–20,000 is a fair estimation. Thus the number of Jews from the annexed territories who served in the Red Army was 30,000–40,000, and the total number of Jews in the Red Army was 490,000–520,000, although not at all times throughout the war. This number includes Jewish soldiers who fell in the first weeks of the war and those who were enlisted near the end of the war and served for only a short time. In addition, 17,000–20,000 Polish Jews were drafted into the Polish army established in the Soviet Union, some of them in General Anders' army and others in the Polish People's Army (Armia Ludowa).[11]

According to an official Soviet source relating to the national composition of 200 fighting divisions in the summer of 1943, 1.5–1.6 percent of all such soldiers were Jewish.[12] That does not take into account those who hid their Jewish identities for various reasons, such as anti-Semitism and the fear of what would befall them should they be taken prisoner. Therefore, it can be estimated that about 1.78 percent of those divisions were Jewish, similar to the percentage within the population of the Soviet Union. In 1944, when Byelorussia and the western Ukraine were liberated, thousands of Jewish partisans who had fought

---

Between 25,000 and 30,000 of them were males born between 1919 and 1922.

10. Levin, "Facts and Estimates," 85–86. In the Yad Vashem archives there are testimonies from Jewish Red Army soldiers relating to the same period, who recount their attempts, and on occasion successes, to remain in the fighting army.

11. *Register of Jewish Survivors*, vol. 2, *List of Jews in Poland* (Jerusalem: Jewish Agency, 1945), lists the names of more than 57,000 Jews who were in Poland in August 1945. It notes that the Polish People's Army contained 13,000 Jews. The numbers of those who fell and were wounded and released and a few thousand from Anders' army should be added.

12. Artyomov, *Bratskii Boyevoi Soyuz Narodov S.S.S.R. v. Vielikoi Otechestvennoi Voyne* (Moscow, 1975), 55–59.

the Germans in the forests enlisted, as well as those Jews who had survived the Nazi camps, or who had lived with forged documents or in hiding.

Jewish Generals and Heroes of the Soviet Union

The Soviet Union did not publish the numbers and national data of generals (and similar navy ranks) who served in the Red Army during the Second World War. According to names collected by historian Colonel Fyodor Davidovich Sverdlov, who was an outstanding officer during the Great Patriotic War, there were 305 Jewish generals.[13] Most of these generals received their rank during the war, nine commanded armies, 12 commanded corps and 34 commanded divisions.[14]

There are no exact numbers for Jews awarded the title of Hero of the Soviet Union. Gershon Shapiro gives the names and biographies of 150 Jews who were decorated as Heroes of the Soviet Union.[15] Colonel Sverdlov gives the names of 120 who were awarded the decoration and notes 20 others who were half-Jewish and listed as Russian, Ukrainian or other nationalities. He also gives the names of 11 Jews who received the award before the war and two after it.[16] However, neither Shapiro's nor Sverdlov's list was complete. On occasion new names are discovered. A pilot's daughter sent the following letter to Israel: "I know that in Israel a book called *Jewish Heroes of the Soviet Union* was published. My late father, Pyotr Danielovich Prosvetov, was given the award. His name does not appear in the aforementioned book. My father hid his nationality and Jewish identity. I would like to have him remembered. He died in 1993." In fact, a Soviet publication about Heroes of the Soviet Union names Prosvetov as having served in the 23rd Air Regiment of the Fourth Air Corps, and as having flown 290 missions during the war and receiving the title of Hero of the Soviet Union on June 29, 1946.[17]

---

13. Sverdlov, *Evrei Generaly*, 14.
14. Ibid., 270–72.
15. Gershon Shapiro, *Under Fire: The Stories of Jewish Heroes of the Soviet Union* (Jerusalem: Yad Vashem, 1988), see table of contents. The number includes some who received the title before the war.
16. F.D. Sverdlov, *V Stroiu Otvazhnykh, Ocherki o Evreyakh-Geroyakh Sovetskogo Soiuza* (Moscow: Kniga, 1992), 9–10.
17. Arkady Timor ed., *Journal of the Soldiers and Partisans Disabled in the War against the Nazis* 16 [Hebrew] (2002): 94.

3. National Divisions and the Idea of Jewish Units

National Divisions in the Red Army

On March 7, 1938, on the eve of the Second World War, the Central Committee of the Communist Party and the Council of People's Commissars decided to establish national divisions within the Red Army: Georgian, Armenian, Azeri and Turkman. During the war, 17 infantry divisions were established, as well as five additional national divisions of cavalry. These divisions were all called by their national names.

There were also Baltic divisions, Lithuanians, Latvians and Estonians,[18] which began organizing toward the end of 1941, in accordance with an edict issued by the Soviet government. The decision to organize Baltic divisions was political, intended to show the world that the Baltic peoples fighting to liberate their countries were loyal to the Soviet Union, although they had been under Soviet rule for only one year.

The 201st Latvian division was composed of the remains of the 24th Latvian territorial corps, and the 16th Lithuanian division from those of the 29th Lithuanian territorial corps. Most of the soldiers of both corps had deserted at the beginning of the war, only a small number retreating with the Red Army. Most of the soldiers in the national divisions were refugees who had fled from Lithuania and Latvia when the Germans invaded, or people who had been living in the Soviet Union for years. Russians and members of other nationalities were stationed with them. Among the refugees, the number of Jews who fought in the national divisions was high. According to one source, when the 201st Latvian division was about to be sent to the front in December 1941, there were 3,000 Jews serving in it, almost one third its total number. Another source states that 17-20 percent of the 10,000 soldiers in the division were Jews. Approximately 1,000 Jews served in the 308th Latvian division, which was established later on.[19] At the beginning of 1943, just before the 16th Lithuanian division was sent to the front, it had 10,251 soldiers: 3,717 Lithuanians (36 percent), 3,061 Russians (29.9 percent), 2,971 (29.0 percent) Jews and just over 5 percent of other nationalities.[20]

---

18. Kirian et al., *Slovar-Spravochnik*, 308.

19. Dov Levin, *With Their Backs to the Wall: The Armed Struggle of Latvian Jews against the Nazis, 1941–1945* [Hebrew] (Jerusalem: Institute of Contemporary Jewry, Hebrew University, 1978), 88–90.

20. Dov Levin, *They Fought Back: Lithuanian Jewry's Armed Resistance to Nazis, 1941–1945* [Hebrew] (Jerusalem: Institute of Contemporary Jewry, Hebrew University,

In the Estonian division, there were only a few hundred Jews, in proportion to their very small representation in Estonia.

The strong national identity among the Lithuanian and Latvian Jews and their relatively large numbers in these divisions lent Jewish overtones to daily life. Yiddish was spoken, Yiddish songs were sung and observant soldiers conducted religious practices. There was great solidarity, even between commanding officers and ordinary soldiers – a situation utterly unique within the Red Army.

The Idea of Establishing Jewish Divisions

With the formation of national divisions in the Red Army, it was suggested to the Jewish Anti-Fascist Committee (JAFC)[21] that an effort should be made to establish Jewish fighting divisions. In December 1941, Yosef Kalmanovich, who lived in Frunze in the Republic of Kirghizstan, wrote a letter to Solomon Mikhoels, saying:

> I am a Jew, [I have been] a member of the Communist Party since 1919, an old fighter. During the Civil War, I was the military commissar of the First Irkutsk division in the Far East. There are special military units composed of different nationalities: Czechs, Poles, Greeks and others. The situation of our people is of course completely different, and we must fight within the ranks of our valiant Red Army. But in addition to this I think it would be appropriate to create several Jewish divisions. It seems to me that our people must separately display their military bravery in this great battle.... The Nazi beast must also be defeated and destroyed by special Jewish divisions within the Red Army.... All this gives us the right to prove that in the Country of Soviets, the military valor of bygone days has been reborn among

---

1974), 60. According to another estimation, about 50 percent of the soldiers in the division were Jews.

21. Solomon Mikhoels was appointed to chair the not-yet-officially established JAFC in mid-December 1941. Officially JAFC was established by the Soviet government in April 1942. Mikhoels was an actor and director of the State Jewish Theater in Moscow. JAFC's primary function was spreading propaganda among world Jewry. It was subordinate to the Soviet Information Bureau, an institution whose job was to spread official Soviet information and propaganda within the Soviet Union and abroad.

the people whom ancient Rome, conqueror of the entire world, once required two-thirds of its armed forces to defeat.… I am deeply convinced that effective military units could be formed in a very short time, and they would receive tremendous moral and material support from fellow Jews throughout the entire world.[22]

The issue of such national divisions was raised in a speech given by Peretz Markish, one of the senior members of JAFC, in a plenary session held between February 18 and 20, 1943. He said he had visited the front and a Jewish colonel who commanded a tank unit said to him, "I am a Jew and would like to fight as a Jew. I would like to approach the appropriate authorities with a suggestion to form separate Jewish units." Markish then asked him what would be the effectiveness of such units, and the colonel answered: "The maximum. Jewish soldiers have only one possibility: either kill the enemy or perish.…"[23]

On March 25, 1944, Senior Lieutenant Semyon Grinspoon, a soldier in the engineering corps, wrote a long letter to Ilya Ehrenburg. He described the fighting in the area of Kiev in September 1941, being taken prisoner, the murder of the Jewish prisoners of war, his escape across the front line and subsequent return to the fighting. At the end he wrote:

> Comrade Ehrenburg, perhaps I am wrong, but the following matter interests me: It seems to me that Jewish divisions should be established within the national divisions. I am convinced that the Jews will fight the Fascists with a hatred ten times greater, both as patriots of the motherland and as the avengers of the blood of their brothers, sisters, fathers and mothers, wives and children. For there is not one single Jew who, in addition to the national account he wants to settle with Fascism, does not have a personal account to settle with the Fascist beasts. Awaiting your reply. Greetings from the battlefield. Death to the German invaders.[24]

---

22. Shimon Redlich, *War, Holocaust and Stalinism: A Documented History of the Jewish Anti-Fascist Committee in the USSR* (Luxemburg: Routledge, 1995), 184–85.

23. Aron Shner, *Plen* [Russian], vol. 2 (Jerusalem, 2003), 55; Redlich, *War, Holocaust and Stalinism*, 210.

24. Mordechai Altshuler et al., ed., *Sovetskie Evrei Pishut Ile Erenburgu 1943–1966* (Jerusalem: Yad Vashem and Hebrew University, 1993), 132.

Such appeals, driven by the awareness that the Jewish fate was unique, reflected the desire of many Jewish soldiers and officers. A. Shner, in his book *Plen* ("Captivity"), recounts what Abram Margolis, the commissar of 328th Infantry Division, said in conversation with a group of Jewish officers in Krasnodar after its liberation on February 12, 1943. There they discovered, possibly for the first time, that a Jewish population had been entirely annihilated. They were horrified, and what they said may be understood as a reaction to that horror. According to the testimony of one of those present, Margolis said:

> I say to you as Jews, we must have a state of our own. If we had one now, and if it had its own army, with tanks and planes, the Fascist villains would not have carried out such a genocide…. We must have a Jewish army…. Damn it, the Czechs organized their army in our country, so did the Poles. We must organize a Jewish division, like the Latvian and Estonian [ones]. But to say such a thing aloud, and worse, to put it into writing – you'll pay with your head…." And Margolis continued in a lower voice, "I hope you won't inform on me."[25]

Margolis's comments were probably not unique. When Jewish soldiers passed through liberated territories and found the mass graves of their families and fellow Jews, they realized the uniqueness of the Jewish fate and awoke to their national identity. At the same time, Margolis's fear of the Soviet régime's reaction to merely raising the topic of Jewish nationality and sovereignty, and the establishment of separate Jewish units, was not without cause. If found out, Margolis risked being punished or even executed.

Those who appealed to JAFC genuinely believed that it was strong enough to influence the establishment of national Jewish fighting divisions, but neither the committee nor Ehrenburg raised the issue with the Soviet government. Both knew in advance that there was no chance Stalin and others in the government would agree, and that an appeal of that nature would only lower the committee's status and even endanger its very existence. The committee had been established by the Soviet government as a tool for its war propaganda needs, not to represent the Jews of the Soviet Union in their dealings with the authorities or operate in their national interest.

---

25. Shner, *Plen*, 55. Shner quoted from an article in the Russian-language newspaper published in Israel, *Novosti Nedeli*, on April 13, 2000, written by S. Dikhne, who was present at the discussion in Krasnodar.

The subject of Jewish units fighting at the Soviet front arose in the committee's first plenary session on May 28, 1942. However, the speeches discussed the units of Jews living in other countries who would fight Nazi Germany, some of them on the Soviet front, rather than units of Soviet Jews. At the meeting, Y. Nussimov said that it was "necessary to organize armed Jewish forces beyond the borders of the Soviet Union. The Jewish youth who fought [in the Civil War] in Spain can also take part in this war in various ways." At the same meeting, Lina Shtern, a member of the committee, appealed to world Jewry, saying, "It seems to me that our appeal should include the demand for the formation of Jewish legions which will be sent to us. We must state that the Soviet Union, on Soviet territory, is where [the war] will be decided. They send us tanks. But if only their volunteer divisions might appear! There can be privates among them, there can be medical men. That is, not only donations of money, but help in every possible form."[26]

There were Jewish units and the Jewish Brigade from Eretz Israel in the British army, but Jewish fighting divisions were never formed, neither in the Soviet Union nor anywhere else in the world. However, it should be mentioned that except for Eretz Israel, it was only among Soviet Jews, and especially among those who fought at the front, that the subject of forming Jewish military units arose. In no other country of the Allied forces – including the United States and Britain, which had large Jewish communities – did the issue ever arise.

4. The Shock of the Surprise Attack: June 22, 1941

At dawn on June 22, 1941, Nazi Germany attacked the Soviet Union. The Germans had 150 divisions, 41 of them armored and mechanized, with about 3,500 tanks. They were backed up by about 4,000 planes. The attack was carried out along four main axes: Army Group North attacked through the Baltic states, with the aim of conquering Leningrad. Army Group Center attacked through Byelorussia and targeted Moscow. Army Group South had as its targets the Ukraine, south Russia and the Caucasus. The German 11th Army, together with two Romanian armies, attacked through Bessarabia along the northern shore of the Black Sea; its targets were Odessa and the Crimean peninsula. The total number of invading Germans was 3,200,000, reinforced by some hundreds of thousands of Romanian, Hungarian and Finnish forces. On June 22, 1941, they were opposed by close to

---

26. Redlich, *War, Holocaust and Stalinism*, 208; Shner, *Plen*, 53–54.

3,000,000 Soviet soldiers in the Baltic states, Byelorussia and the Ukraine, about 100,000 of whom belonged to the NKVD border guards.

The German attack took the Soviet Union by surprise, despite information received from various sources for many months. By July and August 1940, and thereafter at an accelerated pace, the NKVD, NKGB and military intelligence had all sent scores of reports about large German troop concentrations in the *Generalgouvernement* in Poland and details of their infantry and tank strength, of the preparation of air fields, of plans for possible attack dates and other information, clearly indicating that the Germans intended to invade. Soviet Border Guard units reported that German reconnaissance planes had crossed the border to photograph the area, and that teams of saboteurs had penetrated, some of them caught coming from the German border.[27]

A Soviet intelligence report from Berlin dated March 24, 1941, stated that:

> An employee of the German Air Ministry told our source that intensive activity was taking place in the German Air Force on the chance that there might be a military action against the Soviet Union. Bombings of central targets in the Soviet Union are planned. The first targets will be bridges.... There are plans to bomb Leningrad and Kiev.... Among the officers of Air Force headquarters the general assumption is that the attack on the Soviet Union has been set for the end of April or early May....[28]

Reliable information about preparations for a German attack during the second half of June 1941 reached Moscow from many sources (see below, section 16). The British government also passed information to Moscow about German preparations to attack the Soviet Union. Stalin did not believe any of the warnings. At the beginning of June 1941, Stalin received Marshal Semyon Timoshenko, the people's commissar for defense, and Georgy Zhukov, chief of staff of the Red Army, who presented him with documents containing information about German preparations for an attack. Stalin told them he had documents that indicated the opposite.[29] On June 17, 1941, five days before

---

27. S.V. Stepashin, ed., *Organy Gosudarstvennoi Bezopasnosti SSSR v Velikoi Otechestvennoi Voine* (Moscow: Kniga, 1995), Document nos. 151, 153, 161, 163, 164, 168, 170, 171, 173, 175, 180, 182, 183, 184, 190, 195, 196, 197, 200, 201, 206, 201.

28. Ibid., 61–62, Document no. 168.

29. Georgy Kumanev, "June 22, 1941," *Pravda*, June 22, 1989. Kumanev was the head of the department for the history of the Second World War in the Historical

the German attack, the NKGB informed Stalin of important information: "The source, a man who serves in the German Air Force headquarters, says that all the preparations in Germany for a military action against the Soviet Union have been completed, and the attack can be expected at any moment." On the document Stalin penciled: "Comrade Merkulov, you can send your 'source' from the German Air Force to hell. He's no 'source,' only a source of disinformation. Y. St[alin]"[30] (Vsevolod Merkulov served as Beria's deputy of NKVD and was in charge of intelligence). Stalin opposed putting the army on alert and calling up the reserves, lest such steps be interpreted by the Germans as provocation and intent to attack. He also forbade firing on German reconnaissance places crossing the border during the weeks leading up to the war.[31]

Stalin opposed a war at that time. He was correct in his assessment of the German army, having seen what it was capable of in Poland and in Western and southern Europe. He was also aware that the Red Army had been weakened by the officer purges of 1937–38, as had been made evident by the war with Finland in December 1939–March 1940. The Red Army was still reorganizing and absorbing thousands of new tanks and planes. Stalin also believed that the Germans would avoid waging a war on two fronts and would not attack the Soviet Union before the summer of 1942, and by then not only would the Red Army be much stronger, but the war with Britain would have drained Germany's blood. That would enable the Soviet Union to deal a preemptive blow against Germany and take over Europe. A document from Red Army headquarters, dated May 15, 1941, first published in Russia in 1996, contains a Soviet strategic plan for deploying Red Army forces to attack and fight a preemptive war against Germany. It does not note a date for the strike, but considering the time necessary to prepare for such an attack, it is reasonable to assume it could not have taken place before 1942.[32]

Stalin knew that the Germans would attack the Soviet Union and that war was inevitable, but he believed that Germany would respect their agreement until Britain capitulated, especially since the economic agreement accompanying it – which the Soviets honored fully – provided Germany with many benefits. The Soviet Union paid a heavy price for Stalin's mistakes. The Red Army made

---

Institute of the Soviet Union Academy of Sciences.

30. Afanasev, *Drugaia Voina*, 206.
31. Tucker, *Stalin in Power*, 621–22; Bullock, *Hitler and Stalin*, 712–14.
32. Afanasev, *Drugaia Voina*, 175–84.

no preparations for defense. Only at 12:30 a.m. on the night of June 22, 1941, after more information had been received about the upcoming German attack, did Stalin permit Timoshenko and Zhukov to put the military districts bordering Germany on alert and to warn that the Germans might attack on June 22 or 23. The order reached the troops three hours after the German attack had begun.[33]

The news first reached Red Army headquarters at 3:30 a.m. on June 22. Zhukov immediately informed Stalin. Zhukov later wrote: "The Commissar for Defense [Timoshenko] ordered me to phone Stalin. I started calling. No one answered. I kept calling. Finally I heard the sleep-dulled general on duty of the security section. I asked him to call Stalin to the phone. About three minutes later Stalin picked up the receiver. I reported the situation and requested permission to start retaliation. Stalin was silent. The only thing I could hear was the sound of his breathing. 'Do you understand me?' Silence again… 'Tell Proskrebishev [Stalin's secretary] to summon the entire Politbureau.'"[34] The Politburo meeting began at 4:30 a.m. Molotov, after speaking with the German ambassador to Moscow, Count Von der Shulenburg, announced that Germany had declared war on the Soviet Union. Zhukov wrote, "Stalin sank down into his chair and lost himself in thought. There was a long, pregnant pause."[35] A decision was reached to order the western military districts, where the Germans had initiated their attack, to counterattack and destroy the invading enemy forces. The order was completely divorced from the catastrophic reality on the front and issued by Red Army headquarters in accordance with Stalin's instructions, who knew nothing about the real condition of his troops in the border area.

Radio Moscow informed the Soviet people of the attack at noon on June 22, but it was Molotov who made the announcement, not Stalin. Stalin was heard for the first time in a speech to the Soviet people on July 3, 1941. In this speech he justified the Ribbentrop-Molotov pact, claiming it had given the Soviet Union more than a year and a half of peace and the opportunity to strengthen the Red Army, and called for partisan warfare behind German lines. Completely ignoring the army's difficult straits at the time, he said, "The enemy's best divisions and best air force units have already been pounded to bits" – an assessment that was far from the truth.[36]

---

33. Kumanev, "June 22, 1941."
34. Georgii Konstantinovich Zhukov, *The Memoirs of Marshal Zhukov* (New York: Delacorte, 1971), 235.
35. Ibid., 236.
36. Joseph Stalin, *O Velikoi Otechestvennoi Voine Sovetskovo Soyuza* (Moscow, 1950), 20, 27.

5. THE CRUCIAL PERIOD –
RETREAT AND ATTEMPTS TO CHECK THE GERMAN ADVANCE:
JUNE 22–DECEMBER 5, 1941

The Wehrmacht's Victories

During the first stage of the Great Patriotic War the Germans won substantial victories, and by the end of November 1941 their army was at the gates of Moscow. Germany planned a short war and swift victory, certainly by the beginning of winter. Writing in his diary on June 16, 1941, Goebbels noted that "the Führer has assessed the [military] operation at four months; I think it will be less. The Bolsheviks will fall like a house of cards."[37] In truth, the first weeks and months of the war justified the German assessment.

During the first month of the war, the Army Group North advanced 400–450 kilometers (250–80 miles), conquering Lithuania, Latvia, part of Estonia and territories in northern Russia, and reached Leningrad. The uprising of the soldiers of the 29th Lithuanian Territorial Corps and the desertion of the 24th Latvian Territorial Corps made the rapid advance of the German army in the Baltic states even easier. The Panzers of the Army Group Central advanced 450–600 kilometers (280–375 miles) and in mid-July reached Smolensk, on their way to Moscow. The Army Group South advanced through the Ukraine somewhat more slowly because of large Red Army concentrations, but by the end of the first month of the war had penetrated to a depth of 300–350 kilometers (185–215 miles), having conquered the western Ukraine and parts in the east. Odessa was blockaded and cut off from the rest of the Soviet Union on August 5, 1941.[38]

Despite the determined fighting of some of the Red Army units, their defenses were breached in the western areas of the Soviet Union, entire armies were surrounded and hundreds of thousands of Soviet soldiers were captured.

---

37.   Hans-Heinrich Wilhelm, *Rassenpolitik und Kriegfuhrung* (Passau, 1991), 111.

38.   There were stronger Soviet forces in the Ukraine for two reasons: Firstly, the Red Army command estimated that if Germany were to attack, its main thrust would be through the Ukraine for economical reasons (Ukraine and the Don region housed many food supplies and raw materials, and Caucasia contained petrol). Secondly, according to Red Army plans submitted to Stalin in May 1941, the main Red Army counterattack would start from the Ukraine, from there moving to the west and north and along the Carpathian Mountains.

On July 8, Franz Halder, head of the German Army General Staff, presented Hitler with German military intelligence's most optimistic assessment of the situation. He noted that 84 Soviet divisions (of a total of 164) had been destroyed and the Red Army had at its disposal no more than 45 divisions that could be called battle worthy.[39] In the middle of July, Halder wrote in his diary that it would not be an exaggeration "to say that the victory in the Russian campaign will be achieved in two weeks." In the middle of July, Hitler, also feeling that the Soviet Union had already been defeated, ordered the German military industry to give priority to the air force and navy at the expense of the ground forces; he intended to plan the war against Britain and the United States, where air and sea power would be determining factors.[40]

In August 1941, Hitler decided to temporarily halt the push toward Moscow and to move Guderian's Panzer Army to support Army Group South in capturing the Ukraine and Kiev, and Hoth's Panzer Army in capturing Leningrad. He gave priority to the conquest of the Ukraine and Crimea because of their agricultural produce and raw materials, which were vital for Germany. There were two reasons for his desire to conquer Leningrad: the first was to ensure that its industrial products could not be used by the Red Army; the second was to prevent the Soviet Navy from having a Baltic naval base that could be used to disrupt supplies of steel from Sweden, which were important for Germany's war industry.

In the Ukraine, Guderian's tank forces advancing from the north and the tank forces of Army Group South created an enormous pocket around Kiev. On September 19, Kiev fell to the Germans and over 600,000 Red Army soldiers were taken prisoner.

Further south, the German army took over the Crimean peninsula, with the exception of Sevastopol. Odessa repelled the combined German and Romanian attack until October. When the German army began its conquest of Crimea, the Soviets decided to evacuate the forces in Odessa by sea to reinforce the defense of Sevastopol. Kharkov was conquered on October 25, and Rostov-on-Don on November 21.

---

39. Christopher Ailsby, *Images of Barbarossa: The German Invasion of Russia, 1941* (Dallas: Potomac, 2002), 72.

40. Richard Overy, *Russia's War: A History of the Soviet Effort, 1941–1945* (New York: Penguin, 1998), 94.

In the north, the attempt to take Leningrad failed, but the Germans, supported by Finnish forces from the northwest, surrounded the city. The Germans succeeded in reaching Lake Ladoga in September and cut off its land routes. The ensuing situation was appalling, and Stalin removed Voroshilov and on September 11 sent Zhukov to organize its defenses. The German attempts to take Leningrad failed. At the beginning of October 1941, Hitler decided to starve it into submission and use artillery and air attacks to destroy it. Priority was again given to the capture of Moscow, and Guderian's and Hoth's armored armies were returned to Army Group Center.

In October the German army renewed its attack on Moscow. Despite the German victory in encircling five Soviet armies west of Moscow, the German advance was halted 40 kilometers (25 miles) from Moscow. At the end of October it began to rain, and the roads, which were vital to the mechanized German army, turned into mud. The fierce cold and the early winter complicated matters for the Germans, who had not prepared for a winter war. The determined resistance of the Red Army, the lengthening supply lines, the losses suffered, the rain and the winter forced the German army to stop in its tracks. The plans to take Moscow and Leningrad by the winter and to bring about the collapse of the Soviet Union failed. The German army had to make arrangements for a long, drawn-out war, with all its logistical implications and complications.

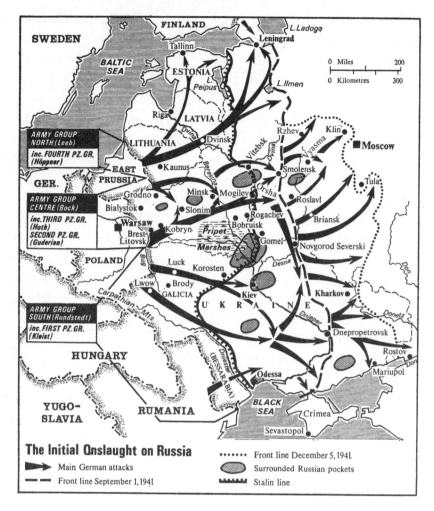

The Initial Onslaught on Russia

▶ Main German attacks

━ ━ ━ Front line September 1, 1941

••••••• Front line December 5, 1941

⬭ Surrounded Russian pockets

▬▬▬ Stalin line

MAP OF THE GERMAN ADVANCE

The Red Army also suffered extremely heavy losses. According to Soviet data, by the end of 1941 there were more than 800,000 soldiers dead and more than 1.25 million wounded. The number of those whose fates were "unknown," primarily prisoners of war, was 2,335,500 million. Thus the Red Army's total losses at that time were approximately 4,473,820.[41] According to German figures, the number of Soviet prisoners at the time was 3,350,300, one million more that the official Soviet figure.[42]

41.   Krivosheyev, *Grif Secretnosti*, 141–43.
42.   Theo J. Schulte, *The German Army and Nazi Policies in Occupied Russia* (New York: Berg, 1989), 203; Dallin, *German Rule*, 427. It is safe to assume that the

The Reorganization of the Soviet Military

Both the Red Army and the Soviet government reorganized to face the German onslaught. Three Soviet fronts were established against the three German Army Groups: the northwest, the west and the southwest. During the war and following military developments, the number and names of the fronts changed. On June 24, 1941, the Soviet government ordered the establishment of special military units composed of local residents who had not been drafted for reasons of age, health or economic situation. They were to fight against Germans who had infiltrated or parachuted behind Soviet lines and against local hostile elements, and defend bridges and factories close to the front. They were called "extirpation units" (*istrebitelnye otriady*).[43] Their members continued working at their jobs, and when necessary were called to support the internal security forces (the militia and the NKVD) in fighting hostile elements. [44]

During the first half of July, when the German army advanced toward Leningrad and Moscow, the Central Committee of the Communist Party decided to hastily draft men who for whatever reason had not yet been drafted, and high school students who were too young for the draft, and organize them as combat divisions. They were called the National Guard (Narodnoe Opolchenie). Ten such divisions were established in Leningrad, 16 in Moscow, a total of 60 throughout the country, providing approximately two million additional soldiers.[45] Because the military situation was perilous, they were sent into battle after a short training period and without proper weapons and equipment, and suffered particularly heavy losses. Most of their members came from the big cities and among their ranks was a high percentage of Jews.[46]

German number of Soviet prisoners of war is closer to the truth.

43.   Kirian et al., *Slovar-Spravochnik*, 206.

44.   Ibid.

45.   Ibid., 302–3.

46.   There were four large concentrations of Jews in the Soviet Union: in Moscow, where more than 6 percent of the population was Jewish, 140,000 men were in popular recruitment units; in Leningrad, where the Jews made up 6.3 percent of the population, 130,000 were recruited into the units; in Odessa, where more than 30 percent of the population was Jewish, 55,000 were recruited into the units; in Kiev, where 26.5 percent of the population was Jewish, 35,000 were recruited. It is reasonable to assume that the percentage of Jews in the popular recruitment units in the cities mentioned was not far from their percentage in the general population. The above numbers also include members of the extirpation units.

MOTHER HOMELAND CALLS!

On June 30, 1941, a supreme strategic entity to conduct all aspects of the war was established. Called the State Defense Committee (Gosudarstvennyi Komitet Oborony – GKO), it was chaired by Stalin. On July 10, 1941, the Headquarters of Supreme Command (Stavka Verkhovnogo Glavnokomandovanya – SVGK, known as Stavka) came into being. Headed by Stalin and composed of the chief commanders of the Red Army, the Stavka was the body responsible for all military operations. On July 19, 1941, Stalin assumed the role of people's commissar of defense, replacing Marshal Timoshenko, and on August 8 he assumed the role of supreme army commander. In view of the catastrophic military situation, the Supreme Command issued Order No. 270 on August 16, 1941, which stated the following:

> Commanders and political staff members who remove their insignia during battle and surrender should be regarded as malicious deserters, whose family is to be arrested as being related to someone who violated his oath and betrayed the Motherland. Such deserters are to be shot on the spot.... If a unit is surrounded it must fight to the end and to try to break out and reach our forces. If any commander or soldier suggests surrender instead of continuing to fight, he should be destroyed in any way either by ground forces or with planes. The families of soldiers who are taken prisoner should have all government support taken from them.... This order should be read to all the battalions, batteries, staffs....[47]

A description of the terrible situation at the front that dictated this order was given by a senior commander of a Soviet counterintelligence agency in the army known as SMERSH (Death to Spies). It stated:

> The conditions during the first year were particularly terrible, especially during the retreat. Morale was at its lowest. Many defected to the enemy. In some instances the men killed their commanders and entire units surrendered. Often the soldiers in a platoon came from the same area and it was easy for them to talk among themselves [about deserting]. We monitored the situation and disbanded such units.... We were very worried about soldiers who deliberately wounded themselves so they would be evacuated, for example, some shot themselves through their canteens or through wet towels so there would be no traces of gunpowder, and some exposed their arms so they might be wounded.[48]

---

47. O.A. Rzheshevski et al., *Velikaia Otechestvenna Voina, Sobytia, Liudi, Dokumenty* (Moscow: Politizdat, 1990), 423–24.

48. Vadim Abramov, *Smersh* [Russian] (Moscow: Yauza and Eksmo, 2005), 91–92; Catherine Merridale, *Ivan's War: Life and Death in the Red Army* (New York: Metropolitan Books, 2006), 105, 111–15. The book describes the panic and desertion in the Red Army during this time.

In the battles fought during the retreat, the Red Army High Command decided to give a special title to divisions demonstrating bravery and military skills and to call them Guards. The first such titles went to four infantry divisions on September 18, 1941.

Evacuating Institutions and Military Industries

One of the most successful and important operations carried out by the Soviet government during the first months of the war, under conditions of frantic retreat, was the dismantling and moving of military industries – including the workers and their families – from the territories conquered by the Germans to behind Soviet lines. (For the evacuation of the industries, see chapter 2.) Whatever could not be moved was blown up or destroyed.

Approximately 12,000,000 Soviet citizens were evacuated, of them about 780,000 Jews, the overwhelming majority of whom had worked in the factories and in government, party and cultural institutions. Tens of thousands were not part of the organized evacuation but fled of their own accord. No evacuation of the Jews was carried out by the Soviet government to save them from the horrors of the Nazi occupation. The percentage of Jews evacuated was higher than that of the general population because of the relatively high percentage of Jews working in industry and government institutions, and also because there were many non-Jews, workers in the evacuated plants, who preferred to remain under the German occupation rather than to leave their property and go off into the unknown in the Ural Mountains or Siberia.[49]

The Jewish Soldiers' Motivation to Fight

The Jews in the Red Army fought shoulder to shoulder with their non-Jewish comrades in arms who were Russian, Ukrainian, Byelorussian or who belonged to any of the dozens of nationalities that made up the Soviet Union. Nevertheless, the Jews were different, and their fighting was unique. During the Red Army's retreats in the second half of 1941, it became clear that the loyalty and readiness to fight of some of its soldiers was low, and many of them, especially from Baltic, Asiatic and Caucasian nations, deserted to the Germans. The Red Army's political leadership (GPUKA) issued instructions to intensify indoctri-

---

49.　For the evacuation see Yitzhak Arad, *The Holocaust in the Soviet Union* (Lincoln: University of Nebraska Press; Jerusalem: Yad Vashem, 2009), chapter 7, 72–87.

nation in the units in which such soldiers served.[50] The most loyal elements in the Red Army during that difficult phase of the war were mostly Russians defending their homeland ("Mother Russia") and Jewish soldiers.

By the first weeks and months of the war it had become clear to the Jewish soldiers that not only were they fighting the Germans as Red Army soldiers, they were fighting them as Jews. German propaganda flyers containing anti-Semitic slogans and vicious cartoons were dropped from planes. Stalin was depicted in them as an oppressive tyrant, the Jews as enjoying themselves and raking in money, the Russian kolkhozniks as suffering and the soldiers as giving up their lives for Stalin and the Jews. The flyers called upon the soldiers not to fight in a war that was not their own, to desert the Jewish commissars and to go over to the German side. From such flyers and from the accounts of soldiers who had escaped from German captivity and returned to the Soviet lines, the Jewish soldiers learned of the fate awaiting them as war prisoners. As the months of the war passed, they also learned of the mass murders of the Jews in the German-occupied territories. The families of many soldiers had remained behind, and the soldiers were anxious about their fate. The desire for revenge was strong.

The Jews' basic loyalty to the Soviet state combined with their unique position as Jews provided the Jewish soldiers with strong motivation to fight. There was no need to remind them of the Red Army regulation or Order No. 270, which declared that surrender was not an option even in the face of death. The Jewish soldier did not have the choice of captivity or death; for him captivity *was* death. Therefore they fought with utmost devotion. The historian Catherine Merridale in her book *Ivan's War* writes:

> In 1941, Jews signed up in the thousands for the Soviet cause. Students from Moscow set their books aside; young Communists in government roles asked to be assigned to the front. Jews were among the keenest volunteers for every kind of army service. Not all the volunteers were Soviet-born. Refugees streamed east from Poland and from western Ukraine in the spring of 1941, finding their way into the Red Army by summer. As they would learn when their families perished in the old homelands, their loyalty to Stalin`s cause was justified.... Jews were indeed among the most determined combatants on every Soviet front.[51]

---

50. *Artyomov, Bratskii Boyevoi Soyuz*, 72, 81–83, 97–98.
51. Merridale, *Ivan's War*, 288, 297.

The number of Jewish soldiers who were declared Heroes of the Soviet Union, the highest award given by the Soviet state, is proof of the role played by the Jews in the war against the Nazis. According to the 1939 census, the Jews were seventh in number in the Soviet Union, but fifth among Heroes of the Soviet Union. At least 154 Jewish officers and soldiers received the award. According to official Soviet data, 160,722 Jewish soldiers were decorated; Jews were in fourth place among the decorated, after the Russians, Ukrainians and Byelorussians.[52]

From the first days of the war, the Jewish soldiers were always those who continued to fight their way back to the Soviet lines. The acts of sacrifice and bravery of the Jewish soldiers described further in this chapter are only samples of a broad subject that cannot be comprehensively presented in one volume.

Jews in the Defensive Battles on the Roads Leading to Moscow

One of the most famous battles, and one in which Soviet soldiers demon-strated exceptional valor, took place during the first days of the war. It was widely dealt with in Soviet war literature and is known as the Brest-Litovsk defense. The Brest-Litovsk fortress stood on the German-Soviet Union border and commanded one of the main roads to Minsk and Moscow. At 4 a.m. on June 22, 1941, the soldiers in the fortress were surprised to find themselves at-tacked from the air and on land. After artillery fire and aerial bombing, they were attacked by German assault troops. Approximately 3,500 soldiers from the various units organized themselves within the fortress and repelled the German attacks for more than a week. The leading spirit behind the defense of the fortress was Haim Fomin, a Jewish commissar from the 82nd Brigade; and among the defenders were scores of Jewish soldiers. The names of many of them are mentioned in material issued by the Soviet Union about the heroic battle, including A. Gordon, Sergeant G. Heikin and Junior-Lieutenant Y. Iskovich.[53] The German general Guderian, whose Panzer forces attacked the Brest-Litovsk region, wrote in his memoirs:

52. Shapiro, *Under Fire*. The book includes the biographies of 150 Jews who received the title Hero of the Soviet Union and names four others for whom biographi-cal material could not be found; F.D. Sverdlov and A. Ya. Vainer, *Voiny Evrei na Frontakh Velikoi Otechestvennoi* (Moscow: Izdatelstvo Fonda Holocaust, 1999), 14.
53. P.N. Pospelov et al., *Istoria Velikoi Otechestvennoi Voiny Sovetskogo Soiuza 1941-1945*, vol. 2, 18; Aron Abramovich, *V Reshaiushchei Voine* (Tel Aviv, 1981), 84-87. Abramovich mentions dozens of names and estimates the number of Jew-ish defenders, of whom only a handful survived, as one hundred.

We had managed to take the enemy by surprise along the entire Panzer Group front.... The enemy, however, soon recovered from his initial surprise and put up a tough defense in his prepared positions. The important citadel of Brest-Litovsk held out with remarkable stubbornness for several days, thus depriving us of the use of the road and rail communications across the Bug and Muchaviec.[54]

By June 29–30 the Germans had begun a concerted assault on the fortress and blew up some of its fortifications. Many of the defenders were buried under the ruins, others were removed and captured, among them the wounded Commissar Fomin. One of the captives pointed him out as the Jewish commissar who had ordered them to fight to the bitter end. The Germans pulled him away from the others and shot him. For his leadership and bravery at Brest-Litovsk, Fomin was posthumously awarded the Order of Lenin. A Soviet source described the defense of Brest-Litovsk as follows:

> The staff which organized the defense of the fortress was headed by Captain Y.N. Zubchev and Commissar Fomin. They not only defended [the fortress] but even counterattacked as long as they could. The Soviet fighters' determination prevented large enemy forces from advancing. It was the miraculous success of sons who loved their motherland and were willing to sacrifice their lives for it.[55]

At dawn on June 22, German forces that broke through from eastern Prussia approached the town of Grodno and put the Soviet 10th Army in the region of Bialystok in danger of encirclement. At the end of a day of battle, the 10th Army collapsed and retreated. Moscow and the Western Front Command in Minsk knew nothing of the situation and sent unrealistic commands to counterattack and push the enemy back over the border. The only force within the 10th Army that had not been seriously damaged was the 6th Motorized Corps commanded by Major General Michael Khatskelevitch, who was Jewish. Khatskelevitch was one of the first tank division commanders and had commanded the 6th Corps since 1940. On June 23–24 his tanks counterattacked and were locally successful, but remained without ammunition and fuel. The Germans had complete control of the air, and their planes strafed and damaged many of Khatskelevitch's

54. Heinz Guderian, *Panzer Leader* (New York: De Capo, 2001), 154.
55. Kirian et al., *Slovar-Spravochnik*, 66; Aron Abramovich, *V Reshaiushchei Voine*, 83–85.

tanks. He went to 10th Army headquarters to demand supplies, and General Ivan Boldin, second in command of the Western Front, wrote the following in his memoirs:

> Khatskelevitch arrived looking very worried. He said, We are firing our last shells and we will have to destroy our tanks. Yes, I answered, there doesn't seem to be anything else to do. If we cannot save the tanks, it is better to destroy them. Looking into the eyes of that brave man we could not imagine that on the same day we would lose not only the tank corps but its wonderful commander as well. General Khatskelevitch died a hero's death on the battlefield.[56]

Marshal Zhukov mentioned the death of Khatskelevitch (who burned to death in his tank) in his memoirs, praising his courage and his excellence as a commander.[57] As to the results of Khatskelevitch's counterattack, the Soviet historian Apfilov has written: "The counterattack of the tank corps in the Grodno region did not achieve decisive results.... Nevertheless, it had great importance.... The enemy's plans and schedule for advancing troops toward the Dnieper were obstructed."[58]

On June 25, 1941, a group of cadets from the officers' training school in Vilnius commanded by a Jewish cadet named Wolf Vilensky (who was later named a Hero of the Soviet Union) managed, for a short time, to delay German units trying to cross the Vilya River in the region of Molodechno on the way to Minsk. Vilensky had joined the Lithuanian army in 1940. When Lithuania became a Soviet republic in July 1940, he was sent to an officers' training school whose members retreated eastward when the Germans approached Vilnius.[59]

Individual acts of bravery and those of entire but isolated military units could not change the situation at the front, which was catastrophic. The main German force advanced swiftly toward Moscow. At the end of June, the Germans conquered Minsk and surrounded and destroyed dozens of Soviet divisions in western Byelorussia. The Red Army made desperate attempts to establish a defensive line along the Dnieper River. To gain time, the Red Army

---

56. Abramovich, *V Reshaiushchei Voine*, 81–82. Khatskelevitch had served in the Red Army since 1918 and fought in the Civil War; Merridale, *Ivan's War*, 86–88.
57. Zhukov, *Memoirs*, 253.
58. Abramovich, *V Reshaiushchei Voine*, 82.
59. Shapiro, *Under Fire*, 617–19.

tried to delay the enemy west of the Dnieper on the Berezina River. The mission was given to the 1st Moscow Motorized Infantry Division, which was commanded by Major General Yakov Kreyzer. Kreyzer had volunteered for the Red Army in 1921 when he was 16. He served in the Moscow Proletarian Infantry Division stationed near Moscow and was appointed to command the division in the spring of 1941. The division was one of the first to receive T-34 tanks, then considered superior to the German Panzers. In the attempt to delay the enemy at the Berezina River, he received command of all the Soviet forces operating in that sector. During the first days of July his troops attacked the German 18th Panzer Division which has crossed the Berezina, and despite the Germans' superior forces and complete air control, for two days he halted their advance from a bridgehead erected east of the Berezina. General Guderian, to whose army the 18th Panzer Division belonged, wrote:

> I went on to the 18th Panzer Division at Borisov.... On the wireless operators on my armored command vehicle heard news of an attack by Russian tanks and aircraft on the Berezina crossing at Borisov.... The attack was beaten off with heavy losses to the Russians, but not before a considerable impression had been made on the 18th Panzer Division: this was hardly surprising. Since here, for the first time the enemy employed his T-34 tank, against which our guns were largely ineffective at that time.[60]

Zhukov wrote about the Borisov battle: "General Y.G. Kreyzer...succeeded in holding up the enemy's reinforced 18th Tank Division for more than two days. At that time this was of great importance. In his fighting General Kreyzer proved himself a magnificent commander."[61] When Kreyzer was forced to retreat from the region of Borisov, his division fought a delaying action for ten days.

GENERAL YAKOV KREYZER

The time gained was vital for the Red Army to

---

60. Guderian, *Panzer Leader*, 162.
61. Zhukov, *Memoirs*, 262. Yakov Kreyzer was the Jew with the highest rank in the Red Army, that of colonel general, as well as being an army commander (one rank below marshal). He continued in the army after the war, serving in various capacities. He passed away in 1969 at the age of 64.

strengthen its positions on the Dnieper and along the roads that led to Moscow. The German attempts to surround Kreyzer's division failed. Flyers were dropped on his division reading, "Russian soldiers! Into whose hands are you putting your lives? Your commander is the Jew Yankel Kreyzer. Do you believe Yankel will save you from us?"[62]

There were other Jewish soldiers in Kreyzer's division. Among the commanders who distinguished themselves in the Borisov region were the commander of the artillery battalion, Captain Abram Botvinik; the battery commander, Lieutenant Semyon Gomelski, who later died in battle; the tank battalion commander, Captain Semyon Pronin, who fell in battle and was posthumously awarded the Order of Lenin; the division's operations officer, Captain Vladimir Ratner, and many others.[63] In the middle of July, Kreyzer was wounded and hospitalized. On July 22, he was named a Hero of the Soviet Union. On July 23, 1941, the Red Army's newspaper, the *Red Star*, wrote that "Yakov Kreyzer is the first of the valorous land forces commanders to receive the high order for the bravery and courage he displayed while fighting Fascism and for skilful command of his units in battle, while providing a personal example to his subordinates." Kreyzer's division was one of the first to be awarded the title of Guard Division. After he recovered he was appointed to command the 3rd Army, which fought in the Bryansk region southwest of Moscow.[64]

The German Panzers continued their advance south of Borisov with the intention of crossing the Dnieper to conquer the city of Mogilev. The Soviet 13th Army battled to delay them. An artillery battery commanded by Boris Khigrin, also a Jew, took positions on the Minsk-Mogilev road near the Druth River. Approximately 40 Panzers with air cover stormed forward. Khigrin aimed his artillery fire directly at them, hitting six and halting their advance. He personally fired a canon whose crew had been injured and fell in the battle. On August 31, 1941 he was named a Hero of the Soviet Union. On September 1, Pravda wrote that "our people will reverentially remember the act of bravery performed by Hero of the Soviet Union Captain Khigrin, who battled an enemy tank column of greatly superior numbers and destroyed six of them."[65] In the same region, during the second half of July, the commander of the 110th Infantry Brigade,

62. Shapiro, *Under Fire*, 277.
63. Abramovich, *V Reshaiushchei Voine*, 91–92 .
64. Shapiro, *Under Fire*, 318. For Kreyzer's role in the Borisov battles, also see Pospelov et al., *Istoria Velikoi*, vol. 2, 39.
65. Sverdlov and Vainer, *Voiny Evrei*, 32.

Major K.A. Reiner, of the 53rd Infantry Division, repelled the enemy for ten days. He fell defending the Dnieper.[66]

Having crossed the Dnieper, the Germans continued their advance toward Smolensk and Moscow. In the middle of July, to ease the situation of the forces fighting at Smolensk (which were in danger of being surrounded), the Red Army counterattacked in the southern wing of the sector. The leading force in the counterattack was the 25th Armored Corps, commanded by Lieutenant General Semyon Krivoshin. In September 1939, the tank brigade under his command participated in the invasion into Poland. On September 22, 1939, the city and fortress of Brest-Litovsk were transferred from the German Panzers which had occupied them to Krivoshin and his brigade. German General Guderian and Jewish Krivoshin shook hands and stood on the podium together saluting the tank units passing in formation before them. It was apparently the only instance in the history of the Second World War in which a Jewish general and a German general shook hands and held a friendly conversation while reviewing troops.[67]

GENERAL GUDERIAN AND
LIEUTENANT GENERAL KRIVOSHIN
AT BREST-LITOVSK

---

66. Abramovich, *V Reshaiushchei Voine*, 94–95.
67. Guderian, *Panzer Leader*, 83. For the meeting between Krivoshin and Guderian, see Leonid Sheinker, *Geroism Evreev na Voine* (Tel Aviv: Krugozor, 2003), 135. Krivoshin had joined Budyonny's cavalry in 1918 and participated in the battles against Denikin, Wrangel and Pilsudski's Polish army. After the Civil War, Krivoshin remained in the army and commanded an armored battalion and brigade. In 1936 he was sent to Spain to command the Soviet tanks fighting Franco. When he returned in 1938 he commanded a tank unit in the battles with the Japanese

In a counterattack in the middle of July, Krivoshin's forces crossed the Dnieper and advanced west toward Bobruisk, fighting bloody battles with Guderian's attacking Panzers. That forced the Germans to bring in additional forces, which to a certain extent slowed and weakened their main thrust toward Moscow. A tank battalion commanded by Captain David Dragunsky fought valiantly in the battles in the Smolensk district in July; during the war he was promoted to the rank of general and was twice named a Hero of the Soviet Union. In the middle of August, surrounded by the Germans and attempting to break out, Colonel A.L. Feigen, chief of staff of the 63rd Infantry Corps and the commander of the corps, fell in battle near Smolensk.[68] Units of the National Guard established in Mogilev, Gomel and other places along the axis of the German advance toward Moscow also participated in the battles. One of the Mogilev regiments, composed of militiamen, was commanded by Z. Klugman. Soldiers who fought outstandingly in defense of Mogilev were Yakov Siegel, secretary of the local Komsomol; and Naum Shpolyansky, one of the local National Guard's organizers. Both fell in battle. The local regiment of the National Guard fought outstandingly in the defense of Gomel under the command of Captain P. Utkin; he also fell in battle.[69]

Jews in Defense of Leningrad and along the Roads Leading to It

The German Army Group North advanced through the Baltic states toward Leningrad. On their way north along the Baltic Sea, they surrounded the port city of Libau (Liepaja). The main Soviet force defending the city and the naval base was the 67th Infantry Division. On June 25, after the division commander was mortally wounded, the command passed to the chief of staff, Colonel Vladimir Bobowitz, a Jew. When the city could no longer be held after several days of battle, Bobowitz received the order to break out in the direction of Riga. He was critically wounded in the battle but managed to extricate part of his troops.[70]

With the beginning of the war, the local authorities in Riga hurriedly established a "workers' guard" to defend institutions and facilities, and many volunteered to join the unit. A squad of the 9th Battalion of the workers' guard was commanded by Lev Meirovitch. On June 25–28, he and his squad fought

---

in the Khasan Lake district.

68. Abramovich, *V Reshaiushchei Voine*, 114.
69. Ibid., 96, 115–16.
70. Ibid., 102–3.

local saboteurs and participated in destroying a German paratroop unit that had landed near the city, and on June 29, with his squad and additional forces, he helped halt German forces that had crossed the Daugava River. Many of his men fell in battle; he himself suffered a head wound and was evacuated behind Soviet lines.[71] Members of the workers' guard units from Latvia retreated with the Red Army and were included in the Latvian division of the Red Army.

An attempt to halt the German advance toward Leningrad near the cities of Pskov and Novogorod was successful. The 1st Armored Corps was commanded by General Michael Tsherniavsky, a Jew, and his tanks delayed the Germans at Ostrov, an important crossroads on the way to Leningrad. However, without infantry support and with dwindling supplies of ammunition, on the night of July 6, after having suffered heavy losses, he was forced to retreat. The Soviets counterattacked between July 14 and 18, with Tsherniavsky's corps in the lead, retaking the city of Soltsy southwest of Leningrad on July 17 and halting the German advance toward Leningrad.[72]

For three weeks, from August 7–28, 1941, Tallinn, the capital of Estonia, repulsed German attacks. Its defense was transferred to the Baltic fleet. Baltic fleet ships were active in the city's defense, especially through the use of cannons on the warship decks. The commander of the cannons both on board and at the naval base, and second in command of the defense of Tallinn, was First-Class Naval Captain Nikolai Feldman. The fleet's most important artillery-firing warship was the cruiser Kirov, whose guns were commanded by First Lieutenant Yosef Schwartzberg and whose anti-aircraft guns, which repelled the German air attacks, were commanded by Lieutenant Naum Leubwein. Among the Jewish officers aboard ship were also Lieutenant-Captain Brainaizen, First Lieutenant Bassin and others. The 10th Infantry Corps of the 8th Army, whose chief of staff was Major General Lev Berezinsky (later chief of staff of the army on the Volkhov front) played an important role in defending the city. [73]

---

71. Ibid., 105.
72. Ibid., 106, 118; Sverdlov, *Evrei Generaly*, 233. Between 1942 and 1943, Tsherniavsky was second in command of the 3rd Armored Army, and between 1944 and 1945 he served as commander of the armored forces of the second Baltic and second Byelorussian fronts. Tsherniavsky served in the Red Army from 1917 and had taken part in the Civil War.
73. Sverdlov, *Evrei Generaly*, 29; Aron Abramovich, *Leningradskaia Bitva* (Tel Aviv, 1990), 9. Major General Berezinsky was wounded at the front and died of his wounds in July 1943.

The 1st Latvian Volunteer Regiment[74] fought in the Tallinn battles. It was partially composed of soldiers from the workers' guards who had retreated from Latvia, and about 20 percent of its members were Jewish. The regiment suffered heavy losses, including Commissar Solomon Bauman. The forces that defended Tallinn were evacuated to reinforce the defense of Kronstadt, Leningrad's naval base. The evacuation was carried out through the Finnish straits, where the Germans had complete air supremacy and which were full of mines that had been planted by the Germans and Finns. Of the 195 ships that took part in the evacuation, 53 were sunk, and of the 23,000 men aboard, 4,767 were lost at sea.[75]

The Soviet military base at Hanko in southwest Finland was important in the battles for control of the Baltic Sea and the battle of Leningrad. According to the peace treaty signed after the Soviet-Finnish war, the Soviet Union leased Hanko from Finland. Hanko's garrison held 25,000 soldiers, half of them serving in the navy. The commissar and deputy commander of the base was a Jew named Arseny Rasskin. On July 1, 1941, the Finnish army attacked the base but was repelled. For 164 days the garrison force was under siege and was bombarded by Finns and Germans. The base's warships prevented German freedom of action in the Baltic Sea and enabled the Soviets to attack enemy ships. Rasskin distinguished himself in directing the battle and personally commanded the capture of various islands nearby. The base commander, General S.I. Kabanov, wrote of him that "he kept looking for opportunities to take an active part in the battle. No matter how often I told him there was no need for him personally to participate in the fighting and that as commander of the defense of the peninsula he had a different role, nothing helped."

Other Jews were outstanding in defending the base, among them Captain Lev Tuder, commander of a shore battery of heavy guns (305 mm), who in September had been appointed commander of the island of Khorsen, which was part of the base at Hanko; Sergeant Semyon Levin, deputy commander of an infantry platoon who demonstrated particular valor in defending the island of Elmholm; and Major Peter Roitberg, chief of staff and acting commander of the 13th Air Force Brigade. In November 1941, it was decided that the base would be evacuated and its defenders transferred to Leningrad. The evacuation was carried out by sea under extremely difficult conditions. Many ships hit mines

---

74. A standard infantry regiment was composed of three infantry battalions, with no support units of artillery, engineers, etc.
75. Abramovich, *Leningradskaia Bitva*, 9–10; Pospelov et al., *Istoria Velikoi*, vol. 2, 83–85.

and sank, among them the minesweeper *Gordy*, commanded by Yevgeny Yefet, a Jew, who went down with his ship.[76]

The National Guard divisions contributed greatly to the defense of Leningrad. They were approximately 135,000 strong and had been mobilized from the city's residents into infantry divisions and dozens of artillery, engineering, air defense and other brigades. Approximately 6 percent of them were Jewish, similar to the percentage of Jews in the city's population. Many of the members of the division of the Vasileostrovsk quarter were professors, lecturers, students and employees of the university, the Academy of Art and other academic institutions in the neighborhood. Many of them were Jewish.[77]

Of the hundreds of Jews in the 2nd National Guard Division (which later became the 85th Infantry Division) was its commander, Major General Ilya Liubovtsev, who was later replaced by Colonel Isaak Lebedinskii. The division's artillery commander was Lieutenant-Colonel Grigory Brusser. He was later appointed artillery commander of the army and then, from 1943 on, artillery chief of staff of the Leningrad front, holding the rank of major general while in that capacity. The division showed particular valor in defending the bridgehead at Oranienbaum, west of Leningrad, which covered dozens of kilometers along the southern shore of the Finnish Gulf. The bridgehead, called the Naval Operations Group, was cut off from Leningrad's main defenses after German forces conquered an area along the Finnish Gulf of about five kilometers between Leningrad and Oranienbaum. The bridgehead was important for the defense of Kronstadt, which was the Soviet Navy's most important naval base on the Baltic Sea and which supported the ships evacuating Tallinn and Hanko. It held out for more than two years and kept large enemy forces in place, until the German forces were driven back from Leningrad.

In the defensive battles around Oranienbaum and in local counterattacks, an important role was played by a tank brigade commanded by Major Aron Oskovsky. Major Haim Krasnukotsky, who was named a Hero of the Soviet Union during the Finnish war, commanded the 59th Regiment of the 85th Infantry Division, showing unusual valor at the Leningrad front. Krasnukotsky

---

76. Abramovich, *V Reshaiushchei Voine*, 129–131; Kirian et al., *Slovar-Spravochnik*, 479. Rasskin, after his valor defending and evacuating Hanko, where he was one of the last to leave, was appointed the head of the political department of the Black Sea Navy. He died in a plane crash in December 1942.
77. Abramovich, *Leningradskaia Bitva*, 12.

was promoted to colonel and fought at Leningrad and later in Latvia.[78] In the southern sector, the 42nd Army defended the city; its chief of staff was Lieutenant General Lev Berezinsky, who had been chief of staff of the 10th Infantry Corps during the defense of Tallinn.[79]

The only supply route to besieged Leningrad was by ship through Lake Ladoga, and over the ice when the lake froze in the wintertime. The route was called the Road of Life (*Doroga zhizni*) and was used to bring in food and weapons and to evacuate half a million Leningrad residents. The evacuation was effected to reduce the number of mouths to be fed, and most of the evacuees were children. The imported food could not prevent a famine, and according to official Soviet sources, 632,253 people died of hunger and approximately 17,000 civilians were killed by bombs and artillery fire. According to other estimates, the number of dead was one million of the three million residents living in Leningrad and its suburbs when the Germans isolated it from the rest of the Soviet Union. In January–February 1942 alone, there were 199,187 deaths in the city, approximately three to four thousand a day. The small quantities of food that did arrive were given, for the most part, to the soldiers defending the city and to the workers in factories that continued manufacturing weapons and ammunition, although it was rationed in extremely small portions.[80]

There were many Jews involved in both planning and operating the Road of Life. During September and the beginning of October 1941, ships brought supplies into Leningrad during relentless attacks of German fire. The commander of the Soviet flotilla that secured the movement of the supply ships was a Jewish rear admiral named Pavel Trainin, who had previously commanded the Soviet naval base at Riga. In October the lake began to freeze over, and it was important to know as soon as possible when the ice was strong enough to bear the weight of motorized vehicles. Ice-depth measurements were taken by a Lieutenant Colonel Yakov Yoselev, who headed the front's meteorological service. Army engineer B.V. Yakubovsky was put in charge of preparing the ice route.

---

78. Shapiro, *Under Fire*, 258–61; Sverdlov, *V Stroiu Otvazhnykh*, 150–51; Abramovich, *Leningradskaia Bitva*, 11–12.
79. Abramovich, *V Reshaiushchei Voine*, 126. Major General Berezinsky had joined the Red Army in 1918, participated in the Civil War, and was wounded at the front and died on July 13, 1943.
80. Alexander Werth, *Russia at War: 1941–1945* [Hebrew] (Tel Aviv: Maarakhot, 1968), 231–32, 237; Abramovich, *Leningradskaia Bitva*, 33–34.

On November 21, the first attempt was made to bring in supplies on wagons hitched to horses. F.G. Zinger was one of the wagon drivers who managed to bring sacks of flour into the besieged city, despite German artillery fire and heavy subsequent losses. On the following day, November 22, the ice route was officially opened and the first attempt was made to use motorized vehicles. The caravan was led by the transport battalion commander, Major Biberman. Hundreds of other Jews dealt with the supervision of the ice route. During its operation, hundreds of trucks were hit and sunk. Between November 23 and December 1, 800 tons of flour were brought in but 40 trunks sank.[81] Mordukh Katzman, who was released from army service for reasons of health, volunteered in September 1941 and was stationed with the 332nd Transport Battalion, where he served as a driver for the ice route. He recounted that "every vehicle had two drivers. At night we went via the Ladoga Lake with only a short distance between them. We kept our headlights off and our doors open so that we could jump out if the ice began to crack."[82]

Zhukov wrote of the Road of Life that "the story of the famous life-road connecting besieged Leningrad with the mainland is an epic in itself. By that road, which lay across Lake Ladoga, provisions and ammunition were delivered to the Leningraders by cross-country vehicle, horse-drawn carts and every other means available."[83]

In August 1941 the northern front was divided: north of Leningrad was the Karelian front and in the south was the Leningrad front. Major General (later Lieutenant General) Lev Skvirsky was appointed chief of staff of the Karelian front. The Karelian front, in the far north, defended the access to Murmansk and repulsed heavy attacks by the German "Norwegian" mountain corps and by the Finnish army forces which attacked from north of Lake Ladoga. On the Karelian front in the region of the city of Suoiarvi and its crossroads, during the first half of July 1941, the 52nd Regiment commanded by Colonel Mark Birman,

---

81. Abramovich, *Leningradskaia Bitva*, 40–41.
82. Ibid., 42.
83. Zhukov, *Memoirs*, 318. To defend the city the army needed fuel, which was also necessary to run vital factories within the city. In the spring of 1942 a pipeline was laid on the lake bed and the city was assured a supply of fuel. The German attempts to damage the pipeline using depth charges failed. A cable was also laid on the lake bed to bring electricity from the power station at Volkhov southeast of the lake, which the Soviets had retaken from the Germans.

together with additional forces, halted the advance of the German and Finnish forces, stabilizing the front in that sector for a significant amount of time.[84]

Jews in the Battles of the Ukraine

In the southern Soviet Union, the German Army Group South attacked the Ukraine, intending to conquer Kiev and the Donbas industrial region and proceed to Kharkov. On the southern front, the Germans were met with greater resistance than elsewhere and they advanced more slowly. From the first day, units of the 87th Infantry Division headed by Colonel Michael Blank fought to delay the enemy near the city of Luboml, to the east of the Bug River. On the third day of the war, the division commander, Major General F.F. Aliabushev, was killed, and the division, which had suffered heavy losses, found itself surrounded. Some of its units dispersed; others surrendered. Blank organized the remains of two regiments and for eight days, continuously clashing with German troops, he led them through the woods to the front (which was far to the east) and managed to rejoin the Soviet forces. During those days when entire Soviet armies disintegrated and hundreds of thousands of Soviet soldiers were captured, Blank's action was extraordinary.

On July 8 his force (which had become an independent battle group) was ordered to take defensive positions in the outskirts of Novograd-Volynskii. After a few days, he was forced to retreat eastward. He proved his leadership and bravery, and on August 20, while still a colonel, he was appointed commander of the 15th Infantry Corps, which fought in the Chernigov region. The corps, having fought and suffered losses, was below standard and could not even be called a division. In the same sector, German Panzers crossed the Desna River from the southwest and established a bridgehead on the eastern bank. Blank received orders to drive the enemy forces to the western bank of the river. He personally led the counterattack and was killed in the assault. General Ivan Fediuninskii, commander of the 5th Army, to which the corps belonged, wrote of Blank as follows:

> We were very sorry [to learn of] the death of this brave, vigorous officer, who demonstrated will power and courage while leading the

---

84. Abramovich, *Leningradskaia Bitva*, 17–18. Skvirsky had served in the Red Army since 1919 and took part in the Civil War. During 1943–44, he commanded an army.

units of the 87th Division out of the blockade. Colonel Blank was a brave commander and was always found in the most dangerous localities. He fell in the counterattack while leading it, rifle in hand, like an ordinary soldier....[85]

The 64th Infantry Corps under the command of Major General Zinovey (Ziama) Rogoznyi took part in the battles waged south of Kiev in July–August 1941. From the middle of July, his troops halted the enemy's advance toward the Dnieper and defended it. At the beginning of August, the 2nd Airborne Brigade, which was attached to the 64th Corps, went into action in the counterattack. It was commanded by Colonel K.P. Stein. The brigade, which was made up of elite Red Army units and noted for its fighting spirit, rushed the enemy's positions and fought bayonet to bayonet with the Germans, forcing them to retreat.[86]

However, the military acts and sacrifice exhibited by many of the commanders and soldiers were not enough to change the general situation on the front. In the middle of September 1941 the Red Army suffered one of its worst defeats. Kiev was captured and 600,000 Soviet soldiers surrendered. Small groups, sometimes improvised from soldiers belonging to various other units – among them a high percentage of Jews, for whom the war was a matter of life and death – continued fighting and attempted to break out of the pocket and reach Red Army lines. Colonel Isaak Kushnir, commander of the artillery of the 31st Corps, his forces having scattered, collected a few hundred soldiers from various units and, moving only at night, tried to escape the blockade. For ten days the improvised force moved eastward behind the German lines, sometimes coming upon German forces, and in a clash with German tanks Kushnir was killed. On the same front Colonel Grigori Reutenberg, commander of the 37th Cavalry Division, retreated toward a bridge on the Psel River that was in German hands. On September 12, his forces took the bridge and held it until all the soldiers had crossed, at which point they blew it up. The 6th Airborne Brigade, commanded by Pavel Mendelevich Shafarenko, also continued fighting behind German lines, and on September 18, after having been surrounded for ten days, they broke through enemy lines and joined the main force.[87]

---

85. Abramovich, *V Reshaiushchei Voine*, 110–111, 146.
86. Ibid., 142–43. Major General Rogoznyi had joined the Red Army in 1918 and fought in the Civil War.
87. Ibid., 149–51.

Odessa, which had a Jewish population of more than 200,000, was besieged for 73 days, from August 5 until October 16. The main defense forces of Odessa were the 25th Chapeyev Division and the 95th Moldavian Division. They were joined by the division of the Popular Guards of Odessa, in which many Jews served. After the city was cut off, its defense was turned over to the command of the Soviet fleet in the Black Sea, and approximately 8,000 sailors joined the land forces. Cannons on the decks of warships were also used to defend the city. Opposing them were seven infantry divisions and one armored division of the Romanian army, supported by German air cover. Both sides suffered heavy losses in the ensuing battles. During the second half of September, the Soviet command brought divisions from the Caucasus by sea. Soviet sources note that about 40 percent of the soldiers were killed and wounded and that losses among the officers and the battalions of sailors were even higher. The Romanian army also brought in reinforcements, and according to Soviet data, about 18 Romanian divisions took part in the battles in Odessa.[88]

Many Jews participated in defending the city and the naval base, both soldiers and civilians. Captain Mikhail Tshetshelnitsky commanded the armored train "For the Homeland" (*Za Rodinu*). The commissar of the First Sailors Battalion was Semyon Yzus, who fell while attacking an enemy position in a hand-to-hand battle on September 27. In a Romanian attack on the defending sector of one of the battalions, both its commander and commissar were badly wounded. Senior Lieutenant Peter Aronski took upon himself the command of the remaining force and, fighting hand-to-hand with the enemy, forced them to retreat, leaving scores of dead and wounded. Aronski was promoted to captain and appointed second in command of a regiment. The commander of the 422nd Howitzer Battalion of the 157th Division, which had been sent as reinforcement from the Caucasus, was Captain Alexander Meyerson. In the counterattack at the end of September 1941, Meyerson's guns caused severe losses to the enemy and forced them to retreat.[89]

Head of the medical service in the besieged city was Colonel Dr. David Sokolovsky. The central post of defending the city and organizing the civilian population to aid the army was filled by the secretary of the City Committee of the Communist Party, Naum Gurewitz. General (later Marshal) Alexei Nikolaivich Krillov, one of the commanders of the city's defense, wrote about

---

88. Pospelov et al., *Istoria Velikoi*, vol. 2, 113–18.
89. Abramovich, *V Reshaiushchei Voine*, 161–62.

Gurewitz: "Heading the [civilian] operational group was N. Gurewitz, Secretary of the City Committee. The group dealt with all aspects of organizing local sources of aid for the army – building barricades, organizing fighting regiments, civilian anti-aircraft defense, keeping order in the besieged city...and all the problems connected with the local manufacture of weapons."[90] During the siege, the factories in the city produced 55 tanks assembled on tractors, weapons and ammunition. The idea and implementation of turning tractors into tanks were the province of an army engineer Urii Kogan. When the city airport was shelled by enemy mortars, it was urgent to prepare an alternative airport. With Gurewitz's help, a volunteer brigade of women commanded by Asia Fishman was set up, and, working around the clock, within a week they had prepared the new airport. Many of the Jewish defenders of Odessa were later decorated. Some of them managed to evacuate by sea; however, many of them died defending the city.[91]

The commander of Odessa's large naval base, Colonel Samuel Dityatkovsky, showed particular valor when the city was being evacuated. Between October 1 and 16, more than 80,000 soldiers and about 15,000 civilians were evacuated from Odessa and transferred to the defense of Sevastopol in the Crimea.[92] Odessa was not evacuated because of enemy pressure but because the 11th German Army, commanded by General Manstein, had conquered most of the Crimea, and the forces in Sevastopol were in urgent need of reinforcements to defend the city and the main Soviet naval base in the Black Sea.

On October 30, 1941, the German 11th Army reached the outskirts of Sevastopol. Until the reinforcements arrived from Odessa, Sevastopol was defended by the remnants of the forces that had retreated from other sites in the Crimea, the local garrison and forces sent from Novorossiysk, a port city on the eastern shore of the Black Sea. Those forces repelled an attempt made by the German Army to take the city at the beginning of November 1941. Among the reinforcements arriving from Novorossiysk was the 8th Marine Brigade (Morskaia Piekhota) commanded by Colonel Vladimir Vilshensky. On November 7, the brigade counterattacked and retook the two hills commanding the city. The city's military situation improved when the forces arrived from Odessa and counterattacked to retake German positions controlling the city. During

---

90. Ibid., 159–60.
91. Ibid., 165–66; Pospelov et al., *Istoria Velikoi*, vol. 2, 115.
92. Rzheshevski et al., *Velikaia Otechestvenna Voina*, 59.

the 7th Marine Brigade's counterattack, a battalion commanded by Captain Moise Prosyak captured one of the German positions and repelled the German counterattack; Prosyak was seriously wounded in the battle. On December 17 the Germans again launched an assault on Sevastopol. Vladimir Vilshenky's 8th Marine Brigade stood fast in the face of superior forces and repelled the attack in hand-to-hand combat, but lost 1,700 soldiers in two days. Haim Khislevski, the commissar of one of the battalions, fell in battle. The 7th Marine Brigade was sent into battle to defend the Chorgun Valley (Chorgunskaia Dolina), where the situation was critical. The brigade's chief of staff, A.K. Kerner, fell in the counterattack. The German second assault on Sevastopol, which lasted until the end of December, ended in failure.[93]

Forces of German Army Group South continued advancing eastward in the Ukraine and reached the outskirts of Kharkov during the second half of October 1941. The Red Army's 10th Armored Brigade, commanded by Benyamin Buntman, participated in the battles near the city of Dergachi, west of Kharkov, and its counterattack halted the advance of the 6th German Army for a time. The 169th Infantry Division of the 38th Army, commanded by Major General Samuel Rogachevsky, defended the city's southern outskirts. The Popular Guard in Kharkov, among them the 1st Regiment, commanded by Zilper and containing other Jewish members, fought in the street battles that took place between October 23 and 25. The city was occupied by the Germans on October 25, 1941.[94]

Jews in the Defense of Moscow

On September 30, 1941, the Germans renewed their attack on Moscow after Guderian's armored army (which had been sent to the Ukraine) was returned to Army Group Center. The Germans surrounded large Soviet forces in the Bryansk region southwest of Moscow and in the Viazma-Rzhev region west and northwest of the city, endangering the Soviet capital. The situation was critical, and Zhukov, hurriedly called to Leningrad on October 10, returned and was put in command of the defense of Moscow.

On the Moscow front, as on others, Jewish commanders and soldiers played prominent roles. The 242nd Infantry Division in the Rzhev region was severely hit and surrounded. Major Y.M. Samoilovich, commander of the 897th

---

93.   Abramovich, *V Reshaiushchei Voine*, 264–65, 269–72.
94.   Ibid., 153–54; Artyomov, *Bratskii Boyevoi Soyuz*, 35–37. Rogachevsky joined the Red Army in 1918 and had fought in the Civil War.

Regiment, which defended the division's southern flank, fell in battle. When the division was surrounded and both its commander and commissar were wounded and the artillery commander killed, Lieutenant Colonel V. Glebov was made commander of the division, and David Dragunsky, who had been commander of the tank brigade that had been attached to the division, was appointed chief of staff. The divisions battled for ten days to break out of the encirclement. When Glebov became ill, Dragunsky took it upon himself to command the remains of the division, which totaled about 3,000 soldiers, and managed not only to extricate them but to deploy them in a new defensive line. On November 25, in the Klin region north of Moscow, a tank battalion of the 8th Armored Brigade, commanded by Leonid Motsarski, repelled enemy tanks and prevented them from conquering Rogachevo.[95]

On October 8, the tank battalion of the 18th Brigade, commanded by Grigori Kogan, was deployed to halt the enemy in the Mozhaysk region on the main road to Moscow. The battalion fought until all its tanks had been hit. In an attempt to cover the infantry's retreat, Kogan attacked the Germans with his last two tanks, both of whose cannons had been hit. He fell in the attack. To the north, on the Volokolamsk road, the famous 316th Division of General Panfilov defended the outskirts of Moscow, with many Jews fighting in its ranks. Among them were Major K. Hoffman, the division's operations officer; Major Shechtman, commander of the 1077th Brigade, who was badly wounded; and Major Vladimir Ogsburg, chief of staff of the 857th Artillery Battalion, who fell at an observation post while directing cannon fire.[96]

On the Volokolamsk road, in the 18th Division's defensive sector, artillery private Haim Diskin distinguished himself in action and was awarded the title of Hero of the Soviet Union. When all the men in his anti-tank battery were wounded, Diskin, alone and wounded as well, continued firing shells and hitting enemy tanks until he lost consciousness. In the region of the city of Kalinin, north of Moscow, Captain Yosef Makovsky demonstrated exceptional valor in commanding his tanks in battle and was awarded the title of Hero of the Soviet Union. In a counterattack he commanded and in which he was wounded, two villages were recaptured.[97]

---

95. F.D. Sverdlov, *Encyclopedia Evreiskogo Geroizma* (Moscow: Dograf, 2002), 223; Abramovich, *V Reshaiushchei Voine*, 183, 202.
96. Abramovich, *V Reshaiushchei Voine*, 194–99.
97. Shapiro, *Under Fire*, 103–106, 363–67. Makovsky later fought in Stalingrad, where he was seriously wounded a second time.

To the south, on the Bryansk front, the Germans advanced in the direction of Tula and Moscow, where Guderian's 2nd Armored Army attacked. The Soviet 3rd Army, commanded by General Yakov Kreyzer, and other large Soviet forces were surrounded south of Bryansk. On October 7, the order was given to break out, and for the next four weeks Kreyzer's forces moved east without a stop, clashing with the German forces blocking their way. Kreyzer's forces succeeded in breaking through the encirclement and redeployed in a new defensive line, where they halted the enemy's advance on Moscow from the southwest. The 42nd Tank Brigade was also surrounded, and after 11 days of tank battles they had neither fuel nor ammunition; later on, they had to abandon their tanks as well. The brigade disintegrated. Major Grigory Klein, who was its deputy chief of staff, gathered the remaining soldiers and led them out of the pocket. Klein described the events and his meeting with General Kreyzer and his retreating forces as follows:

> In the forest I gathered the remains of the brigade and told them that from now on I was their commander. I divided them into companies and platoons and appointed commanding officers. The backbone of the unit was the brigade's tank crews. I demanded the strictest discipline....
>
> We moved by night, and only on dirt side-roads; during the day we camped in the forests. When we came upon small enemy units we joined battle with them. It was like that for 10–12 days. One day we entered a small village and a soldier came running up to me and said, "Comrade Major, General Kreyzer has sent for you." It turned out that Yakov Kreyzer, the commander of the 3rd Army and his staff and some of his units were trying to break through the encirclement....
>
> I reported to him immediately and received the order that from that moment on I was under his command. I was very glad to be under the command of such a gallant commander. All the officers, including the Army's commander, advanced on foot, especially at night. The number of men grew constantly, and on the way entire units which were also looking for a way out of the encirclement joined us. All were armed. On November 5 we reached the city of

Yefremov and joined our army.... Our brigade was reorganized. I was appointed chief of staff of the 14th Tank Brigade.[98]

In the vast stretches of the battle arena that were largely wooded and had no continuous front line, it was possible for determined, enterprising commanders not to surrender, but to infiltrate or break through the surrounding German forces and join the main Red Army at the front. The actions of General Kreyzer, Major Klein, Captain Dragunsky and many others proved that was so. They were motivated by their loyalty to their country and army, and their sense of duty toward their soldiers, but it is also certain that the fact that they were Jewish and the knowledge of what awaited them as German prisoners of war influenced their fortitude and determination.

Guderian wrote about the attempts made by Kreyzer's 3rd Army and other Red Army forces to break through the encirclement:

> On October 9th, the Russian attempt to break out near Sisemka succeeded.... A small number of Russians succeeded in breaking free across the Seredina Buda–Sevsk road.... On October 11th the Russians attempted to break out in the Trubchevsk encirclement along either bank of the Navlia [River].... There was heavy fighting and the enemy succeeded in creating a gap in our defenses. At the same time heavy street fighting took place in 24th Armored Corps area, in Mzensk.... Russian T-34 tanks went into action and inflicted heavy losses on the German tanks, and the situation changed.... The prospect of rapid decisive victories was fading in consequence.... On October 13 the Russians continued their attempts to break out between the Navlia and Brasovo.... A group of about 5,000 Russians succeeded in fighting their way through as far as Dmitrovsk.[99]

Although during the first stage of the war the Red Army suffered severe defeats, the Germans could not realize their plan to conquer Moscow and bring the Soviet Union to their knees before the winter. By the end of November the German advance toward Moscow had been halted. The autumn rains and muddy roads, the early winter with its freezing temperatures, the determined fighting of the Red Army and the failure of the German army to have prepared

---

98.   Abramovich, *V Reshaiushchei Voine*, 188–90.

99.   Guderian, *Panzer Leader*, 236–39.

for winter fighting conditions all resulted in their attack grinding to a halt. Guderian wrote:

> Our attack on Moscow had broken down. All the sacrifices and endurance of our brave troops had been in vain. We had suffered a grievous defeat which was to be seriously aggravated during the next few weeks, thanks to the rigidity of our Supreme Command: despite all our reports, those men far away in East Prussia could form no true concept of the real conditions of the winter war in which their soldiers were now engaged. This ignorance led to repeatedly exorbitant demands being made on the fighting troops. A prompt and extensive withdrawal to a line where the terrain was suitable for defense and where positions had already been prepared seemed the best and most economical way of rectifying the situation.... But this was exactly what Hitler refused to allow.[100]

6. THE SOVIET COUNTEROFFENSIVE ON THE MOSCOW FRONT AND IN THE SOUTH: DECEMBER 6, 1941–MARCH 1942

Repelling the Germans from Moscow

While conducting a defensive war on the roads that led to Moscow, the Soviet High Command prepared a counteroffensive to force the enemy retreat from the outskirts of Moscow. On December 6, 1941, the Red Army initiated the offensive, which lasted until the end of March 1942. To that end the Soviet High Command brought in fresh troops from the Soviet-Japanese border in the Far East. They had been transferred after Soviet military intelligence reported Japan was planning to attack the United States, and at that point the Soviet Union was not in danger of a Japanese attack through Siberia. Moreover, the Soviet command would have certainly considered the removal of the enemy from the gates of Moscow an issue of greater priority than a Japanese threat in the Far East.

The main counteroffensive was in the northern, western and southern sectors of the Moscow region. The cities of Kalinin, Kaluga and many others were liberated. The Red Army advanced to the west and reached the region of Velikye-Luki north of Vitebsk, thus removing Moscow from immediate

---

100. Ibid., 259.

danger. In the south, by the end of November 1941, the Red Army had conquered Rostov. It was Nazi Germany's first major defeat in the Second World War and proved that the German army was not invincible. Tens of thousands of German soldiers were killed, wounded or taken captive, and the Germans lost hundreds of tanks and an enormous amount of equipment. In the wake of the defeat, Field-Marshal Walter von Brauchitsch resigned as commander of the land forces, and in December 1941, the commanders of the German Army Groups North, Central and South were replaced. Hitler took upon himself the role of commander of the land forces, in addition to already being commander of all the German armed forces, including air and sea forces.

The Soviet winter attack, which was crowned with impressive success, petered out in March 1942. The Red Army, which had also suffered heavy losses, did not have the strength to maintain the initiative and needed a respite to reorganize. However, Stalin, despite the advice of Zhukov and other General Staff officers, decided to continue attacking – and not through a concerted effort in one sector, but rather in three separate sectors: in the Kerch peninsula in the Crimea, in the Kharkov region and on the Volkhov River front, southeast of Leningrad. The attack on the Volkhov River sector was commanded by General Andrei Vlasov, commander of the 2nd Army Strike Force (Vtoraya Udarnaya Armya). It began at the beginning of May, but after initial successes Vlasov's forces were surrounded and the attack ended in failure. He and his men surrendered to the Germans.[101] All three attacks failed and the Red Army suffered heavy losses in terms of personnel and arms, a situation which made itself felt in the summer of 1942.

Jewish Soldiers in the Counteroffensive on the Moscow Front

On December 12, 1941, the tank battalion commander of the 8th Armored Brigade, Captain Leonid Mocharski, fell while attacking the enemy in the battle at Klin (northwest of Moscow). He had fought in the sector from the second half of November, when his battalion repelled a German tank attack, preventing the

---

101. As a prisoner of war, General Vlasov collaborated with the Germans. Flyers signed with his name were issued by the Germans, calling upon Soviet soldiers to desert and fight against Stalin's Jewish-Bolshevik dictatorship. In 1944 he established the Russkaia Osvoboditelnaya Armia (Russian Liberation Army) within the German army. When Germany surrendered, he was captured by the Allied forces and deported to the Soviet Union, where he was tried, found guilty of treason and hanged.

enemy from advancing eastward toward Klin and threatening Moscow from the north. On December 20, an infantry regiment commanded by Major M. Shteinlucht of the 331st Infantry Division participated in the street fighting in the key city of Volokolamsk (which lay on the main highway to Moscow). The Soviet soldiers found a gallows in the city with the bodies of six young men and two young women who had been sent to carry out sabotage missions behind enemy lines in November. They had met a German force and, in the ensuing exchange of fire, were wounded and caught. Among the youths were two Jews, Nikolai Kagan and Yevgenia Poltawska. The entire group posthumously received the Order of Lenin for its bravery.[102]

The 201st Latvian Infantry Division (as part of the 33rd Army) went into battle for the first time in the counteroffensive to the west and southwest of Moscow at Naro-Fominsk and Borovsk. As noted above, there were many Jews in the division. It began actual fighting only a few months after it had been organized and without having finished basic training. In the attack on Naro-Fominsk on December 20, dozens of Jewish soldiers of the 122nd regiment fell, among them Junior Lieutenant Samuel Grinfeld and Hersh Bitker, politruk of the 3rd company. On the same day, two other regiments of the division (the 92nd and 191st) went into battle at Ermolino, supported by the 200th Artillery Regiment commanded by Major Peter Kushnir. The company commander, Reuven Admor, distinguished himself in battle and was the first in the division to be decorated with the Order of Red Banner. After a fierce battle, Naro-Fominsk was liberated on December 26. Isaak Pliner, the commissar of the 201st Engineer Battalion, fell liberating the city. On January 4, 1942, the 92nd and 191st regiments broke into Borovsk and liberated it. Many of the soldiers in the regiments fought bravely and many fell, among them Junior Lieutenant Isaak Borok, Lieutenant Hanan Zicherman and others. On January 11 the division conquered the fortified region of Fedotovo, and on January 15, having suffered heavy losses, it was taken out of the battle for reorganization.[103]

The goal of the Soviet counteroffensive southeast of Lake Ladoga was to open the railway to Moscow, making it possible to bring supplies to besieged Leningrad. The railway ran through the German-held city of Tikhvin, an important crossroads between Moscow and Leningrad. In the middle of December the Volkhov Front was set up to command all the Soviet forces operating southeast

---

102. Abramovich, *V Reshaiushchei Voine*, 202, 211–12.
103. Ibid., 214–16.

of Lake Ladoga; General (later Marshal) Kiril Meretskov was in charge, and the chief of staff was Major General Grigori Stelmach. In his memoirs, Meterskov wrote the following about Stelmach:

> I relied entirely on his great experience, which had proved itself many times in the past. He carried out every mission brilliantly. He was widely knowledgeable, knew the military profession very well and also excelled in personal valor.... To our great sorrow he was cut down at the height of his creative activity. About a year after the Tikhvin mission he fell on the Stalingrad front.[104]

Tikhvin was liberated on December 9. For his distinguished service in the operation, Stelmach received the Order of the Red Banner. Many Jews took part in the battles on the Volkhov front, among them chief of staff of the 65th Infantry Division, Major Grigori Kutik; engineers' company commander Lieutenant Yu Shaikevich; tank company commander Senior Lieutenant Constantine Lasman; and anti-tank battery commander Senior Lieutenant M. Zeichman. The 44th Infantry Division was transferred from the Leningrad front through Lake Ladoga to reinforce the troops at the Volkhov front. An advance unit of 300 men of the division's artillerymen, commanded by Lieutenant Samuel Abezgauz, was brought into battle as infantry before their guns arrived. After a few days of battle, the unit found itself surrounded by Germans. Clashing with enemy units, Abezgauz led his soldiers through the forests to the Red Army lines, at temperatures reaching -30° Celsius (-22° Fahrenheit). During one of the clashes he was seriously wounded but continued leading his men. They reached the Red Army in the Novaia Ladoga region; of his entire unit, only 49 men remained.[105]

On January 9, 1942, the 4th Army attacked from the region of Ostashkov in the direction of Toropets, in the northwestern sector south of the Volkhov front, forcing the Germans to retreat to the west. On January 21 the army conquered Toropets and Zapadnaia Dvina. Colonel Benjamin Beilin, who was later promoted to major general and division commander, headed the army's operational branch.[106]

---

104. Ibid., 222. Stelmach had volunteered for the Red Army when he was 19 and fought in the Civil War. On December 21, 1942, he fell in battle in the vicinity of Kalach on the Don River.
105. Ibid., 221–23.
106. Ibid., 228; Sverdlov, *Evrei Generaly*, 24.

The 158th Infantry Division of the 22nd Army participated in the attack on the Kalinin front. The mission of occupying the village of Zhigarevo was given to the 881st Regiment; the attack took place on February 22, 1942. The Soviet soldiers came upon a fortified enemy position. Machine guns were fired from a bunker, forcing the attackers to the ground and preventing them from advancing. Artillery fire had no influence on the position. Private Abram Levin ran to the enemy bunker and covered the sights of the machine gun, his body taking the bullets. The machine gun was silenced and the soldiers of the unit rose up cheering, rushed forward and occupied the village. A monument was erected in the village to Abram Levin's bravery.[107] A year later, in February 1943, a Russian private named Alexander Matrosov performed the same act of self-sacrifice in the region of Pskov. The Soviet media turned him into a symbol of heroism and of boundless devotion to the Soviet homeland, and years later, when the history of the war was written, Matrosov's act was widely noted. He was awarded the title of Hero of the Soviet Union, and the battalion in which he fought was named after him. The act of bravery performed by the Jewish soldier Abram Levin, performed exactly one year before, was never mentioned.

On the night of January 23, 1942, a counteroffensive was launched southwest of Kaluga, south of Moscow. A platoon of soldiers using snow gliders infiltrated behind enemy lines for a night attack to occupy the village of Khludnevo near Sukhinichi and prevent the enemy forces on the front from receiving reinforcements. The platoon consisted of 25 men who belonged to the NKVD's Special Missions Brigade. They had been ordered to hold the village until the main Soviet force, which was attacking on the front, joined them. They reached the village and attacked the superior German forces, fighting all night long. The main attacking forces did not arrive from the front, and the entire platoon perished. The last to die was the sharpshooter Private Eliezer Papernik. When his ammunition ran out he blew himself up with his last hand grenade, along with the German soldiers who approached him. For his act of bravery he was awarded the title of Hero of the Soviet Union. His certificate was signed by Zhukov, who was then commander of the western front, and by Colonel General Nikolai Bulganin, a member of the front council. It stated that

> On January 22, 1942, in an action of the snow-glider platoon, the soldier Lazar Haimovich Papernik broke into a fortified enemy village of Khludnevo whose garrison numbered 400 men. In a battle with

---

107. Abramovich, *V Reshaiushchei Voine*, 229.

superior German forces, his platoon killed and wounded more than 100 of the enemy, and upon being surrounded, it fought through-

out the night. At the critical moment, when Comrade Commissar Egortsev died a hero's death, Comrade Papernik assumed command. With a small group of soldiers he bravely fought far-superior enemy forces. Remaining the only one alive, he did not surrender to the Germans, who did their best to capture him, and shouting "Bolsheviks do not surrender!" he blew himself up with a hand grenade.[108]

PRIVATE ELIEZER PAPERNIK

Three days later the Soviet forces captured Khludnevo, after which the events of Papernik's heroic death came to light.

Jews in the Battles on the Southern Front: Rostov-on-Don and the Crimea

At the end of October 1941 forces from the German Army Group South reached the outskirts of Rostov-on-Don. The city was located at a strategic junction on the road to the Caucasus. The Soviet government established a defense committee headed by the first secretary of the District Communist Party, Boris Davinsky. The committee organized dozens of battalions from among local residents, who participated in the defense of the city. The 343rd Infantry Division halted the advance of the German Panzers and distinguished itself in battle. The commander of the cannon battery of the 1151st Artillery Regiment was Lieutenant Joseph Radchenko, who aimed his cannons directly at the enemy tanks and hit four of them. In the battles for Rostov, a fleet of fast Coast Guard cutters came from the Sea of Azov, commanded by Jewish Major Tsezar (Tsadok) Kunikov. The boats were equipped with machine guns and light cannons. They operated along the shore held by the enemy and at the Don estuary.[109] On November 21, 1941, the Germans occupied Rostov. To prevent their advance to the Caucasus, the Soviet forces counterattacked and on November 29, reconquered the city.

---

108. Sverdlov, *V Stroiu Otvazhnikh*, 206–8.
109. Abramovich, *V Reshaiushchei Voine*, 226–27.

After the Soviet victory in the Rostov region, between December 25, 1941, and January 2, 1942, the forces at the Caucasian front landed on the Kerch peninsula and in the port city of Feodosia to ease German pressure on Sevastopol and to create conditions for the Crimea's liberation. The 51st Army forces were brought to the Kerch peninsula and the 44th Army forces to Feodosia by the Sea of Azov fleet, whose chief of staff was Captain Arkady Sverdlov and whose commissar was V.A. Lizinsky. Their boats belonged to the naval base at Kerch and were commanded by Read Admiral Pavel Trainin (see above, "Jews in Defense of Leningrad and along the Roads Leading to It"). Among the ships leading the landing force in Feodosia was the minesweeper *Schyt* commanded by Lieutenant Captain Vladimir Grangros; the commissar of the landing flotilla (six vessels) was Joseph Weissman. The flotilla commissar of the ships providing covering fire for the landing force was Joseph Prager. Captain Michael Shtarkman distinguished himself in the battle of the Feodosia region. In Kerch, Lieutenant Joseph Bolshinsky was wounded in the assault and died of his wounds. The landing there was successful and the Soviet force held the position. At Feodosia, the Germans counterattacked with forces brought in from the Sevastopol front and recaptured it on January 3, 1942.[110]

After the German failure to capture Sevastopol in December 1941, local battles were waged and artillery, which was important in the defense of the city, was used on both sides. The commander for the coast defense artillery (including 305-mm guns) was Colonel B.A. Fein. Commander of the medical service for the defense of Sevastopol was M.Z. Zelikov, who previously had been commander of the medical service at the naval base in Odessa.

7. THE GERMAN ATTACK ON STALINGRAD AND THE CAUCASUS: JUNE 1942–JANUARY 1943

The Renewal of the German Offensive in Southern Russia

Despite its heavy losses in equipment and personnel and the loss of ground during the Soviet winter attack, the German front did not collapse. It took the German army some months to reorganize and concentrate its forces for a renewed offensive. It was obvious to the German High Command that it could not attack simultaneously along all of the front line as it had in the summer of

---

110. Pospelov et al., *Istoria Velikoi*, vol. 2, 309–313; Abramovich, *V Reshaiushchei Voine*, 273–74.

1941. Hitler decided that the main thrust would be in southern Russia, in the direction of Stalingrad and the Caucasian Mountains, and not toward Moscow.

Economic considerations had influenced the choice of sector and goals, which were Stalingrad and the Caucasian oil fields. After the United States entered the war, economic considerations, especially oil, became more important for Hitler, as he realized he was facing a prolonged war. At the same time, the capture of the Caucasian oil fields would cut the Red Army off from its main fuel sources. The second stage of the plan, after the capture of Stalingrad, was to turn northward and advance along the Volga, reaching Moscow from the east and southeast. On July 16, 1942, Hitler transferred his headquarters from east Prussia to the Ukraine, near Vinitsa, to be closer to the front and to the attacking forces.

The Soviet High Command was of the opinion that the Germans would renew their attack in the spring of 1942, either on Moscow, Leningrad or the southern front. Stalin, who made the decisions, estimated it would be Moscow. Thus the Soviet reserves, which had dwindled in the abortive attacks in the spring, were concentrated on the fronts defending Moscow and not in the south.

In the middle of May 1942, before launching their attack toward Stalingrad and Caucasus, the Germans pushed the Red Army out of Kerch, causing them heavy losses. The Soviet High Command blamed the commanders of the forces there for the defeat and removed them from their commands. Among them was Lev Mekhlis, High Command representative of the Crimean front, who was dismissed as head of the Red Army's political administration and as deputy commissar for the defense of the Soviet Union. He was demoted from first class army commissar to corps commissar.[111]

The German attack toward Stalingrad and the Caucasus began on June 28, 1942. Army Group South forces advanced southeast between the Donets and Don Rivers. The 6th Army, commanded by General von Paulus, led the attack toward Stalingrad and Army Group A, commanded by Field Marshal von List, advanced toward the Caucasus, while the 17th Army attacked Rostov-on-Don. The Red Army was taken by surprise, its defenses cracked and the troops retreated.

The northeastern flank of the forces advancing along the Don's western bank were secured by Romanian, Hungarian and Italian troops, whose arms

---

111. Rzheshevski et al., *Velikaia Otechestvenna Voina*, 355–56.

and fighting spirit were greatly inferior to those of the Germans. In July the Germans captured Voronezh and Voroshilovgrad, and recaptured Rostov. In the beginning of September the German 6th Army reached Stalingrad and fighting began in the city. In August, Army Group A conquered Krasnodar, Novorossiysk and the oil center of Maikop. Nalchik, on the northern Caucasian slopes, was captured at the end of October 1942. The German advance was halted near Grozny in Chechnya. In the northern Caucasus, especially in the autonomous republics of Kabardino-Balakar and Chechnya, the Germans were welcomed by the indigenous Muslim population. Uprisings broke out there and retreating Soviet troops were attacked.[112]

On July 28, 1942, after the collapse of the Soviet southern front, Stalin issued Order No. 227. It forbade any retreat, regardless of the conditions, without orders. Anyone who retreated without receiving an order from a superior command authority was a traitor to the country and would be punished as such, i.e., executed. The commanders of armies whose units retreated without orders from the front command were to be arrested and face a court martial. The order also stated that in each army formation, three to five blocking units of 200 men each had to be organized and positioned behind divisions that had demonstrated weakness in battle. Without hesitation, they were to shoot soldiers trying to escape or cause a panic. Stalin stressed that the German army, after its defeats in the Soviet winter offensive, had taken similar disciplinary steps which had achieved their goal, and that the Red Army should learn from them.[113]

The Defense and Fall of Sevastopol

On June 7, 1942, after massive artillery and air strikes, the 11th German Army and the Romanian Mountain Corps attacked Sevastopol. The Germans controlled the air, and before the attack they brought in heavy artillery to destroy Soviet defensive positions. After several days of battle, the Soviets suffered from a serious lack of ammunition and fuel. Using submarines to bring in supplies did not ameliorate the situation. The defenders of Sevastopol could not withstand the superior enemy forces. The Soviet High Command in Moscow did not fully appreciate the gravity of the situation, obvious from the fact that on June 22–26, instead of evacuating the troops as quickly as possible, an infantry brigade was brought in by sea as reinforcement. Only on June 30 was the order given to

---

112. Dallin, *German Rule*, 244–47.
113. Rzheshevski et al., *Velikaia Otechestvenna Voina*, 435–36.

evacuate Sevastopol by sea, but unlike the evacuation of Odessa, it came too late. The city had already been encircled and the Germans prevented Soviet ships from reaching it. They used planes and torpedo boats to lay underwater mines. During the night of June 30, a few hundred senior officers were evacuated by plane and submarine. Fierce battles were waged until July 4, when the Germans took over the city. The last of the defenders held out and fought along the shore until July 9 in the hope that boats would come for them. During the next nights only a few hundred soldiers were rescued by swimming to boats that managed to approach the shore. Small groups tried to break out or slip through the German lines to reach the mountains where partisan units were operating, but only a very small number succeeded. The rest of the defenders were doomed, and either fell in battle or were captured. The defense of Sevastopol lasted 250 days.

According to official Soviet sources, 106,625 Soviet soldiers took part in the defense of Sevastopol. A few thousand wounded were evacuated by sea. The hundreds or even thousands of Jews who defended the city fell in battle or were murdered in German captivity. One of the fallen was Colonel Frol Grossman, commander of the 25th Chapaiev Artillery Brigade, who commanded the division's last soldiers after their original commander was wounded. Another was Commissar Isaak Kadeshevitch, who organized a regiment from the remaining soldiers of the 95th Division, and along with most of his soldiers, fell in the last battle. Captain Giorgi Alexander, commander of a battery of coast artillery, was taken prisoner by the Germans and executed when one of the captives revealed his Jewish identity. On July 2, Commissar Giorgi Shafransky and his second in command, Michael Neiger, were wounded and captured; both were shot to death. A similar fate befell many of the Jews who were captured by the Germans.[114] The defense of Sevastopol was recorded in Soviet history as one of the most courageous battles of the Great Patriotic War.

Jews in the "Strategic Defensive Operation" at Stalingrad

Pressured by German forces in July–August 1942, the Soviet 64th Army retreated to defensive positions south of Stalingrad. The retreat was covered by the 126th Infantry Division, which arrived from the Far East, commanded by Colonel Vladimir Sorokin. The commander of the 64th Army, Major General M.S. Shumilov, wrote: "We managed to delay the Germans thanks to the ar-

---

114. Rzheshevski et al., *Velikaia Otechestvenna Voina*, 98–100; Abramovich, *V Reshaiushchei Voine*, 278–89; Boris Gelman, *Prichina Smerti-Rasstrel* (Sevastopol, 2004), 169; Pospelov et al., *Istoria Velikoi*, vol. 2, 407–9.

rival of the 126th Infantry Division.... The commander of the division was Colonel V.E. Sorokin, a commander with outstanding talent, courage and strong character."[115]

The 62nd Army, commanded by General Chuykov, was responsible for defending Stalingrad. The battles continued until November 19, when the Soviets began the counterattack. The Germans conquered most of the city, but the Red Army succeeded in defending three small bridgeheads on the western bank of the Volga. The German 6th Army, however, was exhausted and decimated.

Thousands of Jewish soldiers fought in and around Stalingrad. The tank units of the 62nd Army were commanded by the Jewish Lieutenant Colonel Matvey Vaynrub, whom General Chuykov praised highly in his memoirs. According to the official Soviet history of the Second World War:

LIEUTENANT COLONEL
MATVEY VAYNRUB

The tank crews of the 62nd Army, commanded by deputy commander of the Army in charge of the armored and mechanized forces, Lieutenant Colonel Matvey Vaynrub, displayed extraordinary inventiveness and exploited the tanks most effectively in street fighting. Having a limited number of tanks, he deployed them in small groups of one and two in the important defensive sectors, and in cooperation with the infantry and artillery carried out local counterattacks or repelled the enemy. Immobilized tanks became stationary firing positions.[116]

Vaynrub was not content with merely directing armored forces, but personally commanded the tanks in street fighting. On October 14, after enemy forces had captured an important position, he led a tank and infantry counterattack and recaptured the position.[117]

---

115. Abramovich, *V Reshaiushchei Voine*, 313–17. Sorokin was severely wounded in the Stalingrad battle on August 29, 1942. He was captured by the Germans, and died or was executed by them.

116. Pospelov et al., *Istoria Velikoi*, vol. 2, 443; also see Vasily Chuykov, *The War for Stalingrad* [Hebrew] (Tel Aviv: Maarakhot, 1970), 179–89.

117. Shapiro, *Under Fire*, 598–99. After the Battle of Stalingrad, Vaynrub participated

In his memoirs, General Chuykov praised Colonel Michael Kreitzman, commander of a tank brigade, and Colonel Michael Herman, head of army headquarters' intelligence section.[118] Some of the privates and others of low rank who fought at Stalingrad were also decorated, among them Private Wolf Rimsky. His commanding officer was killed and he took command of the platoon and led the assault; he was then appointed platoon commander. He led his platoon in the capture of the Workers Union Building (Dom Profsoyuzov), which changed hands several times, fighting from floor to floor using hand grenades until the building, which had major tactical significance, was taken. On September 19, his platoon suffered heavy losses and he was left with only a few soldiers, who fell one by one until he was left alone. When a German tank approached his position he wrapped himself in hand grenades, rushed at its tread and blew himself up. Rimsky had four brothers at the front: one of them, Lev, also fell in battle, and the two others distinguished themselves in battle and were decorated.[119]

The official history of Stalingrad mentions the story of the Pavlov Building, named for Sergeant Pavlov, commander of a group of 16 soldiers, who repelled German attacks for 58 days. The last German attack was on November 24 and all 16 soldiers, among them the Jewish soldier Yidel Khayat, fell in battle. The official Soviet history of the war mentions the names and nationalities of 12 of the soldiers who fell there, but Khayat's name does not appear.[120]

Among soldiers who distinguished themselves at Stalingrad were Lieutenant Isaak Waxman, who commanded a battery of 45-mm guns in street fighting. In November 1943, he distinguished himself in the Ukraine and was awarded the title of Hero of the Soviet Union. Sergeant Mikhail Grabsky was wounded in Stalingrad, and later, in the Ukraine, was awarded the title of Hero of the Soviet Union. During street fighting in Stalingrad both sides used snipers, and among the most proficient was Giorgi Krassitsky of the 96th Infantry Battalion, who, according to Soviet sources, killed and wounded 45 German soldiers.[121]

---

in the liberation of the Ukraine and Poland, and in March 1944 was appointed commander of the Armored Corps and promoted to the rank of major general.

118. Abramovich, *V Reshaiushchei Voine*, 330–31; Chuykov, *Stalingrad*, 292.

119. Abramovich, *V Reshaiushchei Voine*, 322; Sverdlov and Vainer, *Voiny Evrei*, 113–14.

120. Pospelov et al., *Istoria Velikoi*, vol. 2, 54; Chuykov, *Stalingrad*, 151; Abramovich, *V Reshaiushchei Voine*, 328–30.

121. Abramovich, *V Reshaiushchei Voine*, 332; Shapiro, *Under Fire*, 174–78, 183–85, 586–87.

The supply lines to Stalingrad came through the Volga, enabling the 62nd Army to receive reinforcements, ammunition and food, and to evacuate the wounded. The Volga flotilla carried out all these missions, chiefly by night. Chuykov wrote of the Volga flotilla that "if they had not existed, the 62nd Army would have perished for lack of ammunition and food." During the ten days between September 15 and 25, 1942, the main Volga crossing was under heavy German artillery and mortar fire, while flares lit the area at night so German planes could bomb the boats moving on the water. Nevertheless, the flotilla brought in more than ten thousand soldiers and a thousand tons of ammunition, and evacuated five thousand wounded soldiers.

Among the soldiers of the flotilla, as in every other place where there was fighting, there were Jews. The commander of one of the boats was Senior Lieutenant Yakov Veiner. Under continuous fire, he persisted in delivering supplies and reinforcements from one bank to the other every night. One night his boat was in the middle of the river, carrying soldiers from the 13th Guard Division and a shipment of ammunition. The Germans attacked and the surface of the water became covered by a burning oil slick. Suddenly the motor of his boat stalled and fire broke out below decks, making the ship a stationary target. Veiner ran to the hold, extinguished the fire and managed to start the motor. He reached shore safely, the ammunition was unloaded and the boat crossed to the opposite shore under heavy bombardment to take on another load. He survived the battles in Stalingrad but fell months later, serving in the Dnieper flotilla and landing a Soviet force in the region of Pinsk in Byelorussia. Another Jew of the Dnieper fleet who was killed during the same mission was Lieutenant Rafael Arons.[122]

There are no official Soviet statistics regarding the losses sustained in Stalingrad before the Germans surrendered on February 2, 1943. Such statistics as there are relate only to those between the initial German attack on July 17, 1942, and November 19, 1942, when the Soviet counteroffensive began – the period known in Soviet historiography as "the strategic defensive operation" of Stalingrad. The losses relate to all the Soviet forces participating in the operation, including the 62nd Army. In accordance with the data, 323,850 soldiers belonging to 56 divisions and 33 independent brigades were considered "irrevocable losses" (*bezvozvratnye potery*) – a term that included both the dead and those taken prisoner. The data recorded 319,986 wounded soldiers, most

122. Sverdlov and Vainer, *Voiny Evrei*, 115–17.

of whom returned to the fighting once they had recovered.[123] Thus, considering the percentage of Jews in the army, the number who fell in battle can safely be estimated at about 4,850 (including prisoners, who were murdered by the Germans). The numbers do not include those who fell in Stalingrad between November 19, 1942 and February 2, 1943.

8. THE TURNING POINT – FROM STALINGRAD TO THE KURSK SALIENT: NOVEMBER 19, 1942–JULY 12, 1943

The Battles of Stalingrad and Leningrad

While fighting in the city, the Red Army was preparing for a counteroffensive, which became the turning point of the war. It began on November 19, 1942, when the Red Army attacked from northwest of Stalingrad, across the Don River, to overcome the Romanian 3rd Army, whose forces had been deployed for defense; a second force attacked from the southeast. On November 23, the two Soviet forces met to the west of Stalingrad in the Kalach region and the 6th Army was surrounded. The German forces, commanded by General von Manstein, tried to attack from the west to save the 6th Army, but they were repelled. The Red Army advanced westward and defeated the Italian 8th and the Hungarian 2nd armies. The 22 divisions of the German 6th Army surrendered on January 31, 1943. More than 90,000 German soldiers were taken prisoner and more than 150,000 died in battle.

After the German failure at Stalingrad and the Red Army's advance toward Rostov, the German Army Group A, commanded that time by General Kleist, was in danger of being cut off. As a result, it quickly retreated from the northern Caucasus. At the beginning of February 1943, the Red Army liberated Kursk, and Rostov-on-Don was liberated in the middle of the month. After an advance of hundreds of kilometers west, the Red Army was forced to halt, chiefly for logistic reasons. In early spring of 1943, the front line in the south was stabilized east-northeast of Kharkov and west of Rostov.

---

123. Krivosheyev, *Grif Secretnosti*, 178–79.

FROM THE CAUCASUS TO KIEV

A few weeks before the victorious end of the Stalingrad campaign, the Red
Army in northern Russia began the relief of the siege of Leningrad. It was carried out from two directions: from within the city and from the east by forces
of the Volkhov front. The mission was to oust the German 18th Army from
the southern shore of Lake Ladoga, between Shliselburg in the west and Lipka

in the east, in order to regain the land route to Leningrad. On January 12, 1943, the Soviets attacked, and on January 18 the Leningrad front and Volkhov front forces met. As a result, a land corridor 8–11 kilometers (5–7 miles) wide was created. Railroad tracks were quickly laid and a road was paved, thus providing a continuous route between the besieged city and Soviet territory. The blockade was partially relieved, but German forces continued to threaten and bombard the city from the south. Among the forces leading the attack from the besieged city were the 152nd Tank Brigade, commanded by the Jewish Aron Oskotsky, and the 220th Tank Brigade, commanded by the Jewish Joseph Shpieller. Once a land corridor had been established, these tank brigades defended the route against German forces trying to break through from the south.[124]

Jews in the Battles from Stalingrad to the Kursk Salient

On January 31, 1943, von Paulus, the commander of the German 6th Army, and his staff surrendered at Stalingrad to Lieutenant Colonel Leonid Vinokur, a Jew who was second in command of the 38th Brigade of the 64th Army.[125] The Soviet Jewish newspaper *Einkeit* (Unity) described the meeting of Vinokur and von Paulus in the following terms:

> At dawn on January 31…Vinokur's soldiers neared the central department store building where the headquarters of the German 6th Army were located, the headquarters of Field Marshal von Paulus.… At 6:40 a.m. the department store was surrounded and the brigade command proposed the Germans surrender. The Germans rejected the proposal and the attack was renewed. After 15 minutes the Germans agreed to open negotiations. Lieutenant Colonel Vinokur went into the basement where the 6th Army headquarters was located, accompanied by Major Yagorov…and a few soldiers with submachine guns. The large courtyard was filled with German soldiers and there was a machine gun at every door. Major General Roske [the commander of the surrounded German force, who was in charge of what was left of the German 71st Infantry Division, which defended the army's headquarters] accompanied the Soviet Lieutenant Colonel to a large, semi-dark room, its walls covered with carpets and its floor

---

124. Sverdlov and Vainer, *Voiny Evrei*, 179–80.
125. Abramovich, *V Reshaiushchei Voine*, 356–57.

with cigarette butts and scraps of paper. As soon as they entered, an unshaven man with a gray face rose from a bed lying near the wall and stood up. "*Heil*," he greeted Vinokur.... For a moment they faced one another silently, the Soviet officer, Vinokur, the Jewish boy from Odessa, broad-shouldered and strong, and the defeated German Field Marshal in his wrinkled general's uniform.... At nine in the morning on January 31, the battles in the center of Stalingrad stopped.[126]

Among the forces on the Don front, which cut off Stalingrad from the northwest, was the 2nd Guards Army, whose second in command was General Yakov Kreyzer. As a result of his exceptional direction of forces during the campaign, he was given command of the army, promoted to lieutenant general and awarded the Suvorov Order. Colonel Izrail Beskin also fought on the Don front, commanding the 65th Army's artillery, and was later promoted to the rank of lieutenant general and awarded the title of Hero of the Soviet Union.[127]

In the middle of January 1943, the Red Army attacked on the Voronezh front, a region held mostly by Italian and Hungarian forces. The Red Army's 7th Cavalry Corps penetrated deep behind enemy lines. The Corps's 31st Cuban Cavalry Brigade, commanded by Colonel Haim Popov, advanced more than 140 kilometers (87 miles) in four days and took over the Valuiky Train Station on the Oskol River, helping to cut off and destroy large enemy forces. For its action, the corps was awarded the title of Guards.[128]

In December 1942, the Lithuanian 16th Infantry Division, was attached to the 3rd Army. On February 21, 1943, amid terrible winter weather, they reached the front near the village of Alexeyevka, southwest of the city of Oriel. The soldiers were exhausted when they arrived, having marched for five days through freezing snowstorms with almost no food; the maintenance and kitchen units and even the artillery were lagging behind them. Their mission was to break through the enemy's defenses and advance toward the city of Zmievka, south of Oriel. On February 24, the division attacked without sufficient artillery support. They faced a fortified German defensive line which commanded flat snowy expanses that the attacking soldiers had to cross. After a few days the attack

---

126. *Einkeit*, February 21, 1948, vol. 584, no. 23.
127. Shapiro, *Under Fire*, 271–305. Beskin joined the Red Army in 1918, fought in the Civil War and continued in the professional army in the Artillery Corps. Before the Stalingrad campaign, he had commanded artillery divisions on various fronts.
128. Abramovich, *V Reshaiushchei Voine*, 392–93.

ended in failure. The division suffered extremely heavy losses, with about 50 percent of its troops either wounded or killed. Among them were 1,500 Jewish soldiers.[129] Private Grigori Ushpolis, who took part in the battle and was later awarded the title of Hero of the Soviet Union, wrote:

> For generations the village of Alexeyevka became the place of our shameful baptism of fire. Here, in the village center next to the destroyed church, we buried the division's soldiers; among them rest a large number of Jews. In the earth of Oriel, in graves both marked and unmarked, lie the bodies of hundreds of Jewish frontline soldiers from the Lithuanian 16th Division. We went into battle fully aware that we were contributing our part in defeating the hated enemy. I have already mentioned that within the division's units, we Jews were mostly simple soldiers. In certain units [of the fighting companies], more than half of the soldiers were Jewish. This was the reason that such a high number of our coreligionists fell in battle.[130]

The command of the 3rd Army was responsible for the failure and losses. It had sent the division to attack a fortified enemy position without artillery or air cover and without enough training. The division was removed from the front for reorganization, its commander and head of staff were replaced and it received reinforcements. Because of the heavy losses and the lack of Lithuanian Jews of draft age behind the Soviet front, the percentage of Jewish soldiers in the division decreased.

While German Army Group A was retreating from the Caucasus after the defeat at Stalingrad, the troops on the northern Caucasian front initiated an attack to recapture the port city of Novorossiysk on the eastern shore of the Black Sea. They planned on staging a landing from the sea and establishing two bridgeheads to support the attack – the main one at Iuzhnaia Ozereika and the second at the Stanichka Bay, a Novorossiysk fishing beach. Both forces left from the port of Gelenchik, southeast of Novorossiysk, and landed on February 4, 1943. The main force attacked at Iuzhnaia Ozereika but, encountering strong resistance, failed to complete its mission. The marine battalion (composed of sailors and volunteer marines) that established the bridgehead at Stanichka was commanded by Major Tsezar (Tzadok) Kunikov. He was considered one

---

129. Levin, *With Their Backs to the Wall*, 53–56.
130. Grigori Ushpolis, *Trevozhnoe Vremia* (Tel Aviv, 1997), 101.

of best officers in the Soviet marines and had demonstrated outstanding ability during many previous incursions behind German lines. The Germans mounted a desperate counterattack, bombarding the marines in the hope of putting Novorossiysk out of danger, but Kunikov and his men stood firm and enabled more Soviet reinforcements to land. The persistence of the soldiers at the bridgehead became famous throughout the Soviet Union, and in Soviet historiography it is referred to as "the small land" (*malaia zemlia*). In official Soviet history, Kunikov is mentioned in the following terms:

> Kunikov, previously an engineer, volunteered for the front. In the fall of 1942 he was considered an outstanding marine officer. For his courage, bravery and leadership qualities he was awarded the Order of Alexander Nevsky. He prepared his troops with an exalted sense of responsibility and great enthusiasm. The command of the operation permitted him to choose men from all the ships of the fleet and from all the marine units. Kunikov personally spoke with each soldier before accepting him into the unit, for which 800 of the bravest and most daring soldiers were chosen....[131]

MAJOR TSEZAR (TZADOK) KUNIKOV

Kunikov was wounded in the bridgehead battle and died on February 14, 1943. After his death he was awarded the title of Hero of the Soviet Union, and the fishing village in the middle of the bridgehead was named Kunikovka in his memory. More Soviet troops were landed on the "small land" bridgehead and for months it held out against German attacks, until September 19, 1943, when Novorossiysk was liberated.[132]

---

131. Pospelov et al., *Istoria Velikoi*, vol. 3, 93–96.
132. Shapiro, *Under Fire*, 324–37. In some sources about Kunikov he is refered to as being Russian by nationality. In a letter to the Moscow magazine *Sovetish Heimland*, Kunikov's sister Yevgeniya Finkelshteyn, from Leningrad, made known her brother's Jewish identity. Kunikov's father was Lev Moiseevich and his mother, Tatyana Abramovna.

9. THE KURSK SALIENT – THE LAST GERMAN STRATEGIC OFFENSIVE AND ITS FAILURE: JULY 5–13, 1943

The Largest Tank Battle of the Second World War

During the first half of July 1943, the Germans made a last attempt to regain the initiative on the eastern front. The strategically important operation, code-named Citadel, began in the Kursk-Oriel sector, where the Germans had concentrated their best armored forces. Kursk had been liberated by the Red Army at the beginning of February 1943, creating a salient to the west. The German plan was to attack the Kursk salient from the north and south, to cut off and destroy the Soviet forces and then to attack northeast in the direction of Moscow, or to the south. Attacking from the north was given to Army Group Central and from the south to Army Group South. The Germans concentrated about 50 divisions numbering 900,000 soldiers for the attack, including their best SS divisions, 2,700 tanks – many of them the particularly powerful Panther and Tiger tanks – 2,000 planes and 10,000 artillery guns. The Soviets had exact intelligence about the sector and attack plans. They concentrated more than 1,330,000 soldiers, 3,444 tanks and 19,000 artillery guns there. The Soviet plan was to let the enemy bleed to death in an attempt to attack their defensive lines and then to take the offensive.[133]

The German attack began on July 5, as scheduled, under massive Soviet artillery fire and against an entrenched defensive deployment waiting for the enemy. Suffering heavy losses, the Germans managed to advance only a few kilometers from both directions and were finally halted on July 12. On that day, near the village of Prokhorovka in the southern sector, the largest tank battle of the Second World War took place, 850 Soviet against 600 German tanks. The battle was waged at close range, where the Soviet T-34s had a relative advantage over the heavy German Panthers and Tigers. The tanks rammed each other and both sides lost hundreds of tanks, but the Soviets received reinforcements and the Germans did not. The Germans were forced to retreat. The Soviet counteroffensive began on July 13 and lasted until August 23. Oriel and Belgorod were liberated on August 5 and Kharkov on August 23, and the Red Army quickly advanced westward to the Dnieper.[134]

---

133. Overy, *Russia's War*, 201.
134. Ibid., 203–10; Zhukov, *Memoirs*, 336–45.

At that point in the war – the summer of 1943 – the modern tanks, planes and artillery supplied by the Soviet industry proved their worth, and the American Lend-Lease Act provided the Soviet Union with large amounts of war material. Particularly important to Red Army mobility were the tens of thousands of Lend-Lease Studebaker trucks, which enabled maintenance units to supply the advancing tanks with fuel and ammunition, as well as the tens of thousands of wireless sets for tanks and other military units, which enabled commanders to control their units better during battle and increase their fighting effectiveness.[135] General Guderian wrote of the results of the Oriel-Kursk battle that Operation Citadel was a decisive failure, that the armored formations which were organized and re-equipped with great effort lost many men and much equipment, and that from that time onward the initiative was in the hands of the Red Army.[136] General Walter Warlimont, deputy chief of operations of OKW, wrote: "Operation Citadel was more than a battle lost: it handed the Russians the initiative and we never recovered it again right up to the end of the war."[137]

Jews in the Kursk Salient Battle

Thousands of Jews fought in the battle of the Kursk salient. The 3rd Mechanized Corps of the 1st Armored Army, commanded by Semyon Krivoshin, was deployed as part of the defense of the Kursk salient's southern sector, where the Germans' 4th Panzer Army attacked. On July 6 the Germans managed to break through the first defense line of the Soviet 6th Army. On July 6–10 the 3rd Mechanized Corps, as well as other units of the 1st Armored Army, was engaged in battle with large German tank forces, among them the SS Adolf Hitler Panzer Division, the SS Death's Head Panzer Division and the SS Reich Panzer Division. Krivoshin's corps demonstrated extraordinary valor during the battle and received the title of Guard Corps. Two weeks later he was promoted to the rank of lieutenant general and received the Suvorov Order.[138]

On July 12, Lieutenant Colonel Mikhail Goldberg fell in the great tank battle near Prokhorovka. He had commanded the 55th Tank Regiment of the

---

135. Overy, *Russia's War*, 193–96, for information about the scope of American aid to the Soviet Union under the Lend-Lease agreement.

136. Guderian, *Panzer Leader*, 312.

137. Warlimont, *Inside Hitler's Headquarters*, 334.

138. Shapiro, *Under Fire*, 307–10. The Suvorov, Kutuzov and Alexander Nevsky orders were established during the Great Patriotic War and given to officers who made outstanding contributions on the battlefield.

5th Armored Corps. D. Kleinfeld, commander of the 51st Tank Regiment of the 10th Armored Brigade fought in the same battle. The 26th Airborne Regiment, commanded by G. Kashpersky, defended an important hill during the battle. Senior Lieutenant Katseleman, who commanded an artillery battery, was also killed when, on the third day of the German attack, the infantry in the sector retreated and his battery was left to face enemy tanks alone. They damaged 14 tanks and most of the men were either killed or wounded, Katseleman among them.[139]

An infantry regiment under the command of Major Leonid Buber, who was a Hero of the Soviet Union, also participated in the Kursk salient battle. Speaking before members of the Jewish Anti-Fascist Committee in Moscow on April 2, 1944, he recounted the story of the battle:

> Many enemy planes appeared over our positions and there were 20 enemy tanks coming toward us. When they were ten meters [about 11 yards] from our positions, our soldiers rushed toward them with anti-tank grenades. Some of the tanks were hit and others retreated.... I led my men forward in an assault, and we repelled the Germans in hand-to-hand combat. I was wounded in the chest but stayed with my soldiers until the battle was over.[140]

A battalion of T-34 tanks commanded by Senior Lieutenant Matvey Pinsky defended the region of the villages of Rakovo and Shepelevka. On the first day of the attack, the battalion stood firm in the face of enemy's heavy Tiger tanks. Pinsky's tanks were well-camouflaged, and he allowed the Tigers to approach. When he could clearly see their flanks, which were vulnerable to the T-34s' guns, he gave the order to open fire. The enemy tanks and accompanying infantry were hit and retreated. Pinsky was awarded the Order of Alexander Nevsky.[141]

After reorganization in the summer of 1943, the Lithuanian 16th Infantry Division, subordinate to the 48th Army, was deployed in defense of the northern sector of the Kursk salient, where the Germans were about to attack. Grigori Ushpolis, a member of a 76-mm gun team, was positioned in front of the infantry to fire directly at the advancing enemy. He wrote:

---

139. Abramovich, *V Reshaiushchei Voine*, 437–40.
140. Ibid., 57–58.
141. Shapiro, *Under Fire*, 435–36.

The Germans stationed loudspeakers along the front and broadcast the voices of Lithuanian deserters, who called upon the Lithuanians in the division to defect to the German side. They promised that every defector would be returned to his family in Lithuania. They threw leaflets at our positions calling upon us not to fight and promising that the Lithuanians would not be harmed in German prisoner-of-war camps but would be returned to their homes. Their propaganda was to no avail. They had not counted on the fact that almost one third of the division were Jews, who were prepared to fight valiantly and would not retreat from their positions, not even one step. Not only that, most of the Lithuanians in the division were Soviet patriots, and about 20 percent of the soldiers were Russians, Ukrainians or other nationalities.... The German attack began after intensive artillery pounding of our positions that lasted more than an hour.... This time we were fully prepared to repel the enemy.... When their infantry approached our positions we fired shrapnel shells at them... and our counterattack forced the enemy to return to their starting positions after having suffered heavy losses. We also sustained many losses, and the commander of our battery was killed.... Before our attack on the village of Panskaia, our gun crew, which was commanded by Kalman Shur, was ordered to destroy three enemy machine gun positions by firing directly at them. During the capture of the village our soldiers encountered no fire from those positions.... In the battle for the liberation of the township of Nikolskoe, many of our soldiers were wounded and killed, and I myself was seriously wounded....[142]

The Soviet artillery played an extremely important part in the Kursk salient battle and was nicknamed "the god of war" (*bog voiny*). The generals in command of the artillery of the 65th Army and the 2nd Armored Corps were both Jewish: Izrail Beskin and Grigori Plaskov. The 12th Artillery Division was commanded by General Moise Korkovsky.[143] Among the hundreds of Jews who were decorated for their part in the Kursk salient battles, 13 received the Order of Lenin, which was awarded to members of the armed forces for exemplary service.

---

142. Ushpolis, *Trevozhnoe Vremia*, 108–18.
143. Sverdlov and Vainer, *Voiny Evrei*, 136.

10. THE EXPULSION OF THE GERMAN ARMY FROM THE OCCUPIED TERRITORIES OF THE SOVIET UNION: SUMMER 1943–SUMMER 1944

Crossing the Dnieper and the Campaign to Liberate Soviet Lands

After the victory at Kursk, the Red Army attacked along the German Army Group Center's front and by October 1943 had liberated the districts of Kalinin, Smolensk and eastern Byelorussia. During the 1943–44 winter, the front stabilized at Byelorussia, east of the cities of Vitebsk, Orsha, Mogilev and Bobruisk.

In the Ukraine, during the summer of 1943, the Red Army advanced westward to reach the Dnieper River as quickly as possible and capture bridgeheads on its western bank before the Germans could set up defensive lines. The Dnieper was the chief obstacle to the Soviet advance, and therefore the obvious place for the Germans to try to stop the enemy. Their plan was to establish a defense line, the so-called "eastern wall," along the Dnieper, from Smolensk in the north to the Black Sea in the south. In order to encourage soldiers and officers to reach and cross the Dnieper as quickly as possible, Stalin issued Order No. 9 on September 9, 1943, according to which those who were first to cross the Dnieper would be awarded the title of Hero of the Soviet Union.[144]

The first Soviet unit reached the river on September 20, crossing it on boats and rafts to the north and south of Kiev. From the bridgeheads they established on the western bank, they began the October–November offensive to liberate the Ukraine. The important city of Dnepropetrovsk was liberated on October 25, 1943. In the southern Ukraine the Soviets forced the Germans out of the Donbas industrial region and cut off the Crimea. On November 6, Kiev, the Ukrainian capital, was liberated. They were then halted by German reinforcements, which had been brought to the front for a counteroffensive to recapture Kiev and reestablish a defensive line along the Dnieper. German Army Group South failed in its mission to halt the Soviet advance.

Between March 26 and April 14, 1944, the Red Army liberated Transnistria, including the city of Odessa. Lvov was liberated on July 27, 1944, thereby achieving the liberation of the Ukraine. On April 8, 1944, the Red Army penetrated into Crimea and by May 12, 1944, the entire peninsula was in Soviet hands.

---

144. Zhukov, *Memoirs*, 485–86.

The liberation of Byelorussia and most of the Baltic states was one of the greatest and most successful strategic operations of the war. It lasted for more than two months, from June 22 to August 29, 1944, beginning on the third anniversary of the German invasion of the Soviet Union and two weeks after the Allies landed in Normandy. The operation, which was nicknamed Bagration (after the Russian general Pyotr Bagration, a hero of the War of 1812 against Napoleon, who fell in the battle at Borodino), liberated all of Byelorussia and parts of Lithuania and Latvia. Minsk, the Byelorussian capital, was liberated on July 3. Vilnius, the capital of Lithuania, was liberated on July 13, 1944. The German army had established a defensive line in the west of Lithuania to protect its land bridge and its forces in Latvia and Estonia. The Red Army had reached the borders of east Prussia, the Vistula River and the outskirts of Warsaw. Hitler forbade Army Group Center from retreating in time, and as a result the German losses were greater than those suffered at Stalingrad, and included 350,000 killed and captured and hundreds of thousands of wounded, as well as enormous quantities of equipment.

Jews in the Battles to Liberate the Occupied Territories

In the middle of September 1943, in the battles in the Demidov region in the district of Smolensk, the 2nd Infantry Battalion of the 973rd Regiment found itself heavily under fire from fortified enemy positions and was forced to halt. Three 45-mm guns were brought forward by Senior Lieutenant Mikhail Gurevich, who fired directly at the enemy positions, silencing four of their machine guns. The battalion continued to advance when suddenly the enemy opened fire from behind and Gurevich and his men found themselves surrounded. He aimed his cannons and fired directly at the attacking German infantry. The battle was fought at short range, and one by one Gurevich's soldiers were hit and he himself was wounded in the shoulder. Left alone, he grabbed a machine gun and continued firing. He was wounded again, this time in the stomach, and while trying to throw a hand grenade at the oncoming Germans, who were only a few meters away, he was hit in the head. When the battalion finally repelled the German counterattack, the bodies of Gurevich and his men were found, mutilated by the Germans. Only with difficulty was his body identified. The story of his death was told by one of the soldiers who, wounded, had managed to crawl to a nearby forest without being detected.[145]

---

145. Shapiro, *Under Fire*, 194–95.

There were many Jews who were among the first to cross the Dnieper. The forward units of the 17th Infantry Corps reached the river north of Kiev near Chernobyl, where the Pripets River meets the Dnieper. One of the first to lead a crossing at night was the company commander, Senior Lieutenant Yuri Dolzhansky, who employed two boats and a few rafts. The Germans, using floodlights and flares to illuminate the area, discovered the troops on the river and shelled them. Dolzhansky, a veteran of Stalingrad and the Kursk salient, led his soldiers in an assault on the enemy and in hand-to-hand combat captured some of their positions. They stood firm under a German attack that lasted the entire night. Three weeks later Dolzhansky was awarded the title of Hero of the Soviet Union. One month later he fell in battle near Zhitomir.[146] Captain Zalman Vikhnin commanded a forward unit of the 288th Infantry Regiment of the 181st Division, which crossed the Dnieper on September 22. His mission was to capture the village of Beriozki. He led the assault on the village and captured it but was killed by a landmine. His regiment crossed the Dnieper and held the western bank; he was posthumously awarded the title of Hero of the Soviet Union.[147]

The 4th Regiment of the 6th Division, commanded by Colonel Boris Lev, reached the Dnieper where it converges with the Pripets. On September 23 he crossed the river with his forward company. For his bravery, for providing a personal example and for establishing the bridgehead, he was awarded the title of Hero of the Soviet Union. He was later promoted to the rank of major general and appointed division commander.[148] Company commander Senior Lieutenant Rafail Lev distinguished himself while crossing the Dnieper near Lyutezh, leading the advance force of the 989th Infantry Regiment of the 226th Division and holding the bridgehead until the entire regiment had crossed, on October 17, 1943. For his actions he was awarded the title of Hero of the Soviet Union. Some months later, in December 1943, the regiment was involved in fierce battles near Chopovichi station (southeast of the city of Korosten and west of the Dnieper). When German tanks endangered the regiment's defenses, Senior Lieutenant Rafail Lev saved the situation. Lieutenant General S.

---

146. Sverdlov and Vainer, *Voiny Evrei*, 160; Shapiro, *Under Fire*, 83. Dolzhansky was killed in a battle for a bridgehead south of Chernobyl.
147. Sverdlov and Vainer, *Voiny Evrei*, 161; Shapiro, *Under Fire*, 614.
148. Sverdlov and Vainer, *Voiny Evrei*, 162: Shapiro, *Under Fire*, 344.

Andryushchenko, commander of the 38th Army, who was responsible for the sector, wrote about him as follows:

> If the company commander had lost control of the fighting, the Germans would have crushed our defenses in this sector. Fortunately this did not happen. Senior Lieutenant R.F. Lev proved to be an intelligent and decisive commander. He had fought at the Kursk salient, where he had encountered the Tigers and Ferdinands more than once, and he knew how to resist them. Quickly assessing the situation, this officer decided to move the anti-tank gunners to a more suitable position: a small elevation with an excellent field of view. At the same time he moved a group of tank fighters and a battery of 57-mm anti-tank guns to the right with the intention of destroying the enemy tanks by firing at their flanks....[149]

During the battle, which lasted for a few days, Senior Lieutenant Rafael Lev was killed.[150]

On September 21, the 10th Tank Corps of the 40th Army reached the Dnieper near the city of Pereyeslav. With a view to crossing the river, the corps ordered the 183rd Tank Brigade to send a six-man reconnaissance unit to the western bank of the river to examine the enemy's deployment. One of the soldiers in the group was Private Grigori Garfunkin. The unit sailed across the river on the night of September 22. They found German bunkers and anti-tank guns, mortars and artillery positions – information that was vital to crossing the river. As they returned to the boat they were discovered and attacked by the Germans. One of the soldiers had to remain on the bank to cover the boat as it crossed eastward, and Private Garfunkin volunteered. He shot at the Germans until the boat pushed off. When it had distanced itself from the west bank, he dove into the water and tried to swim across the river, but the Germans shot and killed him. In January 1944 he was named a Hero of the Soviet Union.[151]

Colonel Arkady Kaplunov was second in command of the 54th Tank Brigade. At the end of September the brigade reached the Dnieper, southeast of Kiev. A small bridgehead held by infantry soldiers had withstood heavy pressure from attacking Germans, and it was necessary to reinforce it with

---

149. Shapiro, *Under Fire*, 348.
150. Sverdlov and Vainer, *Voiny Evrei*, 163.
151. Sverdlov and Vainer, *Voiny Evrei*, 164–65; Shapiro, *Under Fire*, 146–48, 348.

tanks as quickly as possible. When the pontoon bridge was finished, the first tank to reach the western bank was Kaplunov's. The bridgehead was ready to collapse but Kaplunov and a few of the tanks that had come after him joined battle with the Germans and forced them to retreat. He died fighting. He was posthumously awarded the title of Hero of the Soviet Union. There is a street named after him in the city of Pereeslav-Khmelnitski, where he is buried.

Sergeant Semyon Gelferg commanded an anti-tank section. As a Kiev native he wanted to be among the city's liberators, and when his battalion reached the Dnieper, he was one of the first to land on the western shore. In the battle near the villages of Lukovitsy and Grigorevka, the section under his command destroyed two enemy tanks. In the battle on September 29, aimed at taking a position that would command the bridgehead, he led the entire platoon in the assault, destroyed a German tank and hit a number of enemy soldiers. Sergeant Gelferg did not live to see his native Kiev liberated, as he fell in the battle. He was posthumously awarded the title of Hero of the Soviet Union.[152]

Among the tanks leading the assault on Kiev was the т-34 tank company commanded by Lieutenant Izrail Kuperstein, of the 52nd Tank Brigade. For several days Kuperstein's tank supported the infantry as it repelled the Germans counterattacks on a bridgehead. For the assault on Kiev the brigade was moved to the Liutezh bridgehead north of the city. On November 3 the assault on Kiev began, and the 167th Infantry Division was supported by the 52nd Tank Brigade. The tanks were to capture the resort town of Puscha-Voditsa, a few kilometers northwest of Kiev, and subsequently take the Sviatoshino suburb and cut off the Kiev-Zhitomir road. After Puscha-Voditsa had been captured, Kuperstein's tank led the assault and conquest of Sviatoshino. The Germans, who had tanks and assault guns, attempted to break out from the city to the west. In the ensuing battle Kuperstein's tank destroyed a Ferdinand assault gun and two anti-tank guns, wounded scores of enemy soldiers and completed the mission by cutting off the road. Kiev was liberated the following day. The 52nd Tank Brigade moved west and, along with other units, took the city of Fastov on November 7. Fastov was located 60 kilometers (37 miles) southwest of Kiev, and commanded a railroad junction. Kuperstein's tank was among the first to enter Fastov, where it destroyed a German Panther. For his fighting on the Dnieper and the conquests of Sviatoshino and Fastov, Kuperstein and his entire

---

152. Sverdlov and Vainer, *Voiny Evrei*, 164–65; Shapiro, *Under Fire*, 149, 213.

tank crew – including Jewish gun-loader Mikhail Grabsky, a Kiev native – were awarded the title of Heroes of the Soviet Union.[153]

Soviet artillery played an important role in crossing the Dnieper and repelling the German counterattacks. The 24th Guard Brigade, commanded by Colonel Nikolai Izrailevich Brozgol, used their fire power to cover the Liutezh bridgehead, from which the attack and conquest of Kiev began. Colonel Brozgol personally reached the bridgehead and from there directed the guns positioned on the eastern side of the Dnieper. On November 3, when the assault on Kiev began, his heavy guns hit and silenced three German artillery batteries. For his distinction in battle and successful direction of gunfire he was awarded the title of Hero of the Soviet Union. The award was also given to Jewish battery commanders who fought on the Dnieper: Senior Lieutenant Yefim (Haim) Berezovsky, Senior Lieutenant Yevgeny Birbrayer, Senior Lieutenant Isaac Vaksman and Lieutenant Yefim (Haim) Stern. Birbrayer and Vaksman fell in battle on the Dnieper and were granted the awards posthumously, Stern fell in the battle for Kirovograd in March 1944. Both Sergeants Haim Zlatin and Naum Zholudev were awarded the title of Hero of the Soviet Union. Zholudev, who was wounded, positioned his mortar on a raft and, while crossing the Dnieper south of Kremenchug, fired and hit Germans who tried to prevent the force from landing. Zlatin, who was also wounded, landed with his crew on an island in the Dnieper near Kiev along with the first infantry unit, and fired his mortar to repel an enemy counterattack.[154]

It was the soldiers of the engineering corps who operated the boats carrying the troops to the western bank of the Dnieper. On September 24, Private Lev Margulyan and another soldier were in the first boat carrying infantry troops to capture a bridgehead. Most of the crossing was carried out under the cover of darkness. Margulyan and his comrade repeatedly crossed the river while subjected to heavy, continuous gunfire and over a period of days brought additional troops and entrenching equipment. On one of the crossings, Margulyan was hit and died instantly. For his bravery under enemy fire he was posthumously awarded the title of Hero of the Soviet Union.

Another member of the engineering corps, Captain Benjamin Ruvinsky, commanded the unit that brought troops and equipment through the Dnieper.

---

153. Sverdlov and Vainer, *Voiny Evrei*, 165–66; Shapiro, *Under Fire*, 184–85, 338–41.
154. Sverdlov and Vainer, *Voiny Evrei*, 168–70; Shapiro, *Under Fire*, 44–45, 48–49, 539–40, 586–87, 638–39, 642.

He was always in the lead boat. When there was danger that the bridgehead might fall, he managed to improvise boats to bring a tank battalion to the west bank. The tanks enabled the Soviet troops to repel the Germans and enlarge the bridgehead. For his actions he was awarded the title of Hero of the Soviet Union. Captain Pinhas Turyan was also awarded the title for his bravery in crossing the Dnieper and for staying with his soldiers when, surrounded by Germans, they mined the Petrovskoe–Svistunovo bridgehead. Wounded, he repelled the enemy and managed to extricate his encircled troops.[155]

In the battle for the town of Melitopol on October 18, 1943, Junior Lieutenant Abram Zindels, commander of an infantry platoon, drove the enemy out of two blocks, destroying a number of machine-gun emplacements. The Germans moved in some tanks and two platoons of submachine-gunners against Zindels' platoon. Zindels' men repelled the attack, and he personally hurled Molotov cocktails at a Tiger tank, which went up in flames. However, Zindels found himself surrounded by German soldiers and most of his soldiers wounded. When he was himself alone and the Germans called out to him to surrender, he answered, "A Soviet officer does not surrender!" and as the Germans approached him he threw his last hand grenade and blew up both German submachine gunners and himself. For his actions he was posthumously awarded the title of Hero of the Soviet Union.[156]

The 8th Mechanized Corps participated in the battles known in Soviet historiography as the Zhitomir-Berdichev Campaign. Commanded by Semyon Krivoshin, it had taken the city of Kazatin south of Berdichev on December 25, 1943, and repelled counterattacks by the German 4th Panzer Army. Junior Lieutenant Vladimir (Volodya) Vayser was a commander of a т-34 tank platoon in Krivoshin's corps. Vayser was killed in a battle near the city of Chopovichi, southwest of Korosten. His death was described by a friend, a nurse named Nina, who before the war had gone to school with him in their home town, Proskurov (Khmelnitski). The letter was sent to a fellow classmate:

> You must surely remember Volodya Vayser…. Already in school I fell in love with him…. It was near the Stalingrad front I heard about him from the patients. I was working in the hospital and he was fighting…. Finally, in January 1943, when our soldiers were chasing the Germans

---

155. Sverdlov and Vainer, *Voiny Evrei*, 170–71; Shapiro, *Under Fire*, 390–91, 463–65, 581–82.
156. Shapiro, *Under Fire*, 640–41.

from the Don region, I met Volodya. He came to our hospital to visit a friend. I was astonished when I saw him. This was not the boy I had known at school but a real soldier, singed with the fire of many battles.… When I went up to him, however, he recognized me at once and his eyes shone, his face softened and became tender, as it used to be. All through 1943 I was in a unit together with Volodya.… During our meetings Volodya would say, "As soon as we liberate the Ukraine we will ask for a two days leave and go to Proskurov, we will go to our school and sit at our old desks. Won't that be great?" I was always worried about what would happen to him. He was a junior lieutenant and commanded a tank. He had already destroyed several German tanks.…

On December 20 fighting broke out near Chopovichi station in the Zhitomir region. Our tank brigade had occupied this station and blocked the road to Kiev from the SS Adolf Hitler's tank division. Volodya's company had been given orders to hold the station. Our first-aid post had been moved into a half-destroyed brick factory at the station and the tank unit took up the defense 300 meters [330 yards] in front of it. I myself saw how Volodya set fire to a Panther with two shots. His tank caught fire as well. I saw him jump out of the tank, smother the flames with his jacket and jump in again. Volodya's T-34 tank moved from place to place. He would shoot from a hill or bush and maneuver again. The Germans had about 40 tanks and it was hard for our company to cope with such numbers. Volodya set fire to another Tiger and knocked out an armored carrier, but his tank again caught fire. He jumped out and started to drag his wounded comrades out of the tank.…

German planes nose-dived at us. Forgetting my fear I ran to him to help. When I reached him he had already placed the wounded in a shell hole and was trying to extinguish the flames in the tank. It was dreadful to look at him. His face was burned, he was black, smoke was billowing from his uniform.… "You're hurt," I said. "Let me bandage you," but he did not seem to hear me. Extinguishing the flames, the boys again climbed into the tank.… They knocked out another Tiger and then a Panther.… Again the tank was burning, but its crew continued to fight. I cried and screamed: "Crawl out, crawl out," as if they could hear me in that hell.… One of the wounded said,

"Vayser will fight to the last shell." Finally the guns were silenced. We all waited in vain for Volodya and his men to jump out of the tank. In the evening, when the Germans had been pushed back and the fighting was stopped, the remains of the heroes were buried in the village of Chopovichi.[157]

For his distinction in the fighting at the Chopovichi station, Vayser was post-humously awarded the title of Hero of the Soviet Union. For their roles in crossing the Dnieper and taking part in the battles in the region, 900 soldiers, among them 27 Jews, were awarded the title Hero of the Soviet Union. Among those who received the award for the Dnieper campaign, Jews were third after Russians and Ukrainians.

On January 15, 1944, in the battle to expel the Germans from Leningrad and relieve the partial siege still in force, the 59th Regiment of the 85th Infantry Division of the 42nd Army, commanded by Colonel Haim Krasnokutsky, led the assault from the south of the city in the region of Pulkovo and captured the besieged area of Alexandrovka. The regiment continued fighting in the battles in the Pskov region, in the liberation of Estonia and Latvia, and in the siege of the German forces in Kurland in western Latvia until the surrender on May 9, 1945. He was promoted to the rank of major general after the war.[158]

West of the 42nd Army's attack sector, from the region of the Oranienbaum bridgehead on the southern shore of the Finnish Gulf, the 2nd Army attacked to the south. The attack was supported by artillery consisting of 300 long- and medium-range guns, which was commanded by Colonel (later Major General) Haim Gurevich. The 152nd tank Brigade, commanded by Colonel Aron Oskotsky, played an important part in the breaking through enemy lines. On January 17, the brigade captured enemy positions in the village of Gliadino after a battle with German tanks. From there it continued the attack through Ropsha and Kipen, where it joined the forward forces of the 42nd Army, which was attacking from the direction of Leningrad. The forward force of the 42nd Army was the 220th Tank Brigade commanded by Joseph Shpieller. It was a meeting of two tank brigades, both commanded by Jews. As a result of their joining forces, the enemy forces in the region of Petergot-Strelno were surrounded and destroyed.[159]

---

157. Ibid., 606–9.
158. Abramovich, *Leningradskaia Bitva*, 94, 106.
159. Ibid., 86–94.

The 51st Army, commanded by General Yakov Kreyzer, took part in the liberation of Donbas industrial area and of the city of Melitopol, cut off the Crimea in the region of Perekop and played a decisive role in liberating the Crimea in the spring of 1944. The 17th German Army, supported by Romanian forces, defended the Crimea – all in all about 200,000 troops. The Soviet attack began on April 8, 1944, on the well-entrenched German defense lines west of Perekop and east of the Straits of Sivash. Kreyzer's army broke through the defenses in the Sivash, and together with the 19th Tank Corps they liberated the Crimean capital of Simferopol on April 13, reaching Sevastopol on April 15. A large concentration of forces was vital for the assault on Sevastopol, which began on May 5. Kreyzer's army conquered the Sapun ridge, which commanded the city. There were several days of street fighting, and by May 9 the entire city had been liberated.[160]

One of the officers who distinguished himself in the battle of Sevastopol was Lieutenant Israel Yakubovski, commander of an anti-tank infantry platoon that had been equipped with rifles and anti-tank grenades. During street fighting on May 7, Yakubovski and some of the men of his platoon, who had three anti-tank rifles between them, were engaged in a battle with five enemy tanks. Yakubovski hit a tank, setting it on fire. The battle continued, Yakubovski was wounded and remained in command of only five soldiers, the others having been killed or wounded. When he saw the enemy was about to attack, he took an anti-tank rifle and fired, hitting the tank and ending the assault. He was awarded the title of Hero of the Soviet Union for his bravery under fire.[161]

---

160. Shapiro, *Under Fire*, 293–96. Hitler was afraid that the fall of the Crimea might have a negative influence on Romania as a German ally. With the Crimea in Soviet hands it could become a base from which Soviet planes could bomb the Romanian oil fields at Ploesti, which were vital to Germany. The 17th German Army was given the order to defend the Crimea at any cost and to prevent its capture.

161. Ibid., 631–33.

11. THE GERMAN DEFEAT –
FROM THE VISTULA TO BERLIN:
AUGUST 1944–MAY 1945

Political and Military Changes

During the second half of August 1944, the Red Army entered Romania. The pro-German government in Bucharest was removed, and on August 24 the new government declared war on Germany. On August 31 the Red Army entered Bucharest and advanced toward Hungary. On September 4 the Finnish government announced it had severed relations with Germany and ended its military activity against the Soviet Union. Bulgaria, which had been allied with Germany, declared war on Germany on September 8, 1944.

In October 1944, the Red Army broke the defensive line in the west of Lithuania, reached the shore of the Baltic Sea and cut off the German army's land routes in Latvia. By the end of September 1944, Estonia had been liberated. Between September 14 and October 22, almost all of Latvia was liberated, including Riga, the capital. The Germans held Kurland in western Latvia and the port city of Liepaja until the final surrender on May 9, 1945.

The Red Army on the Vistula River and
the Polish Uprising in Warsaw

Following the attacks on the Byelorussian and Ukrainian fronts, the Red Army entered Poland, and at the end of July–beginning of August 1944 they neared Warsaw. On August 1, 1944, the Polish underground Armia Krajowa (the Home Army) rose up in Warsaw against the Germans. The Armia Krajowa operated as an arm of the Polish government-in-exile in London, which disagreed with the Soviet government regarding various matters concerning the future of Poland and its borders. Militarily, the rebellion was directed against the Germans, but politically against the Soviet Union. Its objective was for Poles to liberate Warsaw, presenting the arriving Soviet forces with a *fait accompli*. After Warsaw's anticipated fall, the Poles planned on liberating additional areas of Poland, bringing them under the rule of the Polish government in London. Stalin, however, wanted Poland ruled by the pro-Soviet government he had established in the Soviet Union.[162]

---

162. Tadeusz Bor-Komorowski, *Armia Podziemna* (London: Studium Polski Podziemnej, 1989), 203–7.

Even when the Red Army took control of the Praga suburb of Warsaw and the east bank of the Vistula, only a few hundred yards from the rebel-held Old City, the Soviet soldiers stood idly by, watching as the German army put down the rebellion and destroyed the city. The rebellion failed and cost the lives of 300,000 Warsaw residents; the rebels surrendered on October 2, 1944.[163]

Along the Vistula, which was the last natural obstacle before Germany, the Germans established a well-entrenched defensive line running south from Warsaw. The Soviet Supreme High Command announced that those who distinguished themselves in building bridgeheads along the Vistula would be awarded the title of Hero of the Soviet Union, as it had previously done regarding the crossing of the Dnieper.

Jews in the Battles to Cross the Vistula

During the attack of July–August 1944, the forces of the First Ukrainian Front reached the Vistula and established a bridgehead near the city of Sandomierz. The 55th Tank Brigade Guards of the 3rd Tank Army, commanded by Colonel David Dragunsky (see above, "Jews in the Defensive Battles on the Roads

COLONEL DAVID DRAGUNSKY

Leading to Moscow"), distinguished itself in the operation. Dragunsky's brigade advanced rapidly toward the Vistula, and when they arrived on July 30, it became clear that the Germans had not yet established defenses on the west bank. Without waiting for the construction of an amphibious bridge, Dragunsky ordered his men to collect fishing boats and build rafts to take an infantry battalion and tanks across the river in order to establish a bridgehead. Before the Germans could counterattack, Dragunsky's entire tank brigade, an additional armored brigade and an infantry brigade had established themselves at the bridgehead.

The Germans viewed the bridgehead as the source of a possible attack against

---

163. Afanasev, *Drugaia Voina*, 345–51.

Germany and Berlin, and in August, the Germans' North Ukraine Army Group began a fierce counteroffensive with massive air and artillery support. Despite heavy fighting and losses on both sides, the Germans were unable to capture the Sandomierz bridgehead. Additional Soviet forces were brought in and the bridgehead was extended to a width of 70 kilometers (44 miles) and a depth of 60 kilometers (38 miles). During the fighting on September 24, Dragunsky and the two other brigade commanders who had established the bridgehead were awarded the title of Hero of the Soviet Union. A second bridgehead was established on the Vistula at Magnuszew, south of Warsaw, near where the Pilitsa River empties into the Vistula. On August 1, Lieutenant Grigori Zlotin was with the first force landing near Magnuszew on the Vistula's west bank. He led the platoon's assault and repelled a German counterattack, personally destroying a German self-propelled gun, and was awarded the title of Hero of the Soviet Union. He fell at the Oder River in February 1945. Infantry battalion commander captain Haim (Yefim) Tsitovski, who established and defended a bridgehead on Vistula and enabled the 79th Infantry Guards Division to cross, was also awarded the title of Hero of the Soviet Union for his part in the crossing.[164]

Between September 1944 and January 1945 local battles were waged, but they did not result in any significant changes in the front lines along the Vistula or in the Soviet bridgeheads from Warsaw to the south. North of Warsaw the front ran along the Narev River and from there to Klaipeda, where there were also no significant changes until January 1945.

The First Arrivals on German Soil

On October 17, 1944, the soldiers of the Third Byelorussian Front crossed the East Prussian border, and the war on German soil began. A Jewish soldier with the first forces to enter East Prussia wrote:

> The platoon commander told us that we were going to enter Germany (Prussia). We were briefed to be careful of surprises…. However, he said nothing about our conduct within Germany as he had before we entered other regions. I had my own interpretation of his orders and took what he said to mean that we could do what we wanted to as long as we were careful not to be surprised…. We were under heavy fire until we took over the first settlement in Prussia…. Some of the residents fled with the retreating soldiers….

---

164. Sheinker, *Geroizm Evreev*, 123, 127.

In the daylight we discovered a very beautiful place, the likes of which we had never seen. It was a large, orderly village with a lot of white buildings of more than one floor, yards, cowsheds and very well-equipped stables. The differences between Russian and Polish settlements and this one was very striking. There was great wealth inside the buildings as well: nice clothing, fancy furs, expensive kitchen tools, sets of china dishes, crystal goblets, pictures on the walls. Seeing everything was like being stabbed through the heart: had it all been taken from murdered Jews? The people who had stayed in their homes were very frightened. They huddled in corners and didn't say anything.... We went into several similar villages in Prussia. It is impossible to describe the joy of our soldiers whenever they took German prisoners. The Germans begged for their lives, saying they had small children at home and that they were all against this cursed war.... I was happy to see those German soldiers, members of the "master race," begging me, a Jewish soldier, for food, water and cigarettes.[165]

The Campaign from the Vistula to the Oder

On January 12, 1945, the great Soviet offensive began along the Vistula and Narev fronts. Its goal was to reach Berlin and force a German surrender. The assault began from the Sandomierz bridgeheads toward Krakow and Silesia, and from the Magnuszew and the Pulawy bridgeheads toward Lodz, Poznan and Berlin. From the Narev north of Warsaw, Soviet forces attacked northwest to reach the Baltic Sea at Gdansk (Danzig) and cut off the German forces fighting in east Prussia. The German front in Poland was crushed and the Red Army rapidly advanced west and northwest. The German forces retreated from Warsaw before the city could be surrounded, and it was liberated on January 17, 1945.

---

165. Yosef Leshch, "In the Trenches and Strong Points," *Voice of the Disabled*, ed. Gad Rosenblat [Hebrew] (November 2003): 8.

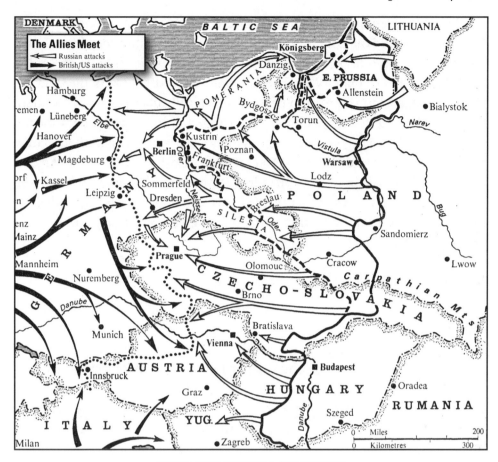

FROM THE VISTULA TO BERLIN

The August 1944 attempt on Hitler's life undermined his faith in the army commanders. On January 24, 1945, he decided to put Himmler (who had no military experience) in charge of the Army Group Vistula which was then being organized. He did so against the better judgment of Guderian, chief of staff for the land forces. The Army Group Vistula's mission was to defend the main routes leading to Berlin. Hitler rejected Guderian's suggestion that the German forces still in Kurland (Latvia) and Norway be evacuated, which would bring in about a half million additional troops to defend Berlin. To overcome the severe shortage of soldiers caused by heavy losses at the front, and since all males between the ages of 17 and 45 were already in uniform, Hitler decided to set up the Volkssturm militia of men over 45 and younger than 17, especially youths who belonged to the Hitler Youth, to equip them with Panzerfaust anti-tank weapons and rifles, and to use them in defensive and street battles.

When the German front along the Vistula collapsed, they decided to deploy their forces behind the last natural barrier before Berlin, the Oder River. Hitler ordered some cities to be turned into fortresses, and soldiers were ordered to fight there to the last man. When Himmler failed to take control of the situation, Hitler transferred the command of Army Group Vistula to General Gotthard Heinrici. On March 28, 1945, after Hitler raged at his commanders for not stopping the Red Army's advance and Guderian tried to defend them, Hitler turned to him and said, "Oberst-General, your health requires you to take an immediate leave of six weeks." Thus he dismissed the last man in his Berlin entourage who understood that the war was lost. Hitler, Keitel and others in the Berlin bunker built a fantasy world and waited for military and political developments to save the situation.

Jewish Soldiers in Battles in Germany

The 1st Mechanized Corps, commanded by Lieutenant General Semyon Krivoshin, was among the Soviet forces on the First Ukrainian Front, which had broken out from the Magnuszew bridgehead on the Vistula in January. The corps was subordinate to the 2nd Guards Tank Army. There were many Jews with high positions in his corps, among them Chief of Staff Colonel David Biberman and the commander of the 291st Tank Brigade, Colonel Yevsey Vaynrub. Krivoshin's corps advanced westward at the rate of 40–50 kilometers (25–30 miles) a day, cut off the Warsaw–Poznan highway near Klodava and reached the Oder on January 31, 1945. Without delay the corps crossed the river north of Frankfurt-an-der-Oder. From Kustrin-an-der-Oder, Vaynrub's brigade was sent north and on February 5, after savage battles, captured the town of Koenigsburg near the Oder, south of the city of Shchechin. After three weeks of battles and having crossed a thousand kilometers (620 miles), Krivoshin's corps left the front to reorganize in preparation for the assault on Berlin.[166]

Another force from the Magnuszew bridgehead was the 8th Guards Army (previously the 62nd Army, which fought at Stalingrad), commanded by General Chuykov. It included the 8th Tank Corps, which was commanded by Major General Matvey Vaynrub – Colonel Yevsey Vayrub's brother. Chuykov appointed Vaynrub to command an armored force that included a tank brigade, a tank-destroyer brigade and two tank battalions, assigning him the mission of breaking through enemy defense lines, bypassing defended regions, pen-

---

166. Shapiro, *Under Fire*, 316–18.

etrating deep behind enemy lines and cutting off transport routes. On January 14 they carried out the mission successfully and quickly arrived at the Lodz suburbs. When Vaynrub left his tank to make observations of the area, he was hit by enemy fire and wounded for the fourth time during the war. When he recovered he was made second in command of the army and fought with it until Berlin was captured. Three days before the German surrender, on April 6, he was awarded the title of Hero of the Soviet Union. The Vaynrub brothers, Yevsey and Matvey, one a colonel and the other a general, met twice during the war. The first emotional meeting was at the Magnuszew bridgehead in August 1944 and the second in Berlin just after the war.[167]

The 1st Tank Brigade, commanded by Colonel Abram Temnik, belonged to the 8th Mechanized Corps of the 1st Tank Army, commanded by General (later Marshal) Mikhail Katukov. It was subordinate to Zhukov's First Byelorussian Front. Temnik had a long career as a tank crew member beginning with the battles against the Japanese in 1939, and after the German invasion he fought as the commander of a tank battalion in Stalingrad and the Kursk salient, and from there to the Vistula, the Oder and on to Berlin. In the fall of 1944 he was appointed commander of the 1st Tank Brigade. General Katukov had commanded the brigade during the battle for Moscow and had a special respect for it. He wanted it led by a brave, talented officer, and chose Temnik because he knew him from previous battles.

Advancing toward the Oder, Temnik crossed the Pilitsa River, bypassed Lodz from the south and captured the town of Alexanderov to the west of Lodz. Fearing they would be surrounded, the German forces left Lodz, and the city fell on January 19, 1945 without a shot fired. Temnik's brigade bypassed Poznan from the south to avoid getting involved in street fighting and sped west. After a fierce battle they captured the city of Kunersdorf, close to Frankfurt-an-der-Oder. In March the brigade, along with the 1st Tank Army, was transferred to the Second Byelorussian Front to destroy the German forces at Pomerania, where hundreds of German Panzers were concentrated. The Germans initiated a counteroffensive there on February 16, which endangered the northern flank of the Soviet forces moving toward Berlin. Temnik's tank brigade participated in repelling the Germans and capturing Gdansk, after which they returned to the First Byelorussian Front in preparation for the attack on Berlin.[168]

---

167. Ibid., 593–98.
168. Ibid., 556–63; Sverdlov, *Encyclopedia Evreiskogo Geroizma*, 302–4.

Private Leonid Blatt distinguished himself in the battles around Gdansk. During a battle that lasted for two days, he repaired 30 field telephone lines under heavy artillery fire, enabling Soviet artillery fire to continue. Carrying reels of telephone cable, he crossed the Peene River under heavy enemy fire and set up communication lines for the front artillery officers, who provided cover fire for the assaulting forces. The division commander, the army commander and Marshal Rokossovsky, the front commander, all recommended that Blatt be awarded the Slava ("Glory") Medal, First Class, for his bravery.

The Slava Medal was a new medal, instituted by the Supreme Soviet of the Soviet Union on November 8, 1943. It could only be given to privates and sergeants who had displayed extreme bravery in action. There were three classes, and for distinguished conduct in battle and exceptional acts under fire for the first time, the Third Class medal was awarded. For distinguished conduct in battle the second time, the Second Class medal was awarded, and only the third time could the First Class medal be awarded, at which point the soldier was referred to as a Cavalier of the Slava Decoration. Those who had been awarded all three were automatically given a promotion and granted a larger pension should they be incapacitated, and their children were allowed to study at the universities without cost. Blatt had other medals and decorations from previous battles, including the Red Star. He was awarded the Slava Medal Third Class on June 25, 1944, for distinguished service on the Leningrad Front, where he reconnected telephone lines under enemy fire many times. He was awarded the Second Class during the battles near the Narev River north of Warsaw in January 1945, where in a critical situation caused by a German counterattack, he secured communication lines with the artillery and the attack was finally repelled. He was awarded the First Class medal, as noted, during the battle at Gdansk.[169]

Other Jewish soldiers were awarded Slava Medals First Class in the battles on the Oder. Shimon Burman, a machine gunner, had fought on the Ukrainian front at the beginning of the war and later at Moscow, Stalingrad and Kursk,

---

169. F.D. Sverdlov, *Soldatskaia Doblest, Ocherki o Voinakh-Evreiakh-Polnykh Kaval-erakh Ordena Slavy* (Kniga, 1992) 15–17. The foregoing is a detailed booklet of the names and deeds of 12 Jews who were awarded the Slava Medal, but there were many more. One of the missing names is that of Sergeant Boris Margolin, who received the Slava First Class in the battles near the city of Labiau in eastern Prussia, near Koenigsberg (today Polessk). See *Voice of the Disabled* (May 2002): 22. Margolin fell in battle in March 1945, a few weeks after the medal was awarded.

and had been wounded several times. He received the Slava Medal Third Class during the battles in the Praga suburb of Warsaw in the middle of September 1944 and the Second Class during the battles near the German city of Doich-Krone in February 1945. During the assault in the Alt-Kustrin region at the end of March 1945, where the enemy held a bridgehead on the east bank of the Oder, he received command of a machine-gunner platoon after its commander had been wounded. Leading the assault, his fire enabled the company to carry out its mission. That night, with three other soldiers, Burman took a boat and landed on a small island in the middle of the river and there destroyed an enemy unit with hand grenades. He continued to the west bank and fired his machine gun, repelling an enemy counterattack and hitting dozens of enemy soldiers.

On April 14, in a battle near Frankfurt-an-der-Oder, unit commander Nikolai (Nathan) Gizis was awarded the Slava Medal First Class. Gizis fought in Moscow, Stalingrad and Kursk. He was awarded the Slava Medal Third Class in the battles near the Vistula on August 17, 1944, and the Second Class near Poznan in Poland in January–February 1945. On the Oder River, Gizis, together with three other soldiers, infiltrated the no-man's land between the forces and from there, even though he was wounded, he aimed precise mortar fire at the enemy's positions. Only after the battle would he agree to evacuate for medical treatment.[170]

On February 8, 1945, two German infantry battalions supported by tanks attacked the village of Karlsbisee at the bridgehead on the Oder near the city of Vritsen. The Panzers advanced along a narrow road and endangered the headquarters of the 990th Infantry Regiment of the 230th Infantry Division, which was defending the village. Nineteen-year-old Mikhail Ocheret, who had been drafted only in 1943, saw the enemy tanks nearing his position. He checked his grenades and arranged them around himself. A column of tanks were approaching and the narrowness of the street prevented them from maneuvering. Putting the first tank out of commission would halt the column. He threw grenades at the first tank but it continued moving toward him. Ocheret seized his remaining grenades and threw himself under the treads of the enemy tank. The demolished tank blocked the road and the column slowly turned back. The headquarters was saved and the attack on the village and bridgehead was repelled. Ocheret was posthumously awarded the title of Hero of the Soviet Union.[171]

---

170. Sheinker, *Geroism Evreev*, 22–28, 172–82.
171. Ibid., 416–17; Shapiro, *Under Fire*, 25.

The Polish city of Poznan, on the main road to Berlin, was one of the fortified cities Hitler had ordered to be defended and fought for to the end. There were 60,000 soldiers in the city garrison. The attack began on January 24 and lasted for a month, with Poznan falling only on February 23. For nine days before the assault, Soviet guns roared and loudspeakers announced that defense of the city was hopeless, and that the only way the Germans could save themselves would be by surrender. Captain Shaltiyel Abramov, a Caucasian Jew, distinguished himself in the battle. When the battalion commander was killed, he took command and fought until the fortress was captured, climbing to the top of the fortress and planting the Red Banner. He was awarded the title of Hero of the Soviet Union for his courage and capable leadership.[172]

Breslau (Wroclaw) on the Oder River was another city Hitler had ordered to be defended and fought for to the last man. The forces of the First Ukrainian Front, having crossed the river and advanced to the west and northwest, surrounded the city in the middle of February 1945. The battle lasted 82 days and 40,000 Germans fought in it, some of them Volksstrum. Breslau was finally taken on May 6, four days after the fall of Berlin.

Major Yakov Chapichev was a member of the small ethnic group of Crimean Jews (called Krimchaks). He had fought in Leningrad where he edited a military front newspaper, wrote propaganda-oriented articles and belonged to the political staff of an armored division. After having been wounded at the front, he was appointed deputy commander for political affairs of the 2nd Battalion of the 243rd Infantry Regiment, which participated in the street battles in Breslau. On March 9, 1945, during one of the battles, Chapichev personally commanded a group of soldiers assaulting a fortified three-story house. Under covering fire he broke into the house and led his men through the ground floor, using hand grenades to kill the Germans there, and was killed while securing rooms on the second floor. His men continued the mission and cleared the Germans out of the house. Yakov Chapichev was posthumously awarded the title of Hero of the Soviet Union.[173]

Lieutenant Yosef Bumagin also distinguished himself in street fighting in Breslau. When the war broke out he was working in an automotive factory, and despite his pleas to enlist was ordered to remain at his job. He was drafted in May 1944, and on reaching the front he distinguished himself in battle. He

172. Shapiro, *Under Fire*, 25.
173. Sheinker, *Geroism Evreev*, 70–73, 128.

was quickly promoted from private, given an officer's rank and command of an infantry platoon. On April 24 he led the assault on a fortified German position that blocked Soviet advance through the streets. The enemy opened fire and a number of soldiers were wounded. Bumagin crawled toward the position and tossed in hand grenades, silencing the German machine guns. Another bunker opened fire and though Bumagin's men kept close to the ground, he was hit. Nevertheless, he crawled toward the bunker and with his body covered the embrasure through which the gun was firing, enabling his troops to capture the enemy position. Bumagin was posthumously awarded the title of Hero of the Soviet Union.[174]

Conquering Hungary and Crossing the Danube

After the removal of the pro-German government in Romania in August 1944, the Red Army rapidly crossed the country, and at the end of September the soldiers of the Second Ukrainian Front reached the Hungarian border.

The Danube was a natural barrier for advance into Hungary, Czechoslovakia and Austria. The 99th Infantry Division reached it in the beginning of December 1944. Senior Lieutenant Boris Veinstein, deputy commander of a battalion of the 99th Division, distinguished himself at the crossing south of Budapest and in the defense and enlarging of the bridgehead. On December 6, 1944, under the cover of darkness, he led the first force across the river, sailing in boats and on improvised rafts, and held a position on the opposite shore. The bridgehead was reinforced and withstood German and Hungarian counterattacks. When the battalion commander was wounded, Veinstein assumed command, repelled the attack and held the bridgehead, and from there the attack on Budapest was eventually begun. During an enemy attack, he led a reserve company and repelled the Hungarians in hand-to-hand combat. However, he was hit by machine-gun fire and killed. For demonstrating initiative and leadership at a critical moment, he was posthumously awarded the title of Hero of the Soviet Union.[175] At the end of December the Soviet forces surrounded Budapest, and after fierce street fighting the city was finally captured on February 13, 1945.

Junior Lieutenant Semyon Kheyfets, the commander of an infantry platoon, distinguished himself during a Danube crossing west of Budapest near the city

---

174. Ibid., 121; Shapiro, *Under Fire*, 59–60.
175. Shapiro, *Under Fire*, 411–12, 603–5; Sverdlov and Vainer, *Voiny Evrei*, 238–39.

of Komarno. On March 30, 1945, he was one of the first to reach the south bank of the river, cross it and hold the north bank, which was in Czechoslovakia. Kheyfets and his men repelled a German tank-assisted counterattack and he was awarded the title of Hero of the Soviet Union.[176] Junior Lieutenant Mikhail Valyansky, also Jewish, commander of a machine gun platoon, participated in the same battle. On the night of March 29, 1945, leading a 30-man landing force, he crossed the Danube and captured a bridgehead. He and his platoon participated in the liberation of the city of Komarno in Czechoslovakia. For his distinguished conduct, he was awarded the title of Hero of the Soviet Union.[177]

In October 1944, in the area of Debretsen-Seged (east and southeast of Budapest), the advancing Soviet forces met strong German-Hungarian opposition and counterattacks. The 320th Infantry Division, commanded by Colonel Yosef Burik, and the 1055th Infantry Regiment, commanded by Yosef Sledya, captured the fortified area of the city of Seged.[178] For his distinguished conduct in the battles in the Debretsen region, Senior Lieutenant Nikolai Moiseevich Molochnikov, commander of an anti-tank artillery battery, was awarded the title of Hero of the Soviet Union. He was a young man recruited during the war and only reached the front in 1944. On October 12, 1944, after most of the infantry soldiers securing his battery had been wounded, he remained without backup to face an assault of German tanks and foot soldiers. Only two or three men remained at each gun. Molochnikov, himself wounded, fired an anti-tank gun, hitting several German tanks. When the German foot soldiers approached, he personally operated a machine gun and the attack was repelled.[179]

Sergeant Grigori Bogorad served in the battles south of Debretsen as a member of the engineering corps. At the end of October 1944, he used inflatable rubber dinghies and other crafts to transfer his squad (the force that held the other side of the Tisse River) under heavy enemy fire, together with the force leading the attack on the enemy positions commanding the passage. At a distance of less than 100 meters (110 yards) from enemy positions, he personally laid a minefield to protect the bridgehead. Attacking Panzers hit the mines and had to retreat. He had received the Slava Medal Third Class in January 1944 for his distinguished conduct in the battles for the city of Uman in the

---

176. Shapiro, *Under Fire*, 235–36.
177. Sheinker, *Geroism Evreev*, 152–53: Shapiro, *Under Fire*, 588.
178. Sverdlov and Vainer, *Voiny Evrei*, 236.
179. Ibid., 236–37; Shapiro, *Under Fire*, 411–12.

Ukraine, when he and a few others crawled to enemy positions and captured a prisoner for interrogation. He had received the Slava Medal Second Class in March 1944 in the battles southwest of Kirovograd in the Ukraine, when under heavy fire he broke through an enemy mine field the Soviet tanks would have to pass. For his bravery in the battles south of Debretsen he was awarded the Slava Medal First Class.[180]

The Attack on Berlin and the German Surrender

The offensive against Berlin began on April 16 and ended on May 2 with the fall of the city. It began from the bridgeheads on the Oder and involved Zhukov's First Byelorussian Front forces, which attacked from the west, and Konev's First Ukrainian Front forces, which attacked from the southeast. Marshal Rokossovsky's Second Byelorussian Front forces were also supposed to join the attack by securing the northern flank of Zhukov's forces. However, they joined the battle four days after it started because they had been wiping out the last German forces in Pomerania and capturing Gdansk and Gdynia. Stalin ordered the attack to begin as soon as possible, without waiting for Rokossovsky's forces, to prevent the Americans and British from reaching Berlin before the Red Army. Zhukov wrote that Stalin had told him that according to intelligence sources, the Germans had proposed a separate peace agreement to the Americans and British which would allow them [the Allies] to enter Berlin before the Soviets.[181]

According to Soviet data, 2.5 million soldiers, 42,000 cannons and mortars, 6,250 tanks and 7,500 airplanes took part in the attack on Berlin. According to the same source, there were one million German Army Group Vistula and Army Group Center troops, 10,400 cannons and mortars, 1,500 tanks and assault cannons and 3,300 airplanes.[182]

In the battle for the Oder, the Germans did not deploy along the river, where they kept small mobile forces, but were well entrenched on the Seelow Heights to the west, along the Reichsstrasse which led westward to Berlin. It was the last line of defense on the way to the German capital. At dawn of April 16, 1945, thousands of Soviet guns opened fire on the German front line. However the main German force, which was on the Seelow Heights further to the rear, was not badly damaged. The result was that when the Byelorussian Front forces

---

180. Sverdlov, *Soldatskaia Doblest*, 18–21.
181. Zhukov, *Memoirs*, 586–88.
182. Kirian et al., *Slovar-Spravochnik*, 54.

began their assault, they encountered a strong rear deployment, suffered heavy losses and advanced only slowly toward Berlin. To overcome German resistance on the Seelow Heights, Zhukov was forced to send into battle the reserves he had meant to keep for the attack on Berlin. He wrote:

> The Seelow Heights towered over the entire surrounding terrain: they had steep slopes.... They rose as a continuous wall before our advancing troops, closing the plateau where we would fight the last battle before advancing to Berlin.... By one p.m. of that day I realized quite distinctly that the enemy defenses on the Seelow Heights had basically remained intact.... After consultations with the army commanders we decided to send into action additionally both tank armies under Generals M.Ye. Katukov and S.I. Bogdanov....[183]

Following the delay in the advance of Zhukov's forces, Stalin ordered Konev's First Ukrainian Front to move toward Berlin. That caused a fierce rivalry between Zhukov and Konev, both of whom wanted to capture Berlin, and they raced to see who would arrive first.

Captain Nathan Polyusuk, who had participated in the defense of Moscow, had distinguished himself in the battles of the Volga and the Kursk salient. On April 18, 1945, as second in command of a battalion of the 301st Infantry Division, Polyusuk led his forces in an assault of a fortified hill of the Seelow Heights. Two attacks by the battalion were stopped by fire from bunkers on a commanding hill. Unseen by the enemy, he led a small group of volunteers through bushes and a ravine, reached the bunkers and silenced them with hand grenades. Carrying a red flag he ran forward, raised his voice and shouted, "The hill is ours, the way is open! On to Berlin!" Those were his last words. Shrapnel from a shell hit him and he was killed on the spot. He was posthumously awarded the title of Hero of the Soviet Union.[184]

Part of Katukov's tank army, which was deployed in the assault of the Seelow Heights, were the 1st Tank Brigade commanded by Abram Temnik and the 11th Tank Regiment commanded by Benyamin Mindlein. The assault was carried out on steep paths, and the local German counterattack cost Temnik's brigade heavy losses. The capture of the Seelow Heights was accomplished on April 18, enabling the advance toward Berlin to be renewed. On April 20,

---

183. Zhukov, *Memoirs*, 605.
184. Shapiro, *Under Fire*, 449–53.

Zhukov's forces reached the eastern suburbs of Berlin and began heavy artillery bombardments. Zhukov sent a telegram to Katukov: "You have the historic mission to enter Berlin first. Send the best brigade from every corps to enter Berlin and raise the flag of victory...." Katukov chose Temnik's brigade to lead the charge, cross the Spree River and take the Tempelhof airport in the center of the city, and from there to attack the Reichstag. The mission was carried out, although as the brigade advanced, pockets of German resistance were left behind. Tempelhof and its many aircraft were taken and the brigade repelled German counterattacks. Temnik's brigade fought hard street battles against a desperate enemy and the brigade suffered heavy losses.

On April 24, Temnik led the attack on the Reichstag. His tank went over a mine and he was critically wounded, dying the following day. He had fought in many battles, from Stalingrad to Berlin, and fell only a few days before the end of the war and the Allied victory. He did not succeed in waving the flag over the Reichstag. He was posthumously awarded the title of Hero of the Soviet Union.[185]

Lieutenant Colonel Naum Peysachovsky led the assault on the Reichstag, commanding the 164th Rifle Regiment of the 33rd Division of the 3rd Shock Army. He had fought in Byelorussia in 1941, and in Smolensk and Viazma in the battles for the liberation of Latvia and Poland, and from there he was sent to Berlin in April 1945. He and his troops cleared German forces from the Pankow quarter in northern Berlin and from the Moabit region in the center of the city near the Reichstag, where he was seriously wounded in hand-to-hand combat fought in one of the buildings. For distinction in battle, he was awarded the title of Hero of the Soviet Union.[186]

Staff Sergeant Ilya Spiashvilli, a Georgian Jew, was awarded the Slava Medal First Class for distinguished conduct in street battles in Berlin in April 1945. Commanding an anti-tank gun, he aimed directly at enemy positions and destroyed them. When he ran out of shells he used a machine gun, was wounded three times and continued fighting until he lost consciousness. Only then was he evacuated for medical treatment. He had received the Slava Medal Third Class in 1944 for repelling a German tank attack in the city of Wolomin

185. Ibid., 564–68; Sverdlov, *Encyclopedia Evreiskogo Geroizma*, 303–4.
186. Sverdlov, *V Stroiu Otvazhnykh*, 209–10.

in Poland, and the Second Class for his actions in the battle near the German village of Brausendorf in March 1945.[187]

General Semyon Krivoshin's 1st Mechanized Corps was part of the 2nd Guards Tank Army. It crossed the Oder and attacked Berlin from the northeast. Yevsey Vaynrub's 219th Tank Brigade was part of Krivoshin's corps, which had fought in the capture of Bernau, and from there advanced to Berlin. On April 21 it reached the outskirts of Berlin and the following day captured the northeast fortified suburb of Weissensee. In fierce street fighting on April 27, the corps took the Siemensstadt areas northeast of the city and crossed the Spree River from north to south. For distinction in battle in Berlin, Krivoshin was awarded the title of Hero of the Soviet Union. Yevsey Vaynrub was also awarded the title of Hero of the Soviet Union, and his brigade received the honorary title of the Berlin Brigade.[188]

The 55th Guards Tank Brigade, commanded by Hero of the Soviet Union Colonel David Dragunsky, reached the outskirts of Berlin from the southeast, as part of the 3rd Guards Tank Army commanded by General Pavel Rybalko. Dragunsky and his brigade had fought in many battles, from the bridgehead at Sandomierz on January 12, 1945, through Krakow and Silesia, across the Varta River and finally in Germany. In 20 days the brigade had fought its way across 600 kilometers (370 miles). On April 30, 1945, as part of the First Ukrainian Front, they cut off the Potsdam-Berlin road and joined Krivoshin's 1st Mechanized Corps, which had come from the north. Berlin was surrounded. For distinction in battle in Berlin, Dragunsky was awarded Hero of the Soviet Union a second time.[189]

In Berlin there was fierce street fighting until May 2, when the German army in the city surrendered. Hitler committed suicide in his bunker on April 30, and on the same day the Soviet flag was flown over the Reichstag. Despite the surrender, battles persisted against small German units that tried to break out of the city to reach the Americans and surrender to them; these continued until May 5. On May 8 German representatives signed a formal surrender. On May 9, 1945, the last German units in Kurland, Latvia, and southwest of Gdansk in Pomerania surrendered.

---

187. Moshe Shpitsburg, "*Trizhdy Slava Synu Gruzinskogo Evreistva*," in *Golos Invalidov Voiny* 170 (2002): 28–29.
188. Sheinker, *Geroism Evreev*, 135; Shapiro, *Under Fire*, 318–20, 601.
189. Shapiro, *Under Fire*, 98: Sheinker, *Geroism Evreev*, 13–14.

The last to surrender were the German soldiers in Czechoslovakia. The commander of the First Ukrainian Front sent Dragunsky's 55th Guards Tank Brigade and other troops to destroy the German forces in Czechoslovakia and support the Czech revolt in Prague. In both Prague and Dresden, in southwest Germany, there were still large German forces belonging to the Army Group Center, about 900,000 men in all. The Soviet leadership assumed that the United States and Britain wanted to reach Czechoslovakia for political reasons connected to the future government in the country, and that the German forces would hold out until the Americans arrived. On May 6, an attack was initiated against the Germans in both regions, the First Ukrainian Front and the Polish Popular Army attacking from the north, and the Second Ukrainian Front from the south. That same day the German forces in Breslau surrendered. On May 9, Dragunsky's tanks entered Prague. The 309th Infantry Division of the First Ukrainian Front commanded by Hero of the Soviet Union Lev Davidovich was diverted from the fighting in Berlin to Prague. Davidovich had fought during 1941–43 on the Volkhov front, participated in the battles of the Kursk salient, crossed the Danube and fought in Berlin. He finished with the surrender of the German soldiers in Prague. The battles lasted for two days after the official German surrender on May 9, with the last German units surrendering on May 11, 1945.[190]

12. Jews in the Red Army's Political Administration

The political administration of the Red Army, or as it was officially called, the Institution of Commissars and Politruks, was established during the Civil War. As a result there was essentially a double command in every division and unit, since the commissar had decision-making authority equal to that of the commander. In 1940, after the war in Finland and in accordance with demands made by Timoshenko, the people's commissar for defense, the commissar's status was limited and preferred status was given to the military commander. In July 1941, during the period of great defeats, the Central Committee of the Communist Party decided in a "recommendation to the army" that the powers of the commissars would be expanded to strengthen the party's influence and supervision of the army – meaning a reinstitution of the double command. During the first

---

190. Shapiro, *Under Fire*, 97–99, 344–46; Pospelov et al., *Istoria Velikoi*, vol. 32, 317–30; Sverdlov, *V Stroiu Otvazhnykh*, 108–9, 170–72.

three months of the war, 132,000 party and Komsomol members were enlisted to fill the posts of commissar and politruk.

The double command persisted throughout the difficult phase of defeats and retreats until the Germans were halted at Stalingrad. It can be said the commissars contributed to the Red Army's morale and fighting spirit and its ability to withstand setbacks during those difficult times. They were no longer necessary when the army began to chalk up victories. The double command was basically contradictory to the essence of command and its unique responsibility for decision-making in battle, in matters of discipline and military order. During the first 15 months of the war, the officer corps of the army proved its loyalty to the Soviet state during difficult times of defeats, and there was no longer a need for the commissars' close supervision and monitoring. On October 9, 1942, in the middle of the battle of Stalingrad, the commissar institution, which had an enormous influence in the army, was abolished. The commissars received the title of "deputy unit commander for political affairs," making them subordinate to the unit commanders, who now had the final say in military and operational matters, including overall responsibility for political indoctrination in their units.[191] The change strengthened the status of the regular army officers. At the same time, many commissars who had battle experience were appointed as ordinary commanders of units at all levels, from battalions to divisions and higher.

No official data has ever been published about the number or percentage of Jews in the political staff of the army on the eve of or during the war. According to data dating from 1926, 10.3 percent of the commissars then serving in the army were Jewish. However, following the developments between 1926 and the beginning of the war, the percentage decreased. It can be assumed that the number of Jews serving as commissars and politruks at varying ranks during the war was relatively great compared with other roles carried out by Jews in the army, since the former were filled by members of the party and Komsomol. From the partial data concerning the number of Jews in the Communist Party on the eve of the war, it can be concluded that about 5 percent of all party members were Jewish, almost three times the number of Jews in the Soviet Union's population, and it is logical to assume that the same percentage served in the army's political ranks.

---

191. Rzheshevski et al., *Velikaia Otechestvenna Voina*, 115.

The most prominent figure in the Red Army political ranks was Lev Mekhlis. During the Civil War he was a member of the Communist Party and the commissar of a Red Army division that fought in the Ukraine. Between 1921 and 1936 he filled various posts in the Communist Party bureaucracy. Between 1937 and 1940 he was head of the Red Army's political administration, to whom the entire army political administration was subordinate. When the Germans attacked the Soviet Union, he was reappointed head commissar of the army and deputy commissar for defense. He served in that capacity for a year, until June 1942, when following the failure at the Kerch peninsula in the Crimea (which he was partly responsible for, see above, "The Renewal of the German Offensive in Southern Russia"), Stalin dismissed him and replaced him with Alexander Shcherbakov. While Mekhlis was still in office, the political staff regained equal status with the army commanders. He also organized the recruiting of 132,000 party and Komsomol members to the ranks of the commissars and politruks. After Stalin dismissed him, he served in senior positions in the military councils of the various fronts, and in 1944 was promoted to the rank of colonel general.[192]

A certain indication of the number of Jews on the political staff of the army can be gained from studies of the war dealing with the defense on Sevastopol, which lasted 250 days, and the siege of Leningrad, which, until it was finally relieved, lasted 900 days. Under difficult conditions of the long sieges, the firm stance of the defenders had to be bolstered by indoctrination activities of the commissars, and their work was extremely important.

The defense of Sevastopol was divided into four main sectors, each of which with its own headquarters and propaganda department. Two sectors had Jewish commissars: Aaron Khatskevich served in Sector No. 1, and Yakov Melnikov in Sector No. 4. Melnikov was also commissar of the 95th Infantry Division, which fought in the sector. S. Abramovich was the commissar of the 241st Brigade of the same division, and the deputy commander of the 161st Brigade was Commissar Samuel Libshein. The commissar of the 172nd Infantry Division, which fought in Sector No. 2, was Giorgi Shafransky. The division withstood heavy German assaults in December 1941. The commissar of the 7th Marines brigade's 5th Battalion was Z. Shapira, and the commissar of the 40th Cavalry Division was Abram Margolis.[193]

192. Rzheshevski et al., *Velikaia Otechestvenna Voina*, 355–56.
193. Abramovich, *V Reshaiushchei Voine*, 270–71, 285–86, 289.

A political department headed by Matvey Bassovsky was set up in besieged Leningrad at the Oranienbaum bridgehead. The bridgehead had been cut off and isolated from the city's main defense line. The department was set up by the Navy Command of Oranienbaum, which considered that the morale of the isolated bridgehead needed active political indoctrination. In December 1942, after the commissariat had been abolished, Bassovsky was appointed "deputy commander of the Oranienbaum bridgehead for political matters" and given the rank of colonel.

Jews were in key positions in operating the Road of Life on Lake Ladoga – repairing damaged and stalled vehicles, preserving security, maintaining first-aid stations for the wounded and treating the wounded – all performed under continuous enemy fire which had to be dealt with by thousands of soldiers under the worst possible conditions. The political staff dealing with the Road of Life played an important role in bolstering the soldiers' morale. Three of the commissars of the units operating the Road of Life were E. Hershkowich, F.G. Furel and M. Halperin. Head of the political department of the Leningrad front was Commissar Mikhail Orlovsky. The head commissar of the Baltic submarine fleet based at Kronstadt was Ilya Rivchin.[194] The large number of Jewish commissars in the units fighting at Sevastopol and Leningrad shows the enormous contribution of Jews to the political staff of the entire Red Army.

The aforementioned names of Jewish commissars are indicative of only a fraction of the Jews who served on the political staff of the defenses of Sevastopol and Leningrad. Many other names are known, but even more are unknown. Many commissars distinguished themselves in battle and many of them were killed. The Jewish commissars taken prisoner by the Germans were among the first to be murdered, their Judaism usually informed on by soldiers from their own units who had also been captured.

13. JEWS IN THE SOVIET AIR FORCE

The Soviet air force was hit hard at the beginning of the war, and most modern Soviet planes located in airfields in the western Soviet Union were destroyed while they were still on the ground. The Germans enjoyed complete control of the air until the winter of 1941. Nevertheless, the planes in the airfields that had not been hit, among them the Baltic fleet planes based on islands, tried to hit back. They made efforts to bomb strategic German targets, including Koe-

---

194. Abramovich, *Leningradskaia Bitva*, 11, 23, 42–43.

nisberg, Berlin and the Ploesti oil fields in Romania. Despite the Germans' air superiority, Soviet pilots, making many personal sacrifices and flying technically inferior planes, successfully defended the skies over Moscow and supported the army in the defensive battles.

There were many Jews among the founders of the Soviet air force, and many of the pilots were Jewish as well and participated in the aforementioned aerial activities. During the first weeks of the war, planes of the 43rd Squadron of the Baltic fleet, commanded by Captain Vakhterman, attacked German ground forces advancing through Lithuania and Latvia and participated in the defense of the port city of Libau (Liepaja). Planes of the 40th Air Battalion, commanded by Captain Mogilevsky, attacked Koenisberg, Klaipeda and other cities.

On June 27, 1941, Lieutenant Izaak Presseizen died a hero's death. As he attacked an enemy convoy near the Byelorussian city of Radoshkovichi, his plane was hit and caught fire. He aimed it at a concentration of German tanks and vehicles, crashed into them and inflicted many losses. He was posthumously awarded the Lenin Order for his heroic act.[195] Another case recently reported was the heroic death of Captain Isaak Yirzhak, the deputy commander of the Baltic Sea fleet air squadron, who on January 17, 1944, crashed his damaged plane into a German army convoy. His commanders recommended that he be awarded the title of Hero of the Soviet Union, and Lieutenant General S. Gulaev, commander of the air force of the Baltic Sea fleet, wrote:

> In the region of Oranienbaum during the battles to lift the siege of Leningrad, Comrade I. Yirzhak repeated the brave deed of N. Gastello and died a hero's death. As he led a group of IL-2 planes in a dive-bomb attack on enemy soldiers…the Fascist enemy directed their anti-aircraft fire at the leading plane. A shell hit the plane and set it on fire. At the last moment, and with a supreme effort, Captain Yirzhak turned his burning plane toward a structure around which a large enemy force had gathered with their weapons and crashed the plane and its bombs in their midst. The pilots in the planes accompanying him saw a great explosion…. For his bravery above and beyond the call of duty, I have recommended that Comrade Yirzhak be awarded the title of Hero of the Soviet Union."[196]

---

195. Sverdlov and Vainer, *Voiny Evrei*, 48–49; Abramovich, *V Reshaiushchei Voine*, 102–4, 172–74.

196. Timor ed., *Journal of the Soldiers* 20 (2006): 86–87. The commander of a squad-

The recommendation was made at the end of the war. Yirzhak was not awarded the title, but he was awarded the Patriotic War Medal, First Class.

On the night of August 8, 1941, Captain Mikhail Plotkin flew in the first Soviet air strike on Berlin. The best pilots of the Baltic fleet were chosen to carry out the mission and the planes took off from the Baltic Sea island of Saaremaa. An official Soviet publication stated that on the night of August 8, a special group from the Baltic Fleet's 1st Air Regiment for sowing marine mines, commanded by Colonel A.N. Preobrazhensky, took off with 12 DB-3 planes for the first bombing of Berlin. With the Swedish coast to their right, the planes crossed the Baltic Sea to avoid flying over areas protected by anti-aircraft guns. Plotkin led the first group of three attacking planes. The planes returned to base safely. On August 13, five days after the attack on Berlin, Plotkin and four other pilots were awarded the title of Hero of the Soviet Union. The Germans, who did not believe the Soviet air force capable of such an attack, reported that the British had bombed the city. Plotkin continued his activity in the Leningrad and Baltic Sea regions. On March 6, 1942, his plane was hit while he was sowing mines at the entrance to a German harbor in the Baltic sea and he was killed.[197]

A test pilot named Mark Galay distinguished himself in defending the skies over Moscow at the beginning of the war. The first German air strike on Moscow was carried out on July 22, 1941, a month after the invasion. Galay flew one of the planes that repelled the attack. In June 1943 his plane was shot down while attacking a German airfield near Bryansk. He and his navigator managed to parachute to safety in a region controlled by partisans, and they returned to Soviet lines. He continued flying both in battle and in test missions with new planes and received three Orders of Lenin, and after the war he was awarded the title of Hero of the Soviet Union.[198]

During the first year of the war the Soviet air force gained experience in battle and learned operational and organizational lessons. Emphasis was placed on reconnaissance and aerial intelligence, and on attacking the enemy's transport routes, troop concentrations and air fields. Between May and November 1942, the

---

ron of bombers, Captain Nikolai Gastello, mentioned by Lieutenant General S. Gulaev, aimed his plane, which had been hit, into a group of enemy tanks on June 28, 1941. He was posthumously awarded the title of Hero of the Soviet Union.

197. Abramovich, *V Reshaiushchei Voine*, 175–77; Shapiro, *Under Fire*, 438–48; Rzheshevski et al., *Velikaia Otechestvenna Voina*, 46.

198. Sverdlov and Vainer, *Voiny Evrei*, 50; Abramovich, *V Reshaiushchei Voine*, 175; Shapiro, *Under Fire*, 136–39.

air force was organized into aerial divisions supporting the fronts where important operations were taking place. Many of the pilots got experience in air-to-air battles, in bombing and in providing close support for the ground forces. During the second half of 1942, the Soviet military industry began supplying the air force with modern planes equal in quality to those of the Germans. Among them were advanced models of the Il (Ilyushin), La (Lavochkin), MiG (Mikoyan and Gurevich) and others (see chapter 2:3, "Jews in the Aviation Industry and the Development of Aircraft"). The more time passed, the greater their numbers grew.

At Stalingrad, the Soviet air force hit many of the German planes parachuting supplies to the surrounded 6th Army, almost completely preventing the German planes from accomplishing their mission. Soviet air superiority over the Germans was proved at the strategically important Kursk salient battle. While the Soviet air force became progressively stronger, the German air force was unable to cover its losses of planes and pilots on the eastern front. The American and British bombings also damaged Germany's manufacturing capabilities, and the German air force was to a large degree restricted to defending German cities. In attacks on Berlin and on the Dnieper, Vistula and Oder rivers, the Soviet air force gradually gained air superiority and supported the ground forces in achieving victory.

There are no statistics regarding the number of Jewish pilots and air crews in the Soviet air force during the war, but without a doubt their numbers were in the hundreds and possibly in the thousands. What is known is that 20 of the 154 Jews who were awarded the title of Hero of the Soviet Union during the war were pilots. According to Soviet data, Captain Vladimir Levitan, commander of a fighter plane squadron, shot down 20 enemy planes; Captain Abrek Barsht shot down 18. Captain Yakov Vernikov flew more than 300 missions, participated in 64 air battles and shot down 16 planes. His plane was shot down in an air battle near the Don River in the summer of 1942 but he parachuted out, managed to return to Soviet lines and continued fighting. On April 23, 1944, Captain Ilya Katunin was killed in battle in the North Sea, where he led eight Ilyushins to attack a convoy of German ships that had set out with air cover from the Varanger Fjord in Norway. His plane was hit and set on fire. He aimed his burning plane at an enemy ship and sank it. His gunner was killed with him. Captain Boris Lunts flew weapons to partisan fields behind enemy lines and returned with wounded fighters. Kovpak, the famous legendary partisan commander, mentioned him in his memoirs.[199]

CAPTAIN PAULINA
GELMAN

There were also Jewish female pilots who distinguished themselves, such as Captain Paulina Gelman, who flew hundreds of combat missions during the war. When the war broke out she was studying history at Moscow University. She volunteered for the army, trained as a pilot and served in an air force regiment composed entirely of female pilots. The regiment was equipped with light, low-flying PO-2 night bombers. She fought in the Crimea, where she bombed enemy targets at Kerch and Sevastopol, and later in Byelorussia, East Prussia and Berlin. For her distinguished service she was awarded the title of Heroine of the Soviet Union.[200]

Another female pilot who distinguished herself in battle was Lily Litvak, who served in the women's squadron commanded by Heroine of the Soviet Union Marina Raskova. Litvak fought over the Rostov and on the Stalingrad front, was wounded and returned to her squadron once she recovered, and carried out many combat missions. On August 19, 1943, her plane was shot down over territory controlled by Germans. She was 21 years old at the time. Her commander recommended she be awarded the title of Heroine of the Soviet Union, but since neither her body nor plane was ever found, she was suspected of having been taken prisoner, and therefore the award was not granted. During the 1960s, on a joint initiative of a journalist and her family, her plane was located, and in 1990 she was awarded the title of Heroine of the Soviet Union.[201] The few names mentioned are but a sample of the large number of Jewish pilots and air crew members who fought in the ranks of the Soviet air force and distinguished themselves in battle, many of them sacrificing their lives in the process.

199. Shapiro, *Under Fire*, 31–32, 214–18, 356–57, 359–62, 610–11.
200. Ibid., 151–58: Sheinker, *Geroism Evreev*, 106.
201. Timor ed., *Journal of the Soldiers* 16 (2002): 29 (appendix).

14. JEWS IN THE SOVIET NAVY

During the war, the Soviet navy was active in both the offensive and defensive battles waged along the various shores, in collaboration with and closely supporting the ground forces. Most of their activity was carried out along the shores of the Baltic, Black and Azov seas, and in the lakes and rivers where there was fighting. The Soviet fleet also had air power it could call upon. But the Great Patriotic War was waged and won on land, with the Soviet navy playing only a secondary role. Tens of thousands of sailors were taken off their ships to fight in battalions and brigades – mainly in Leningrad, Odessa and Sevastopol, but in other places as well. Nevertheless, Soviet submarines and light, fast torpedo boats attacked the enemy's sea routes.

One of those serving in the Soviet navy was Arseny Rasskin, deputy commander and commissar of the naval base on the Hanko peninsula in southwest Finland (see above, "Jews in Defense of Leningrad and along the Roads Leading to It"). After Hanko was evacuated, he was appointed chief commissar of the Soviet fleet in the Black Sea. He died at the end of December 1942 in an air crash.[202]

Under-Admiral Pavel Aaronovich Trainin was the highest-ranking Jewish officer in the Soviet navy at the beginning of the war. He commanded the fleet base of Riga, and after it was evacuated he was appointed commander of the fleet in Lake Ladoga. In the fall of 1941 he was transferred to command the naval base at the Kerch peninsula in the Crimea, where the fighting was fierce. His ships supported the ground forces with covering fire in landing and evacuating troops. After the retreat from Kerch, he commanded naval forces at the Taman Peninsula and at Novorossiysk.[203]

Another Jewish sailor who distinguished himself was Captain Arkady Sverdlov, chief of staff of the Azov Sea squadron. He directed the evacuation of the forces from Kerch to Taman in November 1941. At that time the commander of the Soviet fleet was Nikolai Kuznetsov, who wrote that "during the evacuation from Kerch, the chief of staff of the [Azov Sea] squadron Captain A. Sverdlov…personally directed the operations of the ships that evacuated the retreating units through the Kerch Straits to Taman. At that time more than 120,000 soldiers were transferred from the Crimea to Taman." Sverdlov's boats also landed Soviet forces on the Kerch peninsula at the end of December

202. Abramovich, *V Reshaiushchei Voine*, 129–30, 133.
203. Ibid., 138, 266, 371–72.

1941. There were many other Jewish naval personnel who participated in the operation.[204]

After the Germans occupied the Baltic states during the first months of the war, and until the summer of 1944, Leningrad was the Soviet fleet's only base in the Baltic Sea. The German navy and air force made it difficult for the Soviet fleet to operate in the Baltic, and the active vessels were submarines and small, rapid torpedo boats. In addition, the Germans and the Finns mined the Gulf of Finland, blocking the exit from Leningrad and Kronstadt and greatly endangering Soviet naval activity in the Baltic Sea. Nevertheless, Captain Abram Sverdlov, commander of a torpedo boat squadron, managed to navigate between the mines and evacuate the last of the Soviet forces from the Hanko Peninsula, and to carry out attacks in the Baltic Sea. On the night of July 1, 1944, his torpedo boat squadron joined battle with German boats in the Gulf of Finland near the Gulf of Vyborg. The squadron's mission was to prevent the German ships from landing forces for the recapture of Narvi, the island commanding the entrance to the Gulf of Vyborg, which had been taken over by the Soviets. For three days Sverdlov's torpedo boats prevented the enemy from reaching the islands. For his leadership, skill and achievements in sinking German ships in this battle, on July 24, 1944, he was awarded the title of Hero of the Soviet Union.[205]

CAPTAIN VOLF
KONOVALOV

A number of Jewish submarine commanders distinguished themselves in the Baltic Sea. One of them was Captain Third Class L. Smolar, who commanded an s-306, which hit a mine and sank with its crew. Captain Volf Konovalov, commander of an l-3 submarine, was awarded the title of Hero of the Soviet Union for his many successful missions, among them the sinking of two ships near the Gulf of Gdansk. Thousands of German refugees and soldiers were on board the two ships, evacuated from east Prussia during the second half of April 1945. One ship, the *Goya*, was carrying about 6,700 refugees and soldiers of the 35th Panzer Regiment. On April 16, 1945, two

204. Ibid., 263, 266, 272–73.
205. Ibid., 138; Shapiro, *Under Fire*, 546–48; Sheinker, *Geroism Evreev*, 102–3; Pospelov et al., *Istoria Velikoi*, vol. 4, 458.

torpedoes hit it, tearing it in half and sinking it in four minutes. There were 183 survivors; the others perished. After the war, Konovalov was promoted to the rank of Vice-Admiral.[206] In January and April 1945, an SHCH-3 submarine, commanded by Captain Third Class Samuel Bogorad, sank a total of three German ships evacuating troops from Kurland in Latvia. For those actions, he was awarded the title of Hero of the Soviet Union.[207]

Captain Second Class Israel Fisanovich, who commanded an M-172 submarine in the North Sea near Murmansk, hit 12 enemy ships. In the summer of 1944, four of the Soviet Union's best submarine crews were sent to England to take over various Italian war ships – among them four submarines – which had been divided among the Allied fleets after Italy surrendered. Two crew commanders were Jewish: Israel Fisanovich and Isaak Kabo. The submarines sailed from England to their new base in Murmansk, but only three of them arrived. The fourth, commanded by Fisanovich, did not. All hands on deck were lost at sea, the result of unknown circumstances.[208]

Among the Jewish commanders in the Black Sea were Izrail Izrailovich, who commanded a D-4 submarine, and Ysai Zelbet, who commanded an SHCH-210 submarine. The names of 15 Jewish submarine commanders who fought in the North, Baltic and Black seas are known.[209] The large number of Jewish submarine captains and crew members, as compared with other vessels, is explained by the fact that the submarines formed a new arm of the Soviet fleet, and as a rule Jews tended to enlist in the newer corps because there were not veteran soldiers or experienced commanders standing in the way of their advancement.

15. Jews in the Medical and Engineering Corps

Many Jews also served in the medical and engineering corps (some of them in high-ranking positions), for medicine and engineering were professions in the Soviet Union with especially large numbers of Jews. According to the 1939

---

206. Shapiro, *Under Fire*, 244–47.
207. Ibid., 53–55.
208. Ibid., 110–127.
209. Mikhail Lerner, "Jewish Submarine Officers in the Soviet Union Fleet during the War against the Nazis," *Voice of the Disabled* (November 2005): 18–19. Lerner planned and for a time was responsible for the construction of submarines at the Krasnoye-Surmovo shipyards, where he worked for 36 years. His article included the names of the 15 Jewish submarine captains and the names of scores of other Jewish officers in the submarine fleet, including vice-admirals.

census, out of the 360,000 Jews who were defined in Soviet terms as belonging to the "intelligentsia," 14.4 percent, or 52,000 Jews, worked in the medical professions (doctors, nurses, medical orderly); engineers and architects made up 6.8 percent of Jews, or 25,000.[210] In the army, most of them were sent to the medical and engineering corps.

The Medical Corps

Among the Jewish doctors serving in the Red Army, those in the highest ranking positions of the medical corps were Major General Miron Vovsy, the chief army physician; Major General Vladimir Levit, the deputy chief surgeon; Major General David Antin, the head stomatologist; and Lieutenant General Leonid Ratgauz, who, as of 1941, was second in command of the sanitation service.[211] Hundreds of Jews directed hospitals at the front and behind the lines, and thousands of other Jewish doctors worked in the hospitals in various capacities. Medical staff members worked at first aid stations on the front lines, in field hospitals and on the trains evacuating the wounded to hospitals on the home front. Their contribution is attested to by the following statistics: Out of the students graduating from the Leningrad military medical academy between the years 1925 and 1944, 473 graduates fell in war. Ninety-seven of these, i.e., 20.5 percent, were Jewish, despite the fact that Jews at the academy made up 12–15 percent of the student body. In besieged Leningrad, 27 academy graduates were killed, nine of them Jewish – i.e., 33 percent.[212]

With the exception of the medical staff, women were not drafted. According to official statistics, during the war 800,000 women served in the Red Army, 20,000 of whom, i.e., 2.5 percent, were Jewish; of those, close to 6,000 were doctors, nurses and orderlies.[213] Constantly in danger, they provided first aid on the front lines and tens of thousands of soldiers owed them their lives.

---

210. Benjamin Pinkus, *The Jews of Russia and the Soviet Union* [Hebrew] (Sdei Boker: Ben-Gurion University of the Negev, 1986), 205.
211. Sverdlov, *Evrei Generaly*, 59, 133, 177, 256. Major General Vovsy had served in the Red Army since 1918 and had fought in the Civil War; Major General Levit had served in the Red Army since 1918, and had been a regimental surgeon in the Civil War; Lieutenant General Ratgauz had joined the Red Army in 1919 and served in the Civil War.
212. Shner, *Plen*, vol. 2, 34.
213. Ibid., 29.

Riva Orman (nicknamed Rivochka at the front) was 18 when the war broke out. She joined the army as a volunteer and in July 1941 was posted to the medical battalion at Smolensk:

> After a few days her battalion was sent to the battlefield. At first the guns could be heard from afar, but soon shells began exploding nearby. The first wounded were brought in. Riva worked in a tent, and there was a stretcher on a wooden tripod that served as an operating table. Shells were exploding all around. When she took the bandage off the arm of one of the wounded, she practically fainted [when she saw] a mixture of infected shreds of skin, pieces of quivering flesh and broken bones. When the operation was over she could not bear to touch the amputated arm, which was lying on the table not far from the wounded soldier. Dr. Efrem Ginzburg took it and threw it into the refuse bin....
>
> The Russian forces were forced to retreat. The medical battalion retreated as well, leaving a squad behind to collect the last of the wounded from the battlefield. Riva was with the squad.... As they left to carry out their mission, the Germans attacked them with machine guns. It quickly became clear that they were surrounded and would have to find their own way out. They filled their knapsacks and pockets with medical supplies and set out. They wandered through the forests.... On the way they met a group of tank-crew soldiers and members of the engineering battalion, and they joined forces as a fighting team.... As they quietly crossed a field they were suddenly under heavy fire. "Get the wounded out, quick, into the forest," shouted Riva.... Her blouse was stained red by the blood of the wounded soldiers she had treated the previous night.... She finally managed to rejoin her unit....
>
> January 1943.... During one of the attacks near Sidelchovo, she saw thick smoke issuing from all the openings of a tank. As fast as she could, she ran to the burning tank. She climbed up the side, and smoke billowed out and covered her face. At first, she pulled back.... "The driver and commander are dead. Pull me up!" cried someone from inside. It was the wireless operator. Riva grabbed him under the arms.... With a tremendous effort she managed to push him

out head first and hold him without falling from the tank. Then she dragged him far from the burning tank....[214]

Riva Orman treated hundreds of wounded soldiers on the front, saved the lives of many of them, reached Berlin and survived the war. Her story is typical of the conditions under which the members of the medical corps worked on the front.

Arkady Kaplan, a Jewish surgeon, had a unique experience and many months of anxiety when he operated on Marshal Rokossovsky (at that time a lieutenant general, he commanded the 16th Army), who had been critically wounded by a shell in March 1942. Kaplan described his experiences in an article entitled "An operation under SMERSH supervision":

On March 10, at two in the morning, in the middle of Rokossovsky's operation, I was informed that in an hour I had to take a telephone call. A. Poskrebishev [Stalin's personal secretary] called – I knew his voice quite well. He was calling to find out about Rokossovsky's condition. He repeated everything I said, I suppose because he was dictating to a secretary. When I said that Rokossovsky's temperature was 38.7°C [101.6°F] I heard a loud voice with a Georgian accent say, "Why does he have a temperature?" It was the voice of the ruler of the country [Stalin]. Poskrebishev informed me that the next day at three [in the afternoon] he would call again. Early in the morning I was told that some commanders had arrived who demand[ed] that I present myself before them....

I entered the room and three military men were waiting for me. One was sitting at a table and two others stood behind him. I knew one of them, he was the SMERSH representative at the hospital. I introduced myself and welcomed them; they neither answered nor extended their hands for me to shake. The man sitting at the table asked, "What is Rokossovsky's condition?" I answered in a few sentences. He continued in the same tone of voice, "Is it clear to you that you are responsible for his health, his life, and have you done everything necessary?" I later learned that the man asking the questions was the head of SMERSH for the western front. He most

---

214. Arkady Timor, *Comrades in Arms: Jews Fighting in the Soviet Army, 1941–1945* [Hebrew] (Tel Aviv: Maarakhot, 1971), 54–57, 65–66.

likely was convinced that a military doctor with the "strange" [i.e., Jewish] name of Kaplan had to be suspect. Two days later I happened to discover that Rokossovsky's chart, which I had personally filled out…had disappeared. It had been taken by the hospital's SMERSH representative. I lived in anxiety…until Rokossovsky recovered and returned to the front on May 25.[215]

Kaplan went on to recount his friendship with Rokossovsky and the conversations they had during his recovery. What is noteworthy is Stalin's interest in the health of the high-ranking officers wounded at the front. The story also highlights the anti-Semitic stereotype and the suspicion of the "plots" the Jews were suspected of concocting, in this case Jewish doctors, even when they were carrying out their tasks faithfully in the best way possible to save the lives of soldiers and officers (for anti-Semitism in the army, see below).

The Engineering Corps

MAJOR GENERAL
LEONID KOTLER

Major General Leonid Kotler, who had served in the Red Army since 1920, was one of the senior officers of the engineering corps. Until the Germans attacked, he was chief of staff of the corps and head director of fortifications. He was responsible for erecting the defense lines and fortifications around Moscow in the fall of 1941, the difficult days when the German army approached the city. In the counterattack on the Stalingrad front, he commanded the engineering forces of the southwestern front that crossed the Don. At the beginning of 1943 he was appointed head engineering officer of the Third Ukrainian Front. He ended the war with the senior rank of colonel general and was awarded the title of Hero of the Soviet Union for the excellence of his command of the engineering units during the capture of Berlin.[216]

Fortifying Moscow entailed laying mine fields, as well as the placing of bombs and side charges to be detonated by remote control. Engineer Lieutenant

215. Timor ed., *Journal of the Soldiers* 13–14 (1998): 56–57.
216. Shapiro, *Under Fire*, 253–54; Rzheshevski et al., *Velikaia Otechestvenna Voina*, 338.

General Mikhail Joffe was in charge of the operation. His targets were bridges and installations in areas the enemy was expected to occupy, and the explosives were detonated when the Germans were either close to or at the targets. Yakov Rabinovich, an expert in laying mines and fashioning electrically operated booby traps, distinguished himself in the Moscow campaign. He was admiringly mentioned in the memoirs of Soviet Marshal V.K. Kharchenko, who was in charge of special-missions operations:

> In the days of our counteroffensive at Moscow, Rabinovich's brigade carried out missions of dismantling objects set to explode in case the enemy approached them. On one of the bridges on the Minsk highway there was a charge that was booby-trapped to explode if anyone tried to defuse it. According to standing orders, in such cases dismantling was forbidden, and the charge had to be blown up with the object. But the bridge was of the highest importance for our advancing forces to put the enemy to flight. Rabinovich dismantled the change and the trigger. He miraculously survived. [217]

During the battles for the access roads to Stalingrad, Joffe commanded the 16th Special Missions Brigade of the engineering corps, which was established in July 1942. It dealt with laying mines and blowing up bridges on the roads into the city and laying mine fields and booby-trapping targets within the city. One of the brigade's battalions had a Jewish commander, Major Yu. Pergament, and there were many other Jews serving as both officers and soldiers in the brigade. When it was necessary to slow the progress of the enemy on the Don River front, Joffe's units blew up 64 bridges. In Stalingrad, the brigade was responsible for mining the Barrikady tractor factory sector, where there was particularly fierce fighting. For their distinguished conduct in Stalingrad they received the title of 1st Guards Brigade for Special Missions. Joffe and his brigade also participated in establishing the defense lines during the Kursk-Oriol battle.

During the second half of August 1942, the 4th German Panzer Army, commanded by General Hoth, attacked Stalingrad from the southwest. Among the forces ordered to halt their advance was a special operations blocking group from the engineering corps commanded by Colonel Yakov Rabinovich. They received the following mention in a book about the Soviet engineering corps during the Great Patriotic War: "The special operations blocking group (*Opera-*

---

217. Abramovich, *V Reshaiushchei Voine*, 242–44, 456.

tivnaia Gruppa Zagrazhdenia) of the High Reserves Command led by Colonel Yakov Rabinovich played a special role in halting the attack of the 4th German Panzer Army. During August, the group (composed of four engineering battalions) laid 140,000 mines and blew up 19 bridges along our forces' retreat routes. The enemy lost 53 tanks and other military equipment in the minefields they laid." In December 1942, Hoth's Panzer Army received reinforcements of Tiger tanks, used for the first time on the Soviet front; it overcame the Soviet defenses near Kotelnikovo, southwest of Stalingrad, with the intention of joining the 6th German Army, which was trapped inside the city. Joffe's brigade, and especially the 8th Engineering Battalion commanded by Pergament, were ordered to lay minefields as quickly as possible and to prepare other obstacles. The Germans, having advanced to a depth of 45 kilometers (28 miles), were not only blocked, but repelled. After the Germans surrendered at Stalingrad, Joffe's brigade was ordered to dismantle the minefields and the many other obstacles they had planted in the Germans' path.[218]

The chief of staff of the engineering corps on the Stalingrad front was Colonel (later Major General) Aaron Shifrin. Beginning with the Kursk battle in July 1943 and until the end of the Second World War, Shifrin was chief of staff of the engineering units on the western front. Colonel Ilya Pruss distinguished himself in preparing the defense lines of the southwest front and in the fighting at Stalingrad.[219]

In addition to the various commanders mentioned above, many Jewish servicemen of the engineering corps distinguished themselves in the various battles.

16. JEWS IN RED ARMY INTELLIGENCE

Leopold Trepper and the Red Orchestra

One of the most important and well-known networks of Red Army intelligence[220] was what the Germans called the Red Orchestra. It was founded and operated

---

218. Ibid., 359–62, 456; Abramovich's quotation is taken from A. Chirlin and P. Biryukov, eds., *Inzhinernye voiska v boyakh za Sovetskuyu Rodinu* (Moscow: Voenizdat, 1970), 130; Rzheshevski et al., *Velikaia Otechestvenna Voina*, 120.

219. Abramovich, *V Reshaiushchei Voine*, 362; Sverdlov, *Evrei Generaly*, 168, 243. Shifrin served in the Red Army and participated in the Civil War.

220. The Chief Intelligence Authority, or the Glavnoe Razvedovatelnoe Upravlene, better known by its initials, GRU.

LEOPOLD TREPPER

by a Jew named Leopold Trepper. He was born in Poland in 1904 and immigrated to Palestine in 1924, where he joined the then-illegal Communist Party. As a result of his political activities he was deported, and went to France in 1929. From there he traveled to the Soviet Union in 1932, where he finished his studies at the Communist Party High Institute for Party Activists from European countries. For a few years he worked for a Yiddish newspaper called *Der Emmes* (The truth). In 1938, GRU head General Yan Berzin sent him to Belgium to set up a spy network that would operate in Western Europe and Germany disguised as a commercial company.

In Belgium Trepper met Leo Grossvogel, whom he knew from his party activities in Palestine. Grossvogel had returned to Belgium in 1928 and entered the family business. The two formed a company with branches in European countries and used them as a cover for their espionage network, most of whose members were local Communists. After France fell in the summer of 1940, the network moved to Paris.

One of the Red Orchestra's most important achievements was setting up a link with an anti-Nazi group in Berlin headed by Harold Schulze-Boysen, a member of the German aristocracy who worked for the German Aviation Ministry. Schulze-Boysen passed along a great deal of intelligence, including information about German plans to invade the Soviet Union, which was transmitted from Red Orchestra offices or through General Susloparov, the Soviet military attaché to the Vichy government. Trepper wrote:

> In May 1941, through General Susloparov...I transmitted the plan for the expected attack to be launched on May 15. I later transmitted the change of date and then the final date.... On June 21 we received confirmation through Schulze-Boysen that the invasion would begin the following day.... With Leo Grossvogel, I hastened to Vichy. Skeptical as usual, Susloparov tried to convince us, saying, "I'm telling you, you are completely wrong. Today I met the Japanese military attaché, who had just come from Berlin. He assured me the Germans were not planning war. He can be trusted".... I demanded that Susloparov send the message....[221]

---

221. Leopold Trepper, *My Red Orchestra* [Hebrew] (Jerusalem: Idanim, 1975), 109–11.

Intelligence about the German preparations to attack the Soviet Union also reached Moscow from Richard Sorge, a Soviet spy in the German Embassy in Japan, as well as from from other sources. In 1990 the Soviets published the biography of General (later Marshal) Filipp Ivanovich Golikov, who was head of Soviet military intelligence during the war. It stated that "on the eve of the war, Golikov felt that Germany would not attack the Soviet Union before it solved the problem of Britain, thus he received the intelligence regarding German preparations to attack the Soviet Union as disinformation. He was not interested in having military intelligence conclusions at odds with Stalin, and in 1941 it was Stalin's opinion that war with Germany could be prevented."[222]

The Red Orchestra transmitted hundreds of messages to Soviet military intelligence in Moscow, including plans for new types of German airplanes, the number of planes in the German air force, the plan of the attack in the direction of Moscow in November 1941 and that the Germans were planning an attack in the direction of the oil in the Caucasus in the spring of 1942.[223] But in the spring of 1942 the Germans discovered the Red Orchestra and began arresting its members, and on November 24, 1942, Trepper was taken into custody. He was interrogated and held until September 19, 1943, when he managed to escape, and he remained in hiding in Paris until the liberation. In January 1945 he was flown to Moscow, where he was arrested and accused of betraying secrets to the Germans. In 1955 he was released and cleared of all accusations.[224]

Lev Manevich's One-Man Spy Ring

Another Jew who worked for Soviet military intelligence was Colonel Lev Manevich, code-named Eten, a native of Chausy in Byelorussia. His official Soviet Union biography describes him thus:

> Born in 1898…and educated in Geneva. Joined the Red Army in 1918. During the Civil War fought on the eastern front and in the Caucasus. Began serving in military intelligence in the middle of the 1920s. Until the 1930s, occasionally operated abroad. Possessed all the qualities

---

222. Rzheshevski et al., *Velikaia Otechestvenna Voina*, 9, 307–8.
223. Ibid., 112–14.
224. In 1957, Trepper moved to Poland with his family, where he headed the Jewish Cultural Society until he immigrated to Israel in 1973, dying in Jerusalem in 1982.

necessary for an intelligence officer, self-control and courage. Arrested by Italian counterespionage agents and sentenced to a long term in prison. In 1943, he was handed over to the Germans. Incarcerated in Matthausen and Ebensee concentration camps under the name Colonel Y.N. Starostin. Liberated on May 6, 1945, by the American army, but died of tuberculosis a few days later.[225]

COLONEL LEV MANEVICH

Behind the short biography was a multifaceted Soviet intelligence agent. In 1910, at the age of 12, he was sent to Switzerland to join his eldest brother, who had been forced to flee Russia for fear of being imprisoned for his revolutionary activities. There Manevich learned French, German and Italian. In 1917 the brothers returned to Russia, and one year later Lev volunteered for the Red Army, where he fought and commanded a special intelligence unit. In 1924, after the Civil War, he graduated with honors from the High Military Academy. He was sent to China for a time, where he served in the Red Army delegation aiding and supporting the organization of Mao Tse-Tung's Chinese Revolutionary Army. Returning to Russia, he trained as a pilot and almost became a squadron commander in the Soviet air force. However, he was summoned by General Y. Berezin, head of military intelligence, who said, "You studied in Switzerland and have visited other countries, and you know many languages. We propose you work for intelligence." Manevich accepted. In view of his talents and abilities, it was decided that he would work in Europe alone and not as part of an intelligence network.

He opened a patent registration office in Vienna in 1932 as Konrad Kartner and had an account in a large German bank. He utilized his pilot's knowledge to make contacts in aviation and as part of his business visited Germany, Spain and other countries. He moved his main offices from Vienna to Milan, where he also represented German, Austrian and Czech firms interested in selling their goods in Italy. He transmitted a great deal of information to Moscow about German and Italian aid to Franco's Spain, and as a "businessman" visited locations in Spain held by Franco. He also visited Germany several times and,

---

225. Rzheshevski et al., *Velikaia Otechestvenna Voina*, 351–52.

using his business connections, discovered how Germany was arming itself. He transmitted the information to Moscow from Milan.

In 1937 the Fascist Italian counterespionage service got wind of his activities and he was arrested, but they did not manage to discover the exact nature of those activities or for whom he was working. He steadfastly maintained he was an Austrian businessman, but nevertheless was sentenced to 12 years in prison. In September 1943, when Italy surrendered and the Germans took control of the central and southern parts of the country, Manevich fell into German hands. After lengthy interrogations, they sent him to Matthausen as a Russian prisoner of war named Colonel Starostin, which is how he represented himself. From there he was transferred to Ebensee, where he organized an underground group. The SS planned to put a large number of prisoners, Manevich among them, into a tunnel in the mountainside and then blow it up. After the morning headcount on May 5, 1945, the day before the camp was liberated, the prisoners were ordered to enter the tunnel. Manevich, suspecting what the SS was planning, shouted in several languages, "No one is to enter!" All the prisoners understood and disobeyed the order. The same day the SS left the camp, and the following day the Americans liberated the prisoners. Manevich was ill and weighed only 37 kilograms (81 pounds). He died a few days after the liberation and was buried by friends in Linz, Austria. His headstone read "Colonel Yacov Nikitich Starostin." For many years Soviet military intelligence ignored his existence, but comrades from Ebensee who knew he had saved their lives made the effort to find out about the man behind the name Starostin and discovered the truth. In 1965 he was awarded the title of Hero of the Soviet Union for the special actions he performed for the Soviet government during the struggle against Fascism.[226]

Dr. Shandor Rado and the Dora Group

From 1936 until the beginning of 1944, Soviet military intelligence ran an intelligence network in Switzerland headed by a Hungarian Jew named Dr. Shandor Rado, who was a geographer and cartographer. Rado joined the Communist Party in Hungary in 1918 and was recruited into Red Army intelligence in October 1935 by Semyon Oritzky. Rado's mission was to set up a network centered in Geneva whose intelligence gathering would be aimed at Germany and Italy. Oritzky considered these countries to be "aggressive countries which, in the

---

226. Sverdlov, *V Stroiu Otvazhnykh*, 186–87; Shapiro, *Under Fire*, 368–85.

event of war, were liable to be the Soviet Union's principle enemies."[227] The network operated as a scientific cartographical institute code-named Dora and transmitted its information by radio. In the summer of 1939, Shandor Rado sent Moscow the information that Germany was planning to invade Poland. On June 6, 1940, he sent the message that after its rapid victories in Europe, Germany was planning to turn its forces against the Soviet Union. On February 21, 1941, he sent the following message: "According to information from a Swiss intelligence officer, Germany now has 150 divisions in Eastern Europe. In our opinion, Germany will attack at the end of May." On April 6, 1941, the network notified Moscow that all the German mechanized divisions were stationed in Eastern Europe. Exact information for the German attack was transmitted to Moscow on June 2 and 17, 1941.[228]

Between the beginning of the war and November 1943, the network radioed information about forces sent to Germany's eastern front, the number of tanks and planes manufactured in Germany and the locations of German arms factories – both in Germany itself and in the countries of occupied Europe – and about some disagreements between the leaders of the Axis powers. The Rado network agents received information from a source in the German High Command, from employees in the German embassy in Bern, from leading correspondents and from other sources as well. In the fall of 1943, Swiss counterintelligence managed to decode the network's transmissions to Moscow and to arrest some of the agents. Shandor Rado went into hiding and then fled to the south of France in September 1944.[229]

Intelligence at the Battlefield: Masha Volfovna Sinelnikova

Masha Sinelnikova was born in Cherikov in Byelorussia. She was a brave, pretty girl and the first in her town to take up parachuting as a sport. After she finished high school she went to Moscow to study at the Institute for Foreign Languages,

---

227. Shandor Rado, *Pod Psevdonimom Dora* (Moscow: Voenizdat, 1978), 36–37. Semyon Oritzky, a Jew, was born in 1895 and headed Soviet military intelligence from 1935 to 1937. He was arrested on November 1, 1937, in one of Stalin's purges of Red Army officers. He was executed on August 1, 1938, and cleared of all guilt in 1956.
228. Ibid., 89–93.
229. Ibid., 305–8; *Sovetskii Encyklopedicheskii Slovar* (Moscow, 1986), 1096. After the war, Shandor Rado returned to Communist Hungary, where he worked in the sciences. He died in 1982.

and became very fluent in German. When the war broke out, her father, Velvel, and her older brother Abram were drafted into the army. He father served in the infantry and her brother as a paratrooper; both fell in battle at the beginning of the war. She joined the army as a volunteer and insisted on being sent to a course for intelligence radio operators. After the course she was sent to intelligence in the 43rd Army on the Moscow front. Major General F. Maslennikov, the chief of staff of the 43rd Army, wrote in his memoirs, "The worst time of the battle for Moscow was between October 1941 and January 1942. At some missions of the 43rd Army Command, she crossed the front lines a number of times and brought back extremely important information."[230]

During the Soviet counterattack at the beginning of January 1942, Masha and another female soldier took a walkie-talkie and crossed the front to transmit information about German troop movements. She and her comrade situated themselves in the village of Korchazkhino in the district of Kaluga and for two weeks broadcast information about troop movements, the location of the German army front headquarters, and similar matters. On January 17 the transmissions stopped. Masha and her comrade had been caught by the Germans, were interrogated, tortured and shot the following day. For many years nothing was known of their fate, but when some local policemen who were present at the interrogation were caught and revealed what they knew, the women's courage in the face of torture became known: they had not told the Germans anything.[231]

17. ANTI-SEMITISM AND DISCRIMINATION AGAINST JEWS IN THE RED ARMY

Anti-Semitism was well-rooted within the nations of the Soviet Union and among Soviet leaders. The question before us is whether there was anti-Semitism in the army, and whether it was manifested as discrimination against Jews when it came to advancement through the military with regard to promotion, rank, medals, badges, distinctions, etc. It can be stated with some certainty that overt discrimination of the Jews as a policy of the upper echelons in the Soviet government and army did not exist during the war, but did exist as an undercurrent. Colonel Fyordor Sverdlov, who served as an officer during the Second World War and was a historian who lectured at the Frunze Military Academy for many years, writes that as a result of anti-Semitism in the Soviet Union during

---

230. Sheinker, *Geroizm Evreev*, 192–93.
231. Abramovich, *V Reshaiushchei Voine*, 239.

the war, the promotions of Jewish officers was "restrained" (*priderzhivali*). The "restraint" was inspired by Stalin, and supervised and carried out by Lieutenant General Alexander Shcherbakov, secretary of the Central Committee of the Communist Party and close to Stalin. In 1942 he was appointed head of the Red Army's political administration and deputy minister of defense, and at the same time was head of the Sovinformbureau, which determined which information would be issued to the Soviet people and internationally, concerning both the situation on the various fronts and all other aspects of the Soviet Union. During the war, Shcherbakov was prominent and very influential. When awarding medals, especially Heroes of the Soviet Union, criteria beyond acts of courage were taken into consideration, and there had to be proportional representation of all the nations that fought in the ranks of the Red Army. Here as well he discriminated against the Jews. Colonel Sverdlov writes that in 1943 Shcherbakov issued an order reading, "Medals for distinguished conduct are to be awarded to men of all nations, but within limits (*ogranicheno*) with regard to the Jews."[232]

In addition to the policy of "limitation," it was also customary not to inform the media about Jews who had distinguished themselves in battle and been awarded medals, and insofar as was possible, not to reveal the number of Jews who had received them. In 1943 the official publication of the Central Committee of the Communist Party, *Bolshevik*, published an article by Alexander Badaev (who was a deputy chairman of the Supreme Soviet) containing the numbers of the recipients of medals and orders according to nationality. The article referred to 26 separate nationalities and gave the various numbers: Russians, Byelorussians, Ukrainians and smaller nations as well, such as the Chuvashes who had received 1362 awards, the Bashkirs 687, the Lithuanians 29, the Estonians 73, etc. At the end of the list there was a notation that other nations had received awards as well, including Yakuts, Buryats, Kalmyks, Koms and Jews, but no numbers were given. According to extant data, at the beginning of October 1942, a few months before the article appeared, 5,163 Jews had been awarded medals, more than the Armenians, Georgians, Azaris, Uzbekistanis and others whose numbers were specifically mentioned. In June 1943, the number of Jews who had received medals for distinguished conduct was 11,908.

---

232. Sverdlov, *Encyclopedia Evreiskogo Geroizma*, 12. Pinkus, in *The Jews of Russia and the Soviet Union*, 314, wrote: "Even at the beginning of the war, and especially from 1943 on, Stalin and Shcherbakov deliberately discriminated against the Jews, and that policy was evident when it came to promotions, the award of medals for distinguished conduct, and appointments."

The heads of the Jewish Anti-Fascist Committee, Shlomo Mikhoels and Shakhno Epstein, sent Shcherbakov a letter protesting the noninclusion in Badaev's article of Jews who had received awards for valor. The letter, dated April 2, 1943, read:

> The [deliberate] silence regarding the exact number of Jewish soldiers and officers who received awards plays, in our opinion, into the hands of hostile elements both within and outside the Soviet Union.… In our opinion, data published by a figure as central as Badaev, without relation to one of the most impressive statistics [regarding the Jews] will be exploited by Hitler's agents to spread rumors and the libel that "the Jews are not fighting." It is supremely desirable that the latest official statistics about the soldiers and commanders in the Red Army who were awarded medals, and the Jews among them, be published in their entirety by our central communications media.[233]

Despite the policies of "restraint" and "limitation," the percentage of senior Jewish officers was higher than that of Jews in the general population (2.2 percent as opposed to 1.78 percent), and the same was true for Jews who were awarded medals, including Hero of the Soviet Union. That can be explained by the percentage of Jewish officers in the Red Army, including high-ranking officers, which was high between the two world wars, and by the fact that on the fighting front, what might be called "the spirit of comrades in arms" did not permit the full implementation of "restraint" and "limitation," and that such policies were not prevalent among all the commanding ranks. Nevertheless, it is reasonable to assume that without such policies and without widespread popular anti-Semitism in the lower ranks, the percentage of Jews in command positions and among the recipients of medals would have been far greater. Shcherbakov's policy of "limitation" apparently was the reason two Jewish pilots, Presseizen and Yirzhak, whose acts of bravery were described above, were not awarded the title of Hero of the Soviet Union.

The dismissal of Major General David Ortenberg as editor in chief of the *Red Star*, the official publication of the Red Army, on July 30, 1943, was a well-known, conspicuous case of Stalin-Shcherbakov anti-Semitism. His dismissal was part of an anti-Jewish campaign undertaken by the Soviet media to elimi-

---

233. Gennadi Kostyrchenko, ed., *Rossia xx Vek, Gosudarstvennyi Antisemitism v sssr, 1938–1953* (Moscow: Materik, 2005), 35–36.

nate the Jews and give preference to the Russian-national element. Since the summer of 1942 the campaign had been led by the Information and Propaganda Administration of the Central Committee of the Communist Party headed by G.F. Alexandrov. Supported by Shcherbakov, many Jews were dismissed from scientific and cultural institutions and were replaced by ethnic Russians. The "International," the Soviet national anthem, was replaced by a hymn that praised the Russian nation, and was a continuation of the nationalist Russian trend led by Stalin.[234]

During the second half of 1942 and all of 1943, in accordance with Supreme Soviet decisions, orders named for former Russian army leaders were introduced: the Suvorov order, the Kutuzov, the Alexander Nevsky and even one for the leader of the 17th-century pogroms against Jews, Bogdan Chmielnicki. The move expressed the nationalist spirit that began to penetrate the army and was exemplified by Ortenberg's dismissal from the *Red Star*. Ortenberg wrote about his dismissal:

> On July 30, in response to a call from A.S. Shcherbakov, I went to the central committee of the party. He stood up behind his desk, came over to me and said, "The central committee has decided to appoint Talensky as editor in chief of *Krasnaia zvezda* [Red star]. What do you think?" It was a strange question. What importance did my opinion of Talensky have when his appointment had already been decided on? Nevertheless, I answered sincerely, "He is a fitting candidate." We then discussed an appointment for me. Finally Shcherbakov asked, "Does the post of head of the political department of the army seem reasonable to you?" I answered, "Yes, certainly." "Fine," he said, "I'll tell Stalin and inform you of his decision within two days." However, before I left the office I asked him, "Alexander Sergeievich, if the members of the editorial board ask me why I was released from my duties at the paper, what should I tell them?" He took a sheet of paper from his desk and read me the central committee's decision: "'To appoint N.A. Talensky as editor in chief of *Krasnaia zvezda* and to relieve D. Ortenberg [of his duties].' That is what you will tell them, without explanations," he said.... I am still asked today why I was dismissed from the paper....

---

234. Gennadi Kostyrchenko, *Out of the Red Shadows: Anti-Semitism in Stalin's Russia* (New York: Prometheus, 1995), 14–20, 26.

I have thought about it a lot, about what happened at the end of July 1943, and asked myself whose idea it was, Stalin's or Shcherbakov's.[235]

Ortenberg does not give a direct answer as to who was responsible for his dismissal or what the reasons behind it were. However, he does quote an article written by a senior *Red Star* wartime journalist, a Russian major named Pavel Milovanov:

> The web of anti-Semitism comes from the Father of Nations [Stalin]. During the war my editor, D. Ortenberg, was dismissed from his post in accordance with a decision of the central committee. A few months previously Shcherbakov told him there were too many Jews on his editorial board and their numbers had to be reduced. Ortenberg was astonished, and told him he had already done so, and that Lapin, Khatsrevin, Rosenfeld, Schur, Vilkomir, Slutzky, Isha, Bernsten and others had been killed at the front. He sarcastically added, "I can reduce one more – myself." What is interesting is that Ortenberg, who held so high a position, knew nothing of the Politburo decision to prevent Jews from attaining high positions. And as a result of their secret decision he was dismissed from his post as editor-in-chief and sent to the front. And that was the strange thing, that in his work for the motherland behind the front lines he caused damage, but it was permissible for him to fight and die for it."[236]

After Shcherbakov dismissed Ortenberg, he prevented the promotion of Jews to command positions. In October 1942, the institution of military commissars was abolished, and they became deputy commanders for political affairs in the units they served in. As part of the reorganization following the order, some of the political staff who had acquired experience in battle were also appointed commanders of units and divisions, and others were sent to military training courses and afterwards appointed to command units. During the reorganiza-

---

235. David Ortenberg, *Takaia Vypala Mne Sudba* (Jerusalem: Nevo Art, 1997), 307–9. Ortenberg continued in the army until 1950 when he was discharged without being given the reason. For Stalin's attitude toward the Jews during the Second World War, see Louis Rapoport, *Stalin's War against the Jews: The Doctor's Plot and the Soviet Solution* (New York: Simon and Schuster, 1990), 55–79.

236. Pinkus, *Jews of Russia*, 305. Milovanov's article appeared in the newspaper *Gudok* on February 15, 1992.

tion, Shcherbakov directed Jewish former commissars to be appointed to roles and ranks lower than those they previously held.[237]

Twenty years of Soviet rule did not eradicate the widespread popular anti-Semitism among the people of the Soviet Union. The Jews were often accused of cowardice and evading active service, and there were insulting jokes about how the Jews fled to areas far from the fighting. A popular expression of the times was "The Jews are fighting on the Tashkent front," meaning that instead of fighting on the front the Jews were in Tashkent, the capital of Uzbekistan, thousands of kilometers to the east. There was more anti-Semitism behind the Soviet front than where the fighting was. Someone had to be guilty of the hardships of war and the great suffering of the civilian population, and the Jews, always convenient as scapegoats, were ideal. That was also convenient for Stalin, who vented his frustrations on the Jews. One factor of the strengthening of anti-Semitism was Nazi propaganda, which was disseminated through leaflets dropped from airplanes and in other ways, representing the Jews as being guilty of having started the war.[238]

Grigori Ushpolis of the 16th Lithuanian Division, who was a Hero of the Soviet Union, wrote of the anti-Semitic prejudices of the regiment's new commander, who had taken over in the summer of 1944, and how his prejudices changed during battle:

> Instead of our beloved regiment commander, who was promoted to a higher rank, we were sent Lieutenant Colonel F. Lisenko…. He was particularly unsympathetic to us, the Jews…. When our new commander found out how many Jews were in the regiment, and to his surprise as privates and sergeants in the infantry companies, he loudly told the officers that he was sorry he had to command such a regiment. However, during the first clashes with the enemy when we approached the borders of the republic [Lithuania], he realized he had made a mistake. He had a high opinion of the command ability

---

237. Shner, *Plen*, vol. 2, 36–37.
238. In Tashkent and other places in Asia there were large concentrations of Jewish refugees and others evacuated from the territories occupied by the Germans, which was apparently the source of the expression. However, since the men were in the army, most of them were children, women and the elderly. Nevertheless, that did not prevent the anti-Semites from slandering the Jews. Merridale (*Ivan's War*, 296–98) writes about anti-Semitic expressions among soldiers and civilians.

of Major Volf Vilensky, commander of the 3rd Battalion. Many of the Jewish privates, platoon and company commanders distinguished themselves in battle. That forced him to abandon his prejudices and stop sneering at the Jewish fighters.[239]

In his book *Plen*, Shner recounts anti-Semitic acts in the army. A Jewish soldier named Teivel Morkhovsky was shot to death by a Ukrainian soldier from his own unit in the summer of 1941 when Morkhovsky tried to convince him not to become a prisoner of war. After the war, a Russian soldier told his wife about his comrade in arms, the Jewish soldier Solomon Blankov: "We lay next to each other, wounded on the battlefield. The soldiers of the paramedic platoon were collecting the wounded. When Solomon asked them to take him, he was told, 'We don't take Jews.' He remained lying on the battlefield and bled to death." Such an event was perhaps extraordinary, but it did happen. The case in which a Russian captain named Ronin struck a Jewish officer while shouting anti-Semitic slurs appears in a report sent to the counterintelligence department of SMERSH. The report also notes that in several previous instances Ronin had made anti-Semitic remarks, and that General Kuznetsov, commander of the 29th Infantry Division, was also an anti-Semite.[240]

Anti-Semitism and anti-Semitic remarks became more frequent among ordinary soldiers after the liberation of the Ukraine, Byelorussia and the Baltic States, with the mobilization of hundreds of thousands of men who had spent several years under Nazi occupation and been indoctrinated with anti-Semitic Nazi propaganda.

A Jewish soldier who had been at the front since the beginning of the war and had fought on the Don and at Stalingrad was wounded early in 1944 in the battles near the city of Krivoy-Rog in the Ukraine. His leg was amputated in a field hospital at the front, and he was evacuated to a hospital in Baku on the Caspian Sea. He recounted a conversation he had with another wounded soldier, characteristic of the prejudices among many soldiers regarding Jews:

> We arrived in Baku. Most of the wounded were Ukrainians. When the Ukraine was liberated, they were immediately drafted and sent to the front. As they slowly recuperated they spent their time playing chess or checkers, and some of them even played cards. Most of the

---

239. Ushpolis, *Trevozhnoe Vremia*, 138–39.
240. Shner, *Plen*, vol. 2, 151.

time the Ukrainians discussed the Jews. "The Jews don't want to fight," said one. "How do you know that?" I asked. "Look," he said, "there are almost 500 wounded here and almost none of them are Jews." "Well," I said, "what is the entire population of the Soviet Union?" "About 200 million," he answered. "And how many of them are Jews?" I asked. "About two million," he said. "About one per cent," I said, "and of the 500 wounded here, how many Jews should there be?" "I guess about 5," he said. "All right," I said, "take a look. In these two rooms there are three Jews and 38 wounded. In every block you will find about 20 men." "So what," he said, "they are fewer than the Ukrainians."[241]

A soldier who fought at Stalingrad and was wounded at the end of February 1945 near Koenigsberg in East Prussia was sent to a military hospital near Moscow. He wrote: "The wounded soldiers were openly and viciously anti-Semitic. They kept claiming that the Jews didn't fight and evaded every battle. The arguments became so violent that I was sometimes hit by a wounded soldier. On the other hand, there were also expressions of solidarity and friendship."[242]

In addition, the fact that there were many Jewish doctors in the military hospitals who saved soldiers' lives did nothing to prevent anti-Semitic comments toward them. A Jewish soldier who was wounded while clearing an enemy minefield near Kerch in the Crimea and who was brought to a hospital behind the frontline wrote the following:

> I was lying in a room with a Russian soldier, two Ukrainians and two Georgians. Once in the middle of a conversation one of them turned to me and said, "You are a good fellow, you fought the way I did, but if you check the nationality of the workers here you will find that the hospital director is Jewish, and all the doctors, or almost all of them are Jewish as well, and the man in charge of stores is a Jew.... The doctor taking care of us is apparently Jewish too, because you are the only one she prescribed blood for and you are the only one who gets potatoes."[243]

---

241. Abram Shpitkovsky, "In the Red Army," in *Facing the Nazi Enemy: The Fighters Speak, 1939–1945*, vol. 1, ed. Shmuel Burshtein et al. [Hebrew] (Tel Aviv, 1961), 316–17.
242. Abram Parchuk, "From Stalingrad to Koenigsberg," in *Facing the Nazi Enemy*, 156.
243. Dan Landman, "Fighting in the Crimean Peninsula," *Voice of the Disabled* (2003): 5.

Another Jewish soldier, who fought from the beginning of the war in 1941 in Byelorussia, in Smolensk and in the defense of Moscow, and was wounded a number of times, was sent to a unit in the Vitebsk area in the summer of 1944. He wrote:

> Here the anti-Semitism is overt because a lot of the soldiers who were drafted had lived under the German occupation and were poisoned by Nazi propaganda. Their hatred has influenced others. I was amazed more than once to hear, from young men born in the Soviet Union, that the Jews used Christian blood in [making] matzoth. It is often said that the Jews evaded fighting.... We approached Minsk.... After Vilna was liberated I received the Slava Medal Third Class....
>
> All the men who were between 20 and 30 who had battle experience were sent to a sergeants' course. I was one of them. During the course we also felt overt anti-Semitism, and more than once we had to beware of a bullet or other attack from our comrades in arms. Appeals to the officers did no good and the few Jewish sergeants told us that they found themselves in the same situation.[244]

ILYA EHRENBURG

At a plenary session of the Jewish Anti-Fascist Committee held on February 20, 1943, the writer Ilya Ehrenburg raised the subject of anti-Semitic remarks, especially those referring to Jewish evasion of direct participation in the fighting. In his speech he said:

Only yesterday I returned from the front at Kursk. There we again met a situation which causes us a deep pain, but also great pride.... An elderly Jew, the father of a famous pilot whose bravery was mentioned in all the military newspapers, appealed to me. He had only one son, and loved him dearly. He said to me, "I spoke with a certain civilian. He asked me to explain to him why there were no Jews at the front, why they weren't

---

244. Moshe Elishkavich, "As Our Fathers Commanded Us: Four Years in the Red Army," *Voice of the Disabled* (2003): 349.

fighting. I didn't even answer him.... It was hard for me to speak. That was four days after I received notice from the commander of my son's unit that he had died a hero's death." All of you must by now have heard the statement about the Jews, that you don't see them at the front. Many of the fighters didn't feel that they were Jews until they started getting letters from their families. The letters said they didn't understand why there were rumors that the Jews weren't fighting. And when they read the letters at their trenches or on the way to a battle, the Jewish man at the front feels unease at the insult. For the Jewish soldiers and officers in the Red Army to be able to fulfill their sacred duty – to strike the enemy – with tranquil hearts, it is our duty to tell the world how Jews fight at the front....

For that reason it is up to us to publish a book, as fast as possible, in which we must recount the part played by the Jews in this war. Statistics are not enough, we need real stories, real pictures, we need an anthology about Jewish heroes.... The truth must be told, the simple truth, and that will suffice.[245]

During the war, there were many Jewish soldiers in the Red Army who tried to hide their national identity, especially in fear of what would happen to them should they be taken prisoner. A short time after the war broke out, it became clear to the Jews that if they were captured by the Germans, they would be killed immediately. A secondary reason for hiding their identity was the anti-Semitism in the army. Some of the Jewish soldiers had Slavic names or names of the nationalities among which they lived, Georgian, Azars, etc., and for them it was easy, especially for those who did not look typically Jewish. There were also soldiers who changed their names during war. The Jewish Soviet writer Hershel Veinrub wrote as follows:

At the front, even I had a typically Slavic name. Once it happened that I came to Moscow from the front for a number of days, and I paid a visit to the Jewish Anti-Fascist Committee. The poet Leib Kvitko, who was one of the heads of the committee and edited the paper *Einkeit*, rebuked me, asking me why I was calling myself by a goy name and lowering the number of Jewish fighters at the front. After I explained

---

245. Sheinker, *Geroism Evreev*, 4–6.

what I was doing at the front and my situation, he agreed and even insisted that I not say anything at the front about being Jewish.[246]

There were also Jewish soldiers who preferred to appear with names common among the Muslim nations of the Soviet Union to ensure that although they were circumcised, they would not be identified as Jews if taken prisoner by the Germans. Hiding Jewish identity on the front was not by any means marginal. A contributing factor was the assimilation of Jews in the Soviet Union, which had existed before the war. As a result, there seemed to be fewer Jewish fighters at the front than there actually were, which encouraged anti-Semitic slurs such as "There are no Jews at the front." However, Jewish soldiers from the territories annexed to the Soviet Union during 1939–40 identified much more strongly with their Jewish roots, and as a result virtually none of them hid their Jewish identity.

Popular anti-Semitism had a broad base in Soviet society, and prejudices regarding the desire and ability of the Jews to fight were common even among Red Army soldiers. Boris Grigorevich, born in Kiev, said in regard to prejudices that "I was afraid of being thought a coward. I knew that I was a Jew, and so I had to prove that I was not afraid."[247]

However, the high percentage of Jews at all levels of command, including generals, who were promoted during the war by non-Jewish commanders, and the number of medals and awards given to Jewish soldiers, including Hero of the Soviet Union, bear witness to the fact that in general, as an official policy of the army, there was no broad, overt discrimination against Jews. There were certainly instances of discrimination, but they were not widespread. Not many descriptions of anti-Semitism appear in the testimonies and memoirs of Jewish soldiers. When the question was put to 220 Jewish veterans of the Red Army, only 16 responded that they had experienced overt hostility, anti-Semitic remarks or jokes made at Jewish expense by non-Jewish comrades in arms.[248] It is reasonable to assume that when Jewish and non-Jewish soldiers fought together, defending and attacking or as part of the same tank crew, experiencing the same trials and horrors of war together, overt, crude anti-Semitism was neither widespread nor significant.

---

246. Levin, "Facts and Estimates," 103; Joseph Guri-Podryatchik, *Soviet Jews in the War against Nazi Germany* [Hebrew] (Masua and Sifriat Poalim, 1971), 54–57.
247. Merridale, *Ivan's War*, 297–98.
248. Shner, *Plen*, vol. 2, 147.

The trend was to minimize the heroism and achievements of Jewish soldiers and commanders in battle, and here and there to limit their advancement through the ranks, but it would appear that Stalin and Shcherbakov's anti-Semitism was only partially responsible. Rather, the idea was that the war should not be seen by the suffering Soviet population and by the soldiers who were spilling their blood as a war in which the Jews were prominent. That would only serve the German propaganda machine, according to which the war was being fought and its victims were being sacrificed for the sake of the Jews.

On the other hand, the trend of minimizing the fighting and distinguished conduct of Jewish soldiers and commanders, and of preventing those acts of bravery and distinguished conduct from being reported in the Soviet media, which were completely party controlled, did succeed. To a certain extent it also fanned the flames of anti-Semitism and led to statements like "You don't see Jews on the battlefront."

18. CONCLUSION: STATISTICS OF LOSSES

For many years detailed statistics relating to the Soviet Union's losses during the Great Patriotic War were not published in the Soviet Union. Only in 1993, after the collapse of the Soviet Union, a book entitled *Grif Secretnosti Sniat* (The secret seal removed) was published.[249] It enumerated Soviet losses during the war according to corps, fronts and ranks, but not national identities. In the absence of official data relating to nationality, only the most general estimation can be given. The book gave the number of soldiers killed (i.e., those who fell at the front, died in hospitals of their wounds, were killed in accidents, were executed for crimes committed, etc.) as about 6,885,000. That does not include prisoners of war who died or were killed by the Germans. It is generally assumed that the number of Jews killed in the war was 1.78 percent (in accordance with the percentage of Jews in the Soviet population and in the army), that is, more than 120,000 of the 490,000–520,000 Jewish soldiers who served in the Red Army fell during the Great Patriotic War. In addition to this number, 75,000–80,000 Jewish soldiers were murdered in German prisoner-of-war camps.[250] The total

---

249. *Grif Secretnosti Sniat*, issued by the military publishing house (Moscow: Voennoye Izdatelstvo, 1993). The book's editor in chief was Lieutenant General G.F. Krivosheyev.
250. Arad, *The Holocaust in the Soviet Union*, 377–81.

losses of Jewish soldiers in the Red Army during the Great Patriotic War can therefore be estimated at around 200,000.

The price the Jews paid on the battlefield was enormous. There were very few Jewish families untouched by the death of a soldier, or by someone wounded or crippled in battle. Many families lost both father and sons, with only the women remaining. Miriam Berestitsky lost her father and three brothers in the war. Originally from Slutsk in Byelorussia, she reached Kazakhstan as a refugee. Miriam writes as follows:

> My father, Isaiah, was drafted into the Red Army at the beginning of 1942. He participated in the battles on the Stalingrad front and his fate is unknown.… My brother Tuvia was drafted into the Red Army in 1940 and served in Vilna in a tank unit. He fought at Stalingrad and his fate is unknown. My brother Jonah was drafted into the Red Army on March 20, 1940. We received a letter from his commanding officer informing us that he was wounded on December 27, 1944, and evacuated to a field hospital. From then on, his fate is unknown. My youngest brother Yaakob (Yasha) was drafted into the Red Army in May 1944. We received a letter from the commander of his unit informing us that he was killed while displaying exceptional valor during the siege of Berlin and buried in a mass grave in the city of Kustrin on the Oder River."[251]

---

251. The testimony of Miriam Berestitsky, including documents and pictures of her father and three brothers, are in the Yad Vashem archives. The term "fate unknown" (*propal bez vesti*) refers to all those who fell in the war whose places of burial are not known or soldiers who perished in German prisons.

CHAPTER TWO:
JEWS IN THE WAR INDUSTRY AND WEAPONS DEVELOPMENT

1. THE SOVIET WAR INDUSTRY

The political developments in Europe of the 1930s, Hitler's rise to power and the beginning of the Nazi-German expansion in Western Europe (the Saar in 1935 and the Rhineland in March 1936) and the outbreak of the Spanish Civil War in July 1936 all led the Soviet Union to take steps to increase its military power. In order to accomplish this, the Soviet Union instituted the Five-Year Plans (*Piatiletka*) to hasten industrial development.[1]

The industrialization of the Soviet Union was planned to enable factories to fulfill the needs of a war economy and develop its military capabilities. On July 15, 1939, the Soviet government (the Council of People's Commissars) issued a decree stating that representatives of the People's Commissariat for Defense would be placed in large industrial plants in order to supervise the implementation of orders and contracts for the defense establishment, plan the plants' operations during the war and exploit all their potential to meet the army's needs. On July 31, 1940, a decree was issued stating that there would be an eight-hour work day and a seven-day work week. In addition, no one could quit or change jobs without authorization.

Within the first months of the German invasion, between the end of June and November 1941, the German army conquered vast territories in the western Soviet Union, reaching the outskirts of Leningrad and Moscow, the Ukraine and the mining and industrial regions of the Don River. This meant that most of the Soviet industry, including its military industry, was located in occupied areas or those in danger of occupation. The Soviet government had to rapidly evacuate their institutions, thousands of factories and millions of workers from these regions. On June 24, 1941, two days after the invasion, the Council for Evacuation was established, headed by Lazar Kaganovich, the people's commis-

---

1. The Five-Year Plan was, as its name suggests, a program to hasten Soviet industrialization and turn the Soviet Union into a modern industrialized state. The first Five-Year Plan lasted from 1928 to 1933, and a new plan was instituted every five years thereafter.

sar for transport. On June 27, the Central Committee of the Communist Party and the People's Council of Ministers decided on the evacuation's priorities:

- "Important industries (equipment, machinery and tools), valuable raw materials (metals, fuel and food), and other nationally important economic commodities;

- Qualified workers, engineers and officials who work in the factories to be evacuated, inhabitants – priority given to youngsters who are suitable for military service, and senior government and party workers. All the important property, reserves of raw materials and supplies that cannot be evacuated and might be exploited by the enemy...are to be destroyed and burned."[2]

On July 3 the order was given to evacuate areas near the front, including animals, tractors and trade school students.[3] At the beginning of July it became obvious that there were problems greater than transportation, and the Council for Evacuation was reorganized and expanded. Kaganovich was replaced by Nikolai Shvernik, a member of the politburo, and other members of the council were Aleksei Kosigin, Anastas Mikoyan and senior representatives from the army, NKVD and from the various people's commissariats. The council determined all the aspects of the evacuation: the areas to be evacuated according to the situation at the front, transportation, the areas of relocation and the evacuees' subsequent absorption and recommencing of operations. The practical aspects of the evacuation were in the hands of the councils for evacuation established in the various republics in danger of occupation and the local authorities, in accordance with instructions received from the councils. "Evacuation points" were established along the evacuation routes to deal with the absorption, food and medical needs of the evacuees.

Because of the Soviet Army doctrine stating that if a war did break out, it would immediately be fought on enemy soil, no advance evacuation plans had been prepared. A possible retreat from Soviet soil had not been contemplated. Therefore, it was necessary to improvise a plan for the evacuation of thousands of industries – especially those vital to the war effort – and millions of individuals, while retreating in disarray under aerial bombings. In addition, the order of the

---

2. *Sovetskaya Ukraina v Gody Otechestvennoii Voiny* (Kiev: Naukova Dumka, 1985), vol. 1, 251–52.
3. Ibid., 253–54.

State Defense Committee was "to continue production until the last minute, and to begin the dismantling [of the factories] only in accordance with the orders of the local representative the State Defense Committee or of the ministry to which the factory belonged.[4] As a result, many factories began dismantling when the enemy was very close, and sometimes there was no time to evacuate all the necessary equipment, the workers and their families. Sometimes the evacuation was also postponed till the last minute because the authorities did not want to create panic in an area about to be overrun by Germans.

The Soviet government hid the gravity of the military situation from the population, directing the media to broadcast optimism and an imminent victory. On July 3, 1941, Stalin, in his first speech of the war, said, "As a result of our resistance, the best divisions of the German-Fascist army were smashed by our Red Army...."[5] Such disinformation was broadcast to the population and was another reason for the delay in evacuation preparations. The decisions to evacuate, along with the order of priority in evacuation, were accepted during the first days and weeks of the war, but several months passed before an organized evacuation campaign could operate efficiently.

Only 109 factories were evacuated from Byelorussia, since most of the region was overrun during the first two or three weeks of the war. The majority of the evacuated factories were from the eastern regions of the republic – Vitebsk and Gomel – which were occupied later. From the Ukraine, whose occupation was completed by the Germans only in October 1941, 419 industrial factories and power plants were evacuated, among them enormous plants with thousands of workers. In the Moscow and Leningrad regions, between July and November 1941, 1523 factories were evacuated, 1360 of them producing for the military industry. The authorities in charge of evacuation included cultural institutions such as theaters, museums, archives and research facilities.[6] By the end of 1941, when the German advance was halted, approximately 12 million people had been evacuated.[7] That number included hundreds of thousands from Moscow and Leningrad. A much smaller evacuation was carried out during the sum-

---

4. Ibid., 143.
5. Stalin, *O Velikoi*, 17.
6. Pospelov et al., *Istoria Velikoi*, vol. 2, 148; Nikolai Voznesenski, *Voennaia Ekonomika SSSR v Period Otechestvennoi Voiny* (Moscow: Gosudarstvennoe Izdatelstvo Politicheskoi Literatury, 1948), 41.
7. *Sovetskii Tyl v Pervyi Period Velikoi Otechestvennoi Voiny, Sbornik Dokumentov,* (Moscow, 1988), 139.

mer and fall of 1942, when the German army advanced toward Stalingrad and the Caucasus.

The main evacuation was carried out during the first five months of the German invasion, July–November 1941, under particularly difficult conditions of hurried retreat and defeats on the front. Trains carried machines, equipment, and workers and their families to the designated absorption areas, which often took weeks of travel. Some of the trains were bombed by the Germans, while others remained stuck at depots along the way for endless periods of time.

The factories in their new locations were completely dependent on the availability of raw materials (metals of all kinds) and sources of energy (coal, etc.) Many sources of raw materials and their factories remained in the regions occupied by the Germans by the end of autumn 1941. Even those that had been evacuated required months of work before they were up and running. According to one Soviet source:

> As compared with 1940, at the end of October 1941, 33 percent of cast iron had been produced, 42 percent of the steel, 42 percent of the rolled iron. At the end of December steel production decreased by two-thirds.... We lost all our coal mines in the Don and Moscow basins: non-ferrous rolled metals were completely lacking and general industrial production had decreased by about half as compared with June. During the last months of 1941, the production of all the industrial branches was at the lowest point of the war. In October the production of airplanes began to decrease; the factories that had been hit had to be moved.... At the front, the lack of armored vehicles was felt because some of the evacuated factories still had not initiated manufacture and others had not yet been set up [in their new locations]...and the same was true for ammunition factories.... The loss of the Don basin with its well-developed chemical industries and the evacuation of the chemical industries from Moscow and Leningrad caused a sharp drop in the production of explosives...and the factories experienced a severe shortage of workers....[8]

Nevertheless, the factories that did reach their destination were set up and began operation. In many instances the machines were turned on before the factory's walls and roofs had been completed. By the end of 1941, the military industry

---

8.   Pospelov et al., *Istoria Velikoi*, 160–61.

had already supplied the Soviet Army with 4,800 tanks and 9,700 planes, but the losses on the ground and in the air were heavier. On the other hand, during 1942, and especially during the second half of the year, the military industry manufactured about 24,500 tanks and about 25,500 planes, far more than what had been manufactured by the German war industry and also more than Soviet losses. In 1943 the same number of tanks were produced, but the number of planes rose to 34,845, and the following year, the total was 29,000 tanks and more than 40,000 planes; the number of artillery guns increased as well.[9]

Such achievements, carried out under the most difficult conditions imaginable and without equal in the military industries in other countries participating in the Second World War, were thanks to the people who kept the factories going: the directors, engineers and workers. They came from all the nations of the Soviet Union – Russians, Ukrainians, Byelorussians, and others – but the Jews among them played a particularly prominent role.

2. JEWS INVOLVED IN FOUNDING AND DIRECTING THE DEFENSE INDUSTRY

Many years before the war, Jews had held prominent positions on all levels of the planning and technical development of the Soviet Union's defense industries. There were Jewish people's commissars and weapons designers, factory directors and simple workers. The industry struck root during the 1920s when thousands of young Jewish students enrolled in Soviet universities, after the Communist Revolution had opened the doors of higher education to the Jews. At the beginning of the 1930s, between 12 percent and 15 percent of university students were Jewish, while the total Jewish Soviet population stood at 1.8 percent.[10] As a result, there was a large cadre of technologically advanced Jewish engineers, a large number of whom held high-ranking roles in the management and development of military industries. At the same time, tens of thousands of ordinary Jews, whose traditional occupations had been destroyed by the Bolshevik revolution, went to work in the factories. Their levels of education were far higher than the many tens of thousands of villagers who streamed into

9. Overy, *Russia's War*, 155, 171. In 1942 the German war industry produced 9,300 tanks and about 15,400 planes. Pospelov et al., *Istoria Velikoi*, vol. 6, 52.

10. Mordechai Altshuler, *Soviet Jewry on the Eve of the Holocaust* (Jerusalem: Ahava, 1998), 122–23; Leonid Mininberg, *Sovetskie Evrei v Nauke I Promishlennosti SSSR v Period Vtoroi Mirovoi: Voiny, 1941–1945* (Moscow: Its-Garant, 1995), 14.

the new industrial centers, and as a result of their education they advanced and received higher positions.[11]

Thousands of Jews, as noted above, were employed in and made a great contribution to the development of the Soviet Union's defense industries. This section relates to only a few of them, those who held key positions in management and who were leaders in the field of weapons development, providing the Soviet Army with the weapons it needed during the war against Nazi Germany.

One of the prominent men in the field was Lazar Moiseevich Kaganovich, whom the Soviet higher echelons considered an excellent organizer, a role he filled many times. Between 1935 and 1944 he served as people's commissar for transport; at the same time, between 1937 and 1940, he also served as people's commissar for heavy industry (fuel, etc.).

Because of the vast distances within the Soviet Union and the underdeveloped road system, most transportation was based on railroads. When the Germans attacked, tens of thousands of railroad cars and locomotives had to be supplied to evacuate the factories and the millions of workers and their families. During those same critical months the railroads had to bring millions of new conscripts to the army, transport reinforcements and supplies to the front, evacuate tens of thousands of wounded soldiers and repair the tracks and bridges bombed by the German air force. In that situation, and especially during the first six months of the war, the commissar for transport proved himself equal to the task. After alternative sources of raw materials were found beyond the Ural Mountains in Asia, railroad lines had to be laid to transport them to the new factories. Despite the many difficulties involved and more than a few failures, the People's Commissariat for Transport succeeded.

After Stalingrad, the Soviet army began advancing westward all along the front, and it was urgent to rebuild the tracks in the liberated territories that had been destroyed. To that end, on April 15, 1943, the railroads were proclaimed a military area and those working on them were subject to military discipline. Infractions and disobedience were tried by court martial. The penalty was dismissal from the railroad and dispatch to the front, sometimes to special punishment units.[12] Concerning the railroads, Marshal Zhukov wrote:

---

11. Yaakov Leshchinsky, *Soviet Russia: From the October Revolution to the Second World War* [Hebrew] (Tel Aviv: Am Oved, 1943), 192–93, 204.

12. G.A. Kumanev, *Voina I Zheleznodorozhnyi Transport SSSR 1941–1945* (Moscow, 1988), 174; Voznesensky, *Voennaia Ekonomika SSSR*, 106.

The operational activity behind the front lines during the war…was, to a great extent, dependent on the existence of a fully functioning railroad system…. Without the railroads frequent operational changes could not have been made during the war, nor would there have been the uninterrupted movement of technological means and materials over vast distances.[13]

The transport system proved it had the ability to provide for the army's and defense industry's needs during the war; Lazar Kaganovich was instrumental in both. Nikolai Vozensensky, who was head of National Planning (Gosplan) during the war and responsible for the entire Soviet economy, wrote: "Despite the enormous difficulties of the war years, the Soviet transportation system successfully carried out its missions and served the needs of the Soviet military and war economy."[14] Kaganovich, besides serving as people's commissar for transport, was a member of the National Defense Committee, a member of the politburo and served in the highest offices of Stalin's state, even though he was a Jew. Although he participated with Stalin in the various purges and mass arrests carried out in the prewar years, involving hundreds of thousands of victims, it is worthwhile to note his contribution to the war effort and victory over Nazi Germany.[15]

In December 1936, the People's Commissariat for Armament was established, and a Jew named Moisei Lvovich Rukhimovich was appointed to head it; before his appointment he served as deputy people's commissar for heavy industry. In this position he laid the foundations for the Soviet defense industries. In October 1937 he was arrested in one of Stalin's purges and executed on July 29, 1938. He was replaced by Mikhail Moiseevich Kaganovich (Lazar Kaganovich's brother), who had held senior posts in the aeronautics industry, and who had been Rukhimovich's deputy. He served as the people's commissar for armament until January 1939, when he was appointed people's commissar for the aviation industry. During the year and a half of his appointment he did not succeed in effecting the revolution necessary for the aviation industry before the outbreak of the Second World War. He was dismissed and received a

---

13. Kumanev, *Voina I Zheleznodorozhnyi*, 57.
14. Voznesensky, *Voennaia Ekonomika*, 107.
15. Rzheshevski et al., *Velikaia Otechestvenna Voina*, 327; Mininberg, *Sovetskie Evrei*, 226–29.

public rebuke from Stalin at the Communist Party conference in February 1941. Some weeks later, just before he was about to be arrested, he committed suicide.[16]

BORIS LVOVICH VANNIKOV

One of the most important contributors to the development of weapons for the Soviet Army was Boris Lvovich Vannikov, the people's commissar for armament from February 1939 till June 1941. In 1938 he was appointed deputy people's commissar for armament, replacing Mikhail Kaganovich. After the beginning of the Second World War, he planned the construction of new factories in the eastern part of the country, far from the border with Nazi-occupied Poland. Those plans proved themselves when the Germans invaded the Soviet Union and it became necessary to rapidly evacuate factories eastward. Vannikov insisted that his commissariat have its own steel mills, which would supply the military industry independently of the People's Commissariat for Metallurgy and Machine Production. He took the same stance in everything connected to construction and worked to establish a construction branch within his commissariat independent of the construction commissariat. By doing so he clashed with the other commissariats and struggled constantly against them.

Superficially it would have seemed that his demands were unjustified, but when the war broke out and factories had to be relocated, there was no need to coordinate between the various commissariats and waste precious time supplying steel. Vannikov even had Stalin order the NKVD that the arrest of a factory director working for a military industry had to be approved by the Council of People's Commissars. That reduced the damage done to the management staff of the military industry, many of whom had been purged during the 1930s.[17]

---

16. Mininberg, *Sovetskie Evrei*, 191–94; Arkady Vaksberg, *Stalin Against the Jews* (New York: Knopf, 1994), 187; Gennadi Kostyrchenko, *Tainaya Politika Stalina* (Moscow: Mezhdunarodnye Otnosheniya, 2001), 200–220. According to Kostyrchenko, both Rukhimovich and Mikhail Kaganovich were dismissed and eventually died because of Stalin's anti-Semitism.

17. Rzheshevski et al., *Velikaia Otechestvenna Voina*, 299; Mininberg, *Sovetskie*

Early in June 1941, a few weeks before the German invasion, Vannikov was dismissed and arrested shortly thereafter. He was accused of being part of a military plot and a German spy, and was beaten and tortured. His stay in the NKVD cellars of the Lubyanka prison in Moscow was short. Held in solitary confinement, on July 17, 1941, he was called upon to present himself before the investigating officer, who addressed him with unaccustomed politeness. Using his name and patronymic, a sign of friendship, he asked, "Boris Lvovich, if war were to break out with Germany and if during its first stages the Germans were extremely successful, where could our military industry's factories be moved to?" Vannikov, apparently in ignorance of the war, was surprised by the question and after a short pause answered, "I cannot answer immediately, but I am very familiar with each factory and within two days I could prepare a document showing how it could be done." The investigating officer said, "Excellent," and left him a notebook and several pencils. Two days later the document was ready. The following day, after his torture wounds had been bound and he had been given new clothing, Vannikov was rushed to the Kremlin and presented to Stalin. Beria and Molotov were there as well. Stalin held up the notebook and said, "Your plan is excellent, give it to People's Commissar for Armament [Dmitrii] Ustinov. You are his deputy and you will both begin carrying out your plan immediately. The Germans are already nearing Smolensk." A moment later he added, "We were wrong [about arresting you], scoundrels made up stories about you, do not be offended." He smiled and said, "I was in prison too." Vannikov answered, "You, Comrade Stalin, were imprisoned by enemies, but I – by our own people."[18] From there Vannikov was driven directly to the Commissariat for Armament and began organizing the evacuation and the reopening of the factories.

In the fall of 1941 the Commissariat for the Production of Ammunition was established, independent of the Commissariat for Armament, and in February 1942, Vannikov was appointed to head it. Under his management in 1942, the manufacture of ammunition increased three-fold and the following year it was four times what it had been in 1941. In 1944 he was promoted to colonel general, the rank second only to marshal. In August 1945 Stalin appointed him deputy chairman of the Atomic Bomb Committee, headed by Beria. Early in

---

Evrei, 212–13. Vannikov joined the Red Army and fought in the Civil War in the Caucasus, after which he studied engineering at the High Technical Institute in Moscow, and from 1926 on directed heavy industry factories in various locations.

18.   Sverdlov, *Encyklopedia Evreiskogo Geroizma*, 250–51.

1946 he was appointed chairman of the Atomic Industry Administration and his deputy was a Jewish physicist named Abraham Joffe.[19]

Major General Isaak Moiseevich Zaltzman held a series of important posts in the tank industry before and during the war. From 1938 to October 1941 he was in charge of the Kirov factory in Leningrad. It was one of the largest producers of tanks, and when the Germans approached, it was evacuated and reopened in Chelyabinsk. On September 11, 1941, the Commissariat for Tanks Production was established and Zaltzman was appointed its deputy people's commissar. In June 1942 he was appointed people's commissar for tanks production. He broadened the scope of the commissariat's activity to repairing tanks that had been damaged and taken out of action. In August 1942, when the Germans were approaching Stalingrad and the city was being heavily bombed, the tank factory was hit. Zaltzman arrived on the scene and organized the repair of hundreds of tanks, which were then returned to battle. He served as people's commissar for a year and then returned to run the factory at Chelyabinsk. (For his actions as director of the Kirov factory in besieged Leningrad, and then as director of the tank factory in Chelyabinsk, see below, "Jews in Tank Production.")[20]

During the war, the people's commissar for construction was Semyon Zacharovich Ginsburg. Between 1937 and 1938 he served as deputy people's commissar for heavy industry, and in 1939 he was appointed people's commissar for construction, a post he held until 1946. During the war he directed the construction of defense plants, preparing the structures for factories that had been evacuated and rehabilitating the economy in liberated areas.[21]

About 30 Jews were deputies in the commissariats that administered the defense industry. Some of them also ran weapons factories at the same time. We

19. Ibid., 252–54; Mininberg, *Sovetskie Evrei*, 214–15; Rzheshevski et al., *Velikaia Otechestvenna Voina*, 299. Vannikov was awarded the order of Hero of Socialist Labor three times and held key posts in the Soviet government until 1958, when illness forced him to retire. He died in 1962.

20. Sverdlov, *Evrei Generaly*, 90; Mininberg, *Sovetskie Evrei*, 220–25, 236–37.

21. Kirian et al., *Slovar-Spravochnik*, 140; Collection of Dmitri Olinsky, Yad Vashem Archive 043/5, p. 21. Ginsburg had fought in the ranks of the Red Army in the Civil War, and during the second half of the 1920s he graduated from the High Technical School in Moscow. From 1946 he was minister of constructing military installations in the Soviet Union. In May 1950, during the anti-Jewish witch hunts, accused of financial misdealings and failure to manage human resources in the factories for which his ministry was responsible, he was dismissed from his post.

have included here some of the most prominent among them. Leonid Belakhov served as deputy people's commissar of the navy during the war. He received the Order of Lenin for transporting oil, vital for the war effort, from the Baku region through the Caspian Sea and from there through a provisory pipeline laid on the decks of boats in the Ural-Caspian channel. During the winter the channel was covered by ice, such that, until the creation of the pipeline, boats with oil could not sail. When the Soviet Army reached the Danube (running through Romania, Hungary and Austria) in the summer of 1944, Belakhov organized the ships on the river and the military supplies through it.

Deputy people's commissar for naval construction, especially of warships, was Grigory Kaplun, who, until his appointment, was director of the large shipyards at Vladivostok. Deputy commissar for the chemical industry during the war was Leon Lokshin. Deputy commissar for steel production was Semyon Reznikov. When the production of one of the main steel mills operating in Novo-Tagilsk was lagging behind schedule, and their steel was vital for the manufacture of tanks, Reznikov took it upon himself to manage the factory and within a short time it became the leader in the field. Deputy commissar for the aviation industry during the war was Solomon Sendler. In addition, Jewish deputy people's commissars were in charge of electricity, the river fleet, heavy industry, the fuel industry, and other sectors.[22]

3. JEWS IN THE AVIATION INDUSTRY AND THE DEVELOPMENT OF AIRCRAFT

The foundations for the Soviet Union's aviation industry were laid at the end of the 1920s and beginning of the 1930s. Most of the research and development work was done in the following institutions: the Central Aerodynamics Institution, the Central Airplane Motor Institution, the Military/Aviation Academy and the military aircraft research centers in Moscow and Kharkov. About 25 percent of the staff in those institutions were Jewish.[23] In 1938, after the fierce battles waged by the Red Army against the Japanese on the Manchurian bor-

---

22. Mininberg, *Sovetskie Evrei*, 231–38, 478–81.
23. Ibid., 20–24, 155–59. Mininberg mentions the names of scores of Jews who contributed to the fields of flight theory, motor and fuselage technology, who were test pilots and who had scientific administrative posts in the research institutions specializing in aeronautical development, etc.

der, and the increasing danger of a European war, the development of a new generation of planes became increasingly urgent.

In the summer of 1939, the Soviet air force had more than 11.000 warplanes, but the overwhelming majority were outdated and far inferior to the German planes. That number included more than 5,000 bombers – only 40 of which (Su-2, Pe-8, Iak-4) were modern and could be described as capable of carrying out their missions – and more than 6,000 outdated fighter planes (I-15, I-16, I-153), which were inferior to the German Messerschmitts in speed, weapons and altitude capability.[24] The Russian air force also had cargo, reconnaissance and other planes. In view of the might of the German air force in September 1939 in the war against Poland, the Soviet aircraft industry needed far-reaching changes.

The aviation industry was given a push forward, and teams of engineers were appointed to plan new models. One of the planning teams was headed by aviation engineer Semyon Lavochkin.[25] Lavochkin began developing fighter planes. His first prototype was the La-1, which was improved and mass produced as the La-3. Until then airplane frames were made of aluminum, of which there was a severe shortage at the time. Lavochkin proposed using tree pith instead. Stalin, when brought a sample, laid his burning pipe on it, then used a knife to scratch it. When it remained intact he agreed it could be used for aircraft frames. On December 7, 1940, the Soviet government and the Central Committee of the Communist Party decided 16,530 aircraft would be manufactured in 1941, 2,960 La-3s among them. They were to be produced in three factories, one of which was making furniture at the time. Despite certain limitations, in the first air battles with the German air force it proved itself equal to the Messerschmitt 9, and could continue flying even when hit. An improved version, the La-5, which could fly 650 kph (about 400 mph) at an altitude of 6 kilometers (about 19,000 feet), appeared for the first time during the battle at Stalingrad. It was superior to the Messerschmitt 9 but not the Messerschmitt 9F.

Lavochkin and his staff worked ceaselessly to improve the plane. At the Kursk salient in the summer of 1943, the La-5FN was introduced. It had a longer range, excellent maneuvering capabilities and could fly at a higher altitude.

---

24. Afanasev, *Drugaia Voina*, 198–99.

25. Lavochkin was born near Smolensk in 1900. In 1918 he served in the Red Army, which sent him to study engineering at the Moscow State Technical University. He graduated in 1927 and from then on worked in aircraft development.

It equaled the German Fokker Wolf 190 and in certain respects was superior. According to official Soviet history, "the new Soviet La-5FN plane was better than all the German fighter planes, including the modern Fokker Wolf 190. More improvements were introduced into the La-7, which had an air- (instead of water-) cooled motor and participated in battle in 1944. The La-9 flew in the victory parade in Moscow. During the war the aircraft industry produced 15,758 planes of designs created by Lavochkin. In 1944 he was promoted to the rank of major general."[26] At Plant 21, where the planes were assembled, the head engineer was David Reznikov, the head technician was Semyon Zaichyk and the factory's deputy directors were Arkady Shulman and Alexander Joffe.[27]

One of the generation of new aircraft was the MiG-3 fighter plane, designed by Artem Mikoyan and Mikhail Gurevich, who was Jewish. Gurevich began designing planes during the second half of the 1920s.[28] The prototype of the MiG appeared in 1940. It could climb quickly to an altitude of 12,000 meters (39,000 feet). The production of 3,600 such planes was planned for 1941. When the war broke out, 900 were ready, but two-thirds of them were destroyed on the ground by the Germans during the first days of the war. The remaining 300 participated in Moscow's air defense, and half of the German planes intercepted over the city were shot down by MiG-3s. In 1942 fewer such planes were produced because various limitations were discovered, such as problems with maneuvering at high and low altitudes. However, the main reason was that the defense industry was not producing enough motors, and priority was given to the Ilyushin-2. Most of the Mikoyan-Gurevich team's developments took place after the war, when they produced the MiG-9, the Soviet Union's first jet fighter plane, and later other MiG models. Gurevich received three Orders of Lenin, and despite his achievements and the important work he did, his name is far less known in the Soviet Union that that of his partner Mikoyan. In many books

---

26. Mininberg, *Sovetskie Evrei*, 25–29; Rzheshevski et al., *Velikaia Otechestvenna Voina*, 345; Pospelov et al., *Istoria Velikoi*, vol. 3, 165–66. After the war, Lavochkin continued developing new models, among them the La-176 jet plane. It was the first Soviet plane to break the sound barrier. He was twice awarded the title of Hero of Socialist Labor and received the Order of Lenin three times. Lavochin died in 1960. Soviet planes were usually named after their inventors, and all the "La" planes were named after him.

27. Mininberg, *Sovetskie Evrei*, 29–30. Jews were also part of the La-series research and development team, including Leonid Zak and Mikhail Arlozorov.

28. Ibid., 32–36; Rzheshevski et al., *Velikaia Otechestvenna Voina*, 313.

and museums where the MiG is featured, only Mikoyan's name appears, with no mention of Gurevich. That is probably due to the wave of anti-Semitism that swept through the Soviet Union after the war, especially before Stalin died. As of the end of the 1980s, encyclopedias dealing with the war have had an entry for Gurevich and his contribution to the development of Soviet aviation.[29]

Sergei Vladimirovich Ilyushin headed a development team, many of whose members were Jewish. They developed the low-altitude, single-seated attack planes called Il-2. Its cabins were armor-protected, and it took part in battle as early as 1941. During the war a double-seated Il-10 was produced. Key Jewish members in the development team were Victor Shaivin and D.V. Leshchiner. Chief designer at the factory that produced Ilyushins in Komsomolsk-on-the-Amur was A.M. Vulman and chief engineer at the factory was Yaakob Khaevsky. Because of their armored cabins, Ilyushins could continue flying even when hit. The Jewish pilot Heinrich Hofmann, a Hero of the Soviet Union who carried out 150 missions in an Il-2, said that his plane had been hit by 600 bullets but managed to return safely to base every time. During the war, 40,000 Il-2s were produced and 6,500 Il-10s, making up 40 percent of the Soviet aviation industry during the years 1941–45.[30]

Among the leading figures of the Iak fighter plane development team were Yosef Zaslavsky and Leonid Shechter, both Jewish. The factory that produced the planes, located in Saratov, had Israel Levin as director and Grigory Pivarov as chief engineer. With the outbreak of the war it began producing improved Iak models. In September 1942, in Stalingrad, the Soviet air force received its first Iak-1 aircraft and later the improved Iak-3. For the first time, planes were mass produced and assembled on a conveyor belt.[31] On the night of May 23, 1943, the Germans bombed from the air and destroyed 70 percent of the factory. At first it seemed that nothing could be done, but under the leadership of Levin and his team it was rehabilitated, and four months later it had returned to its previous production schedule. In his memoirs, Alexei Shakhurin, the people's commissar for the aviation industry, wrote the following about Israel Levin: "Among those who contributed greatly to the defense industry, the man who proved himself in the most difficult situations in the war as a brilliant,

29. Mininberg, *Sovetskie Evrei* , 32–36; Rzheshevski et al., *Velikaia Otechestvenna Voina*, 313.
30. Mininberg, *Sovetskie Evrei*, 36–37; Shapiro, *Under Fire*, 160–61.
31. Mininberg, *Sovetskie Evrei* , 37–38.

thoroughly expert organizer in the field of aircraft manufacture…was Israel Salomonovich Levin."[32]

The head engineer of Aviation Factory 27, Sina Shmerkovich Bas-Dubov, and engineer Heinrich Zaslavsky of Aviation Factory 467, developed a new propeller for fighter planes and bombers, which enabled them to use a shorter runway and climb to higher altitudes. The head designer in Factory 589, S.I. Boianover, developed an instrument for automatic bomb release to improve precision.[33]

A great contribution to aircraft development was made by Major General Yakov Shmushkevich, twice awarded the title Hero of the Soviet Union. He was a fighter pilot, commanded the Soviet aviation squadrons sent to support the anti-Franco republican forces in Spain in the fall of 1936, and acquired experience in air battles against the German and Italian planes and pilots fighting for Franco. When he returned from Spain, he was appointed deputy commander of the Soviet air force and in August 1939 left for the Far East to command the Soviet air forces fighting against the Japanese on the Mongolian-Manchurian border. In November 1939 he was appointed chief of staff of the Soviet air force and in December 1940, its inspector. The experience he gained in Spain and against the Japanese made him instrumental in the planning and development of new types of aircraft. In many meetings with aircraft designers, he brought to bear his own battle experience and that of his pilots, and the designers used his knowledge to improve the various types of aircraft that appeared later, such as the Iak-1, the Il-2 and others, which were mass produced from the middle of 1942. He was unjustly arrested and executed on October 28, 1941, four months after the beginning of the Great Patriotic War, along with twenty-four other senior army commanders.[34]

During the war Soviet aviation industry continually improved the capabilities of their fighter planes and bombers, enabling them to fly longer distances,

---

32. Collection of Dmitri Olinsky, YVA, 043/4; A.I. Shakhurin, *Krylia Pobedy, Vospominania* (Moscow, 1991), 300. In 1950, during the purges of the "cosmopolitans," a Stalin-inspired act of anti-Semitism, Israel Levin was dismissed from his posts in the aviation industries.

33. Mininberg, *Sovetskie Evrei*, 39–41. Among the leading engineers in the development of aviation motors, especially for Ilyushins, were Moise Dubinsky, G.L. Lifshitz, I.L. Fogel and Semyon Arievich Kosberg.

34. For Shmushkevich's part in the Spanish Civil War and in the battle against the Japanese, see chapter 1:1, "Soviet Jews in the Spanish Civil War (1936–1939)."

carry heavier loads and drop bombs with greater precision. At the beginning of the war the Soviet air force was inferior to the German. As a result of the evacuation, and the time required to reopen the factories and find new sources of raw materials, during the first year of the war Soviet airplane production lagged behind Germany. However, from the second half of 1942 it began to provide the army with modern planes equal to and in some respects superior to those of the enemy, and in larger quantities, in many cases thanks to the efforts of Jewish scientists and directors.

4. JEWS IN TANK PRODUCTION

The Great Patriotic War was fought in the air, at sea and on land, but its fate was decided on land warfare, mainly by armored forces. The outcome of tank battles were resolved at the front, but the quality and quantity of the tanks were decisive factors in the outcome, and this was determined by those who developed and produced them.

MAJOR GENERAL
ISAAK ZALTZMAN

Major General Isaak Zaltzman, whose activity as deputy commissar and later people's commissar for tanks has been noted above, was central to the manufacture of armored vehicles. Before the war, the Kirov factory in Leningrad, which he directed from 1938, was one of the Soviet Union's largest heavy industry factories and made locomotives, tractors, tanks and artillery guns. The war with Finland (December 1939–March 1940) showed that the thin armor of Russian T-28 and T-29 tanks could easily be pierced by anti-tank missiles and that heavier armor was required. Already before the war, at the Kirov factory, experiments had been made to produce a heavier tank with armor that afforded the crew more protection.

The prototypes, which were later called the KV series (named after Kliment Voroshilov, the people's commissar for defense), proved themselves in the attack on the fortified Finnish defenses known as the Mannerheim Line. As a result, the diesel-fueled KV-1 went into mass production, weighing 47.5 tons and carrying a 76-mm gun.

When the Germans invaded, the factory increased production and at the end of July turned out ten tanks a day for the army. In August it produced 200, at a time when it was routinely being bombarded from the air. The tanks helped defend the city and were crucial in preventing it from being taken. At that time Zaltzman was a member of the Leningrad Defense Committee. When the Germans were only four kilometers (about 2.5 miles) away, the factory management organized from among its workers a National Guard division; part of the staff took up positions to defend the plant while the others continued their work. They manned tanks they had produced and rode in them to the front. Tanks that were hit were returned to Kirov, where they were repaired. Zaltzman organized a force of workers who manned anti-aircraft guns to defend the factory. The factory was shelled by artillery fire and bombed, and although it suffered direct hits and lost workers, it continued turning out tanks.

In October 1941, Moscow decided that parts of the factory and thousands of its workers would be evacuated to the existing KV tank factory in Chelyabinsk in the Ural Mountains. The evacuation would be carried out with planes and through Lake Ladoga. Before the move, Stalin summoned Zaltzman, informed him that it was vital to move the factory from Leningrad and offered him the appointment of people's commissar for the tank industry. Zaltzman answered that the present time he wanted to continue as factory director. Stalin agreed but informed him that he would be both; as deputy people's commissar for the tank industry he would be responsible for all the tank factories in the Urals.[35] At the beginning of February 1942, Zaltzman, who was in Chelyabinsk, got a phone call from Stalin, who said to him:

> Comrade Zaltzman, all the men in the army say the T-34 is an excellent tank. I know you are in love with heavy tanks [KVs], but my request is that you give priority to the T-34. The commanders at the front call me, armored division generals, and they all ask for more medium-sized T-34s. They move well in deep snow and are more mobile – they fly like swallows. We moved Factory 183 from Kharkov to Nizhni Tagil, and here it is February and no tanks as yet. We dismissed the director

35. Collection of Dmitri Olinsky, YVA, 043/6, Zaltzman file, which includes his autobiography, written in May 1987; Vladimir Sergiichuk, "*Tankovii korol* [King of the tanks]," *Raduga* [Rainbow] 5 (1991): 103. *Raduga* was a periodical that appeared during the first years of glastnost and perestroika in Kiev. Its editor in chief was Vitaly Korotich.

and he will stand trial. Please, be in Nizhni Tagil tomorrow, you have the authority of a deputy people's commissar and the central committee gives you full authority, take all the necessary steps.... The most important thing is that the tanks start rolling out of the factory.[36]

Zaltzman went immediately to Nizhni Tagil, taking with him a team of specialists from Chelyabinsk, and reorganized the factory, mass-producing tanks on a conveyor belt. It was the largest T-34 factory in the Soviet Union and turned out 25–30 tanks a day; in recognition of his work there Zaltzman was awarded the Order of Lenin. He gave priority to the factory at Nizhni Tagil, but it was at the expense of the factory producing the parts for the 76-mm guns which were mounted on the T-34s, a factory in the NKVD's gulag. Beria telephoned Zaltzman and threatened to punish him for it. Zaltzman answered that it was necessary and that he had received authorization from the National Defense Committee (GKO), headed by Stalin. Beria was forced to back down. Zaltzman increased T-34 production, and it became the most important weapon in the Soviet tank arsenal. He began producing them also at the factory in Chelyabinsk without stopping the manufacture of the heavy KVs. In June 1942, in recognition of Zaltzman's abilities, Stalin appointed him people's commissar for the tank industry, a post he held until June 1943. Beria, however, did not forget that Zaltzman had defied him, and at the end of June 1943, when the National Defense Committee appointed Beria inspector of the tank industry, he visited Chelyabinsk, taking Zaltzman with him. In a discussion about increasing production, he made it clear to Zaltzman that it would be best if he returned to the factory and suggested he write to Stalin, asking to be released from his duties as people's commissar so that he could return to his former post. Zaltzman well understood what could happen to him if he refused; he wrote to Stalin, who agreed to the request, and returned to Chelyabinsk.[37]

During the first months of the war, the Germans found out that the T-34 was superior to most of their tanks. General Guderian, the most prominent tank commander in the German army, wrote of the T-34:

In November 1941 the army I commanded was visited by a group of engineers, industrialists and high-ranking ordnance officers to find out first-hand about our experience fighting the superior Soviet T-

---

36. Sergiichuk, "*Tankovii korol,*" 106.
37. Ibid., 106, 110–11.

34s, and to decide what steps could be taken to achieve technological superiority over the Russians. It was the opinion of tank officers at the front that the T-34 should be copied as is, and that that was the fastest way to overcome German tank inferiority. The engineers, however, disagreed, not because of their natural professional pride in products they had designed, but because it was impossible to mass produce the important components, such as an aluminum diesel engine, in a foreseeable time span. We were also at a handicap when it came to armored plates because of the lack of raw materials. Therefore it was decided that the heavy Tiger tank…and the mid-sized Panther would be produced."[38]

Zaltzman turned the Kirov factory at Chelyabinsk into the Soviet Union's largest complex for tank manufacture, and the city was nicknamed Tankograd (Tank city). The complex was comprised of the tank factory of Chelyabinsk, the Kirov factory from Leningrad, the diesel Factory 75 from Kharkov, the "Red Proletarian" (*Krasnaia Proletari*) from Moscow and part of the tractor factory from Stalingrad, and employed 75,000 workers. In 1943 it supplied the Soviet Army with improved T-34s carrying 85-mm guns that could pierce the armor of German Mark-3 and Mark-4 middle-weight tanks. In addition to the KVs and T-34s, Zaltzman began producing a heavier tank, the IS-1 (for Iosif Stalin), which had a 122-mm cannon, and the SU-100 and SU-155 tank destroyers. The latter had no turret and could be fitted with larger-caliber guns to deal with the heavy German Tigers and Panthers.

There was no one in the Soviet Union whose contribution to tank production was comparable to Zaltzman's. In many publications, years after the war, he was crowned "King of Tanks" (*Tankovii korol*). After the war, Zaltzman refused to testify and confirm false accusations against leaders of the communist party from Leningrad (the so-called Leningrad Affair [*Lningradskoe Delo*]) with whom he had worked in the summer of 1941, in the besieged city. He was fired from the Kirov factory and sent to work as a low-grade foreman at a factory. He was lucky not to be arrested during the last years of Stalin's life, as many other prominent Jews were.[39] In the 1988 issue of *Trud*, the Soviet Union's trade

---

38. Guderian, *Panzer Leader*, 276.
39. Collection of Dmitri Olinsky, YVA, 043/6; Sergiichuk, *"Tankovii korol,"* 97–98. Zaltzman administered the Chelyabinsk complex until the summer of 1949, when he was called to Moscow to appear before the Communist Party's Control Com-

union paper, the introduction to an article entitled "The People's Commissar of Tanks (*Tankovyi narkom*)" stated:

> I must admit, I cannot be at all certain that many people know the name of the man this article is about. But during the war his name was well known throughout the country, especially among those familiar with tanks and workers in the defense industry.... I refer to Isaak Moiseevich Zaltzman, a man upon whom fate did not smile."[40]

Many Jews dealt with the development and improvement of armored vehicles. One of the achievements of the Soviet tank industry was the production of a diesel motor to replace the prewar gasoline-powered motors, which would easily catch fire if a tank were hit. One individual who made an enormous contribution to the development of the diesel engine during the 1930s was Yaakov Vikhman. Another was Yaakov Nevyazhesky, who was the chief engineer at the diesel factory in Kharkov and continued in Chelyabinsk after the evacuation. Leonid Mininberg's book notes dozens of Jewish engineers who helped improve armored vehicles and find battlefield responses to the new German tanks, which had better guns and improved armor and mobility.[41]

---

mittee. Beria and Malenkov were in attendance. Zaltzman was called upon to testify against the heads of the Communist Party in Leningrad who had recently been arrested and accused of trying to undermine the authority of the Central Committee of the Soviet Party in Moscow. Zaltzman knew them well from the years he had worked in Leningrad during the first months of the siege, but claimed he knew nothing of any subversive activities they might have engaged in. He was offered the position of minister if he would agree to testify, but refused. The following day the matter was referred to Stalin. He asked what Zaltzman's position at the Kirov factory in Leningrad had been when he started to work there, and when told he had been a foreman of the lowest order, Stalin said, "Let him go back to his old job, but at a different factory." Zaltzman lost his party card. After Stalin died and Beria was executed, Zaltzman was reinstated as a member of the Communist Party. He continued in various positions, but not of the sort he had held during the war. He died in 1988. In the Leningrad Affair, the leadership of the Communist Party of Leningrad were accused of planning to turn Leningrad into the capital of the Russian Soviet Socialist Republic, with a separate Russian government and a more autonomous Russian Communist party, which would be less dependent on the Moscow central government. In 1950 the entire Leningrad Communist leadership was executed.

40.   *Trud*, October 13, 1988, 18.
41.   Mininberg, *Sovetskie Evrei*, 69–86.

During the war the Soviet tank industry successfully competed with the Germans, even surpassing it in certain fields, despite the evacuation of most of its factories and the time required to reopen them. The middle-sized T-34s, especially the models carrying the 85-mm gun, and the heavy KVs, which were impervious to most anti-tank ammunition, surprised the Germans. They were forced to reinforce their mid-range tank armor as quickly as possible and develop heavier tanks. The Soviet tank industry responded with the heavy JS, which was introduced into battle in 1944, and an improved version in 1945, toward the end of the war.

During the first year of the war, the Soviet tanks' greatest limitation was the general lack of radio communication equipment, making it difficult for the commanding officers to control the tanks in battle. However, in 1942 the Soviets received 35,000 radios from the Americans, and they increased commanders' ability to control their units and to conduct tank battles.[42] American (and possibly British) heavy industry was superior to the Soviet, but during the war they did not produce tanks comparable in quality or quantity. German and Soviet tanks were generally equal, but the Soviets produced far more than the Germans. Beginning with the battles of the Kursk salient in the summer of 1943, the combination of quality and quantity tipped the scales against Germany – an achievement that was in large part due to the dedication and ingenuity of the many Jewish tank designers and factory directors, especially Isaak Zaltzman.

5. JEWS IN THE PRODUCTION OF ARTILLERY GUNS

Artillery played a more important role in Soviet military doctrine than in other armies during the Second World War. Soviet offensives included a massive artillery barrage preceding the attack of tanks and infantry. During the offensives of 1941–42, for every kilometer the Soviet Army attack, 70-80 artillery guns were used. The number increased during the war in accordance with the number of guns produced, and when Berlin was attacked there were between 280 and 320 guns for every kilometer of front. Artillery fire included heavy shelling before an attack, support and accompaniment for the forces during an attack, and fire on long-range targets, such as enemy artillery positions and headquarters. The army nicknamed the artillery "the god of war" (*bog voiny*). As with the development and manufacture of other weapons, the Jews were instrumental in the production of artillery guns and mortars.

---

42. Overy, *Russia's War*, 192–94.

During the war Major General Abraham Bikhovsky directed the Lenin machine factory No. 172 in Perm in the Ural mountains, which produced artillery guns. Bikhovsky began his career as a metal worker while he finished his studies at the Technological Institution in Kharkov. He worked at various factory jobs and in 1937 was appointed director at Perm. It mainly produced heavy, large-calibre guns, turning out 30,000 during the war, including 152-mm self-propelled guns, 122-mm howitzers and anti-tank guns. Bikhovsky was awarded three Orders of Lenin.[43] According to the Soviet Encyclopedia:

> The contribution of the Lenin machine factory in Perm…was vital in developing Soviet artillery…. Directed by A.I. Bikhovsky, it underwent a complete change in the shortest possible time at the beginning of the war, so that by the first half of 1942 its output had increased eight-fold. It manufactured 45-mm anti-tank guns, a 76.2-mm field gun, a 122-mm gun, a 152-mm howitzer and mobile SU-152 and ICU-152 as well. During the war the factory provided the front with 48,600 artillery guns.[44]

One of the largest weapons factories, especially for the production of artillery guns, was the Barrikady factory in Stalingrad. From 1939 on, it was directed by Lev Gonor, and specialized in the manufacture of heavy guns, among them the 210-mm gun and 305-mm howitzer, which were used both against the Mannerheim Line in Finland and in the war with the Germans. The production director was L.N. Eisenberg. In 1941 the factory began producing 120-mm mortars. In September 1942 German bombers attacked the factory, killing and wounding many of the workers. Despite the continuous bombing, work continued and only at the end of the fall, when battles were already being waged in the city, were the factory and its workers evacuated from Stalingrad to the Urals. In November 1942, Gonor was appointed director of the Ural Artillery Factory, which continued turning out heavy artillery guns and guns for tanks. In November 1944, he was promoted to the rank of major general. He was awarded three Orders of Lenin and the Order of Kutuzov. However, like many

---

43. Mininberg, *Sovetskie Evrei*, 273–76; Sverdlov, *Evrei Generaly*, 46.
44. M.M. Kozlov, ed., *Velikaia Otechestvennaia Voina 1941–1945 Godov, Encyklopedia* (Moscow, 1985), 554; Collection of Dmitri Olinsky, YVA, 043/3, p. 27.

other Jews during the final years of Stalin's reign, he was imprisoned, and released only after Stalin's death.[45]

Major General Boris Fratkin was the director of Kalinin Factory No. 8
near Moscow, which produced 85-mm anti-aircraft guns; the chief engineer
was Grigory Avtsin. The Germans targeted it from the beginning of the war,
and Fratkin and his men camouflaged it with nets and built a dummy factory
some kilometers away to draw enemy fire. Some anti-aircraft guns produced
there were operated by the workers to defend the factory. In October 1941,
when the Germans approached Moscow, it was moved to the Urals. One month
later, under Fratkin's direction, even before the walls had been built, 45-mm
anti-aircraft guns were being manufactured, and the following month, 85-mm
guns. The difficult conditions and severe cold caused many of the workers to fall
ill. They burned wood fires to keep themselves warm during their 12–14 hour
shifts. They lived in wooden cabins dug into the earth and in public buildings
nearby, and often went hungry as well. Those were the conditions in most of
the weapon factories that were moved behind the front. The workers suffered
from cold and hardship, difficult working conditions, long hours, substandard
housing and greatly reduced food rations. Fratkin was awarded two Orders of
Lenin. At the end of the war, like many other Jews, Fratkin was transferred to
a small ammunitions factory and held other low-ranking positions.[46]

The "Bolshevik Factory" played an important role in the defense of Leningrad. Before the war it produced heavy guns for warships and for coastal defense,
and the necessary ammunition as well. The head engineer was Yaakob Shifrin.
When the Germans took over the Baltic Sea coasts, the production of large warships ceased, and there was no need to manufacture their guns. The directorate
of the Bolshevik Factory and Leningrad's military command decided to mount
heavy guns on open railroad platforms and use them as mobile artillery batteries. Shifrin and his aides designed the necessary technology and produced the

---

45. Mininberg, *Sovetskie Evrei*, 275–78; Sverdlov, *Evrei Generaly*, 73. Gonor was born
in 1906 and graduated as an engineer from the Leningrad Polytechnic Institution
in 1926. After the war he held key positions in the rocket industry and the space
center. In 1952, during an anti-Semitic witch hunt, he was arrested, accused of
misdealings in an institution he directed and of plotting with the Jewish Anti-
Fascist Committee, whose members were arrested and executed. After Stalin's
death, Gonor was released, cleared of all blame and continued in various mana-
gerial positions. He died in November 1969.

46. Mininberg, *Sovetskie Evrei*, 279–81; Sverdlov, *Evrei Generaly*, 218.

mobile batteries. The mobile batteries were very effective, and as a result, the Bolshevik's directorate was asked by the City Anti-Aircraft Defense Command to prepare mobile anti-aircraft batteries mounted on railroad platforms.

At the end of October 1941, Shifrin was appointed director of the Voroshilov Gun Factory near Moscow. His first mission was to move the factory and its workers to Siberia, an enterprise entailing 1,164 boxcars. Parts of other evacuated factories were attached to his factory, with a total of 9,000 workers. The factory was to manufacture underwater mines, 122-mm mortar shells, bombs and other ordnance. Despite many difficulties, Shifrin managed to carry out all the missions entrusted to him and was widely praised. In November 1942 he was appointed deputy director of the Main Office for Artillery Weapons Design, which had to approve every plan and all changes made to guns in all the factories producing artillery. Shifrin was replaced as Voroshilov Gun Factory director by Boris Khazanov. Khazanov had previously served as the Commissariat for Defense Industries inspector of factory activity, an important role not only because the commissariat wanted to know the situation of each factory, but mainly because among the higher ranks of the Soviet regime there was little trust and great suspicion. He had great authority over operations and expanded factory production to aviation bombs. He was promoted to the rank of major general and awarded the Order of Lenin and other orders.[47]

During the war, the giant artillery factory, Factory No. 92 near the Volga (*Privolzhskii Artileriiskii Zavod*), manufactured 100,000 pieces of artillery, 20 percent of all the wartime production. The chief engineer between 1940 and 1947 was Mark (Mordechai) Olevky.[48]

The rocket, popularly called the Katyusha, was one of the most famous weapons in the Soviet Army's arsenal. The units launching them were called the "mortar guards" (*gvardeiskie minomiotnye chasti*) and had two kinds of rockets at their disposal, 82-mm and 132-mm. The units were arranged in batteries, brigades and divisions. A brigade was capable of launching 1,132 rockets in a single volley and a division could launch 3,456 for a total weight of 320 tons. The first such battery was used in the middle of July 1941 in a battle near the city of Orsha. The production of Katyushas was under the control of the

---

47. Mininberg, *Sovetskie Evrei*, 281–86; Sverdlov, *Evrei Generaly*, 220.
48. Mininberg, *Sovetskie Evrei*, 287–88. After the war, Olevsky worked in nuclear weapons, but because of the anti-Semitic witch hunts, he was forced to leave the field in 1949 and was appointed director of a factory for agricultural machinery.

People's Commissariat for Mortars. Some of the directors in Katyusha factories were Jewish: Semyon Tsofin directed the Golts Katyusha Factory and Lazar Boyarsky directed the Engels Factory.[49] Of the 125 factories subordinate to the commissariat, 21 were directed by Jews and 18 had Jewish chief engineers.[50]

6. JEWS IN OTHER DEFENSE INDUSTRIES

The Izhevskoe machine factory in the Ryazan district southeast of Moscow was the main manufacturer of light arms and machine guns for the Soviet Army during the war. At the end of 1941 it produced 5,000 rifles a day, and the following year it increased production to 12,000 a day. Its total output for the Soviet army was about half a million guns. The chief engineer was Solomon Gindenson, and the chief technician was Abraham Fisher.[51] The ZiS automotive factory in Moscow (the Factory in Honor of Stalin – *ZiS-Zavod imeni Stalina*), the largest in the Soviet Union, was required to manufacture weapons as well as vehicles. According to the book *Oruzhie Pobedy* (The weapons of victory):

> During the worst days of the fall of 1941, when the enemy was at the gates of the capital, the National Defense Committee gave the ZiS factory in Moscow the mission of producing weapons vital for the front, among them 82-mm mortars for battalions, model 1941. The mission was announced while the factory was undergoing evacuation. The first serial of the mortars needed improvement. Under the leadership of the chief instructor, Boris Fiterman, technical improvements were made, the mortars became more reliable and it was easier to operate them. The improved ZiS mortars became the army's standard.[52]

The factory, and Fiterman personally, were awarded the Order of Lenin for the mortars. In March 1943 he was appointed the factory's chief constructor. He and his team repaired and presented the army with thousands of vehicles abandoned by the Germans when they retreated from Moscow during the

---

49. Ernst Diupiui and Trevor Diupiui, eds., *Vsemirnaia Istoria Voiny*, vol. 4 (Saint Petersburg-Moscow: Kniga, 1999), 12; Mininberg, *Sovetskie Evrei*, 291; Kirian et al., *Slovar-Spravochnik*, 131.
50. Mininberg, *Sovetskie Evrei*, 316.
51. Ibid., 288–89.
52. YVA, 043/2, pp. 1–2. In March 1952, during an anti-Semitic witch hunt, Fiterman was arrested and sentenced to eight years hard labor. He worked in the coal mines and in 1955 was considered rehabilitated and thus released. He died in 1992.

winter of 1941–42. The vehicles entered the service of the Soviet Army before the thousands of American Studebakers arrived at the end of 1942, enabling the Soviet supply lines to follow the armored divisions.[53]

Special Factory No. 69, which produced optical equipment, was moved to Novosibirsk. It manufactured telescopic rifle sights, distance meters and binoculars for the army. The director was Alexander Kotlyar. The factory produced high-quality items and was the leader in the field within the Soviet Union.[54]

One of the most difficult problems faced by the defense industry during the first six months of the war was ammunition. Many of the ammunition stores located in the western Soviet Union had been captured, while others had either been bombed by the Germans or exploded by Soviet engineers before the withdrawal. Two thirds of the factories producing explosives and gunpowder were out of commission. Moving and reopening the factories also took several critical months. To solve the problem, dozens of factories with no previous experience in manufacturing ammunition were pressed into service.

Dozens of Jewish factory directors and chief engineers were awarded various medals for their contribution to the rehabilitation of the munitions industry. One of them was David Bidinsky, director of Factory No. 59, which manufactured gunpowder. It was situated in the Donbas district in the east of the Ukraine. When the Germans approached in August 1941, the factory's evacuation began, but despite the Germans' proximity and the ensuing evacuation, the workers were ordered to continue production. Shifts were 12–17 hours long and the workers slept in the factory. In October 1941, when battles were being waged quite close by, the factory was evacuated with covering army fire. It was reopened in the Perm region of the Urals and one month later was supplying gunpowder for rockets and mortar shells.[55]

7. JEWS INVOLVED IN SUPPLYING THE DEFENSE INDUSTRY WITH RAW MATERIALS

The defense industry needed raw materials: all types of metals and coal and other forms of energy. Regarding their supply following the German occupation, Soviet sources say the following:

---

53. Mininberg, *Sovetskie Evrei*, 88–92.
54. Ibid., 290–91. Like many other Jews, Kotlyar was arrested in 1948.
55. Ibid., 311–15.

At the beginning of the war, when important industrial areas in the south were occupied by the Fascist Germans, metal production and processing declined: iron by 71 percent, and steel by 60 percent…. The responsibility for supplying metals fell upon the producers in the eastern part of the country…and given the conditions of the war, all production had to be coordinated with the needs of the army. Nevertheless, Soviet metallurgy successfully supplied the needs of war.[56]

Both in management and as engineers, a high percentage of the metallurgists were Jewish. Mininberg's book contains a table of 168 wartime factories subordinate to the People's Commissariat for the Production and Processing of Raw Iron. Nineteen were directed by Jews and 41 had Jewish chief engineers.[57]

One of the three largest metal factories in the Soviet Union was at Novo-Tagilsk in the Urals (the others were at Kuznetsk and Magnitogorsk). During the first year of the war the factory at Novo-Tagilsk did not fulfill its quota, one of the reasons for which was the lack of electricity. To correct the situation, in August 1942 a Jewish engineer named Semyon Reznikov was appointed to reorganize the factory. Prior to his appointment, Reznikov had served as the deputy people's commissar for metallurgy, and between 1938 and 1939 he had run the metal factory in Dnepropetrovsk. He improved the factory's technology, arranged for a steady supply of energy and put more furnaces and rollers into operation, and within a year the factory had surpassed its quota.[58]

Increasing mortar production was dependent on the supply of a sufficient quantity of quality gun barrels. The only factory manufacturing them before the war was the Liebknecht Metallurgical Works in Dnepropetrovsk. It was relocated to Pervouralsk on the site of the local pipe factory. The chief engineer was Israel Pasternak. During 1942, the factory supplied four times the number of gun barrels it had in 1941. There were three Jews in the group of directors, engineers and scientists who shared the Stalin Prize for the technological improvemet of mortar barrels: Israel Zaslavsky, Lev Olshevski and Yaakov Altschuler. According to the official Soviet history of the Great Patriotic War: "The production of the industrial giant – the factory for [mortar] barrel production in Dnepropetrovsk – grew…. In March–April [1943] the factory's

---

56. Pospelov et al., *Istoria Velikoi*, vol. 6, 59–60.
57. Mininberg, *Sovetskie Evrei*, 318.
58. Ibid., 319–20.

team committed itself to preparing a thousand tons of barrels for the Red Army command, far beyond the official program...."[59]

The steel mill at Kuznetsk, one of the largest in the country, supplied a third of the defense industry's steel. Its chief engineer was Leonid Veisberg. According to the Soviet official history of the war:

> During the complex conditions of the war, the mill at Kuznetsk... achieved the highest level of production of cast iron and steel.... The 1943 quota was filled in time and more than 80 thousand tons of iron and 65 thousand tons of steel were produced.... All that was achieved without increasing the number of workers, but by raising the work force's level of efficiency and a more thorough use of raw materials.[60]

The Zlatoustovsk steel mill in the Far East was directed by Mikhail Kremer. Through the introduction of mechanization and new technology, it produced dozens of kinds of steel for different types of weapons. According to the Soviet official history of the war:

> One of the oldest factories in the country was the one at Zlatoustovsk, which produced 10 kinds of steel. However, during the first six months of the war it managed to produce 78 new types, 28 in ordinary furnaces. The Zlatoustovsk metallurgists solved a difficult problem: they increased the weight of a plate of cast steel to 4.5 tons (until then the plates weighed 200–400 kg).[61]

When the war began there was a sharp increase in the need for aluminum, nickel, copper and magnesium. With the loss of the sites of the metal industry, metals had to be built up from scratch, and this was done primarily in the Urals. The Kamensk-Ural aluminum factory, which opened in 1939, was the only one supplying the metal to the defense industry in August 1941. Its production had to be increased six-fold for aviation and the other industries that needed aluminum. That made it necessary to introduce new machines and technology and to train a staff, all in the shortest possible time. This was done by the chief engineer, Yosef Postilnik, and the head metallurgist, Boris Ytsikston. Parallel to its production activity, the factory became a research institute for technology and innovation in the area of aluminum production. According to the official

---

59. Ibid.; Pospelov et al., *Istoria Velikoi*, vol. 3, 161, 177.
60. Pospelov et al., *Istoria Velikoi*, vol. 3, 161.
61. Ibid., 153; Mininberg, *Sovetskie Evrei*, 321.

history of the war, "from a little aluminum factory in the Urals, it became the main producer of aluminum."[62]

The Azovstal factory, directed by Pavel Kogan, made pontoon bridges, aerial bomb casings and grenades. The steel mill at Lysvia, whose chief engineer and for a time director was Arkady Tregubov, produced steel helmets and various types of armor for personal protection. Mininberg's book notes a series of iron and steel mills whose directors and chief engineers were Jewish.[63]

*   *   *

The contribution of Jews to the war effort was enormous. They contributed to the development of planes, tanks, artillery and all types of weapons, to the evacuation of the defense industry to their new location under impossible conditions, and to the industry's operation and management. Jews succeeded in vastly improving the quality and increasing the quantity of the weapons, and in producing and supplying the raw materials from which the weapons were made. The tremendous achievements of the defense industry during the war against Nazi Germany were not only due to the Jews. All the nations of the Soviet Union contributed – Russians, Ukrainians and others. However, it is worthwhile to mention that among all those whose contribution was greatest, the percentage of Jews among them was far greater than their proportional representation in the Soviet population.

The uniqueness of the Jews, as opposed to the non-Jewish comrades with whom they toiled shoulder to shoulder to supply the Soviet Army with the weapons it needed, lay in their fate after the war, the "Black Years" for the Jews of the Soviet Union before Stalin's death. Most of them were dismissed from the high-ranking positions they held during the war and expelled from the Communist Party. Some of them were simply demoted and moved out of the defense industry, some were imprisoned and released only after Stalin's death, and some were forced into retirement and lived in the wretched poverty char-

---

62. Mininberg, *Sovetskie Evrei*, 325–26; Pospelov et al., *Istoria Velikoi*, vol. 3, 513.
63. Mininberg, *Sovetskie Evrei*, 328–55. The metal factory at Chelyabinsk was directed by Yaakov Sokol, the factory at Nizhne-Serginsk by Lev Levin, and its chief engineer was Nahum Berger. The steel mill at Beloretsk was directed by Alexander Nudelman, and the chief engineer at the factory for rolled pipes at Baku was Aaron Grishken. Mininberg's book notes the names of hundreds of Jews who managed various wings and departments within the defense industry and hundreds more of Jewish workers who were singled out for praise during the war for their work.

acteristic of those living on Soviet pensions – as opposed to their comrades who were left at their posts and belonged to the pampered elite of the Soviet state.

Official Soviet historiography gives the names of many directors, engineers and workers who distinguished themselves and contributed to the defense industry, but almost none of the names are Jewish. Their names were erased as part of the anti-Semitic and anti-Israeli witch hunts characteristic of the Soviet Union until its collapse under Gorbachev at the end of the 1980s and beginning of the 1990s.

Chapter Three:
The Background to the Rise of the Jewish Armed Resistance in the Occupied Territories of the Soviet Union

1. The Uniqueness of the Holocaust in the Occupied Territories of the Soviet Union

The uniqueness of the Holocaust in the occupied territories of the Soviet Union and the timetable of the mass-murder *Aktionen* of the Jews in the various localities were determining factors in the emergence of armed resistance in the ghettos. The existence of huge forests and the appearance of Soviet partisan units in these forests also gave the resistance a direction, that is, leaving the ghetto to join the partisans. The activities of armed Jewish resistance organizations in the ghettos and forests of the occupied territories of the Soviet Union can only be understood within the wider context of the Holocaust and the Soviet partisan movement in the forests.

Annihilating the Jews was Nazi German policy throughout Europe; it was the so-called "Final Solution of the Jewish Problem." However, the methods used in the Soviet Union were different from those employed elsewhere in Europe. The overwhelming majority of the Soviet Union's Jews were not deported to death camps; they were shot close to their homes. The killings were carried out almost overtly while the local population looked on. Due to the immense geographical span of the occupied territories of the Soviet Union, as well as the thousands of settlements where Jews lived, the Germans needed and used huge forces to carry out the extermination *Aktionen*. Most of those forces were composed of local residents who volunteered to serve in the police units, in the so-called *Schutzformationen*. Anti-Semitism, which had been deeply rooted in tsarist Russia, was not weakened in the Soviet Union. The German occupation provided popular anti-Semitism with violent ways of expressing itself, and substantial sectors of the population collaborated in carrying out the Nazi's anti-Jewish policies.[1]

---

1.   This chapter is based on my research: Yitzhak Arad, *The Holocaust in the Soviet Union* (Lincoln: University of Nebraska Press; Jerusalem: Yad Vashem, 2009).

The Nature and Demography of the Jews in the Nazi-Occupied Territories

The nature and demography of the Jews in the Nazi-occupied Soviet territories influenced their reaction to the Holocaust. There were two different groups of Soviet Jews under German occupation: Jews who had lived within the "old" Soviet Union's pre-1939 borders; and those in the areas annexed by the Soviet Union in the years of 1939–40, i.e., Lithuania, Latvia, Estonia, western Byelorussia and the western Ukraine, Bessarabia and northern Bukovina.

For over two decades of Soviet rule, the Jews in the "old" Soviet Union had no Jewish national organizations, Jewish communities, or national leadership. The Communist regime had dismantled and outlawed all Jewish organizations, and in those areas the German occupation found a leaderless Jewish population of individuals who faced the Nazi annihilation machine alone and isolated in their struggle to survive. They lived in the more eastern parts of the occupied territories, and for the most part the German army reached them somewhat later, when the men of military age had already been mobilized or evacuated behind the Soviet lines along with the relocated factories and institutions. According to the 1939 census, before the Second World War 3,020,000 Jews lived within the boundaries of the Soviet Union, 2,100,000 of them in territories conquered by the German army. An estimated 1,150,000 were either evacuated, drafted or fled before the Germans arrived, leaving approximately 950,000, mostly women, children and the elderly. This demographic composition of the Jews who remained under occupation was not fit to organize armed resistance against the Germans.

The territories annexed by the Soviet Union had a large indigenous Jewish population, which was increased by approximately 250,000 refugees from German-occupied Poland, bringing the total number to slightly less than 2,150,000. They had a strong national Jewish awareness with an infrastructure of organizations and leaders, which, during the short period between Soviet annexation and German occupation, the Communist regime did not have time to eradicate completely. Most of the refugees, along with what the regime called "anti-Soviet elements" (i.e., property holders and Jewish political, community and institutional activists), were deported to the depths of the Soviet Union. The annexed territories were close to the border and almost all of them were occupied within days or weeks of the German invasion. There was no time for mobilization or organized evacuation, and only limited segments of the Jewish population managed to flee eastward before the Germans arrived. It is estimated that about 1,700,000 Jews in the annexed territories remained under German occupation. The Jewish population there, contrary to that of the pre-1939 Soviet Union, was fairly balanced with respect to age and gender, and it was especially from among the younger members of this group that the underground and partisan groups were organized. Thus the total number of Jews within the June 22, 1941, boundaries of the Soviet Union who remained under German occupation was about 2,650,000.

The German Annihilation Machine

June 22, 1941, the day the Germans invaded the Soviet Union, can be considered the beginning of the last stage of the German "Final Solution" – the stage of annihilation. The Jews of the Soviet Union were the first victims of the annihilation policy, which some months later encompassed the Jews of the other occupied European countries. As the war became a world war and its cruelty intensified, the moral and political barriers that had been in effect in Nazi Germany were obliterated. The decision to annihilate Soviet Jewry was made either on the eve of the invasion into the Soviet Union or during the first two months of "Operation Barbarossa."

The German army set up a military administration in the rear areas of the occupied territories which included regional commands (*Feldkommandanturen*) and urban commands (*Ortskommandaturen*). It controlled every aspect of life and exploited the occupied territories to supply the needs of the German war economy. As the front pushed eastward into the Soviet Union, the rear territories were transferred to the German civilian government, the Ministry for the Occupied Eastern Territories (Ostministerium). The territories under the Ostministerium were divided into two *Reichskommissariats*: the Ostland, which included the three Baltic states and parts of Byelorussia, and the Ukraine.

Einsatzgruppen (literally, "special groups,") were set up within Heydrich's SS Main Office of Security of the Reich (Reichssicherheitshauptamt) before the invasion of the Soviet Union. It was their task to deal with the "enemies of the Reich," which included the Jews. There were four *Einsatzgruppen* – A, B, C and D – each following a different German Army Group, and each the size of a battalion (600–900 men). They were split into smaller units called *Einsatzkommando*, which were about the size of a company (90–120 men). All in all there were approximately 3,000 men in the *Einsatzgruppen*.

The *Einsatzgruppen* followed closely behind the advancing forces of the invading German army and carried out their missions in the occupied territories. In addition to the *Einsatzgruppen*, there were some units of the Waffen-SS directly under the command of Himmler, which were engaged in the murder of Jews in certain areas. Each German army group – North, Central and South – had a Higher SS and Police Commander (HSSPF) in charge of Waffen-SS forces and *Einsatzgruppen* units, in addition to a regiment and a few independent battalions of the German Order Police in each of the army group's operational areas.

The SS forces were reinforced by tens of thousands of local police (*Schutzformationen*), who served in the police stations and in the mobile police battalions of local collaborators. The local police was composed of Lithuanians, Latvians, Estonians and Ukrainians, among them former Soviet prisoners of war who volunteered for German service. Most of the local forces were subordinate to the German Order Police, some of them to the *Einsatzgruppen*. It took months to establish the local mobile battalions, and as time passed their numbers grew until there were 170 such battalions.[2] All of them, as well as the German army, fought the partisans. Some of them were employed, either directly or indirectly, with persecuting and murdering Jews.

The Stages of Annihilation

The annihilation of the Jews in the occupied territories began the day the Germans invaded the Soviet Union and did not stop until the Germans were expelled. The process can be divided into three stages:

- Stage One, which lasted from June 22, 1941, until the end of the winter: most of the Jews in Lithuania, Latvia, Estonia, Bessarabia and northern Bukovina were murdered, as were almost all of the Jews in eastern Byelorussia, the eastern Ukraine and the occupied territories of the Russian Soviet Socialist Republic.

- Stage Two, which lasted from the spring of 1942 until the end of that year: most of the Jews in the western Ukraine, western Byelorussia and

---

2. In October 1942 there were 4,428 Germans serving in the Reichskommissariat Ostland police and 55,562 local people. In November 1942 there were 10,914 Germans serving in the Reichskommissariat Ukraine and south Russian police force and 70,759 local residents.

the areas of southern Russia conquered by the Germans during the summer of 1942 were murdered.

- Stage Three, which began in 1943 and ended when the Germans were expelled from Soviet territories: the Jews who were still alive in some ghettos and labor or concentration camps were massacred. The final acts of annihilation were carried out close to the German retreat.

STAGE ONE

Einsatzgruppe A operated in Lithuania, Latvia and Estonia. There were initially between 203,000 and 207,000 Jews in occupied Lithuania, of whom 160,000 to 163,000 had been murdered by December 1941. There were about 43,000–44,000 Jews in the ghettos of Vilnius (Vilna), Kaunas (Kovno), Siauliai and Svencionys. Of the 74,000–75,000 Jews in occupied Latvia, only about 6,500 were alive in December 1941, and of them about 4,000 men and a few hundred women were in the Riga ghetto. In Daugavpils (Dvinsk) and Liepaja (Libau) about 2,000 remained alive, all the other Lativian Jews having been killed. In Estonia there were about 1,200–1,500 Jews at the time of the occupation, all of whom were murdered by the end of 1941.

Einsatzgruppe B operated in Byelorussia and to the east in central Russia. During the second half of 1941 they murdered no less than 50,000 Jews, but most of those in western Byelorussia lived through the winter. In eastern Byelorussia, with the exception of Minsk and Slutsk, all the Jews had been massacred by the end of 1941. The Jews of central Russia suffered the same fate, with the exception of Smolensk, where a small ghetto remained.

Einsatzgruppe C operated in the Ukraine. In the Volhynia area of the *Reichskommissariat* Ukraine tens of thousands of Jews were killed, but most of the Jewish population remained alive until the spring of 1942. In the eastern Ukraine most of the Jews had been killed by January 1942, including those living in Kiev and Kharkov.

The mass murders of Jews in Bessarabia and northern Bukovina had already begun during the fighting and immediately after the territories fell into German and Romanian hands. Romanian gendarme and army units, in collaboration with *Einsatzgruppe D* and local residents, killed 150,000 Jews in July and August – about half the number of those living there when the war broke out. In September and October 1941, about 120,000 Jews were deported from Bessarabia and northern Bukovina to Transnistria, the area between the

Dnestr and Bug rivers, which Germany handed over to Romanian rule. By the end of 1941, only 20,000 were left in Chernovtsy in Bukovina.

Before the war, 320,000 Jews had lived in Transnistria, about 200,000 of them in Odessa. An estimated 175,000–180,000 did not manage to flee or be evacuated and remained under the occupation. At the end of the winter of 1941–42 only 25,000 of them remained alive, mixed in with the Jews in the camps and ghettos who had been deported from Bessarabia and Bukovina.

Einsatzgruppe D also operated in the Crimea, and by the spring of 1942 they had murdered 35,000 of the 40,000 Jews living there. The remaining 5,000 Jews were in the besieged city of Sevastopol.

Because of the Wehrmacht's failure to conquer Leningrad, most of *Einsatzgruppe A* remained in Lithuania, Latvia and Estonia. The *Einsatzgruppe*, supported by thousands of local police, continued killing Jews without interference and by December 1941 had murdered more than 80 percent of the Jews in those regions. *Einsatzgruppen B* and *C*, which had rapidly advanced eastward toward Moscow and Kiev, did not have time to annihilate most of the Jewish communities in the western Ukraine and western Byelorussia. About 15–20 percent of the Jews living there had been killed by December 1941, and annihilating the rest was left until 1942. In eastern Byelorussia, the eastern Ukraine and the occupied areas of the Russian Republic, the *Einsatzgruppen*, aided by SS and local police units, murdered almost all of the Jewish population there by the end of 1941.

In the area of the western Ukraine known as eastern Galicia, which had been annexed to the *Generalgouvernement* of Poland, tens of thousands of Jews were killed during the second half of 1941. However, the total annihilation began in the spring of 1942, when the mass murder of Jews took place there.

In the Ostland, in the fall of 1941, the German authorities understood that since Moscow had not been captured and the war would not end before the winter, they had to plan for a drawn-out campaign. It was therefore necessary to organize a work force that would serve and support the war economy. The Wehrmacht command in the Ostland demanded that the *Einsatzgruppen* cease killing Jews who worked in industrial plants and shops that served the army's needs. Thus the Ostland *Reichskommissar* Heinrich Lohse, against the wishes of the SS but supported by the army, decided that for the time being the ghettos that still existed in large cities such as Riga, Vilnius, Kaunas and Minsk, and in some of the smaller ghettos, would remain standing. The temporary cessation of the annihilation in the Ostland gave the Jews remaining there time to organize underground units in preparation for an armed struggle. In the areas controlled by the military government and in *Reichskommissariat* Ukraine, the *Einsatzgruppen* and other SS police units continued with the annihilation of the Jews without interference, despite economic exigencies and the demand for workers.

STAGE TWO

During the first months of 1942 the killings subsided. The main reason was the sub-zero weather conditions, which froze the ground and made it difficult to dig large graves. In the spring of 1942 the mass murders resumed, especially in western Byelorussia and the western Ukraine, where most of the Jews had not been killed during the first onslaught. By the end of 1942, hundreds of thousands of Jews in western Byelorussia and the western Ukraine, among them people able to work, had been killed. The need for labor, which had extended the existence of some of the ghettos, did not prevent the annihilation of Jews in others. That is only one of the contradictions that existed within the German authorities in the occupied territories. Some needed the working Jews and wanted to leave them temporarily alive, while others – especially the SS authorities – continued to carry out the mass extermination without reprieve.

On July 31, 1942, Wilhelm Kube, *Generalkommissar* of Byelorussia, submitted a report to *Reichskommissar* Lohse, which stated:

> In all the clashes with the partisans in Byelorussia it has been proved that Jewry…is the main element of the partisan movement.… In consequence the treatment of the Jews in Byelorussia is a matter of political importance owing to the danger to the whole economy. [The issue] must therefore be solved in accordance with political considerations.… We have liquidated about 55,000 Jews in Byelorussia in the past 10 weeks.… Without contacting me, the Army Rear Area Command liquidated 10,000 Jews.… In the city of Minsk about 2,600 Jews from Germany and 6,000 Russian Jews and Jewesses have remained.… There will then be no further danger of the partisans still being able to rely to any real extent on the Jews.… The sd and I would like it best if the Jews in *Generalbezirk* Byelorussia were finally eliminated.… For the time being the essential requirements of the Wehrmacht, the main employer of Jews, are being taken into consideration.[3]

---

3.   Nuremberg Documents, ps-3428.

This report stressed the contradictions between the civilian administration and the SS in *Generalbezirk* Byelorussia, who wanted to liquidate all the Jews in their region, and the army's demand to temporarily leave the Jews employed by them.

The city of Grodno and its adjacent areas of Byelorussia were part of *Generalbezirk* Bialystok. Between November 1942 and January 1943, 30,000 Jews living there were sent to the Auschwitz and Treblinka death camps.

The second stage of annihilating Jews was carried out primarily by local police commanded by their own or German officers. The Smolensk ghetto, one of the last in the area of military administration, was destroyed and its 2,000 Jews were shot on July 15, 1942. In certain places small labor camps remained with a few dozen or hundred "Jewish experts."

In 1942 the German army conquered areas in southern Russia, the northern Caucasus and Sevastopol in the Crimea, where there were both indigenous Jews and refugees who had fled from the occupied western areas and could get no further east. Between August and November 1942, tens of thousands of the Jews there were killed.

"Operation Reinhard," which began in the spring of 1942, was the code name for the annihilation of the Jews of the *Generalgouvernement*, during which most of the Jews in eastern Galicia (western Ukraine), which was part of the *Generalgouvernement*, were murdered. After the pogroms and killings at the end of June and the beginning of July 1941, 572,000–577,000 Jews remained alive there. In the middle of March 1942, the construction of the death camp at Belzec, located near the train line connecting Lublin and Lvov, was completed, and the Germans began sending Jews there.

Most of the east Galician Jews were killed in the *Aktionen* carried out between the spring of 1942 and the end of the following winter. Those who survived worked as slave laborers for the army or in factories manufacturing goods for the war economy. During that time, about 350,000 Jews were murdered outright, in addition to those who died of hunger, related disease and natural causes. In February 1943 there were about 140,000–150,000 Jews in the ghettos and labor camps, some of them "illegals."[4]

---

4.   Aharon Weiss et al., *Encyclopedia of Jewish Communities: Poland*, vol. 2, *East Galicia* [Hebrew] (Jerusalem: Yad Vashem, 1980), 28.

STAGE THREE

After the defeat at Stalingrad and under pressure from the Red Army, the Germans retreated from the occupied territories, and as they did they began killing the last Jews left in the ghettos and camps. By the summer of 1944, when all the regions of the Soviet Union (with the exception of western Latvia) had been liberated, all the Jews were dead except for those who had managed to hide or had taken to the forests, and those remaining in Transnistria.

After Stalingrad, the Romanian government realized the Germans would not win the war and began looking for ways to contact the Americans and British, hoping to change sides. The Romanians understood that annihilating the Jews would not help them gain their objective, and they therefore changed their policy in relation to Jews. In the spring of 1944, when the Red Army liberated Transnistria, there were about 40,000 of the deported Jews still alive, as well as about 12,000 from the indigenous Jewish population. In March 1944, the Red Army liberated Chernovtsy in Bukovina and rescued 16,000 Jewish residents from death.

The Attitude of the Soviet Government and the Local Population to the Jews

In the occupied territories of the Soviet Union there was no organized rescue of Jews, neither by the anti-German underground nor any other organization. Such support, even if limited in scope, did, however, exist in some western European countries and even in occupied Poland. Most of the non-Jews stood by passively and observed, indifferent to the fate of their Jewish neighbors. There were many reasons for their attitude: rampant anti-Semitism existed in those areas; the Germans terrorized and punished those who helped Jews more severely there than in other parts of Europe; the war, suffering and millions of deaths at the front and behind it led to a certain indifference on the part of the local population regarding the fate of the Jews; people were greedy for the property left behind by the Jewish victims. Nevertheless, there were a few supremely brave individuals, some few thousand throughout the entire occupied territories of the Soviet Union, who were willing to help the Jews at the cost of endangering their own lives and those of their families.

The Soviet government was also indifferent to the fate of its Jewish citizens in the occupied territories. No appeal, either by radio or leaflet, was made to the residents of the occupied territories; no directives were given to the Communist underground or the partisans – by the Soviet government or the Communist Party – to aid Jewish Soviet citizens, despite the fact that Jews were the main victims of the Nazi German annihilation policy. It can be assumed that not even once during the war did the Soviet government discuss the tragic fate of the Jews who remained in the occupied territories, and apparently the government was not in the least troubled. The fate of 75–80 million non-Jewish Soviet citizens in the occupied territories did not bother Stalin and his retinue either.

When the Red Army liberated the occupied territories in 1943–44 they found almost no Jews alive. Of the 2,650,000 Jews estimated to have remained in the occupied territories, around 110,000 survived. More than half of the survivors were in Transnistria, which had been under Romanian control. The remaining survivors, who were scattered throughout the occupied territories, had either found a safe haven with gentiles, managed to hide their identities with forged documents, or hidden in the forests or joined the partisans.

2. THE SOVIET PARTISAN MOVEMENT

The First Stage:
From the Beginning of the War to the Spring of 1942

Soviet partisans were active in the forests of the occupied territories. This partisan activity, including the areas in which it operated and the time of its appearance as a real force, influenced the objectives of Jewish undergrounds in the ghettos, as well as the ability of the Jews who reached the forests to fight the Germans or seek asylum in family camps.

Guerilla warfare had a long history in Russia: groups of peasants had attacked Napoleon's army when he invaded in 1812, and Red guerilla units had attacked the anti-Revolutionary White forces during the 1918–19 Civil War. Until the 1930s there were special organized units in the Soviet Union which, in the event of an enemy invasion and war, were supposed to remain in the occupied territories and fight as guerillas. Their members were trained in special schools to wage guerilla warfare. Their identities remained secret and they were organized into small groups of 15–20, with their own secret stores of arms, communications and other equipment. The organization and training of such units was the responsibility of the Red Army's political authority. Groups of their officers had been sent to Spain during the Spanish Civil War to organize partisan activity in the areas held by Franco's forces. Stalin dismantled the units during the second half of the 1930s when the Soviet military's conception changed; the basic assumption became that if a war broke out, the Red Army would fight it on enemy ground. According to the standing orders given to the Red Army in 1939, "every attack on the Soviet Union will be received with a knock-out blow from our armed forces.... We will conduct an offensive war and relocate it into enemy territory...."[5] Many of the commanders of the guerilla units were executed in the 1937–38 purges, and as a result, when the Germans invaded, no preparations had been made for partisan warfare, and the Soviet government had neither the men nor the means to fight it.[6]

Despite the lack of preparation, the partisan war behind German lines began during the first days of the war. At first it was a matter of small groups of Red Army soldiers who, after their units had been surrounded and defeated, did not manage to retreat and remained in the German rear. Some of them took the initiative and began partisan activities in places where the topography and support of the local population enabled them to do so. Among the first partisans were also Communist activists who had not managed to flee.[7]

Parallel to the local initiatives, on June 29, 1941, the Central Committee of the Communist Party and the government of the Soviet Union issued general instructions to the leadership of the Communist Party and the various government bodies in the republics, stating the following:

> In regions occupied by the enemy, partisan units and groups of saboteurs were to be set up to fight against the enemy and spark the partisan struggle everywhere. Bridges and roads were to be blown up, enemy telephone and telegraph communications were to be disrupted and their stores were to be burned. Conditions were to be made intolerable for the Germans and their collaborators, they were to be chased and killed everywhere, all their activities were to be sabotaged. To carry out such activity the first thing to be done was, by the authority of the Party secretaries in the various counties and districts, to set up

---

5. Werth, *Russia at War*, vol. 1, 106; I. Klimenko, ed., *Voina Narodnaya*, (Smolensk: Moskovskii Rabochyi, 1985), 18.
6. Alexei Popov, NKVD *I Partizanskoie Dvizhenie* (Moscow: Olma, 2003), 25–39.
7. Bystrov et al., eds., *Voina v tylu Vraga* (Moscow: Izdatelstvo Politicheskoi Literatury – Politizdat, 1974), 29; Bystrov et al., eds., *Sovetskie Partizany* (Moscow: Izdatelstvo Politicheskoi Literatury – Politizdat, 1961), 315.

underground cells and places where they could meet in every city and town, in railroad depots and kolkhozes.[8]

On July 3, 1941, in his first speech of the war, Stalin also called upon the civilians in the occupied territories "to blow up bridges and roads, cut telephone and telegraph lines, set forests, stores and camps on fire, create intolerable conditions for the enemy and their collaborators, chase and kill them everywhere, do everything [they could] to hamper the Germans operations...."[9] Following those instructions, Communist Party members in Byelorussia and the Ukraine began organizing groups of activists who would remain behind enemy lines and provide the nucleus for a Communist underground in the cities and for partisan units in the forests. In the areas occupied during the first weeks and months of the war, the Soviet government did not manage to organize such activity, but in the areas further east, occupied only later, they did succeed, although only partially. In those areas, where groups of Party and Komsomol members had been deliberately left behind enemy lines, it was done haphazardly and close to the time of the German occupation.

Organizing an infrastructure for anti-German activity involved choosing individuals who were not known to the local population as Communist activists, so that the Germans could not find and arrest them easily. Before the retreat, hiding places had to be arranged in the cities as well as bases in the forests where weapons, equipment and food could be stored. Such preparations took months, and most of the areas had been conquered before they could be finished. In addition, such preparations would transmit to the soldiers and to the population the possibility of Red Army retreat from the area, and this was strictly forbidden. Whoever raised the possibility that the Red Army might retreat or that the Germans might take over territories was considered a traitor and punished accordingly.[10]

---

8. Klimenko, *Voina Narodnaya*, 53; Popov, NKVD, 15.
9. Stalin, *O Velikoi*, 27.
10. At the end of the 1920s and the beginning of the 1930s, the NKVD made preparations for partisan activity in territories that could be conquered by an enemy and trained special units, providing them with bases, weapons and communications. However, following changes in military conceptions and viewpoint, it was thought that a future war would be fought on enemy soil and the units were disbanded. See Popov, NKVD, 160.

Because of the rapid unfolding of events, until the end of 1941 most of the men who were left in the occupied territories for underground activity had not been sufficiently trained for underground or partisan activity. During the first weeks or months of the occupation, the Germans found, arrested and executed most of them. According to official Soviet sources, "at the beginning of the occupation, a series of organized underground groups was completely destroyed…. They had no experience in underground activity…and during the first clashes hundreds of underground organizations and groups were totally wiped out…."[11]

During the summer, fall and winter of 1941, most of the partisan activity centered around the forests of Smolensk and Bryansk, eastern Byelorussia and the northeastern Ukraine, and its extent was small. In the Baltic states, in western Byelorussia and the western Ukraine, there was almost no partisan activity at all. The soldiers and Communist activists who remained behind the German lines at the time invested most of their efforts in surviving and not falling into German hands. Most of the population in those areas was anti-Soviet and welcomed the German army with open arms, hoping that they would be given a certain measure of national independence, and under such conditions partisan activity could not develop. Soviet sources note that in the western Ukraine "the well-established classes of land-owners and capitalists, the reactionary clergy and other anti-popular elements supported Fascism…."[12]

In the Baltic states the situation was even more difficult because most of the population hated the Soviet regime and regarded it as an alien conqueror, and thus was very sympathetic to the German army. Soviet publications, in an attempt to show that the Lithuanians, Latvians and Estonians resisted the Germans, describe underground and partisan activities in those countries, but they are forced to admit that even their limited activity was suppressed during the first months of the Nazi occupation.[13]

In the territories in Byelorussia and the Ukraine that were part of the pre-1939 Soviet Union, conditions were not yet ripe for broad partisan activity. According to an official Soviet source:

---

11. Bystrov et al., *Voina*, 255–56.
12. Bystrov et al., *Sovetskie Partizany*, 447.
13. P. Shtaras, "*Rol KP Litvy v Organizatsii i Razvitsii Partizanskoi Borby*," in *Gitlerovskaia Okkupatsia v Litve*, ed. O. Kaplanas (Vilnius: Mintis, 1966), 187, 191–92.

> It must be admitted that in many instances the local Communist Party did not fully succeed in implementing the orders of the Central Committee of the Communist Party of Byelorussia to prepare in time for a partisan war.... The time at their disposal was very limited, from a few days to no more than two months.[14]

The situation was similar in most of the territories occupied during the first months of the war. The few partisan units that did manage to organize were defeated in their first encounters with the German army, and according to a Soviet source, "only a few units had the time to establish themselves behind enemy lines and develop active fighting."[15]

Close to the front, on the other hand, there was more intensive partisan activity, coordinated with the various commands of the Soviet armies. The front was thousands of kilometers long and open in certain areas, especially in the forests, and movement through those areas was possible, enabling the regular Soviet forces to maintain contact with the partisan units that were beginning to organize behind German lines.[16] However, in the absence of radio contact between the partisans and the Soviet front, supervision of activity, coordination and information was limited until the spring of 1942.

The statistics concerning partisans operating before the spring of 1942 are sketchy at best. A report dated February 15, 1942, sent by the Central Committee of the Ukrainian Communist Party to the Central Committee of the Soviet Communist Party, stated that "according to partial data, behind enemy lines in the areas temporarily under the German invaders' control, there are 716 active partisan units which have a total of 24,690 fighters...."[17] That number should be regarded fairly skeptically. According to a Soviet source dealing with partisan activity in the area of Smolensk, where conditions for such activity were good (i.e., large areas of forests and a Russian population), the information for the period before 1942 was as follows: "It was a period of germination and creation for the partisan movement.... The partisan units organized themselves into fighting units; many of them suffered from a lack of weapons and ammunition

---

14. Bystrov et al., *Sovetskie Partizany*, 326.
15. Klimenko, *Voina Narodnaya*, 54.
16. Ibid., 64–66.
17. V.I. Iurchuk et al., *Sovetskaya Ukraina v Gody Velikoi Otechestvennoi Voiny*, vol. 1, 360.

and they could not communicate with the Soviet front. Their activities were generally scattered and random."[18]

In addition to the Party bodies working to organize partisan fighting, both the Red Army and the NKVD left and/or sent their own units behind the German front. By July 5, 1941, the NKVD had established a special unit to organize intelligence and sabotage. It both recruited and trained special groups, which had been parachuted or infiltrated through the German lines by the end of the summer of 1941. They were armed and had better communications capabilities than the partisan units, but their activities were haphazard and insufficiently prepared, and most of the groups were destroyed by the Germans.[19]

Partisan Activity Gathers Steam: Spring and Summer, 1942

After the defeat of the German army – which until then had been considered invincible – at the gates of Moscow, the Red Army's winter offensive and the liberation of occupied territories (especially along the German Army Group Center), a turning point occurred in partisan activity. Not only did the new situation raise the partisans' morale, but the local population began to understand that Germany was liable to lose the war and that the Red Army might return. This gradually improved the local populations' attitude toward the partisans. The Soviet victories created practical conditions on the ground that greatly aided the partisans, especially those operating in the regions of Smolensk and Byelorussia. As the Red Army approached the area northeast of Vitebsk, a break of about 40 kilometers (25 miles) was created in the front in the wooded regions around the town of Surazh, which was nicknamed the Surazh Gate (*Surazhskie Vorota*). Many partisan groups passed through, both on foot and in vehicles, bringing large quantities of weapons, and approximately 25,000 draft-age civilians, including Jews, also passed through on their way to the Soviet rear. The Surazh Gate was open from April to September 1942, when the Germans brought in troops to close it.[20]

---

18. Klimenko, *Voina Narodnaya*, 67.
19. Alexei Popov, *Diversanty Stalina* (Moscow: Yauza Eksmo, 2004), 76–77; Popov, NKVD, 160.
20. P. Ponomarenko, *Vsenarodnaya Borba v Tylu Nemetsko-Fashistskikh Zakhvatchikov, 1941–1944* (Moscow: Nauka, 1986), 82; Kirian et al., *Slovar-Spravochnik*, 429. For the passage of Jews through the Surazh Gate, see chapter 5:3, "The Forests of Kozyany and Naroch."

Another important development involved placing all the partisan movements under one command. On May 30, 1942, Stalin decided to set up the Central Staff for the Partisan Movement (Tsentralnyi Shtab Partizanskovo Dvizhenia) in Moscow as part of his Supreme Soviet Command (Stavka). It was headed by Panteleimion Ponomarenko, who had been the first secretary of the Communist Party in Byelorussia.[21] The idea of establishing a central headquarters for the partisans had already been suggested at the beginning of 1942, but Beria, who headed the NKVD and wanted to keep both the information coming from the occupied territories and command of the partisan movement in his own hands, convinced Stalin that there was no need for it. With that in mind, on January 18, 1942, Beria established the 4th Administration at NKVD headquarters to command and coordinate partisan activity.[22] However, it quickly became clear that to strengthen and increase control of the partisan units, heighten discipline, organize support and operate efficiently, a separate central staff would be necessary. For each of the Soviet republics occupied by the Germans (Byelorussia, the Ukraine, Lithuania, etc.), separate staffs were established that were subordinate to the central staff.

One of the most important missions of the central staff was to control the partisan movement, and to that end it set up a radio communications network for the partisans and underground groups behind the German front. Graduates of signal schools were sent behind the German front and operated partisan communications. Creating the network with most of the partisan units was a slow process and lasted until the middle of 1943.[23]

The establishment of a central and subordinate republican headquarters was a turning point in the organization and operation of the partisan movement. Until then the partisan groups had been scattered and lacked a unified central command; they had no contact with the Soviet rear and some units suffered from lax discipline. The partisans, most of them independent units, acting without central guidance, were now organized into military units with a clear operational chain of command. The basic partisan detachment was called an *otryad* and was composed of a few dozen to 200 fighters. The *otryad*s were set up in various places when the partisans first became active. In the spring of 1942, and more intensively after the central staff had been established, three to

---

21.   Ponomarenko, *Vsenarodnaya Borba*, 75.
22.   Popov et al., *Diversanty*, 88–89; Popov, NKVD, 161.
23.   Ponomarenko, *Vsenarodnaya Borba*, 80, 87–89.

five *otryad*s were combined to make a brigade of 400 to 1,000 fighters. There were even a few brigades of up to 2,000 men. The brigades were subordinate to the partisan headquarters of the various Soviet republics.

In March 1942 the German army authorities announced that Byelorussian and Ukrainian former soldiers of the Red Army, privates and sergeants, who had been prisoners of war and released, now had to return to the prisoner-of-war camps. Instead of following orders, thousands of them escaped to the forests and joined the partisans, increasing partisan numbers and adding to the movement's strength.[24]

The Soviet Partisan Movement at Its Height: Late 1942 to Summer 1944

In the fall of 1942, with the increasing strength of the partisan movement, partisan-controlled areas (*partisanskie raiony*) began to be created in the forests and the regions near them. Sometimes they covered thousands of square kilometers and included scores of villages. From time to time the Germans concentrated large forces and invaded the areas, but as soon as they left the partisans took over again. Gradually, beginning with the eastern districts and moving westward, according to the administrative division of the Soviet districts, the district Communist Party committees that had left the areas with the retreating Red Army during the second half of 1941 returned to the German rear. They took command and became the central authority for all the partisan units operating in their districts.[25] Thus the Communist Party increased its supervision of the partisan movement, and to emphasize the fact that they were subordinate to the Party and not the army, the partisan units retained the institution of the commissars even after it was abolished in the Red Army on October 9, 1942. With the increase of the number of partisan brigades, they were organized into a "partisan formation" (*soedinenie*), which included two to three brigades.

In the summer and fall of 1942 in western Byelorussia and the northwestern Ukraine, where the first nuclei of Jewish partisan groups were formed, Soviet partisan activity began to make itself felt, but it became firmly organized only in 1943. Between April 1942 and April 1943 the district committee of the Communist Party arrived in the partisan areas from behind Soviet lines.

24.　Jerzy Turonek, *Bialorus pod Okupacja Niemiecka* (Warsaw: Ksiazka I Wiedza, 1993), 111.

25.　Ibid., 124–27; V.E. Lobanok, ed., *Partiinoe Podpole v Belarusii* (Minsk, 1984), 42.

The turning point in partisan activity in the western Ukraine came in the fall of 1942. Until then, the partisans had been active mainly in the northeastern Ukraine in the Chernigov (Chernihiv) and Sumy districts, east of the Dnieper. Partisan units operating there, especially the brigades led by the legendary partisan heroes Sydor Kovpak and Alexander Saburov, received orders to operate west of the Dnieper and to penetrate into the depths of the German occupied territories. In November 1942, the partisans fought their way to Polesie and northern Volhynia. They were followed by additional units, and beginning in the spring of 1943, partisan activity in the area became stronger. In the summer of 1943, Kovpak's brigade carried out a raid through eastern Galicia toward the Carpathian Mountains.[26]

In the spring and summer of 1943, some partisan activity began in Lithuania with the arrival of two operational groups from the Soviet rear. One was headed by Moteius Shumauskas, whose nom de guerre was Casimir, and the other by a Jew named Genrikas Zimanas, nicknamed Jurgis. Their first bases were in the Kozyany and Naroch forests in western Byelorussia. In September 1943 another base was set up in the Rudniki forests in southeast Lithuania, about 40 kilometers (25 miles) south of Vilnius, near the Byelorussian border. Zimanas set up his staff in the Rudniki forests and from there commanded the activities of the Soviet partisans and the underground organizations throughout southern Lithuania, including Vilnius and Kaunas.[27]

In Latvia there was no real partisan activity. Only in 1943 did it develop, primarily in the southeastern part of the country where a large Russian population lived.[28] A genuine fighting partisan movement never took root in Estonia.

One of the factors bringing thousands of young people to the ranks of the partisans in most of the occupied territories of the Soviet Union was that their alternative was slave labor in Germany. On March 31, 1942, Gottlieb Fritz Sauckel, who was responsible for the work force in Germany, ordered workers from the Baltic states to be rounded up and sent to Germany to work in industry and agriculture. At first they tried to enlist them on a voluntary basis, and when that failed they installed a quota system in every city and village. German reprisals were brutal if the quotas were not filled. Thousands of young people

---

26. Bystrov, *Sovetskie Partizany*, 475–77; Ponomarenko, *Vsenarodnaya Borba*, 119–21.
27. Kaplanas, *Gitlerovskaia*, 222–24.
28. A. Kadikis, ed., *My Obviniaem* (Riga, 1967), 99–107; Levin, *With Their Backs to the Wall*, 202–4; Bystrov, *Sovetskie Partizany*, 608–12.

found refuge in the forests and swelled the ranks of the partisans, motivated not by ideology but rather by the desire not to be sent to Germany.[29]

From the second half of 1942, Soviet planes dropped weapons for the partisans – only occasionally at first, but from 1943 on, quite often. In some of the partisan-controlled areas, landing strips were constructed for planes to bring weapons, fighters and Party activists, and evacuate badly wounded partisans.[30] Presses were set up to print newspapers and leaflets, which were distributed to the local population. Not only did the partisans' strength increase, but morale and relations with the local population improved. They were now considered an integral part of the Red Army, which had begun winning the war. As a result, willingness to collaborate with the Germans waned and more of the local people joined the partisans.

The Soviet partisan movement grew, and according to Soviet data, by the middle of 1942 their numbers had swelled to 65,000. This grew to 105,000 in October, more than 120,000 at the beginning of November 1943, and 250,000 by the beginning of 1944.[31]

Conditions of Life in the Forests: Solving Economic Problems

The first, immediate problem faced by the partisans in the forests was finding food. The local peasants were the only source of food and clothing, but they were generally poor, produced little food and had few domestic animals. In the more eastern areas of the occupied territories, where there had been an orderly evacuation, animals and agricultural produce and equipment had been evacuated as well, and what was left had been destroyed as part of the Soviet scorched-earth policy. After the men of the villages had been drafted, there was no one to work the lands, and what could be produced was barely sufficient for local needs.

In addition, it had been German policy that all the food for the 3–4 million German soldiers fighting on the eastern front would come from the occupied territories of the Soviet Union. The German government imposed quotas on the villages and confiscated most of the agricultural produce and animals.

---

29. Ulrich Herbert, *"Zwangarbeit in Deutschland,"* in *Erobern und Vernichten*, eds. Peter Jahn and Reinhard Rürup (Berlin: Argon, 1991), 106–15; Müller, *Deutsche Besatzungspolitik*, 290–92, 297, 303–7.
30. Ponomarenko, *Vsenarodnaya Borba*, 83–84.
31. Ibid., 132; Bystrov et al., *Voina*, 65.

Terrible penalties were imposed if the quotas were not met, and there were even executions. The peasants did their best to hide what they could, both to be able to feed their own families and to sell some of their produce in the nearest city to buy what they needed.

The partisans took foodstuffs, animals and clothing at gunpoint, searching for them if they thought they had been hidden. There was no other way they could survive in the forests and fight the enemy. Often they ordered the farmers to hitch their horses to wagons and, accompanied by partisans, bring what they had taken to the forests. To keep the farmers from knowing the exact location of the partisan base, they left them at the entrance to the forest and took the horses and wagons to the base, later returning the horses with the empty wagons to their waiting owners. These actions for foodstuff were called by the partisans "economic missions."

Insofar as was possible, the partisans tried not to take provisions from friendly villages, but rather from those that had collaborated with the Germans. As time passed, nothing was left to take from the villages close to the perimeters of the partisan-controlled areas, and they were forced to go further afield, sometimes dozens of kilometers away. They usually went out at night, and the danger was great. German security forces had learned where the partisans moved and ambushed them. When the partisans reached a village, they would post guards on its outskirts and conduct searches inside the houses, barns and stables, looking for caches of hidden food. Such "economic missions" could take many hours. The Germans had collaborators among the peasants who, if the partisans arrived, were to run or ride to the closest police station or military post to report. The partisans often had to fight their way out of ambushes or flee from pursuers while still in the village or on their way back to the forest.

As the numbers of partisans grew they needed more food, but the sources of supply dwindled, not only as a result of the "economic missions" but also because of German activity: the Germans confiscated food but also burned villages near the forests in retaliation for partisan attacks, or for collaboration with the partisans or failure to provide information about them. Villages or peasants suspected of collaborating with the Germans could expect similar retaliation from the partisans. In the summer, when the darkness lasted no more than four or five hours, the way back to the forest had to be undertaken when it was light, with all the attendant dangers of German discovery. In the winter, tracks in the snow could lead the Germans to partisans bringing food and even to the discovery of the bases in the forest. Under such conditions, "economic missions" became military operations accompanied by battles, and larger partisan forces were needed to cope with the dangers of the road.

In areas where the population was hostile to the Soviet partisans (especially in the western Ukraine and in Lithuania) the Germans organized the local peasants and gave them weapons so they could prevent the partisans from taking food. As elements hostile to the partisans, they were their preferred targets for food confiscation. In such places the mere act of entering the village was accompanied by a battle, and the German security forces could be expected to appear within a short time. In areas under partisan control, the partisans helped the local population by working in the fields and harvesting the crops. However, those villages, of which there were many hundreds, were the first to be burned in the German anti-partisan war.

In the forests the partisans built huts dug into the ground to live in called *zemlyanka*. The walls and slanted roofs were made of wooden beams and the roofs were covered with a layer of earth. Inside there were wooden bunks with a narrow aisle between them. Such huts had room for 10–15 partisans. In the winter, a wood-burning stove was placed in the aisle for warmth. A typical base had between seven to 15 such living quarters. There was also a kitchen with a big pot where all the unit's food was prepared. The pot, like the foodstuffs, was taken from a village. At the edge of the base there was usually a stable for the horses. Everything was camouflaged to make it invisible from the air, and the bases were patrolled round the clock. In addition, lookouts were posed on the access roads several kilometers from the bases, lest they be taken unaware by approaching German security forces.

Anti-Soviet publications issued after the collapse of the Soviet Union have described the Soviet partisans in the Great Patriotic War as bands of robbers, especially with regard to their "economic missions." The partisans' anti-German activities have also been accused of being responsible for the destruction of villages and the loss of civilian lives in German retaliation actions. An article entitled "Partisans against the People" (*Partizany protiv Naroda*) quoted a Byelorussian writer as saying that "for every act of terrorism or sabotage [carried out by the partisans], hundreds and even thousands of innocent hostages paid with their lives.… Thousands of Byelorussian villages were destroyed by the Germans only because of partisan provocation," and that "the Red partisans also robbed and terrorized inhabitants in other parts of the Soviet Union under German control."[32] There were also Soviet sources that reflect negatively on some of the partisans and discuss their activities in terms of hooliganism and robbery. One of them quotes a letter sent by Beria to Stalin, Molotov and Ponomarenko on January 23, 1943, in which he discusses information received from his agents who were active in Volhynia. He writes:

> Fighters from the 12th battalion of the Saburov brigade are on the rampage; they get drunk, terrorize and rob friendly civilians, among them those whose families are our fighters. After I intervened, the battalion commander and commissar promised me these anti-Soviet activities would stop, but they take only hesitant action and try to shield those acting like thugs. I am trying again to stop it. I ask that pressure be exerted through Saburov [to stop their actions].[33]

There were Soviet partisan units that did engage in robbery, get drunk and run wild at the expense of the local population, especially before the organized Soviet partisan movement took control in the forests. It is also true that thousands of civilian hostages were killed and hundreds of villages were destroyed in German reprisals for partisan activities. However, the German-Soviet Union war was not a "normal" war; Hitler had said before the invasion that it was "more than an armed struggle. It is a clash between two worldviews.…" It was a war of survival for the Soviet Union, and one of its aspects was the warfare waged by the partisans – a total, uncompromising war in which the civilian population paid a heavy price, both in the occupied territories and behind Soviet lines. The "economic missions" involving confiscation of food and clothing were necessary conditions for partisan fighting.

The Germans versus the Partisans

Hitler's first reaction to Stalin's July 3, 1941, public call for a partisan war behind German lines was satisfaction. In a meeting of the German leadership on July 16, 1941, he said, "The Russians have issued an order for a partisan war behind our lines. Such a war has an advantage. It allows us to destroy whoever rises up

---

32. Alexander C. Gogun, "*Partizany protiv Naroda*," in *Pod Okkupatsiei v 1941–1944*, ed. A. Gogun et al. (Moscow, 2004), 5–6. Gogun is a historian from St. Petersburg whose article praises the activity of the Ukrainian nationalists (UPA) and presents the Soviet partisan activity in a negative light.
33. Ibid., 14.

against us…."[34] Hitler meant that by waging war on the partisans, the Germans could destroy and murder as they saw fit. That, in fact, was what happened: tens of thousands of civilians, and even more than that number of Jews, were murdered under the German slogan of war against the partisans.

The war against the partisans was fought by the security divisions of the German army behind the lines of Army Groups North, Central and South, and by SS forces commanded by Himmler, among them battalions and brigades of the German police force (Ordnungspolizei), Waffen-SS brigades and police battalions of Lithuanian, Latvian, Estonian, Ukrainian and Caucasian collaborators. The German forces used extreme measures, and captured partisans were shot on the spot except when their executions were delayed for purposes of interrogation. Hostages were taken from among the local population, and an order issued to the 30th Corps of the German army in the southern Ukraine on November 26, 1941, stated that "for every German or Romanian soldier killed by partisans, ten hostages are to be executed in close proximity to where the event took place. The bodies of the executed are to be left hanging in place for three days."[35] Local residents were warned that the most drastic steps would be taken against them if they did not provide information about the partisans. On December 7, 1941, 6th Army headquarters reported that "the warning given to the population, that all food would be taken from them and their villages would be burned if they did not inform in time about the location of partisans, was completely successful…and during the [anti-partisan] action, more than a thousand people were publicly hanged or shot by the army.[36]

Within a short time the Germans realized that the forces deployed to fight the partisans were insufficient and that more soldiers were necessary to protect vital targets such as railroad crossings, bridges and bases. It was decided that local auxiliary forces would be organized, whose main function would be to help protect those installations. On December 6, 1941, the 285th Security Division, which had been operating in the eastern Ukraine, instructed the military administration to establish "self-protection" (*Selbstschutz*) units from among the local residents and to arm them.[37]

---

34. Norbert Müller, *Die fasistische Okkupationspolitik in den zeitweilig besetzten Gebieten der Sowjetunion, 1941–1944* (Berlin: Deutscher Verlag der Wissenschaften, 1991), 161.
35. Ibid., 231.
36. Ibid., 237.
37. Ibid., 235–36.

In order to strengthen and coordinate the anti-partisan activities, the security police and the SD set up a special wing called Sonderstab Russia (Special Staff Russia). It collected all the information about partisan bases, commanders and the sizes of the various units, and acted to infiltrate agents into partisan units to kill partisan commanders.[38] On July 31, 1942, Himmler issued an order forbidding the use of the word "partisans," replacing it with "gangs" (banden).[39] Following the increase of partisan activity in the summer of 1942, on August 18, 1942, Hitler issued Order No. 46, entitled "Instructions to strengthen the struggle against the nuisance of the gangs in the east." According to the first paragraph,

> The nuisance of the gangs in the east has become intolerable and threatens supplies to the front and the economic exploitation of the area. It is necessary to destroy the gangs before winter comes and to bring calm to the areas behind the front.... The destruction of the gangs necessitates fierce fighting and the taking of the most extreme steps against those who participate in forming the gangs or who are guilty of supporting them....[40]

The order also placed responsibility for anti-partisan activity in the territories under military administration on the army, and in that of the civil administration, on Himmler and the SS.

One of the Germans' main problems was acquiring intelligence about the partisans. The Germans tried to infiltrate their own agents into partisan units and to that end enlisted local people and Soviet prisoners of war. During 1942 and 1943, 16 centers trained 1,538 such agents.[41] After training, four or five agents were sent at a time to areas in which the partisans were active, representing themselves as prisoners of war who had escaped from the Germans. In other areas the Germans even organized partisan units from their own agents who were supposed to join the Soviet partisan movement units and bring back information. From 1942 on, special NKVD teams operated in most of the partisan

---

38. Popov, *Diversanty*, 115.
39. Hermann Erlinger's trial, *Staatsawaltschaft Karlsruhe*, J2 2138/58, no. 332/25.
40. Müller, *Deutsche Besatzungspolitik*, 130–34.
41. Popov, NKVD, 169.

brigades to fight German agents and hostile elements such as deserters and those who violated discipline.[42]

One of the most important partisan missions was attacking German supply lines, especially the railroad, which was the German army's main artery to the front. To make the tracks and trains easier to protect and harder to mine, in areas of partisan activity it was forbidden to come closer than 100 meters (33 yards) to the tracks, and special crossing points were determined for local residents. Where the tracks ran close to the forests, the trees and bushes near the tracks were cut down, leaving a bare area where no one could hide. Armed posts were set up along every few kilometers of track and soldiers patrolled regularly, especially at night.[43]

The Germans' main tactic against the partisans was combing the forests to find and attack their bases. Before such an operation the Germans concentrated thousands of soldiers, police and auxiliary forces, and then surrounded the area, dividing their forces into two battle formations. One combed the area from two or three different directions and the other blocked the way out. Partisans who tried to evade them were forced into the arms of those blocking the way who were deployed at the edge of the forest. There were also reserve forces that would intervene if a large group of partisans tried to break through the cordon. The Germans issued the following instructions to the forces engaged in anti-partisan operations:

> As the searching force advances, each soldier must keep the others in view.... A battalion of 500 soldiers should form a line no longer than 1,000–1,200 meters to prevent partisans from slipping through.... If visibility is bad, a force used to close off escape is better than having the forces advance toward the center.... At night all the forces, including reserves and night-raid forces, will be on alert at their posts....[44]

---

42. Popov, *Diversanty*, 127–29, 184, 201.
43. Ibid., 125–26.
44. Müller, *Die fasistische*, 428. A document of the 3rd Panzer Army containing lessons learned from the campaign against the partisans.

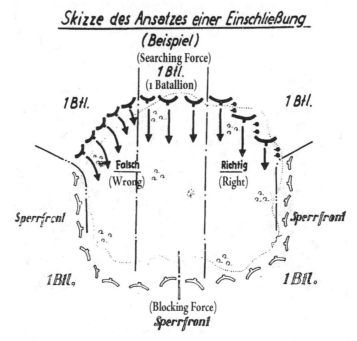

GERMAN ARMY SCHEME FOR A SEARCHING FORCE OPERATION (MODEL)

Partisan strategy was not to engage in battle against the enemy's superior forces. Tactically, the partisans had certain options. When their intelligence discovered German forces organizing a round-up, the preferred tactic was to slip out of the area before it was surrounded, sometimes to forests dozens of kilometers away, and to return when the Germans left. If the partisans were surprised and had already been surrounded, they had two options: one was to try to break out of the encirclement as a group, either through the line of searchers or through those blocking their way, day or night. The other was to divide the partisan unit into teams of three to five men who would try to slip through the encirclement at night. In such cases they would meet in a predetermined part of the forest or village far from the round-up area. Both scenarios cost the partisans losses.

In trying to limit partisan activities, the Germans took hostages from among the local residents. If the partisans attacked, some of the hostages were executed. The Germans also deployed compulsory watch-groups of locals at vulnerable sites and executed them if they did not avert a partisan attack.

With the increase of partisan activity in the spring of 1943, on April 27, 1943, Hitler issued an order noting the military and economic damage they had caused and demanding that the army take more vigorous action against them:

It has been determined that in the army's area of operations (*Operationsgebiet des Heeres*) there are 80,000 active gang members in addition to the many gangs operating in the areas of the civilian administration in the Ukraine and the Ostland. Besides greatly interfering with the movements of trains, they have paralyzed the passage of timber along the rivers. It is therefore absolutely necessary to intensify the struggle against them, especially since we have already deployed a large number of forces to fight them in the area of military operations (about 80,000, of whom 35,000 are German).[45]

Hitler's orders, the activities and round-ups of the German security forces and the terrorizing of the local population were of no avail, and the Soviet partisan movement continued increasing in strength. Instead of deterring the local population, the German reprisals of burning entire villages, mass executions and mass deportations had the opposite effect, and the young peasants joined the partisans. During the first years of the war, most partisan activity took place in the eastern occupied territories, in the districts of Leningrad, Kalinin, Smolensk and Oriel. However, during the second and particularly the third years, after the front had moved westward, most of the partisans were located in the forests of Byelorussia and the northern and northwestern districts of the Ukraine.

It is difficult to estimate the exact number of partisans. Soviet data are exaggerated (one source indicated a million partisans and underground fighters), but their numbers slowly increased, and as the summer of 1944 approached, and with it the liberation, it can safely be said that there were between 250,000 and 300,000 partisans.[46]

The Railroad War (Relsovaya *Voina*)

One of the partisans' main missions was to destroy German supply lines to the front. Because of the enormous distances and bad roads, reinforcements of both men and equipment were brought in by train. In the spring of 1943 the partisan command, in coordination with the Red Army, concluded that in addition to their daily attacks on railroads, it would be effective to concentrate their efforts on the railroad lines to the front where the most important strategic offensive was taking place. Such an action would require thousands of partisans acting

---

45. Ibid., 416.
46. Rzheshevski et al., *Velikaia Otechestvenna Voina*, 351.

simultaneously to blow up sections of track in hundreds of different locations to prevent supplies from reaching the front. The operation was called the Railroad War (Relsovaya *Voina*).

Such a concerted effort had been made once before during a decisive battle in the Kursk-Oriol salient during July and August 1943.[47] An even larger battle in the Railroad War began on June 20 and lasted until July 1944, when the Red Army began its offensive in Byelorussia against Army Group Center, which began on July 23 and lasted until the end of August. In that attack, all of Byelorussia and most of Lithuania were liberated, Army Group Center collapsed and the Red Army reached the borders of eastern Prussia. Tens of thousands of partisans participated, and the entire Byelorussian railroad system ceased functioning until the operation ended.[48] It was the last large-scale partisan operation carried out in the occupied territories of the Soviet Union. By the end of August 1944, the entire Soviet Union, with the exception of western Latvia, had been liberated and returned to Soviet control.

* * *

The German efforts to stop partisan activities failed. The partisan movement grew and its activities increased until the Germans were routed in the summer of 1944. The war was won at the front, but the partisans made a significant contribution. Their activities:

- disrupted and sometimes cut off supply lines to the German forces at the front;

- kept German forces fighting behind their own lines instead of against the Red Army at the front;

- prevented the Germans from exploiting the economic potential of the occupied territories, especially agricultural produce, as had been planned before the invasion;

- lessened the willingness of segments of the local population to collaborate with the occupying authorities – some of them because they feared partisan reprisals, some because they doubted the Germans would be victorious;

---

47. Ponomarenko, *Vsenarodnaya Borba*, 232, 235.
48. Ibid., 257–58.

- raised the morale and provided a tool for Soviet government propaganda among the populations of both the Soviet Union and the occupied territories.

The overwhelming majority of the Jews living in the occupied territories of the Russian Republic, eastern Byelorussia, eastern Ukraine and the Baltic states had been murdered by the second half of 1941, before the partisan movement became active as a real force, and in these circumstances the partisan movement could not have been an encouraging factor for Jewish armed resistance. But in 1942, the most fateful and tragic year for the Jews of western Byelorussia and the western Ukraine, the partisan movement was beginning its activity, and the knowledge that such groups existed in the forest influenced the response and struggle of the Jews in the ghettos. The idea of leaving for the forests to join the partisans was what motivated them and gave them hope when they organized undergrounds in the ghettos.

3. THE UKRAINIAN INSURGENT ARMY (UKRAINSKA POVSTANSKA ARMIA – UPA)

In the forested regions of the western Ukraine, especially in Volhynia, the Ukrainian Insurgent Army was a new, significant factor. The Ukrainian Insurgent Army (Ukrainska Povstanska Armia – UPA) was an arm of the Organization of Ukrainian Nationalists (Orhanizatsia Ukrainskikh Natsionalistiv – OUN). The OUN had been established in Austria in 1929 as an umbrella organization for exiled nationalistic Ukrainian groups, which favored an independent Ukraine made up of the Ukrainian territories that were part of the Soviet Union, Volhynia and eastern Galicia (Polish since the end of the First World War). The OUN, which viewed the Soviet Union and Poland as its chief enemies, was supported by Nazi Germany and supported Nazi anti-Semitism. Their deep-rooted Ukrainian anti-Semitism had an additional dimension in OUN ideology: it viewed the Jews as the main force behind the hated Soviet regime. Publications of leading members of the OUN before the war stressed that "the Russians and the *Zhidi* (Jews) seized the authority in Soviet Ukraine and dominate millions of Ukrainian peasants and workers."[49]

---

49. Alexander Diukov, *Vtorostepennyi Vrag, OUN, UPA I Reshenie Evreiskogo Voprosa* (Moscow: Istoricheskaya Pamyat, 2009), 35–37.

From 1938 on, the OUN was headed by Andrii Melnyk. It operated underground in Poland until the German occupation in September 1939, at which point its actions became overt in the *Generalgouvernement* of Poland. The German *Abwehr* (military intelligence) was the moving factor behind the OUN and helped it set up military units and infiltrate squads of saboteurs into the Soviet Union. The movement split into two factions at its convention in Krakow in 1940. The majority followed Stepan Bandera, whom the Germans had released from a Polish prison, and demanded a more active and independent line. Believing that war between Germany and the Soviet Union was imminent, this group wanted to infiltrate more armed groups into the Soviet Ukraine and to prepare a rebellion that would break out with the onset of the war. The minority faction headed by Melnyk wanted to preserve its forces, keeping them until needed, and to increase coordination and collaboration with the Germans.[50]

In April 1941, at a convention of the Bandera faction of the OUN in the *Generalgouvernement* of Poland, the organization's general objectives and methods of action were determined. Regarding the Jews it was stated: "The Jews of the Soviet Union are the most devoted factor in support of the ruling Bolshevik regime, and are the spearhead of Moscow's imperialism in the Ukraine.... The OUN is at war with the Jews because they support the Moscow-Bolshevik regime...."[51]

When the German forces invaded the Soviet Union there were two Ukrainian battalions with them, Nachtigall and Rolland, and many groups of saboteurs organized by the two factions of the OUN were infiltrated behind the Soviet front. At the end of June 1941, after Lvov had been occupied, the Bandera faction announced the establishment of a Ukrainian government. Sovereignty was not part of the German plans for the Ukraine, and they disbanded the government and sent its members, including Bandera, to prison in Germany. The OUN leadership went underground. Despite the Ukrainian nationalists' disappointment with German policy, tens of thousands of OUN members participated in the German-established administration, joined the police and continued collaborating. At the same time, armed groups of Ukrainians whose aim was to establish an independent Ukraine began organizing in the forests

---

50. Edward Prus, *Atamania UPA* (Warsaw: Instytut Wydawniczny Zwiazkow Zawodowych, 1988), 12–19; Dallin, *German Rule*, 114–16.

51. Ryszard Torzecki, *Polacy I Ukraincy* (Warsaw: Wydawnictwo Naukowe PWN, 1993), 175–76; *Diukov, Vtorostepennyi Vrag*, 47.

of Volhynia. They assumed that during the war the two sides, Germany and the Soviet Union, would weaken each other, and that at the end of the war a strong, independent Ukrainian fighting force organized in the forests would be able to set up its own state.

The first UPA unit was officially established on October 14, 1942, but by then nationalistic Ukrainian groups had been active in the forests for some time, among them the Poliska Sich headed by Maxim Borovets (whose nom de guerre was Taras Bulba). Roman Shukhevych was appointed head of the UPA; his nom de guerre was Chuprinka. He was one of the Nachtigall commanders, and when the police battalion he served in was disbanded in December 1942, Shukhevych and a group of Ukrainian officers fled to the forests and joined the UPA. The UPA had underground connections with thousands of Ukrainians who had served in the German police, and in March 1943, in accordance with a UPA order, about 6,000 of the Ukrainian police in Volhynia escaped with their weapons and joined the UPA units in the forests. In the middle of 1943 UPA units were organized in eastern Galicia and Bukovina as well. In Volhynia, the center of the UPA's power, they took over large areas with townships and villages. At the height of its power, the UPA had some tens of thousands of fighters, but they enjoyed the support of much of the local Ukrainian population. The basic UPA unit was a battalion of between 400 to 800 fighters.[52]

The UPA regarded the Soviet Union as the main obstacle on the path to its national aspirations, especially since the battle of Stalingrad, when it began to be clear that Germany would lose the war and that Soviet rule would return to the Ukraine. The UPA's war was then directed against the Soviet partisans. During 1943 and until the middle of 1944, when the Soviet army liberated the area, there were bloody battles in the forests. The UPA, as the military wing of the OUN, was strongly anti-Semitic. They murdered Jews hiding in the forests and villages, regarding them as a pro-Soviet element. In the available archival documentation, no document was found regarding orders given by the UPA leadership to murder Jews. But anti-Jewish expressions portraying the Jews as a dominant pro-Soviet element in the Ukraine were pervasive throughout the Ukrainian nationalistic legal and illegal press, the OUN and UPA pamphlets and Nazi propaganda. Combined with the virulent anti-Semitism that was already prevalent among many Ukrainians, these images created the understanding

---

52. Torzecki, *Polacy I Ukraincy*, 234–45.

among the UPA fighters that the murder of Jews was the intention of their leadership and served the Ukrainian national aims.

The UPA also considered the Poles as enemies who should be removed from the Ukraine, and they murdered thousands of them as well. The Poles and the Polish underground fought a defensive war against the UPA.

After the German defeat in the battle of Kursk (July 1943), the leadership of the OUN-Bandera faction concluded that Germany was losing the war. They estimated that among the victorious Allied countries – USA and Great Britain on the one side and the Soviet Union on the other side – there existed contradictory opinions concerning the postwar political division of Europe. Therefore, in order for the OUN to gain support from the USA and Great Britain for an independent Ukraine, the OUN decided to change their anti-Jewish and anti-Polish policy. On the Third Extraordinary Convention, which met at an isolated farm in the Ternopol region on August 1943, they decided that the OUN was officially against imperialism, fascism and racism, and would grant equality of rights to all the nations who were living on Ukrainian soil.[53]

Whether this extreme conversion of OUN policy was only for propaganda purposes or had to some extent a more genuine nature, it did not stop members of the UPA from murdering Jews in the forests and villages of the western Ukraine.[54] Perhaps the change in policy did not reach the UPA units, perhaps it was ignored by them or perhaps the units understood the propaganda character of this pseudo-ideological change.

The UPA also clashed with the Germans, especially when the latter tried to take over certain areas where the UPA had control. However, as the Red Army approached in July 1944, an agreement was signed between the UPA and the Germans, who had supplied them with weapons, ammunition and other military equipment, according to which the UPA would continue fighting behind the Soviet front.[55]

Several hundred Jewish professionals, doctors, nurses, tailors and shoemakers, who had hidden in the forests and villages, ended up with UPA units. Many were brought against their will by UPA units that had need of them, while

---

53. Diukov, *Vtorostepennyi Vrag*, 98–99.
54. For more on the murder of Jews by the UPA, see chapter 5:7, "The Volhynia Forests."
55. After the Germans retreated and Soviet rule returned to the western Ukraine, the UPA began a guerilla war against the Soviets and later against the Polish government in the Lublin regions. It lasted for a few years, and only in 1948 was the UPA finally defeated and Shukhevych killed.

others came voluntarily, hoping for refuge. Most of them were murdered by the UPA on the eve of the Soviet liberation of the area.[56]

4. THE POLISH HOME ARMY (ARMIA KRAJOWA – AK)

Partisan units belonging to the Polish Home Army (Armia Krajowa – AK) operated in the forests of the Grodno-Novogrudok-Bialystok areas of western Byelorussia and in the Vilnius district. The AK was the Polish underground's military wing, subordinate to the Polish government-in-exile in London. That government had not accepted the annexation of western Byelorussia and the western Ukraine to the Soviet Union and viewed both as belonging to Poland, leading to bitter differences of opinion between the two governments. After the exposure of the murder of thousands of Polish officers at Katyn in April 1943, for which the Germans blamed the Soviet Union (which proved to be the truth), diplomatic relations were severed between the Polish government-in-exile and the Soviet Union. That intensified the struggle between the Soviet partisans and the AK units. The activities of Polish partisan units in western Byelorussia emphasized the area's belonging to the Poland that would rise after Germany's defeat.

By the second half of 1942, small groups of AK fighters had begun operating in those areas, but the extent of their operations increased dramatically between the fall of 1943 and the spring of 1944, when the organization had 7,400–8,000 fighters in the Novogrudok district and double that number in organized reserves in underground cells.[57] Their most important bases were in the forests and villages on the banks of the Neman River, where there was a large Polish population. The Soviet partisan movement regarded the AK as a hostile movement to be fought against. During the second half of 1943, Soviet partisan units were transferred from eastern to western Byelorussia as reinforcements against the AK.[58]

---

56. Shmuel Spector, *The Holocaust of Volhynian Jews, 1941–1944*, trans. Jerzy Michalowicz (Jerusalem: Yad Vashem, 1990), 271–73; Eliyahu Yones, *Smoke in the Sand: The Jews of Lvov in the War, 1939–1944* [Hebrew] (Jerusalem: Yad Vashem, 2001), 242–43.

57. Zygmunt Boradyn, *Niemen Rzeka Niezgody* (Warsaw: Oficyna Wydawnicza Rytm, 1999), 37–41.

58. Turonek, *Bialorus*, 120–22.

At the end of October 1943, as the Red Army approached the pre-1939 Polish border, the Polish government-in-exile decided to reinforce its partisan units fighting in western Byelorussia and Volhynia and to expand their activities. Its objective was to take over broad areas and to present the approaching Soviet Army with the region already under Polish control. The operation was called *Buzha* (Storm). The government-in-exile gave the AK units the following order:

> Clashes with Soviet partisan units should be avoided. As far as the regular Red Army units are concerned, when they arrive, the Polish commander, after having fought off the retreating Germans, is to appear openly before them and present himself as in charge of the area. With regard to the wishes of the Soviet army commanders, it should be stressed that the legal authorities are Polish and not Russian, and the nature and extent of Soviet activities should for the Polish citizens be determined by the legal Polish authority.[59]

The order to avoid clashes with the Soviet partisans notwithstanding, the situation on the ground was quite different. The increase in AK activity in western Byelorussia led to more intense fighting between them and the Soviet partisans, whose intention was to prevent the Poles from taking over the territory. The result was mutual slaughter.

At the end of 1943, the German authorities (including security police and military intelligence operatives) in the regions of Vilnius and Novogrudok decided that to toughen the fight against the Soviet partisans, they had to reach an agreement with the AK units and support them with weapons, ammunition and other equipment, and prevent clashes between the German security forces and the AK. The AK commanders in western Byelorussia (Novogrudok-Baranovichi) were Adolf Pilch and Yosef Swida. They regarded both the Red Army approaching the borders of Poland and the Soviet partisans as enemies more dangerous than the retreating Germans, and accepted the German offers, reaching an agreement with them in December 1943. In March 1944, a similar agreement was reached with Alexander Krzyzanowski, the AK commander for the Vilnius district. The agreements, which were kept secret, were made by local AK commanders who had fought against the Soviet partisans and did not have authorization from the supreme AK command in Poland or from the Polish government-in-exile. In certain areas of the Novogrudok district, the

---

59. Bor-Komorowski, *Armia Podziemna*, 174.

German security forces were evacuated. Once the AK units had charge of the area they were able to enlist local Poles and Byelorussians into their ranks.[60]

The AK-German agreements were tactical, military and local, with no political dimension regarding German-Polish relations. Despite the agreements and the weapons received from the Germans, the AK did not overcome the Soviet partisans, and the latter remained the dominant presence in the overwhelming majority of the forests in western Byelorussia. The AK viewed the Jews as a pro-Soviet element and did not accept them into their ranks, murdering many of those hiding in the forests and villages.[61]

60. Boradyn, *Niemen*, 173–81, 206; Zdzislaw A. Siemaszko, *Wilenska AK a Niemcy: Zeszyty Historyczne* (Paris, 1994), 198–222: Turonek, *Bialorus*, 202–7.
61. For the AK's attitude toward Jews, see chapter 5 on Jewish partisans.

Chapter Four:
The Armed Jewish Underground

1. The Conditions Leading to the Organization of the Underground

The Jewish armed underground organized in the ghettos in the occupied territories of the Soviet Union had no parallel in any other Jewish community in Nazi-occupied Europe. It was unique in its size, with thousands of members organized across an extensive geographic distribution. It staged uprisings in dozens of ghettos and succeeded in enabling tens of thousands of Jews to flee to the forests and fight as partisans. The idea of armed resistance had emerged when the ghetto inhabitants became aware of the mass murders of the Jews being carried out around them. The undergrounds' main source of motivation was the realization that Nazi Germany had sentenced the Jews to total annihilation, and that the enemy had to be fought despite its overwhelming numerical and military superiority. The Jews knew they could not prevail, but if in any case they had been sentenced to death it was better to die fighting than by being deported to gas chambers or shot on the edge of an open pit. In addition, there was the hope that an uprising in the ghetto could enable some of them to break away to the forests, which would offer them a slim chance of survival – a hope that at least partially proved itself.

The complete isolation of the Jews in the ghettos and the lack of communication between one ghetto and another formed the character of the Jewish underground movements. It was not a central hierarchic movement, but a series of underground organizations acting independently and under conditions unique to each.

Many factors influenced the organizing of the fighting undergrounds, but the main ones were the following:

- the timing of the extermination *Aktionen*;
- awareness of the Germans' policy toward the Jews, and the point at which they understood they were facing total annihilation;
- the existence of individuals initiating and leading the organizing;
- the possibility of acquiring weapons;
- the proximity of the forests and the partisans, and their attitude toward the Jews.

Since conditions differed from region to region and ghetto to ghetto, the organization and activities of the undergrounds in the various ghettos must be dealt with in particular, before general conclusions be drawn. Underground activity, the search for a plan of action and attempts to organize for armed resistance existed in many ghettos, in the labor camps and at various killing sites. This chapter, however, deals with prominent examples taken from a wide geographical range. It also deals with the actions of Jewish individuals in the non-Jewish Soviet underground. Since the events occurring in each ghetto profoundly influenced the organization and activities of the fighting undergrounds, a summary of those events is given here.

2. THE MINSK GHETTO UNDERGROUND

The Holocaust in Minsk

On June 28, 1941, Minsk, the capital of Byelorussia, was occupied by the Germans, and on July 3 and 4 *Einsatzgruppe B* units arrived. A few days later the city's *Feldcommandant* issued an order that all men aged 18 to 45, regardless of nationality, were to present themselves. They were taken to Drozdy, outside the city, where a camp had been set up in an open field and already held tens of thousands of prisoners of war. It is estimated that at least one quarter of the 40,000 civilian men held there were Jewish.[1] The *Sonderkommando* and members of the German military secret police (GFP) searched the camp for Communist activists and Jews. Shortly after the men were brought to Drozdy, the civilians were separated from the prisoners of war and the Jews from the non-Jews.

Thousands of the Jewish men were murdered in Drozdy; some were released and some were taken to the prison in Minsk and put to work at various tasks. On July 19, 1941, the order was given to establish a ghetto in Minsk, and six days later, 70,000–75,000 Jews, among them those from towns near Minsk and refugees from western Byelorussia, were imprisoned in it. The Germans set up a *Judenrat* and appointed Eliahu Mushkin to head it. Ziama Serebryansky was appointed chief of the ghetto police.

---

1. Jews made up about 30 percent of the Minsk population. Assuming that the number of Jewish men who were evacuated or fled the city was higher than those who were not Jewish, the number of Jewish men in Drozdy was probably no more than about 25 percent.

The *Aktionen* were carried out without respite. On November 7 (the anniversary of the October Revolution) and November 20, a total of about 19,000 Jews were shot in the village of Tuchinka, close to the city. In the Minsk ghetto there remained 49,000–56,000 Jews (7,000 of whom had been brought from the Reich). Throughout the winter the Germans continued killing small groups of Jews. On March 2, 1942, 5,000 more Jews were murdered. The largest *Aktion* carried out in the Minsk ghetto lasted from July 28 to July 31, 1942, during which 25,000–26,000 local Jews and 3,500 German Jews were killed in Maly-Trostinets and Petreshevichi. About 12,000 Jews were left in the ghetto, and their numbers dwindled as they were murdered or starved to death.

At the beginning of 1943 there were an estimated 9,000 inhabitants in the Minsk ghetto. The *Judenrat* was dissolved and an administration was set up chaired by a man named Epstein who, unlike previous heads, had collaborated with the Germans. In September 1943 the final destruction of the ghetto began. About 2,000–3,000 men were sent by train to the *Generalgouvernement* in Poland, the overwhelming majority of whom were taken to the death camp at Sobibor and murdered.[2] The final *Aktion* was carried out on October 21, 1943, at which time the last 2–3 thousand Jews were taken to Maly-Trostinets and murdered. The Germans left about 500 Jews of various occupations, some of whom burned the bodies at Trostinets. They were killed on the eve of Minsk's liberation, July 3, 1944.

The Establishment of the Underground

During the first months of the German occupation, a few groups of Jewish Communists organized in the Minsk ghetto. They discussed how to react to the German occupation and the murder of Jews. One of the groups was led by Hersh Smolar, a refugee who in the past had been an activist in the outlawed Communist Party in Poland. Another group was led by an old Party member named Nahum Feldman, who had fought as a partisan with the Red Army during the October 1917 Revolution. In October 1941, Smolar and Feldman met and decided to join forces and form a fighting underground whose main objective would be to get ghetto inmates to the forests, where they would engage in partisan warfare. They also decided to set up an underground press and print leaflets calling upon the population of Minsk, Jewish and non-Jewish alike, to

---

2. Testimony of Rachel Milchin, yva, 03/9020.

resist the German occupation. It was the first Jewish underground organization in Europe whose objective was to fight the Nazis with arms.

Before establishing their organization, however, they debated whether they had the right to form an underground Communist organization without instructions and authorization from the Central Committee of the Communist Party, which was somewhere behind the Soviet front lines. It was Feldman who asked the question, afraid the central committee might view their independent initiative as a separatist action. Smolar wrote that during his first meeting with Feldman, the latter said to him: "What do you mean, to set up an organization? Who gave you permission to do so? Who ordered you to organize?" Feldman explained that he and his comrades were not a formal organization, only a group of friends who had spoken about leaving for the forests and fighting as partisans, as he had in 1919 and 1920, and for that they did not need the permission of the upper echelons of the Party. Smolar wrote that in another meeting with Feldman, he told him that his organization had connections with "the other side," and Feldman understood that he had permission "from above" to organize.[3] The question of authority and initiative from "above" and Feldman's fear of how Soviet authorities would view them after the liberation were the product of the education and indoctrination of a society in which the Communist Party was the exclusive authority for initiative in every area, and it alone had the right to decide and authorize an action.

The Minsk ghetto underground did not view their organization as an independent Jewish activity, but rather as a part of the overall Communist activity behind German lines. Unlike underground organizations in other ghettos, the Minsk underground did not consider the idea of remaining in the ghetto and organizing a Jewish national uprising. Their plan was to escape to the forests, join Soviet partisans and embark on guerrilla warfare as Soviet citizens. As Red Army soldiers whose units had been dispersed were already engaged in

---

3.   Hersh Smolar, *Soviet Jews behind the Ghetto Barrier* [Hebrew] (Tel Aviv: Tel Aviv University, 1984), 46–54. Regarding Smolar's statement that he had connections with "the other side," see further in this chapter concerning his meeting with Shedletsky, a messenger from a partisan group, in September 1941; Shalom Cholawski, *In the Eye of the Hurricane* [Hebrew] (Tel Aviv: Hebrew University of Jerusalem and Moreshet, 1988), 140–41; memoirs of underground member Rosa Lipska, YVA, 033/2687; memoirs of underground member Sylva Gebelev-Ustashinska, YVA, 033/2688.

partisan warfare in the forests surrounding Minsk, escaping to the forests to join these partisans was a realistic plan.

According to Smolar, Stalin's call on July 3, 1941, to wage a partisan war behind German lines encouraged and influenced the ghetto underground's decision to fight the Germans.[4] The *Judenrat* and the ghetto police chief supported the underground. The *Judenrat* provided the underground members with work in the ghetto and documents, as well as information received from the German authorities. Smolar tended the boiler in the basement of the ghetto hospital and from there directed underground activities. When they began sending groups out to the forest, the *Judenrat* supplied them with food and clothing. Underground members forged work papers, Aryan birth certificates and other documents.

Contact between Smolar and a partisan group that began forming in the forests was made already in September 1941 when a messenger came to the ghetto from the forest – a Jew named Fedya Shedletsky. He met Mushkin, the chairman of the *Judenrat*, at Mushkin's home and told him that he had been sent by the partisan commander Captain Bistrov, who demanded that the *Judenrat* supply the partisans with warm clothing and medicines. Shedletsky warned Mushkin that if he betrayed them, the partisans would execute him.[5] After discussing the matter with Serebryansky, Mushkin agreed to the demand. Through Mushkin and Serebryansky, contact was made between Smolar and Shedletsky and later with the partisans in the forests.[6]

The combination of Smolar's experience in Communist underground activity in prewar Poland and his familiarity with the prevailing conditions of the local Jewish Communists in Minsk, who had no previous underground experience, gave impetus to underground activity in the ghetto. The underground's core was a group of members called "The Ten." During the first months, 12 such

---

4. YVA, 033/2689. Smolar prepared a report about the ghetto underground in July and August 1944, a few weeks after the Minsk region was liberated by the Red Army, submitted to the Central Committee of the Communist Party of Byelorussia. Smolar mentioned Stalin's speech as encouraging them to organize to fight the German invader. For Stalin's speech see chapter 3:2, "The First Stage: From the Beginning of the War to the Spring of 1942."

5. YVA, M41/49, testimony of F. Shedletsky, from Dan Zhits, "The History of the Minsk Ghetto in Light of the New Documentation," [Hebrew] (master's thesis, Bar Ilan University, 1999), 47.

6. Smolar, *Soviet Jews*, 84–85.

"Tens" were set up. At the height of its activity, the Minsk ghetto underground numbered around 450 members. Many of them were murdered in the *Aktionen* of November 1941 and March and July 1942, but new members replaced them. Those who worked at the Krasny Urochishche warehouses, where captured Soviet arms were stored, removed rifles and other weapons and smuggled them into the ghetto. Weapons hidden by Red Army soldiers before they were captured by the Germans were uncovered by the Jewish underground and also brought to the ghetto. The underground operated a radio and relayed the news received from Radio Moscow throughout the ghetto.[7]

ISAI KAZINETS

In late November 1941 the ghetto underground made contact with a non-Jewish Communist underground group in Minsk, headed by an engineer and reserve army officer named Isai Kazinets, a Jew who was passing as a Tatar. His underground name was Slavik. The group's main activities were setting up partisan bases in the forests, sabotaging urban installations and disseminating anti-German propaganda. During a meeting with Smolar, Kazinets asked who had given the ghetto underground the authorization to organize and define its objectives. It was essentially the same question Feldman had asked, a manifestation of the fear of Moscow's reaction to organizations not sanctioned by the Communist Party leadership; Kazinets's question was also prompted by the possibility that prior to the German occupation Soviet authorities had left an underground Communist committee in Minsk. Kazinets stated that for the latter reason the leadership of his underground was called the Reserve Committee (Reservnyi Komitet) – just in case a Communist committee might be found which had been left in place before the retreat. The ghetto underground agreed to become part of the urban underground and subordinate to its leadership, and its main request and expectation was help in getting men into the forests.[8]

---

7. Cholawski, *In the Eye*, 141–42, 145, 150; Smolar, *Soviet Jews*, 95–96; memoirs of underground member Ahron Piterson, YVA, 033/2690.

8. It should be noted that despite Kazinets's apprehension, after the war his Reserve Committee was recognized by the Central Committee of the Communist Party of Byelorussia as the official urban underground committee, and he was posthumously awarded the title of Hero of the Soviet Union.

In the wake of the agreement the ghetto's print shop was transferred to the urban underground and propaganda leaflets were printed and distributed. The urban underground was also in contact with members of the *Judenrat*, including Chairman Mushkin, and the ghetto police commander, Serebryansky, from whom they received support.[9]

At the same time, an underground group of Red Army officers who had remained in Minsk were forming their own organization. Known as the Military Council, they were in contact with the urban underground but retained their independence and focused primarily on getting people into the forests. However, they rejected the ghetto's appeal to help Jews into the forests for purely anti-Semitic reasons: in the first place, "their Jewish appearance" would harm the partisans; and second, Jews did not know how to use weapons or fight. As a result, the ghetto underground severed ties with the Military Council. At the end of February and beginning of March 1942, the Germans uncovered the Military Council. In the course of interrogating them, the Germans discovered the existence of the urban underground, and arrested and shot hundreds of its members. Kazinets was arrested on March 27, and according to one source, he shot at and wounded some of the German security police.[10] After interrogation and torture, which he withstood in heroic fashion, revealing nothing, he was hanged in the Minsk central square on May 7, 1942, along with 27 of his comrades.

The interrogation of the urban underground revealed the existence of the ghetto underground and of the cooperation between the urban underground and ghetto *Judenrat*, among them Mushkin and Serebryansky. Both were arrested and executed, as were others, and the Germans demanded that the *Judenrat* hand over Smolar and other underground leaders. The latter were forced to go into hiding in the ghetto, which they did with the help of the new *Judenrat* chairman, Moshe Jaffe, who was appointed to replace Mushkin.[11]

The *Einsatzgruppe* report dated April 3, 1942, described the exposure of the Minsk underground and noted that

> A Georgian Jew, Mustafa Delikurdgly, who runs the Party apparatus, was arrested.… An illegal group of 60 ghetto Jews…bought weapons and constantly augmented the ranks of the partisans. Sixty to 80 Jews

9. Smolar, *Soviet Jews*, 55–56, 86, 88–89; Cholawski, *In the Eye*, 145–46; YVA, 033/2690, p. 5.
10. Sverdlov, *V Stroiu Otvazhnykh*, 125–26.
11. Smolar, *Soviet Jews*, 117–22; Cholawski, *In the Eye*, 152–55.

joined the partisans. From the apartment of the Jew Delikurdgly a number of weapons, bandages and medicines were confiscated, as well as a functioning printing press and eight typewriters.[12]

And an *Einsatzgruppe* report dated May 8, 1942, stated that

> In August/September 1941, a Jew tried to organize and unite these Communist groups. He was the oil engineer Isai Kazinets, who assumed the name Mustafa Delikurdgly and possessed false papers in that name. Although he was a reserve officer, he was not called up when the war broke out.... Kazinets was the leader of the [Communist] committee and was in charge of matters concerning the ghetto. His job was to maintain connections with the Jews in Minsk, to recruit for the partisans, to collect clothing and to see to it that the ranks of the partisans were kept full.... About 100 Jews were led to the partisans from the ghetto.... The printing workshop was in a dwelling near the ghetto and was managed by a Jew named Chipchin, who lived outside the ghetto.... Currently the partisan movement is mainly financed by donations from the ghetto. Investigations have revealed that practically the entire ghetto was organized and divided into units and sub-units. Investigations in this direction have been restricted for the time being since the plans to dissolve the ghetto there are at an advanced stage.... So far, a total of 404 people have been arrested, including the partisans who were organized in the ghetto. Of these, 212 have already been shot. A large quantity of weapons and ammunition has been seized.[13]

Even before the urban underground was broken up and its members arrested, and after the *Aktion* on March 2, 1942, on its own initiative the ghetto underground sent three groups of its members to the forests south of Minsk to set up partisan bases. Other groups left as well, although they did not belong to the underground.[14]

---

12. Yitzhak Arad et al., eds., *Einsatzgruppen Reports* (New York: Holocaust Library, 1989), 324.
13. Ibid., 339–41.
14. Smolar, *Soviet Jews*, 115, 128, 131; Cholawski, *In the Eye*, 148–49, 151. For further information about ghetto underground members who left for the forests and how they organized there, see chapter 5.

The activities of the ghetto underground were seriously hampered after the urban Communist underground members had been arrested and revealed information about it to the Sipo (Sicherheitspolizei, the security police). The Germans knew their addresses and where their secret hiding places (*malinas*) were. The Germans would enter the ghetto, usually at night, and using specific information would surround buildings and shoot the underground members and anyone else they found inside the building. Under such conditions, Smolar and others in hiding decided to move their activities to the forests as soon as possible. The wide-scale *Aktion* at the end of July 1942, in which the overwhelming majority of the ghetto inmates were murdered, also catalyzed the move out of the ghetto. The July *Aktion* was part of the wave of *Aktionen* carried out by the Germans in *Generalkommissariat* Byelorussia in the summer of 1942. However, it can be assumed that the exact timing of the *Aktion* was the result of the prominent involvement of Jews in the underground activity and the escape to the forests, which was discovered by the Germans in their interrogation of the urban and ghetto undergrounds.

Even after the July *Aktion* and after Smolar had left for the forests, those underground members who still remained in the ghetto were active, and contacts with the partisans continued. Small groups fled the ghetto to join the partisan units even in the spring and summer of 1943. One such escape was unique: A group of ghetto women, some of them deported from Germany, worked at a German air force unit. A German captain named Schultz fell in love with Ilsa Shtein from Frankfurt. To rescue her he contacted the ghetto underground, and on March 30, 1943, he entered the ghetto with a truck, loaded 30 people, including Ilsa Shtein, and on the same day reached a partisan base near Rudensk, southeast of Minsk.[15]

Underground members also continued to carry out sabotage at workplaces. A woman underground member wrote:

> Despite [the German] terror we continued our acts of sabotage. Nadia Shuster and a small group of women worked in the Bolshevik Factory. They damaged leather and parachutes and stole warm clothing for the partisans.... There was a group that managed to get work in

---

15. Zhits, "History of the Minsk Ghetto," 73. Zhits mentions testimonies of M. Tokarsky and D. Travnik, who were among the 30 people taken in Schultz's truck. A film called *Die Judin und der Hauptmann* [The Jewess and the captain] was produced in Germany in 1995.

a German army communications installation where they sabotaged technical equipment and took out arms. Some of their actions were unsuccessful and our people were killed.... We received an order to contact prisoners in the prisoner-of-war camp on Shirokaya Street, which continued organizing escapes.[16]

There are no exact data relating to the number of Jews the underground succeeded in sending to the forests, neither those who joined the partisan units nor the non-combatant population organized in family camps. Besides men who left in organized fashion through the auspices of the underground, at least several hundred Jews fled for the forests, individually or in groups. The total number, according to estimates, was about 4,000–5,000, more than from any other ghetto.[17]

3. THE VILNIUS GHETTO UNDERGROUND

The Holocaust in Vilnius

Vilnius, with its 57,000 Jews, was occupied on June 24, 1941. The *Aktionen* began during the first days of July and continued until December, by which time most of the Jews in the city had been murdered. The killings took place at Ponary (Panerai), about 12 kilometers (7.5 miles) from the city. The ghetto was established on September 6, 1941.

Anatol Fried was appointed head of the *Judenrat* and Jacob Gens was appointed chief of police. At the beginning of January 1942, about 13,000 "legal" Jews – workers in various factories and services and their families – were left in the ghetto, and about 7,000 more "illegal" Jews lived there and hid during the *Aktionen*. The period between January 1942 and the spring of 1943 was relatively quiet, and mass murder *Aktionen* were not carried out. In the spring of 1942 the Germans replaced Fried with Gens as head of the *Judenrat*, giving him the title of "ghetto governor." During that time, the ideology prevailing among the ghetto Jews and preached by the *Judenrat* was that since the ghetto's

---

16. Sofia Sadovskaya, "Sparks in the Night," in *Minsk, Jewish Metropolis: A Memorial Anthology* [Hebrew], ed. Shlomo Even-Shoshan, vol. 2 (Jerusalem, 1985), 354–55.

17. Smolar (*Soviet Jews*, 209) writes that close to 10,000 Jews from Minsk were in the forests, according to a census he and some other Jewish partisans made immediately after they entered the liberated Minsk. This number is exaggerated.

work served the German war economy, there was hope, at least temporarily, that the ghetto and its inhabitants would continue to exist.

On April 4, 1943, about 4,000 Jews from the ghettos of Oshmany, Svencionys, Mikhalishki and Svir in the eastern part of *Generalkommissariat* Lithuania were brought to Ponary and murdered there. At the end of June 1943 and throughout July, labor camps around Vilnius were also liquidated. Some of the camp inmates were murdered outright and some were sent to the Vilnius ghetto. The ghettos in eastern Lithuania and in the labor camps around Vilnius were destroyed as part of the Nazi-German anti-Jewish policy, but their execution occurred when it did as an attempt to prevent more Jews from escaping to the forests and joining the partisans.[18] On June 21 Himmler issued the following order: "All Jews still remaining in ghettos in the Ostland are to be closed in concentration camps.... Inmates of the Jewish ghettos who are not required are to be evacuated to the east."[19] The order was intended to temporarily extend the lives of those who were fit to work, while all the others were doomed for immediate extermination.

Himmler's order was issued a few weeks after the suppression of the Warsaw ghetto uprising, which may have taught Himmler and the SS that in closed concentration camps, where inmates were isolated from the world and supervision was far stricter, it was more difficult to rebel. It seems that the worsening military situation at the front close to the Ostland and the partial breach of the Leningrad blockade by the Red Army also influenced Himmler's decision to issue the order.

On August 1 and 23, 1943, 2,500 Jews were deported from the Vilnius ghetto to labor camps in Estonia. The number was not sufficient and the Germans surrounded the ghetto on September 1, demanding that the *Judenrat* turn over 5,000 men for Estonia. Between September 1–4, Gens and the ghetto police managed to round up 4,000 people, half of them women, for deportation to Estonia, leaving 11,000–12,000 Jews in the ghetto. The Vilnius ghetto was liquidated on September 23 and 24. About 3,000 of the inhabitants were sent to labor camps within the city, men and women of working age were sent to the camps in Estonia and Latvia, and the rest were murdered. On July 2–3, ten

---

18.   Yitzhak Arad, *Ghetto in Flames* (Jerusalem: Yad Vashem, and New York: Anti-Defamation League, 1980), 357–72.

19.   Nuremberg documents, NO-2403.

days before the liberation, the last Jews in the city camps were shot. On July 14, 1944, the Red Army liberated Vilnius.[20]

The Concept of Armed Resistance Crystallizes

The founders of the underground in the Vilnius ghetto belonged to Zionist youth movements which, during the Soviet rule in Vilnius (June 1940 to June 1941), were organized in underground circles, as well as Bund members and Jewish Communists who remained in the city after the German occupation. Until the end of 1941, their main activity consisted of saving their members from *Aktionen*. Facing the reality of extermination, they concluded that the Jewish response to the mass murders should be armed resistance. Mass murders in Vilnius and other Lithuanian towns and villages made some of the Zionist youth movement leaders debate whether the *Aktionen* they witnessed targeted only the Jews of Lithuania (as most of their perpetrators were Lithuanians), or whether they were part of an overall German policy to annihilate the Jews everywhere. The background of this dispute was the information that reached them from Byelorussia and Warsaw in the late summer of 1941, according to which no mass murders of Jews were being carried out there.

The first contact from Warsaw came via a Pole named Henrik Grabovski, who in late September 1941 was sent by the Polish underground, the Armia Krajowa, to contact Polish underground circles in Vilnius. He brought messages from Zionist youth movements in Warsaw describing the situation there, where Jews were closed in a ghetto and suffered from hunger, but where there were no mass murders, and where the Zionist youth movements continued clandestine educational and political activity. The information sharpened the dispute within the underground groups. There were those who argued that it would be better to transfer the members of the Zionist youth groups to Warsaw, where conditions for armed underground activity would be better. On the other hand, there were those who argued that the mass murder of Jews would not be limited to Lithuania but would spread eventually to Warsaw and other territories occupied by the Germans. Therefore, there was no reason to leave Vilnius and that it would be better to remain, organize and fight.[21]

During October and December 1941, emissaries from the Zionist youth movements left Vilnius for the Grodno, Bialystok and Warsaw ghettos to exam-

---

20. Arad, *Ghetto in Flames*, 410, 432.
21. Ibid., 226–30.

ine the situation there, and brought there news of the mass murders in Lithuania. During the fall of 1941, more messengers came to Vilnius from Warsaw, and they established underground connections between them, creating the term "ghetto messengers." Most of them were young women who looked "Aryan," making it easier for them to carry out dangerous missions. The news they brought of the relative quiet (at that time) in the ghettos of Bialystok and Warsaw only honed the dissent between those who wanted to relocate underground activity and those who preferred to stay in Vilnius. The ghetto messengers continued their activity along the Vilnius-Warsaw axis on and off until the middle of 1942, although some of them were caught and executed.[22]

The Establishment of the Underground

On the night of January 1, 1942, a meeting was held in the Vilnius ghetto, attended by representatives of underground groups affiliated with the Zionist youth movements. Jewish youths were called upon to join the armed resistance, with the slogan "We will not go like sheep to the slaughter." Three weeks later, on January 21, 1942, a meeting of representatives of the Zionist youth movements and some Jewish Communists was held. They decided to establish an armed organization that would fight should the Germans attempt to liquidate the ghetto. The name given to the organization was the FPO (Fareinikte Partizaner Organizatzie – United Partisan Organization). They decreed that "resistance [was] a national act, the nation's struggle for its honor." Furthermore, they decided that the organization would bring the idea of resistance to the other ghettos. Yitzhak Wittenberg, a Communist with experience in underground activity that went back to the Polish regime, was elected to command the organization. Other leaders were Zionist: Abba Kovner from Hashomer Hatzair and Yosef Glazman from Beitar, who was deputy of the Jewish ghetto police. Several months later, Bund members joined the FPO. Another Zionist underground group of Hehalutz Hatzair–Dror members, led by Mordechai

---

22. Ibid., 221–26. In April 1942, the sisters Sara and Ruzhka Zilber and Shlomo Antin set off on a mission from Vilnius to Bialystok. The group had to relay the testimonies of Jews who had escaped from Ponary and a manifesto from the Vilnius underground drafted by Abba Kovner to the inhabitants of the other ghettos, calling on them to take up arms and fight the Nazi murderers. The delegation was arrested at the railway station in Malkinia, brought to Warsaw and executed. The last messenger between the ghettos was Irena Adamowicz, a Pole, who came to Warsaw from Vilnius in late June 1942.

Tenenbaum-Tamaroff, had left Vilnius in mid-January 1942 for Bialystok, pre-ferring to transfer the underground activity to the areas where mass murders were not yet being carried out.[23]

Before Tenenbaum-Tamaroff left the Vilnius ghetto, he devised a daring plan to take a group of his men from Vilnius through the Baltic Sea to Sweden. He relied on the help of Anton Schmidt, a pro-Jewish Austrian army sergeant contact who served in Vilnius. The plan was to leave Vilnius in Schmidt's truck, arriving at Liepaja in Latvia, and from there a fishing boat would take them to the Swedish island of Gotland. Tenenbaum-Tamaroff wrote in his diary that "there was an attempt to leave Hitler-land in German vehicles, to Libau in Latvia and from there, in winter, over the ice to Sweden."[24] Hehalutz-Hatzair Dror members never carried out the plan, but the Polish underground used the route to reach England and join Polish military forces organized there.

Though the FPO included almost the entire Jewish political spectrum, from Beitar on the right to the Communists on the left, it functioned harmoniously. It was unique compared with the Jewish undergrounds in Warsaw, Bialystok and other ghettos, which were politically split. At its height it consisted of two battalions, totaling 300 members.

In the spring of 1942, Hehalutz Hatzair–Dror members who had not left for Bialystok established an underground of their own, led by Yehiel Scheinbaum, called Yehiel's Struggle Group. Its objective was to arm itself, make contact with the partisans and leave for the forests. At its height, the group had between 150 and 200 members.[25] During the spring and summer of 1942, as Yehiel's Struggle Group organized and decided upon its objectives, they were influenced

---

23. Ibid., 231–38. Anton Schmidt placed a military vehicle at their disposal. Schmidt, an Austrian, was head of a small military unit whose role was to act as a collection point for German soldiers who had left their units. Some Jews from the ghetto worked in this unit, and during *Aktionen* Schmidt hid Jews, one of whom put him in contact with Tenenbaum-Tamaroff. Schmidt acted as a humanist and friend to the Jews. He was arrested, court-martialed and executed on April 13, 1942. For his deeds, he was recognized as a Righteous Gentile by Yad Vashem. Mordechai Tenenbaum-Tamaroff later commanded the underground in the Bialystok ghetto and fell during the revolt there in the second half of August 1943.

24. Mordechai Tenenbaum-Tamaroff, *Pages from the Fire* [Hebrew] (Tel Aviv: Hakib-butz Hameuhad, 1947), 124.

25. Arad, *Ghetto in Flames*, 239–41, 263–66.

by information that began reaching the ghetto about partisan activity in the Byelorussian forests.

The first weapons obtained by the ghetto underground came from warehouses of captured Soviet arms in the Borbishki suburb where Jews were employed, including some members of the FPO. Dozens of arms were taken out and brought to the ghetto. FPO members who worked outside the ghetto bought weapons from non-Jews and smuggled them in. Yehiel's Struggle Group used similar methods to obtain weapons. Jewish policemen who also belonged to the underground helped smuggle the weapons through the ghetto gates; the weapons were then hidden in *malinas*.[26]

In July 1942, Irena Adamowicz, a leader of the Polish underground Scout Movement, was sent by the Warsaw Zionist underground to contact the FPO. On behalf of the FPO she then traveled to Kaunas and Shauliai to contact members of Zionist youth organizations and instill in them the idea of armed resistance.[27]

Contacts with Non-Jewish Underground Groups

The FPO also made contact with the Armia Krajowa underground in Vilnius, which operated under the auspices of the Polish government in exile, and conducted negotiations about obtaining weapons. The members of the Polish underground asked the FPO various questions about the organization: Were they Communists? Would they favor the Poles or the Soviets in a struggle for control of Vilnius after German defeat? They were answered that the FPO was not a Communist organization; its objective was to fight the Nazis, and the fate of Vilnius after the liberation was not on its agenda. Following several weeks of talks, the request for weapons was denied and ties with the Poles were severed.[28]

In early 1942, the FPO established contact with Polish Communists in Vilnius who had formed a group called the Organization for Active Struggle (Zwiazek Walki Czynnej). It was a small group with few resources, which needed and received support from the FPO.[29]

---

26. Ruzka Korczak, *Flames in Ashes* [Hebrew] (Merhavya: Moreshet, 1956), 94, 100–101.

27. Nissan Reznik, *Budding from the Ashes: The Story of Hanoar Hatzioni Youth in the Vilnius Ghetto* [Hebrew] (Jerusalem: Yad Vashem, 2003), 99–101. Reznik was one of the leaders of the FPO.

28. Testimony of Abba Kovner, YVA, Kovner-3405-291, 7–8; Korczak, *Flames*, 93.

29. Arad, *Ghetto in Flames*, 249–50.

In the spring of 1942 the FPO contacted a group of Soviet paratroopers who operated in the Rudniki forests south of Vilnius. The FPO transmitted information about German military installations in Vilnius, which was in turn passed along to Moscow. At the end of the summer the Germans discovered the group in the forest and destroyed it. In the fall of 1942 the FPO sent two of its female members to cross the front lines and reach Moscow with the information that Jews were being massacred. The assumption was that neither Moscow nor the rest of the world knew anything about the Holocaust. The plan was for the women to reach the Polotsk region, where Soviet partisans were known to be active, and with their help to cross the front line. The two women, Sonia Madeysker and Chesia Rozenberg, armed with forged documents, reached the area close to the front at Velikiye-Luki. They were arrested by the German police but managed to escape and returned to Vilnius.[30]

In late February 1943 a Lithuanian Communist underground group became active in Vilnius. It was led by Juzas Vitas-Valunas, who had been mayor of the city during the Soviet regime. The group was called the Union for the Liberation of Lithuania (Lietuvos Islaisvinimo Sojunga Union). Through Wittenberg, they formed ties with the FPO, and the two organizations decided to establish a coordination team called the Vilnius Anti-Fascist Committee, composed of representatives of the FPO (the largest and best organized group), the Organization for Active Struggle and the Union for the Liberation of Lithuania. The FPO gave the Anti-Fascist Committee a printing press, which they used to print and distribute anti-German leaflets in Polish and Lithuanian.[31] After negotiations in the spring of 1943, Yehiel's Struggle Group joined the FPO as an autonomous unit and Yehiel Scheinbaum joined the FPO staff.[32]

FPO-Judenrat Relations

Until the spring and summer of 1943, the relationship between the FPO and the *Judenrat* chaired by Gens can best be described as peaceful coexistence. The FPO did not oppose the *Judenrat*, which wanted to keep the ghetto economically worthwhile for the Germans as long as possible. Gens, who knew of the FPO and its leaders, did not oppose the underground as long as it did not jeopardize the ghetto's existence. In May 1943, with the increase in partisan activity

---

30. Reznik, *Budding from the Ashes*, 94; Korczak, *Flames*, 118–19.
31. Arad, *Ghetto in Flames*, 366–75; Korczak, *Flames*, 135–37.
32. Arad, *Ghetto in Flames*, 374.

in the forests, German security forces arrested Jews betrayed by local inhabitants whom they had approached to buy weapons. Jewish partisans, former inhabitants of the Svencionys ghetto, came to the Vilnius ghetto in the spring and summer of 1943, contacted the FPO and smuggled several groups out of the ghetto into the forests. The Sipo found out and warned Gens that such acts endangered the very existence of the ghetto, whereupon Gens requested that the FPO leadership to put a stop to it.[33]

YITZHAK WITTENBERG

The first open conflict between the FPO and the *Judenrat* took place during the so-called Wittenberg Affair. In late June 1943, the Sipo discovered the Vilnius Anti-Fascist Committee and arrested its members. During interrogation and torture, one of them revealed their connection with Wittenberg. The Sipo ordered the *Judenrat* to hand Wittenberg over and threatened to liquidate the ghetto if they failed to do so. On the evening of July 15, 1943, Gens arrested Wittenberg and handed him over to the Lithuanian police. On the way to the gates, FPO members attacked the police and took Wittenberg to a hiding place in the ghetto.

The following day, assuming that Wittenberg's arrest had been an attack on the entire organization, the members of the underground barricaded themselves in a few buildings. Gens alerted many of the ghetto inmates and informed them that the ghetto was in danger of being destroyed. An angry crowd surrounded the buildings and demanded from the FPO that they hand Wittenberg over: the lives of 20,000 ghetto inmates should not be endangered because of one man who was involved in Communist activities outside the ghetto, they claimed. The FPO faced the dilemma of either fighting fellow Jews or handing Wittenberg over, and the leadership decided that Wittenberg would have to surrender. Wittenberg accepted the decision and was taken by the Sipo. The

---

33. Ibid., 381–82. In April and June 1943, youngsters from Svencionys came from the forests, met with FPO leaders and offered to transfer people to the forest. In June they brought letters from commanders of the Soviet partisan Markov Brigade, including a proposal to send armed individuals to the forests.

following day he was found dead in his cell, having swallowed a cyanide pill that he had taken with him.[34]

The Germans wanted Wittenberg because he was a member of the urban Communist Committee. At that time they knew nothing of the existence of the FPO or of his role in it. The FPO knew that to protect Wittenberg they would have had to use their weapons against fellow Jews and endanger the existence of the entire ghetto. The ghetto inmates, fearing for their lives, took sides with the *Judenrat* and asked that Wittenberg be handed over; there was nothing else the FPO could have done. To rebel against the Germans because of Wittenberg was against the principles of the "combat regulations" the FPO leadership had prepared in March 1943. One of the regulations was that "the FPO would join battle when the entire ghetto was in danger.… It will not undertake action to protect the life of an individual Jew.… [In such a case] the Jewish public would condemn us as *provocateurs* and we would have to fight our own brothers." The Wittenberg affair led to a deterioration in the relations between the FPO and Gens and the *Judenrat*.[35]

The Dilemma: Uprising in the Ghetto or Leaving for the Forests

After Wittenberg's death Abba Kovner took over the command of the FPO. Witnessing the ghetto inmates' reaction to the Wittenberg affair, the FPO asked itself if their fellow Jews would respond to a call to join the uprising when the Germans came to liquidate the ghetto. In addition, by that time – the summer of 1943 – the forest had become a practical option. There were partisans in the forests, they were in contact with the FPO and they required armed men to join them. In spite of the new situation, the FPO leadership decided that the organization would follow its ideological path of ghetto uprising, and at the same time send a group headed by Yosef Glazman to the forests to establish a partisan base where members of the organization could go after the uprising. On July 24, 1943, Glazman and 21 other FPO members left for the Naroch forests, and on the way were joined by 14 men from the New Vileika (Naujoji Vilnia) camp.[36]

A few days after Glazman's departure, Gessia Gleser (known as Albina) arrived in Vilnius, a Jewish paratrooper who belonged to the leading Operation Group of the Soviet Lithuanian Partisans, commanded by Motiejus

---

34. Ibid., 387–95.
35. Korczak, *Flames*, 146.
36. Arad, *Ghetto in Flames*, 398.

Shumauskas. She had been sent to the city to help reorganize the Communist underground, which had collapsed after Vitas-Valunas's arrest and execution. She entered the ghetto in August 1943 and informed the FPO that the partisan command's position was that they leave for the forests and fight there. However, the members of the Zionist youth movements were dominant in the FPO after Wittenberg's death, and they maintained that they would leave for the forests only after an uprising.[37]

On September 1, 1943, the Germans surrounded the ghetto and demanded that the *Judenrat* supply 5,000 Jews to be sent to Estonia. The FPO leadership regarded the *Aktion* as the liquidation of the ghetto and issued a mobilization order, in response to which two battalions stationed themselves in prearranged positions and some members went to take weapons out of hiding. However, before the FPO could receive weapons, the second battalion in Shpitlana Street found itself surrounded by Germans and Estonians, and were led out of the ghetto. Some of them managed to escape and reach the other battalion, which had received its arms, and deployed along Strashuna Street. The FPO distributed a leaflet telling the inmates of the ghetto not to believe the Germans – that they were not being sent to Estonia to work, but to Ponary to be shot. They called upon the ghetto inmates to join the fighters and resist the Germans. The *Judenrat* claimed that the 5,000 would be sent to Estonia and not Ponary. When the *Judenrat* could not supply the number of people demanded, German and Estonian soldiers entered the ghetto and began searching for Jews. In the evening, when they reached Strashuna Street, the FPO position there opened fire and Scheinbaum, who commanded it, was killed in the exchange of fire. As night fell the German troops left the ghetto.

To prevent another armed clash which was liable to endanger the ghetto's existence, Gens reached an agreement with the Germans whereby he would provide them with the required number of Jews for Estonia. He informed the FPO of his decision, promising that if they stayed where they were the organization would not be harmed. The FPO was again faced with a dilemma: since the ghetto inmates had not responded to the call to join the fighters, but rather believed Gens, the chances that a rebellion would succeed and that they could break out of the ghetto were extremely small. It was also perfectly clear to the FPO leadership that if a rebellion did break out, the ghetto inmates would be massacred, and they could not and did not want to take responsibility for that.

---

37.   Ibid., 409–10.

In the end, they decided to wait until the *Aktion* was over, and only then to send FPO members into the forests. Thus the idea of a ghetto uprising, which the FPO had championed since its inception, could not in reality be implemented, and the organization decided to abandon it.

On September 4, 1943, the required number of people was assembled and deported to Estonia. Between September 8 and 13, 1943, a total of about 150 FPO members left the ghetto for the Naroch forests in Byelorussia, about 80 kilometers (50 miles) northeast of Vilnius. As the last group, commanded by Abba Kovner, was preparing to leave, an order arrived from Zimanas (Jurgis), the Soviet Lithuanian partisan commander in southern Lithuania, sending them to the Rudniki forests, 50 kilometers (30 miles) to the south. The last FPO group left the ghetto through sewer pipes on the final day of the ghetto's existence, September 23, 1943.[38] Throughout the ghetto's existence, a total of six to seven hundred people, almost all of them youths, escaped to the forests.

The Vilnius ghetto was liquidated following an order from Himmler given on June 21, 1943. But in spite of the order, the ghettos of Kaunas and Shauliai in *Generalkommissariat* Lithuania remained largely untouched, while the Vilnius ghetto was completely liquidated. The German Sipo knew about the underground activity in the Vilnius ghetto and about the Jews who had left for the forests. They viewed the ghetto as a nest of underground activity which had to be destroyed as quickly as possible. According to the Sipo reports of September 1 and October 1, 1943, Jews had escaped from the ghetto and resisted the Germans, and, according to the October report, "because of the well-known difficulties in the Vilnius ghetto, it was completely evacuated. A number of times it was necessary to use force to break down the earnest resistance of the Jews."[39]

4. THE KAUNAS GHETTO UNDERGROUND

The Holocaust in Kaunas

Kaunas, with its 37,000 Jews, was occupied by the German army on June 24, 1941. During the pogroms carried out by the Lithuanians, and especially the *Aktion* in the Seventh Fort, by July 8 approximately 6,000 Jews had been murdered. On July 15 the order to enclose the Jews in the ghetto (erected in the

---

38. Ibid., 422–24. For more on Zimanas, see chapter 3:2, "The Soviet Partisan Movement at Its Height: Late 1942 to Summer 1944."
39. Ibid., 438–44, quoted from German reports of the dates noted.

Slovodka suburb) was given, and it was sealed off on August 15. Approximately 1,000 more Jews were murdered before the remaining 30,000 were herded into the ghetto. On August 7, a *Judenrat* (called Altestenrat) was appointed, headed by Dr. Elhanan Elkes. In a series of *Aktionen* carried out from the middle of August to the end of October, 12,500 ghetto Jews were murdered, leaving fewer than 17,000. A period of relative quiet followed, lasting until the fall of 1943.

In September and October 1943, the ghetto was turned into an SS-run concentration camp. Some of the men were sent to labor camps around Kaunas or in Latvia. However, most of the inhabitants stayed in the Kaunas ghetto camp. At the end of March 1944, 1,200 children and some of the elderly were sent to Auschwitz and to the notorious Ninth Fort in the city and were murdered there. Forty Jewish policemen, among them Moshe Levin, the police chief, were murdered at the Ninth Fort for refusing to divulge the location of the ghetto *malina*s. Between July 8 and 11, 1944, the remaining 8,000 Jews in Kaunas and the labor camps around the city were sent to camps in Germany. Kaunas was liberated by the Red Army on August 1, 1944.

The Establishment of the Underground

The idea of armed resistance and the establishment of a united fighting underground came into being in the Kaunas ghetto at a later stage than in Vilnius and Minsk. The Jewish Communists, headed by Haim Yellin, had founded the Anti-Fascist Struggle Organization, which focused on contacting pro-Soviet activists within the local population and sabotaging German equipment in the workplaces. In the spring of 1942 the Zionists established an underground called the Williampola Kaunus Zionist Center, code-named Matzok (Merkaz Tzionei Vilyampole Kovna). Most of their activities were educational and they had close relations with the *Judenrat*.

In July 1942 Irena Adamowicz arrived from Vilnius, sent by the FPO. She met with Matzok members and with the heads of the *Judenrat*, telling them about conditions in Vilnius and the mass murders that had begun in the *Generalgouvernement* of Poland. She told Hashomer Hatzair and Hehalutz Hatzair members about the FPO in Vilnius and about its objective of armed resistance. Her information led to a gradual change in Zionist underground ideology, and toward the spring of 1943 they decided to change the focus of their efforts from culture, education and mutual aid to armed resistance.[40] The change was also

40. Levin, *They Fought Back*, 131–32; Y. Oliesky et al., *Haim Yellin: Ghetto Fighter*

influenced by news of partisan activity in the forests, the shock of the murder of the last Jews in the small ghettos of eastern Lithuania in early April 1943 and news of the Warsaw ghetto uprising.

In the spring of 1943, the ghetto Communists contacted an underground Communist group that had organized in the city at the same time, and the two began collaborating on the distribution of propaganda and on finding a way to contact partisan units. An agreement was reached in the early summer of 1943 between the ghetto Communists and Matzok regarding the establishment of the Jewish Fighting Organization (JFO), which would focus on procuring weapons and organizing groups to leave the ghetto and join the partisans in the forests. Haim Yellin headed the JFO, which at its height had about 400 members.

The JFO also set up a plan for fighting in the ghetto if it faced liquidation before they could leave for the forests.[41] It was not a united organization like the FPO, but rather an umbrella for various political groups, each of which kept its independence and interests. Nehemia Endlin, one of the Communist activists, wrote that "we needed the Zionists [because of their close relations with the *Judenrat*] to be able to preserve our organization insofar as was possible, so that our members would not disperse in the various [labor] camps.... The Zionists needed us for their struggle outside the ghetto with the partisan units."[42]

The JFO maintained contact with the *Judenrat* in the ghetto. The chairman of the *Judenrat*, Dr. Elkes, supported the idea of underground activity. He helped the JFO by providing money for weapons and by enrolling JFO members in the ghetto police and giving them jobs enabling them to establish contacts outside the ghetto. Once contact was made with the partisans, the *Judenrat* supplied those leaving for the forests with clothing and transport.[43]

Contact with the partisans in the forests was made through Albina, who was in Vilnius in summer 1943 and sent an emissary to summon Yellin. Yellin arrived in Vilnius in mid-September 1943 and accompanied Albina to the Rudniki forests to establish contacts between the ghetto underground and the partisans, commanded by Zimanas. He returned to the Kaunas ghetto about two weeks later. In early October 1943, Yellin received a message from Zimanas, ordering the ghetto underground to send groups to the Augustova

and Writer [Hebrew] (Tel Aviv: Igud Yotzei Lita, 1980), 25–27; Nehemia Endlin, *Memoirs of a Jewish Guerilla Fighter* [Hebrew] (Tel Aviv, 1980), 72.

41. Levin, *They Fought Back*, 133–34; Oliesky et al., *Yellin*, 26.
42. Endlin, *Memoirs*, 81.
43. Levin, *They Fought Back*, 133–34, 167.

forests, about 165 kilometers (103 miles) southwest of Kaunas, near the border with east Prussia.[44]

The forests closest to Kaunas (about 150 kilometers [93 miles] away) and the most appropriate destination for the ghetto underground were the Rudniki forests, where partisan bases had already been set up and where Zimanas's headquarters was located. But Zimanas wanted a partisan base established in the Augustova forests to enlarge partisan activity in southern Lithuania. With the exception of military considerations, Zimanas was not interested in having more Jews in the Rudniki forests than the hundreds of FPO members who had already come from the Vilnius ghetto.[45]

Yellin tried to persuade Albina, who was then in Kaunas, that the organization was not yet prepared to leave for Augustova because of the distance, the absence of guides, the dearth of weapons at their disposal and the lack of his group's military training. Albina promised him that they would meet partisans in the Augustova forest and be supplied with weapons. She told Yellin, "Orders are not a subject for debate, they are to be followed!"[46]

The first 18 people left the ghetto on October 21, 1943, armed with a few guns. They got lost and split into smaller groups, some of which were arrested by the German police; the others returned to the ghetto three days later. Nevertheless, it was decided that another group would be sent out. It consisted of 25 people and left on October 28, 1943, and another group left two or three days later. They were unarmed and some of them lost their way and were arrested. Only some of them reached the Augustova forests, and after a few days of fruitless searching for partisan groups, which according to Albina's promises would meet them there, they decided to return to the ghetto. One of those who took part in the abortive attempt wrote as follows:

> We were in the forest for three days and found no trace of the men we were supposed to meet. We combed the forest, assuming there were also people looking for us. We came to the conclusion that they were not there and that it was pointless to wait for them. Not only that, but

---

44. Ibid., 100, 134–35; Alex Feitelson, *The Truth and Nothing but the Truth* (Jerusalem: Gefen Publishing House, 2006), 100; Endlin, *Memoirs*, 89–91.
45. For Zimanas's attitude toward the concentration of Jewish partisans in the Rudniki forests, see chapter 5.
46. Endlin, *Memoirs*, 89–91.

local farmers had already noticed us…and we were in a hostile area. The region was not suitable for partisan activity.[47]

A total of 71 underground members left the ghetto for the Augustova forests. Those caught were taken to the Ninth Fort where they were put to work burning corpses; some were killed on the way and the rest returned to the ghetto.[48]

With almost no weapons, no guide and no partisan experience, using a route that ran through villages of hostile local inhabitants, the JFO's Augustova operation was doomed to failure. The Soviet partisan command was responsible, having made no preparations. Moreover, at that time there were no partisan bases in the Augustova forests for the Kaunas ghetto fighters to join. Nevertheless, the JFO did not abandon the idea of partisan warfare, and in November 1943 the organization received permission from Zimanas to send its people to the Rudniki forests. The first group set out in late November 1943, and was followed by others. By mid-April 1944, the JFO had transferred about 160 of its people to the forests. On April 6, 1944, the Sipo in Kaunas arrested and executed Yellin. That month also saw the failure of another attempt to leave the ghetto and most of the individuals involved were killed. The way to the forests was blocked. One hundred and fifty members of the JFO remained to share the fate of the other Jews in the Kaunas ghetto.[49]

5. THE RIGA GHETTO UNDERGROUND

The Holocaust in Riga

Riga, with its 35,000–37,000 Jews, including refugees, was occupied by the German army on July 1, 1941. During July, 5,000 Jewish men were murdered. On August 25, 1941, a large ghetto was erected in Riga. On November 26, a small section of it was fenced in with barbed wire, and those who lived inside it were ordered to move into the "large ghetto." Once the "small ghetto" had been evacuated, 4,000 working men and a few hundred women who had been listed as seamstresses were ordered to leave their families and move into it. On November 30 and December 8–9, 25,000–28,000 Jews were taken from the large ghetto into the Rumbula forest, 8 kilometers (5 miles) from the city, and shot. Between December 1941 and the spring of 1942, 16,000 Jews were brought to

---

47. Ibid., 100–101, 109.
48. Ibid., 93–109. Endlin was one of those sent to the Augustova forests.
49. Ibid., 122–27, 175; Levin, *They Fought Back*, 136–38.

the large ghetto from the Reich, some of whom were sent to the labor camps in Latvia. The two ghettos, the large one with Jews from the Reich and the small one with the local Jews, were entirely separate and each had its own *Judenrat* and police force.

The number of Jews in Riga dwindled as a result of torture, starvation, diseases and executions. As the Red Army approached in the beginning of August 1944, the last Jews were evacuated, along with those in other camps in Latvia, via the Baltic Sea to the Stutthof concentration camp and from there to various concentration camps in Germany.

The Establishment of the Underground

The armed underground began its activity in early 1942 in the small ghetto in Riga, where some 4,000 men were kept after the *Aktionen* of late November and early December 1941. The first to organize were former Communist activists headed by Mendel Volfovich, who were later joined by members of Zionist youth movements.

The underground planned to organize armed resistance should the ghetto be liquidated and to get their members to the forests as soon as contact was made with partisans. At its peak, the Riga ghetto underground had 150 members, including 28 of the ghetto's 40 Jewish policemen, one of whom was the police chief.[50] Underground members who worked in the Pulver Turm where captured Soviet arms were stored managed to smuggle dozens of weapons into the ghetto.[51]

In the summer of 1942, news reached the ghetto of partisan activity in eastern Latvia near Dvinsk (Daugavpils) and especially further east, in the forests near Pskov in Russia. The organization managed to contact a group of former Soviet prisoners of war hiding in Riga, among whom was Boris Pismanov, a Jewish Soviet army officer who was passing as a Ukrainian. On October 28, 1942, with the help of Pismanov and his comrades, ten armed underground members left the ghetto in a hired truck. Some distance from the forest they were to meet a contact who would lead them to the partisans; four groups intended to leave in that fashion. Shortly after their departure from the city they were ambushed by Germans, and seven Jews were killed in the exchange

---

50.   YVA, M-33/1052, 12 – a Soviet document dealing with the Riga ghetto; Levin, *They Fought Back*, 170–71.

51.   Levin, *They Fought Back*, 175–76.

of fire, two were wounded and taken prisoner and one managed to escape and return to the ghetto. A German agent had informed the Sipo of the ghetto underground–Pismanov connection and of the preparations for escape to the forests, including the route the truck would take.

In a German document dated October 24, 1942, a report of one of their agents noted that on the morning of October 28, eight to ten Jews would leave for Abrehne (in Russian Pytalovo) in a truck, on their way to meet a partisan contact at the seventh kilometer after Abrehne. A similar document dated October 27 contained the information that ten men were already outside the ghetto in an apartment at 28/24 Sadovnikov Street; that the Jewish police had helped them leave the ghetto; that their contact was a man named Borka (Pismanov), who might be with the escapees, and that the German ambush would be located on the Riga-Madona road near the milestone marking the fifth kilometer.[52]

Pismanov and other members of the underground were arrested on October 28, 1942. According to a German report dated November 2, 1942:

> Of the Jews who escaped from the ghetto on October 28, 1942, seven were shot during the arrest.... The two Jews still alive were taken to prison. A further nine were arrested on the same day, including the leader.... They are: Pismanov, known as Borka; a Soviet POW; Lieutenant [followed by a list of the prisoners of war and civilians who were arrested]. Pismanov led and organized the escaping Jews.... At the end of their journey, they were to provide their Latvian escort with confirmation that their journey had been concluded successfully, and then Pismanov was to prepare the second group.[53]

After that no other groups left for the forests. In retaliation for the attempted escape, the Sipo commander in Latvia, *Obersturmführer* Dr. Lange, ordered the execution of dozens of Jews. On October 31, 1942, 108 Jews were murdered in an *Aktion*, including 42 Jewish policemen accused of not preventing the escape and of assisting in it.[54]

---

52. YVA, M-33/1038 – a collection of German documents including reports by the agent who provided the information and records of the interrogation of the wounded prisoners and others who were arrested, including Pismanov. The original documents are in the State Archive of the Russian Federation (GARF), Fond 7021, Opis 93, Delo 3785.
53. Ibid.
54. Ibid. Lange's order was dated October 30, 1942; Levin, *They Fought Back*, 187–88.

During the interrogation of the arrested underground members, Jewish and non-Jewish alike, the German Sipo gained more information about the ghetto underground and where it hid its weapons, including the central arms store exposed on June 11, 1943. Dozens of underground members and suspected members were arrested at the end of June 1943 in the ghetto and the labor camps around Riga. The overwhelming majority were either shot or died in the concentration camps. The arrests effectively put an end to underground activity in the Riga ghetto.[55]

On August 25, 1944, six weeks before the Red Army liberated Riga, the local newspapers published an announcement from the Sipo headquarters in Latvia stating that on August 24, a group of armed Jews – six men and one woman – had been discovered hiding at 15 Peldus Street. They opened fire on the Sipos, killing one. In the ensuing exchange of fire, two of the Jews were killed, and in a house-to-house search conducted under fire, the others were arrested, as were all the residents of the house in which the Jews had hidden.[56]

6. GHETTO UNDERGROUNDS IN WESTERN BYELORUSSIA

The Holocaust in Grodno

Grodno, with its 25,000 Jews, including refugees, was occupied by the German army on June 23, 1941. The occupation was swift and only a few managed to be evacuated or escape. On November 1 the order to erect two ghettos was issued. Beginning in the fall of 1941, Grodno was annexed to *Generalbizerk* Bialystok. Grodno was spared in the first wave of mass murders of Jews, which began with the German invasion and lasted until the spring of 1942, and was relatively quiet until November 1942.

Toward the end of 1942, the Germans began deporting the Jews of *Generalbizerk* Bialystok to the death camps in Auschwitz and Treblinka. Between the beginning of November and the middle of December 1942, 10,500 Jews were sent from Grodno to the Kielbasin transit camp and from there to Auschwitz.

---

55. Levin, *They Fought Back*, 190–94. Levin wrote that by the end of June 1943, 285 individuals had been arrested. See also Max Kaufmann, *Die Vernichtung Der Juden Lettlands* (Munich, 1947), 204–8. Mendel Volfovich, a leader of the Riga underground, managed to escape during the arrests and lived in hiding in Riga until the liberation. In 1973 he immigrated to Israel.

56. YVA, 3/1049. The notice was taken from the Latvian newspaper *Teyija*.

In the middle of December the transports stopped because the German army needed all its trains after the defeat at Stalingrad. Himmler intervened, and from the second half of January 1943, trains were made available and the deportations continued. During two *Aktionen* (January 18–22 and February 13–16), with the exception of 1,000 people, all the Jews from Grodno were deported to Auschwitz and Treblinka. The remaining 1,000, most of them professionals, were transferred to the Bialystok ghetto in March 1943.

The Grodno Underground

At the end of 1941 and the beginning of 1942, ghetto messengers on their way between the ghettos of Vilnius, Bialystok and Warsaw stayed in Grodno for a while. The Zionist youth movements, which until then had been conducting clandestine educational activities, learned from them about the mass murders taking place in Vilnius and other localities. They abandoned education and turned their activity toward organizing for armed resistance. The first ghetto messenger who came from Vilnius was Bella Hazan, who had Aryan documents and lived outside the ghetto, and at the beginning of 1942, Mordechai Tenenbaum-Tamaroff stopped at Grodno on his way from Vilnius to Bialystok.[57] The first step in organizing a fighting underground was establishing a common framework for Hashomer Hatzair and Hehalutz Hatzair–Dror, which had about 50 members, while Beitar and the Communists organized separately. However, because of the relative quiet prevailing in the Grodno ghetto until November 1942 and the lack of an authoritative leader, the organizations were sluggish and did not manage to acquire weapons. Only after the *Aktionen* of November and December 1942, in which thousands were deported to Auschwitz and Kielbasin, did the underground groups become more active.

At that time, Tenenbaum-Tamaroff returned to Grodno and helped organize the underground. He was followed by Zerah Zilberberg, an activist from Bialystok. The two of them tried unsuccessfully to establish a united front of all the underground groups in Grodno, Zionist and non-Zionist. Tenenbaum-Tamaroff left Grodno for Bialystok. After the deportations to Kielbasin, the leaders of the underground suggested transferring members to Bialystok, which was still relatively quiet, but most of the members rejected the idea.[58] In late

---

57.   Tikva Fatal-Knaani, *Grodno Is Not the Same* [Hebrew] (Jerusalem: Yad Vashem, 2001), 230–32.

58.   Ibid., 234–36.

1942 the underground examined the possibility of leaving for the forests. Zipora Birman, of the Hehalutz Hatzair–Dror underground, wrote:

> We sent the first group to the forests.… It was difficult to obtain weapons in the ghetto. We were sure they would obtain weapons on the way.… They went but did not arrive. One returned and four fell. He [the man who returned] described terrible things he saw on the way: hundreds of Jews lying dead in the forests of Martsikonys, dozens… begging to die. It is better to die than live this kind of life. Our hopes for the forest have been dashed for the moment. Without weapons, it is impossible.[59]

After the idea of the forests was shelved, the only option open to the Grodno underground was resistance. Birman wrote,

> There was nothing we could do but die with honor where we were.… Rebellion meant total destruction within a few days.… We don't want to die. The instinct to live is stronger in the face of death. We have decided that the women will move to Bialystok and the men will stay here to undertake the rebellion.[60]

Attempts to kill those carrying out the *Aktionen* (among them Otto Streblow, one of the deportation commanders) failed, as did the attempt to organize a mass escape during a deportation *Aktion* at the second half of January 1943. The Jews did not respond to the call and the deportation was conducted without disturbance. The underground despaired of leading a rebellion in the ghetto and decided to leave Grodno. At the end of January 1943, a group moved to Bialystok and joined the underground there, and other small groups left for the forest in the hope of joining the partisans. Most of the Grodno underground members were killed on August 16, 1943, during the Bialystok ghetto uprising, and the others fell in the forests.[61]

---

59. Zipora Birman, "Bialystok Ghetto," in a document entitled "To My Dear Friends, Wherever They Are, There," Yad Vashem Studies 2: 289–90. Birman died in August 1943, during the uprising in the Bialystok ghetto; Fatal-Knaani, *Grodno*, 234–35. The Martsikonys forest are northeast of Grodno.
60. Birman, "Bialystok Ghetto," 290.
61. Fatal-Knaani, *Grodno*, 236–38. Zerah Zilberberg died in the Bialystok ghetto uprising. A group of 18 left for the forests and were betrayed to the German forces, which surrounded and killed them. A group of 16, who had fled to the Nacha

The Baranovichi Underground

Baranovichi, with its 10,000 Jews, was occupied by the Germans on June 27, 1941, and the ghetto was erected at the end of November 1941. It was divided in half by a narrow connecting passage. On March 3, 1942, German and local Byelorussian police rounded up 2,300 Jews, who were taken outside the city by truck and shot. After the *Aktion,* Jews from neighboring towns were brought to the Baranovichi ghetto.[62] On August 19, 700 young men from the ghetto were sent to work in Molodechno. On September 22, 1942, 3,000 Jews were killed, and on December 17 the remaining 3,000 Jews were killed and the ghetto was liquidated. About 700 Jews remained in labor camps in the city, and they were murdered in various *Aktionen* during 1943.

The underground began organizing after the first *Aktion* in March 1942. The organization numbered about 120 members, among them a large group of refugees who had come to Baranovichi from neighboring towns. The chief of the Jewish police force in the ghetto, a man named Warshavski, and 12 of the ghetto's 20 policemen also belonged to the organization. Warshavski became the organization's central figure; his objective was to lead an uprising and escape to the forests. He even managed to acquire weapons from the German arms stores and to bring them into the ghetto. The *Judenrat* knew about the weapons and demanded they be removed from the ghetto because of the threat they posed. The underground's refusal to meet their demand worsened relations between them.

Within the underground there were Jews who demanded to leave for the forests, but most of the members adhered to the original plan of an uprising. On September 22, 1942, the ghetto was surrounded by German forces and an *Aktion* was conducted. The order to resist was not given because the underground members were not sure that the *Aktion* spelled the end of the ghetto. When it ended, the underground left for the forests. About 450 Jews escaped from Baranovichi and the labor camps to which they had been sent and fled to the forests.[63]

---

forests in 1943, went from there to the Radun forests where they set up a family camp that grew to 80.

62. *Encyclopedia of the Holocaust,* vol. 1, 147–48. Christian Gerlach, *Kalkulierte Morde* (Hamburg, 1999), 691. Gerlach writes that on March 3 and 4, 1942, the Germans and the local police killed 2007 Jews who were unfit for work.

63. Eliezer Lidovski, "*Viderstand Organizatzieh*" (Resistance Organization), in *The Book of Baranovichi* [Hebrew], ed. Stein (Tel Aviv, 1953), 469–71. According to

The Novogrudok Underground

Novogrudok, with a prewar Jewish population of 7,000, was occupied by the Germans on July 3, 1941. In an *Aktion* in December 1941, 4,000 Jews were murdered. A ghetto was then erected and 1,700 Jews were forced into it, joined by a few thousand others from the surrounding towns. About 2,500 Jews were murdered on August 8, 1942. About 1,200 Jews were left in the ghetto, most of whom were murdered by the middle of 1943.

Underground activity began in Novogrudok in the spring and summer of 1942, led by Dr. Kagan. His group numbered about 50. Its objective was to prepare for an armed uprising followed by escape to the forests. A second group of a few dozen members was also active in the ghetto, and planned to join the partisans in the Naliboki forests. In the spring of 1943, several members of that group left for the forests, most of them falling in the partisan attack on the town of Naliboki. After several mass-murder *Aktionen,* the ghetto was transformed into a labor camp. The uprising and escape to the forests planned for April 15, 1943, did not take place because most of the ghetto inmates opposed it. On September 26, 1943, Dr. Kagan led 233 Jews through a 250-meter tunnel which had been dug by the underground. Although most of them were killed during the escape, about 100 escapees made it to the forests and joined the partisans.[64]

The Lida Underground

Lida, with a prewar Jewish population of 9,000, was occupied by the Germans on June 30, 1941. The ghetto was erected during November and December, and 7,000 Jews were forced into it. Their numbers grew as they were joined by Jews from the surrounding towns and refugees from the *Aktionen* in Vilnius. On May 8, 1942, 5,670 Jews were taken from the ghetto and shot in a nearby forest. About 1,500 were left in the ghetto. After the *Aktion,* 2,000 Jews were brought in from ghettos around Lida.

Underground organization began after the May 8, 1942, *Aktion.* The most prominent figure was Baruch Levin, who stored weapons and organized groups

---

some sources, the number of escapees was 750.

64. Shalom Cholawski, *Resistance and Partisan Struggle* [Hebrew] (Jerusalem: Yad Vashem, and Tel Aviv: Moreshet, 2001), 124, 149, 178–81; Yitzhak Zuckerman and Moshe Bassok, eds., *The Book of the Ghetto Wars* [Hebrew] (Lohamei Hagetaot, 1954), 492–93.

to leave for the forests. Halperstein (Alperstein), the *Judenrat* chairman, heard about Levin's activities, asked him to present himself and when he did, told him:

> If there remains in us any kind of dream, it is the dream that a few among us will remain alive. I myself do not hope to be among them. Hopefully someone will remain to describe what happened here when the day comes.... And then a man comes [i.e., Levin] and destroys even this feeble chance.... Large countries bow down before the German and here [there is only] a man who has already lost his family and has only one thing, a rusty shotgun. And one of these days he'll rise up and fire one bullet from his shotgun and put an end once and for all to our only remaining chance.[65]

Halperstein expressed the opinion of many of the ghetto inmates, since for most of them neither combat inside the ghetto nor escape to the forests was a viable option, either for reasons of age, family commitments or lack of weapons. Their only hope for survival, weak though it was, lay in their ability to work and show loyalty to the German administration. Baruch Levin and others continued their underground activity and eventually left for the forests; approximately 500 Lida ghetto inmates escaped to the forests.[66]

The Slonim Underground

Slonim, with its 19,000 Jews (including Polish refugees), was occupied by the Germans on June 25, 1941. In the large *Aktion* of November 13–14, 1941, 10,000 Jews were murdered. Gert Erren, Slonim's *Gebietskommissar*, wrote that "when I arrived there were 25,000 Jews in Slonim, only 16,000 from Slonim itself.... The *Aktion* conducted by the security police on November 13 released me from unnecessary guzzlers (*Fressern unotigen*). The 7,000 Jews remaining in Slonim were put to work, and they work willingly because they are in constant fear of death...."[67] Two ghettos were erected in Slonim in December, one for professionals and workers in German installations and the other for the other

---

65. Baruch Levin, *In the Forests of Vengeance* [Hebrew] (Tel Aviv: Hakibbutz Hameu-had, 1968), 66–67.

66. Ibid., 62–63, 72–74; Shalom Cholawski, *The Jews of Belorussia during World War Two* [Hebrew] (Tel Aviv: Moreshet and Sifriat Hapoalim, 1982), 140–41.

67. Mira and Gerhard Schoenberner, *Zeugen zagen aus: Berichte und Dokumente uber Judenverfolgung in Dritten Reich* (Berlin, 1988), 135–36.

Jews. Between January and March 1942, Jews from the neighboring towns were brought into the Slonim ghetto.

Following the large-scale *Aktion* of mid-November 1941, an underground anti-Fascist committee, which included representatives of various political trends, was established. Jews from Slonim worked in a store containing captured Soviet weapons, enabling members of the ghetto underground to remove dozens of weapons. The underground made contact with partisans operating in the Rafalovka and Volche-Nora forests south of Slonim, who were led by a Red Army lieutenant named Pavel Proniagin, and supplied them with arms and medicine.

The first ghetto underground members left for the forests in June 1942 and joined Proniagin. They were helped by the *Judenrat*, which supplied them with clothing. At dawn on June 29, 1942, local police and a Lithuanian police unit surrounded the ghetto. The *Judenrat* chairman went to the gates to find out what was happening and was shot on the spot. The ghetto inmates ran to hide in the *malinas*. Two thousand Jews were caught on the first day of the *Aktion* and taken to Petrolewich, about 4 kilometers (2.5 miles) east of the city, and shot there. Hand grenades were tossed into *malinas* when they were exposed and many of those hiding were killed. Others were shot trying to escape. The *Aktion* and search for those in hiding lasted until July 15, and resulted in the deaths of 8,000–10,000 Jews.[68]

No armed resistance occurred during the *Aktion* because the underground was unprepared and most of its weapons were hidden outside the ghetto. Following the *Aktion*, with less than 2,000 Jews remaining in the ghetto, about 400 escaped to the forests.[69] Gert Erren reported on September 26, 1942, that "the Jews played a large role in all the destruction and sabotage.... They were active in supplying stolen weapons and in stealing medicine from hospitals [on

---

68. P. Lichtenstein and Y. Rabinowicz, eds., *The Slonim Notebook* [Hebrew] (Tel Aviv, 1962), 93.

69. Cholawski, *Jews of Belorussia*, 122, 132, 167; Sara Shner-Nishmit, *The 51st Company: The Story of the Jewish Partisan Group from the Slonim Ghetto* [Hebrew] (Tel Aviv: Lohamei Hagetaot and Misrad Habitahon, 1990), 38, 41, 56–67, 65–66. Shner-Nishmit quotes Proniagin (Pavel Proniagin, *U Samoi Granitsi*, [Minsk, 1976], 25–26), who wrote about the weapons, radio and other equipment he received from the Slonim underground.

behalf of the partisans]. In a broad-scale operation conducted by *Oberlieutenant* Schroder, it transpired that of the 223 dead bandits, 80 were armed Jews."[70]

The Brest-Litovsk Underground

With the exception of the fortress where Soviet soldiers held out for a few weeks, Brest-Litovsk was occupied the day after the German invasion, i.e., on June 23, 1941. At the time of the occupation there were more than 20,000 Jews in the city, and only a few managed to escape to the east. On June 28 and 29 the Germans rounded up 5,000 men on the pretext of sending them to "work," took them out of the city and shot them. In August a *Judenrat* was appointed and in the middle of December the Jews were imprisoned in a ghetto.

Early in 1942 an underground began organizing. One group included students from the Hebrew Tarbut high school, and another was composed of Communist and Soviet Jews who were trapped in the city. One of these Jews was Arieh Sheinman, a printer. His group had contacts with a Communist in the city who purchased weapons from Italian soldiers stationed there and also stole them from German stores. The underground ran a printing press and had a radio set. Its objective was to stage an uprising when the ghetto was about to be liquidated and then to make a break for the forests.

The underground contacted a group in the forest that represented itself as a Soviet partisan unit headed by a man called Sashka. It later became clear that the "partisans" were thieves who customarily met individuals fleeing to the forests, stole their weapons and clothing and killed them.

On the night of October 15, 1942, the ghetto was surrounded by German forces and the final *Aktion* began. The underground was surprised and did not have time to call up its members or take weapons out of hiding. Only a few small groups managed to arm themselves and escape to the forests. The Brest-Litovsk Jews were taken to the railroad station, loaded onto freight cars and shipped to Brona-Gora, a killing place in the vicinity of Kobryn, northeast of Brest-Litovsk, where they were shot. The searches in the ghetto lasted for a month and about 4,000 Jews in hiding were found, shot and buried in the ghetto.[71]

---

70. YVA, TR-18/808, 209. The Germans called the partisans "bandits."
71. Shmuel Spector, ed., *Encyclopedia of Jewish Communities: Poland*, vol. 5, *Volhynia* and *Polesie* [Hebrew] (Jerusalem: Yad Vashem, 1990), 237.

The Pinsk Underground

The Germans occupied Pinsk on July 4, 1941. About half of its 20,000 Jews – almost all the males – were murdered during the *Aktionen* conducted on August 4 and 7. They were killed near the villages of Ivaniki and Kozlyakovich by soldiers of the 2nd Regiment of the SS Cavalry Brigade. The *Einsatzgruppe* report of August 20 stated that "instigation and incitement by the Jews continue to increase. In Pinsk, Jews shot a guard of the city militia.… In reprisal 4,500 Jews were liquidated."[72] Ten thousand Jews were left in Pinsk, almost all of them women and children. The ghetto was erected on May 1, 1942, and the Jews had only one day to move into it, including those Jews who had been brought in from neighboring towns.

The Pinsk ghetto was the largest in Polesie but its underground activity was limited and information about it is scarce. With the increase in partisan activity in the Polesie region in 1942, several dozen underground members escaped to the forests to join the partisans. The *Judenrat* opposed escape, fearing discovery by the Germans and a subsequent threat to the continued existence of the ghetto. When 20 young people organized to leave, the *Judenrat* threatened their families that if the young people did not change their mind, the *Judenrat* would be forced to turn the families over to the Germans in place of those who had escaped. Between the pressure exerted by the *Judenrat* and their families, the young men returned.

In the summer of 1942 an underground group of about 20 men led by Hershel Levin managed to acquire a small number of weapons. On the eve of the ghetto's liquidation, they planned to set the ghetto itself and workplaces outside it on fire, and use the commotion to cover a mass escape.[73]

According to an order issued by Himmler on October 12, 1942, the Pinsk ghetto was regarded as the main base for partisan activity in the swamp region of Prypyat and had to be liquidated.[74] There was very little truth in what he wrote about underground activities there. On October 22, rumors spread throughout the ghetto that trenches were being dug close to the airport for use in an upcoming *Aktion*. The German administration received information about the

---

72.   Arad et al., *The Einsatzgruppen Reports*, 94. The report apparently refers to one of the *Aktionen* conducted on August 4 or 7. Some of the victims were murdered by members of the *Einsatzgruppen* and others by soldiers of the SS Cavalry Brigade.

73.   Yevgenii Rosenberg and Irina Elenskaya, *Pinskie Evrei* (Brest, 1997), 149–52.

74.   Nuremberg Documents, NO-2027.

rumors and Mirski, the *Judenrat* chairman, was called to the *Gebietskommissar*, where he was promised on "German honor" that the trenches were being dug to provide storage for gasoline tanks and that no harm would come to the town's Jews. The underground decided to postpone the plan to set the ghetto on fire until the situation cleared. The ghetto was liquidated between October 29 and November 1, 1942, before the underground could carry out its plan.

Hundreds of young Jews tried to break through the fences and escape, but almost all of them were shot by the German forces surrounding the ghetto, and about 1,200 were killed inside. On the eve of the *Aktion* and during it, however, several dozen people managed to escape to the forests.[75]

7. GHETTO UNDERGROUNDS IN THE WESTERN UKRAINE

Conditions for Jewish Armed Underground Activity

In the ghettos of east Galicia and Volhynia in the western Ukraine, underground activity was limited since the prevailing conditions did not encourage it. The ideology and aims of all the armed undergrounds in the ghettos in the occupied territories of the Soviet Union were to escape to the forests, join Soviet partisans and start partisan warfare. In the western Ukraine, apart from the areas in the north bordering on Polesie, there were few large forests and there were no Soviet partisans in the region who could provide a target or direction for underground activity. In the areas where there were forests, large segments of the Ukrainian population were anti-Semitic, and either killed Jews escaping from the ghettos or handed them over to the police. In addition, the forests were rife with Ukrainian nationalistic units, especially the UPA, which murdered many of the Jews who fell into their hands.[76] In late 1942, Soviet partisan activity began in the forests of north Volhynia, but by that time most of the Jewish ghettos had been liquidated along with their inhabitants.

The Rovno Underground

On the eve of the war, 25,000 Jews lived in Rovno, the main city of Volhynia. The city was occupied on June 28, 1941, and during July and August, 3,000 of its Jews were murdered. Koch, the *Reichskommissar* for the Ukraine, chose it as the

---

75. Cholawski, *Jews of Belorussia*, 153, 173–74, 223, 248; Nahman Tamir, ed., *The Book of Pinsk* [Hebrew] (Tel Aviv, 1966), 341–43, 349–50.
76. For the Ukrainska Povstanska Armia (UPA), see chapter 3.

capital of the *Reichskommissariat*, which was tragic for the fate of the Jews living there. On November 5, Dr. Beer, Rovno's *Gebietskommissar*, informed the *Judenrat* that the Jews without a *shain* (working license) were to present themselves the following day and would be sent to work. On November 6 and 7, 15,000–18,000 Jews were taken from the city to the Sosenki forest, 6 kilometers (4 miles) away, and shot. Killing on such an enormous scale was exceptional in *Generalbezirk* Volhynia at that time. It was apparently the result of the Germans' immediate need for empty buildings in Rovno, the capital of the *Reichskommissariat*, in order to house their installations and offices, and many employees.[77] The Rovno ghetto was erected in December 1941, and the Jews with *shainen* were imprisoned in it along with their families, a total of about 5,000 people. On July 13, 1942, the ghetto was surrounded and the Jews were taken in freight cars to Kostopol and from there to the forest, where they were shot. On the eve of the ghetto's destruction a few groups of young Jews escaped, some of them reaching the partisans.

There is no information available about a ghetto underground. This was possibly the result of the murder of more than three-quarters of the city's Jews in November 1941, most of whom belonged to the age group that had organized the undergrounds in the other ghettos. There were incidents of individual resistance, of armed men who opened fire and killed German policemen who came to arrest them. During the ghetto's liquidation, hand grenades were tossed from some of the buildings, killing one German and critically wounding two Ukrainian policemen.[78]

The Lvov Underground

The German army occupied Lvov on June 30, 1941. Lvov was the capital of the Galicia district and home to 135,000–160,000 Jews, among them thousands of refugees. When the Germans entered the city, the local Ukrainian population began a pogrom that lasted until July 3 and murdered 4,000 Jews. From July 25 to 28, the Ukrainians carried out another pogrom, killing 1,500 Jews. In September 1941, an SS-controlled labor camp was erected in the northwest of the city on Janovska Street, which became a nightmare for Lvov's Jews. On November 8 the Germans announced that a ghetto would be established and

---

77. Spector, *Holocaust*, 113–15. The sources also give the number killed as 18,000–21,000.

78. Ibid., 212. Spector also mentions two young Jews, Yitzhak Schneider and Niuna Kolilnik, who killed some German policemen.

the Jews were ordered to move into it by December 15. On their way to the ghetto, German and Ukrainian police pulled out 5,000 old and sick Jews took them to a nearby forest and shot them. Between March 19 and April 1, 1942, 15,000 Jews were deported from the Lvov ghetto to the death camp at Belzec. During the second *Aktion,* in August 1942, 50,000–60,000 Jews were taken there and murdered (although some were murdered in Lvov itself), leaving between 50,000 and 60,000 Jews alive in the city.[79]

In the Lvov ghetto, one of the largest in the occupied Soviet territories, there was very limited underground activity. Following the major *Aktion* in mid-August 1942, several groups organized to arm themselves and escape to the forests. The forests with conditions suitable for partisan activity were those near Brody, 80–100 kilometers (50–62 miles) northeast of Lvov. It was virtually impossible to cross such a distance on foot and pass undetected through a hostile Ukrainian population. In late 1942 or early 1943, twenty armed Jews left the ghetto for the Brody forests. The two drivers they hired betrayed them to the police, who ambushed and killed them all in the ensuing exchange of fire. Most attempts to escape failed, and only a few small groups managed to get away and join the partisans.[80]

There were some instances of armed resistance during the liquidation of the Lvov ghetto in June 1943. A group of Jews opened fire on the German and Ukrainian police forces who were searching the ghetto, and the houses in which they were hiding were set on fire or blown up. On June 30, 1943, SS-*Gruppenführer* Katzmann reported the following:

> As the number of Jews decreased their resistance became greater. They defended themselves with all types of weapons, especially those…they bought…from Italian soldiers stationed in the district.… Owing to increasingly grave reports about the growing arming of the Jews, the sharpest possible measures were taken to eliminate Jewish banditry during the last two weeks of June 1943.… In Lvov…to avoid losses to German forces, several houses were blown up or destroyed by fire.[81]

---

79. Tadeusz Zaderecki, *When the Swastika Ruled Lvov* [Hebrew] (Jerusalem: Yad Vashem, 1982), 62–63, 228–33.

80. Yones (*Smoke*, 235, 237) described a small group, led by Dr. Boris Fliskin, which reached the Carpathians mountains and joined the partisans. He also mentioned a group led by a Jewish police officer, Goldberg, which joined the partisans.

81. Nuremberg documents, L-18.

The Polish underground Armia Krajowa was active in Lvov but no organized help was extended to the Jews, although there were instances of help being provided on the basis of personal acquaintance.[82] No fighting underground movements were established in the other large ghettos of eastern Galicia, Ternopol and Stanislavov (Ivano-Frankovsk), but a few small groups of armed Jews did escape to the forests. During the liquidation of the Ternopol ghetto, Jews hiding in a cellar opened fire on German forces, and the Germans responded by tossing in hand grenades. There is no further information about this incident or about the identity of the Jews involved.[83]

8. UNDERGROUND ACTIVITY AND ARMED RESISTANCE IN THE SMALL GHETTOS

The idea of armed resistance in the ghettos whose inhabitants numbered from a few hundred to a few thousand, came, as in the large ghettos, in the wake of a massacre. In contrast to the ghettos in the larger cities, many of the smaller ones were located near forests, tipping the scales in favor of escaping to fight with the partisans rather than open rebellion. In addition, the houses in the small ghettos were made of wood and provided poor shelter for fighters. Revolt in those ghettos was appropriate for one kind of resistance: should the ghetto be liquidated before its inmates could escape to the forests, the houses could be set on fire and the flames might spread beyond the confines of the ghetto. The chaos caused by the flames and smoke could be used for a mass escape from the ghetto, and thus in many of the smaller ghettos it was the chosen form of an uprising.

Organizing for resistance and escape had already begun in some of the small ghettos during the last months of 1941, but most began during the spring of 1942 along with the mass *Aktionen* in western Byelorussia and the western Ukraine. At the same time, partisan groups began organizing in the forests, but only a few of them belonged to the organized Soviet partisan movement.[84] There were dozens of examples of Jews in the small ghettos who resisted, escaped and joined the partisans. Those given below were the more prominent ones,

---

82. Yones, *Smoke*, 243.

83. Ibid., 352; P. Korngrun ed., *Encyclopedia of the Jewish Diaspora: Memorial Book for the Countries of the Diaspora and Their Communities* [Hebrew], Ternopol (Jerusalem: Society for Encyclopedias of the Diaspora, 1955), 413.

84. David Stockfisch, ed., *The Book of Nesvizh* [Hebrew] (Tel Aviv, 1976), 419.

and they demonstrate the way the Jews organized and operated in the ghettos and the problems they were confronted with. For the smaller ghettos as for the large ones, acquiring weapons (and the amount acquired) determined, in great measure, the extent and results of their resistance.

In the Nesvizh ghetto, east of Baranovichi, an underground organized in the wake of the *Aktion* conducted on October 30, 1941, in which most of the town's Jews were murdered; only about 600 remained in the ghetto. As in most of the smaller ghettos, the underground did not organize along political lines, but according to personal acquaintance and the willingness to fight.

In the middle of July 1942, it became known that the ghetto in the neighboring town of Gorodeya had been liquidated, and the underground, which had a certain quantity of weapons, organized to fight. Its members planned to set the ghetto on fire and, during the battle, to break out into the forest with the rest of the Jews. They informed the ghetto residents of the plan because resistance and mass flight demanded their cooperation. On July 20, 1942, a Lithuanian police company arrived, heralding the end of the ghetto. At dawn the following day, the Jewish underground took up defensive positions and the ghetto population prepared to escape, although some of them hid in *malinas*.

The German in charge of the ghetto told the *Judenrat* that he intended to conduct a "selection" and leave 30 Jews whose professions were vital. The *Judenrat* was to aid in the selection. When they refused, the German and Lithuanian police opened fire on the ghetto. The underground returned fire, and a mass escape through the ghetto gate and the fences began. According to one of the escapees:

> Suddenly someone shouted: "Jews, follow me, we'll break through the gate!" …At that moment grenades blew up from the other side of the ghetto.… There were dead and wounded from the first attempt to break through the gate.… The ghetto's weapon was fire. The houses, dry wooden houses, were sprayed with gasoline.… The murderers were confused by the spreading fire, the entire ghetto was going up in flames.… In the Polish street, we saw the Christians carrying their household goods to the fields because the tongues of fire were already licking at their houses.[85]

---

85. Ibid.

As soon as the flames broke out, there was no one to lead the uprising and it was every man for himself. People forced their way out of the gate and through the fences and were killed on the spot, and many others hiding in the *malinas* were burned alive or suffocated by the smoke. Others who managed to escape the burning ghetto were killed by police or local inhabitants. Only a few dozen Jews made it to the nearby Kopil forests. A few policemen were injured in the uprising. On July 22, 1942, the day after the Nesvizh ghetto was liquidated, the Germans also liquidated the ghetto in the nearby town of Kleck. There too, the Jews set fire to the ghetto, burst through the fences and tried to escape, and there too, most of the Jews were killed and only a few made it to the forests and joined the partisans.[86]

Underground activity in the town of Dyatlovo (Zhetl), southwest of Novogrudok in western Byelorussia, began in late 1941. The *Judenrat* chairman, Dr. Alter Dworzecki, established and led the organization. The 60-member underground, which included ghetto policemen, planned the uprising to take place with the liquidation of the ghetto. The first weapons, two rifles, were bought from farmers and smuggled into the ghetto in January 1942. Later more weapons were purchased, and finally they had 12 guns; most of the money came from the *Judenrat*. In the spring of 1942, news reached the ghetto that there were partisans in the forests near the town, and Dworzecki decided that priority should be given to preparations for joining them but without abandoning the idea of an uprising. Following that decision and in view of the danger inherent in bringing weapons into the ghetto, they decided to hide some of them in a forest near the town. In the middle of April 1942, Shalom Fiulon, an underground member, was captured while trying to buy arms; the underground's local contact person had informed on him. He was interrogated and tortured, and Dworzecki, fearing what he might reveal, fled with nine of his comrades to the forests on April 20, 1942. Fiulon, however, had withstood torture and revealed nothing. He threw a note written in Yiddish through the window of his cell which was brought to the ghetto. It read, "They are torturing me terribly, but don't be afraid, I won't give away anything. Rescue me if you can."

The Germans demanded that the *Judenrat* hand over Dworzecki and announced that they would reward whoever brought him in, dead or alive. The affair of the weapons and Dworzecki's disappearance caused bitterness among the ghetto residents, who were afraid of German reprisals. The Germans told

---

86. Cholawski, *Resistance*, 271–72; Zuckerman and Bassok, *Ghetto Wars*, 478–80.

the *Judenrat* that if Dworzecki were not turned in within 24 hours, they would pay for it with their lives. Two days later the Germans murdered the members of the *Judenrat*. On April 30, 1942, the ghetto was surrounded and 1,200 Jews were taken away and shot. The *Aktion* was part of the mass murder of Jews taking place in western Byelorussia at the time, but the discovery of the underground and Dworzecki's escape may have accelerated it.

Dworzecki made contact with one of the non-Jewish partisan groups in the Lipichany forests. On May 11, 1942, they shot Dworzecki and one of his people. The reasons are unclear; they may have shot them for their weapons, or simply because they were Jews. Afterwards, some members of the group returned to the ghetto. Dworzecki's murder and the fact that it had been perpetrated by people who were supposed to be Soviet partisans depressed the ghetto underground but did not stop their activity. Between August 6 and 8, 1942, while the Dyatlovo ghetto was being liquidated, 600 people managed to break out and escape to the forests.[87]

Underground activity in the Svencionys ghetto northeast of Vilnius began in February 1942. The ghetto housed about five hundred Jews who survived the October 1941 *Aktionen*, which killed 2,500. The underground members were youngsters aged between 16 and 19. The group, whose objective was to leave for the forests and join the partisans, quickly grew to 20 members. Some of them worked in the local arsenal of captured Soviet weapons and managed to appropriate about ten guns. On April 13, 1942, two of them were cleaning their weapons when a bullet was accidentally discharged, injuring one of them. They were arrested by the Lithuanian police and the others, fearing that their comrades would be unable to withstand the Sipo interrogation, decided to leave that night. Hundreds of ghetto inmates surrounded the youngsters and begged them to stay, because if the Germans failed to find them they would liquidate the ghetto. The group faced a terrible dilemma, because if they stayed, they faced certain death, and if they left they would endanger the entire ghetto population. They decided to remain. On April 16, 1942, the two who had been arrested were executed. They had withstood torture and not given up the names of their comrades. The group, consisting of 22 young men and women,

---

87. Cholawski, *Resistance*, 169–74; Gefen et al., eds., *The Jewish Partisans* [Hebrew] (Merhavya: Sifriat Hapoalim, 1958), 280–82, 374–80.

left the ghetto for the forests of Adutishki in Byelorussia during the second half of March 1943.[88]

At the beginning of April 1943, the Svencionys ghetto and three other ghettos in the east of *Generalbezirk* Lithuania were liquidated, and almost all of their inhabitants were brought to Ponary near Vilnius and shot. The events were linked to the partisan activity in the areas of Byelorussia close to eastern Lithuania and the Germans' desire to prevent the Jews from joining the partisans. The *Aktion* was described in a report sent by the Sipo commander in Lithuania to the Reich Main Department of Security (RSHA) in Berlin:

> During the month covered by the present report, the Byelorussian areas incorporated into *Generalbezirk* Lithuania, i.e., Svencionys, Asmena…have been cleared of Jews. Those areas which were under constant partisan menace are now completely clear of Jews.[89]

It is uncertain, when they liquidated the Svencionys ghetto, whether or not the Germans knew about the Jews who had escaped to the forests, but the fact that the ghetto was close to an area of partisan activity and that the Jews could join them was, for the Germans, sufficient cause to liquidate the ghetto.

In Mir, southeast of Novogrudok, the underground was established after the *Aktion* on November 9, 1941, in which 1,500 Jews were murdered. Only 850 Jews remained in the ghetto. The local German police employed a man named Josef Oswald as a translator. According to his papers he was an ethnic German, but in fact he was Shmuel Rufeisen, a Jewish refugee from Poland and a member of a Zionist youth movement, whose knowledge of German allowed him to pass as an ethnic German. The ghetto underground made contact with him and he helped them obtain weapons. In early August 1942, he told the underground that an *Aktion* was planned for the next few days, and that on the night of August 10, 1942, most of the local police would leave to hunt for partisans and would be away. He suggested they exploit the situation for a mass escape of the ghetto population. The ghetto people had many reservations: Was the information reliable? If it was, how could they leave with women, children and old people

---

88. Cholawski, *Resistance*, 107–10; Moshe Shutan, *Ghetto and Woods* [Yiddish] (Tel Aviv: Vaad Lehantzahat Halehima Hayehudit, 1971), 25–26, 38–41, 45–46; Yitzhak Arad, *The Partisan* (New York: Holocaust Library, 1979), 67–72, 75–76. The prisoners were Gershon Back (who was wounded) and Reuven Myadziolski, who fired the shot.
89. E. Rozauskas, ed., *Documents Accuse* (Vilnius: Gintaras, 1970), 271–72.

in tow? The underground also had contacts with the *Judenrat*, but they were mainly negative because the *Judenrat* believed their actions endangered the existence of the ghetto.

In the beginning of August, refugee Jews had arrived in Mir, having fled from Nesvizh. They reported that Soviet partisans in the forests were killing Jews and that there was nothing to eat there. The news weakened the ghetto inmates' resolve and desire to escape. Thus on the night of August 10, only 300 of the 850 inmates escaped. Most of them believed that death awaited them on both sides of the ghetto fence and that it was better to stay behind with their families and share a common fate. On August 13, 1942, the Germans annihilated the Jews of Mir.[90]

Kurenets, a township near Vileyka, was occupied on June 24, 1941. Its underground organized during the first months of the occupation and consisted of 12 Jewish youngsters aged 15–19. At first they aided Soviet prisoners of war held nearby, smuggling food to them and helping some of them escape, and later they collected weapons to be able to leave for the forest themselves. Two of them printed underground leaflets in the German printing house where they worked, calling upon the local inhabitants to resist the Germans and sabotage their activities. The leaflets were distributed in August 1941 and were the first in the region. The members made contact with a non-Jewish underground group and in February 1942 jointly sabotaged local bridges. In September 1942, on the eve of the ghetto's liquidation, most of the underground members left for the Rodino forest, and at the end of 1942 joined the partisans. On September 9, when the ghetto was destroyed, 300 of Kurenets's Jews fled, most of them to the Kotlovtsy and Malkevichi forests.[91]

---

90. Cholawski, *Resistance*, 223–28; Zuckerman and Bassok, *Ghetto Wars*, 480–86. After the *Aktion*, the Germans arrested Rufeisen and accused him of informing the Jews. His Jewishness was revealed during his interrogation. He managed to escape and find shelter in a monastery, where he stayed for 16 months. When the search for him became too intense, he escaped to the forests. The Soviet partisans accused him of being a German spy, and only the intervention of some Jews from Mir saved him from execution. Rufeisen adopted Christianity after the war but he identified himself as a Jew. He immigrated to Israel and lived the rest of his life in a monastery. He died in 1998.

91. Moshe Kalcheim, ed., *With Proud Bearing: Chapters in the History of Partisan Fighting in the Naroch Forests* [Hebrew] (Tel Aviv: Irgun Hapartisanim, 1991), 20–21, 131–46.

Glubokoe in northwestern Byelorussia was occupied by the Germans at the end of June 1941, and on October 23 more than 5,000 of the city's Jews were forced into the ghetto. On June 19, 1942, half of the Jews in the ghetto were murdered, and Jews from liquidated ghettos were brought in. After the *Aktion*, an underground organized and groups of young Jews left for the forests. They joined the partisan units, liaised between the ghetto and the partisans, and decided on a mutual plan of action.

In August 1943, the partisans of the Suvorov brigade were supposed to attack the German forces in the town as the 3,000 Jews in the ghetto rebelled. However, the ghetto was liquidated before the plan could be put into action. The *Judenrat* learned of the plan to liquidate the ghetto a few days beforehand, when the Sipo informed them that all the Jews were to be transported to camps in the *Generalgouvernement*. The *Judenrat* passed the information on to the underground and ghetto population, and they prepared for resistance and escape. When the German and local police forces entered the ghetto at dawn on August 20, 1943, they were met with gunfire. Paul Rachmann, the *Gebietskommissar* of Glubokoe, wrote the following in a report to the *Generalkommissar* of Byelorussia, dated August 30, 1943:

> On Friday, August 20, 1943, at five in the morning, there was the sound of heavy gunfire.... An immediate personal investigation of the location revealed to me that the intention was to evacuate the ghetto in Glubokoe and to transfer the Jews to concentration camps in the *Generalgouvernement*.... After the exchange of shots, there was a spontaneous outbreak of fire in some of the houses in the ghetto and the flames spread swiftly [through the houses] that were built of wood and [had] thatched roofs. A strong wind on August 20 increased the general conflagration.... Attempts made by the fire brigade did not prevent the spread of the fire.... Only when the engineering police blew up the buildings was it possible to prevent [its] spread. I have no details as to the extent of the battles in the ghetto. Taking into consideration the general situation in the area during the past weeks, I can state with assurance that the ghetto is a focus of great danger. In my opinion, given the circumstances, it is only fortunate that on August 17, the day of the uprising of the Druzhina unit [Verbandes] in Dokschytse, the ghetto did not become a source of grave danger to Glubokoe, where the security forces were very few.[92]

92. TsGAOR LatSSR (Tsentralnyi Gosudarstvennyi Arkhiv Oktyabrskoi Revolutsii

The battle in the ghetto continued for several hours, and hundreds of Jews escaped under cover of fire and smoke. About 200 people from Glubokoe, some wounded, made it to the forests of Naroch and Kozyany.[93]

Lakhva, in Polesie, with its 2,500 Jews, was occupied by the Germans on July 8, 1941, and the ghetto was erected on April 1, 1942. The ghetto had an organized underground of 30, most of them belonging to Zionist youth movements. The central figure was Yitzhak Rokhchyn, who was in close contact with Dov Luftin, *Judenrat* chairman. News of the liquidation of the ghettos in the region reached Lakhva during the second half of August 1942. On September 2, they heard that pits were being dug in the vicinity of the town and that the ghetto was under increased surveillance. Rokhchyn proposed to Luftin that they attack the German sentries that night and organize a mass escape, but Luftin preferred waiting until the morning to verify German intentions. The following day, when more German forces arrived, their intentions became clear: they were planning to liquidate the ghetto. Luftin ordered that the houses be set on fire and shots were fired at the forces surrounding the ghetto, hitting some Germans. About 1,000 Jews broke out of the ghetto. Most of them were caught and murdered with the help of the local non-Jewish population, and only about 120 reached the forests.[94]

The Germans occupied Tuchin, in Volhynia, on July 6, 1941. The ghetto was erected only in July 1942, and 3,000 Jews, some from the neighboring towns, were forced into it. Following news of the liquidation of the nearby Rovno ghetto in July 1942 and others in the vicinity, an underground was organized. It was headed by the *Judenrat* chairman, Getzel Schwartzmann. *Judenrat* funds were used to buy weapons, and gasoline was stored to set fire to the 60 cramped buildings which held the ghetto's inmates.

On September 23, information reached the *Judenrat* that an SS unit had arrived and that pits were being dug in the vicinity. It alerted the 60 members of the underground, who were divided into fighting and arson squads. The Germans apparently noticed the preparations and on September 24 opened fire on the ghetto. The underground returned fire and began burning houses and several synagogues

Latviiskoi SSR), Fond R-70, Opis 6, Delo 80. Information relating to the Druzhina Verbandes refers to the battalion of German collaborators, which consisted mainly of Russian, Byelorussian and Ukrainian former prisoners of war involved in anti-partisan warfare. In the region of the towns of Dokschytse, the battalion, commanded by Colonel Radionov, turned against the German force from Glubokoe, killed dozens of them and joined the partisans.

93. Gefen et al., *Jewish Partisans*, 180–82; Zuckerman and Bassok, *Ghetto Wars*, 492.
94. Zuckerman and Bassok, *Ghetto Wars*, 477–78; Cholawski, *Resistance*, 303–5.

outside the ghetto which had been used to store grain. People broke out of the ghetto, and about 2,000 Jews, two-thirds of the ghetto population, managed to escape to the Pustomyty forests, northeast of the town. The shooting and arson continued for two days, during which several local and German police were killed, as well most of the Jewish underground. Schwartzmann did not escape, but presented himself to the German commander and said that he was personally responsible for what had happened. He was shot in the Jewish cemetery. Most of the escapees were shot by the police and the local non-Jewish population.[95]

Ilya Ehrenburg described the organized resistance of the Jews who opened fire on the Germans as they were liquidating the ghettos in Ostrog, Proskurov and Yarmolichi in the eastern Ukraine, in which German and local police were killed.[96] Nothing further has been found about those events. Similar acts of resistance and escape took place in dozens of smaller ghettos, and consisted of arson, mass breakouts through the ghetto fences and gates and escape to the forests. They occurred when the ghetto inmates realized that the last day of the ghetto had arrived and that, having nothing to lose, their only chance of survival, slim as it might be, was by uprising. In many instances the *Judenrat* and the ghetto police force cooperated in preparing and carrying out the uprising.

9. JEWS IN NON-JEWISH UNDERGROUND MOVEMENTS

There were many Jews who belonged to multinational Communist underground groups in various cities in the occupied territories. This section describes some of the leaders and underground activists who excelled in their work and whose names were famous throughout the Soviet Union, although their nationality was concealed and they were often allied with other nationalities; German sources frequently referred to Jews as being among captured underground activists.

Some of the undergrounds had been established before the retreat of the Red Army, and stayed behind to carry out subversive activity. Leaving Jews behind German lines for whatever reason was a mistake on the part of the Soviets, who did not know or did not understand that even before they had a chance to fulfill their missions, they would be arrested and murdered along with their coreligionists. The anti-Semitism rife in those areas meant that the local population's support, essential for any underground activity, was not forthcoming.

---

95.   Zuckerman and Bassok, *Ghetto Wars*, 488–89; Spector, *Holocaust*, 214–17.
96.   Ilya Ehrenburg and Vasily Grossman, *The Black Book* (New York: Holocaust Library, 1980), 26–27.

Isai Kazinets, who organized and headed the Communist underground in Minsk, was mentioned in Soviet sources as secretary of the underground Communist Party Urban Committee, but no mention was made of his being Jewish.[97] A small underground was active in Minsk, separate from Kazinets's organization, which helped prisoner-of-war officers to escape. A German patrol arrested and interrogated some of the escapees, and they revealed the identity of the people who had helped them. Consequently, two men and one woman were arrested and hanged in the city center on October 26, 1941. The Germans placed a sign on the young woman in German and Russian reading, "We are partisans who shot German soldiers," and photographed the execution. After the liberation of Minsk, the Soviets found and published the photographs with special emphasis on the young woman, whose behavior in front of her executors was heroic. The executed partisans were identified as Volodya Shcherbachevich and Kiril Trus. The girl, who was classified as "unidentified" (*neizvestnaia*), was Maria Borisova Bruskina, a 17-year-old Jewess, whose mother, Lucia Bruskina, had been murdered in the Minsk ghetto. Photographs of the three were displayed in many Soviet museums, but the Jewish girl continued to be "unidentified."[98]

MASHA BRUSKINA ON THE WAY TO EXECUTION

97.   R.P. Platonov et al., eds., *V Nepokorennom Minske* (Minsk: Belarus, 1987), 7, 50, 209.
98.   G. Shapiro and C. Averbukh, eds., *Ocherki Evreiskovo Geroizma* (Tel Aviv and Kiev, 1994), 97–101.

Masha (Maria) Bruskina worked in a hospital where wounded prisoners of war were treated and did in fact help them escape. A young Jewish doctor, Sonia Idelson, worked at the same hospital and arranged for her to work there. After Bruskina was arrested and hanged, Idelson was arrested and hanged shortly thereafter.[99]

The secretary of the underground Communist Committee in Kiev was Semion Bruz, a central figure in the local underground movement. In June 1942, the Germans exposed the town's underground and arrested most of its members. He shot himself to avoid falling into German hands. Tanya Marcus was Jewish and a heroine of the Kiev underground. Her forged documents gave her the Georgian name Markusidze, and she pretended to be the daughter of a Georgian prince killed by the Communists. As such, and as someone

who hated the Soviet regime, she offered her services to the Germans. She was 20 years old and beautiful, and German officers sought her favors. The information she obtained enabled the underground to kill some of them. In August 1942, when the Germans discovered who she was, she fled but was caught on her way to the partisans in the Chernigov region, interrogated and shot. According to the Sipo report of October 16, 1942, among the central figures of the terrorist groups in Kiev was the Georgian Tatyana Markusidze, who was born in Tbilisi on September 21, 1921. A report by the district committee of the Communist Party in Kiev dated August 15, 1946, describing the

TANYA MARCUS

city's underground activity during the occupation, also mentioned the "brave Komsomol girl who knew no fear, Tanya Marcus, who was known as Markusidze. An active member in the sabotage movement, she personally killed dozens of soldiers, officers and collaborators…. She carried out very responsible operations on behalf of the organization by preparing sabotage operations, etc."[100]

99. Sheinker, *Geroism Evreev*, 189–90. Sheinker writes that a POW named Boris Rudzianko informed on the two woman when he was caught trying to escape. In 1944 he was court martialed by the Soviets and sentenced to death.

100. Leonid Berenshtein and Ster Elisavetskii, *Evrei Geroi Soprotivlenia* (Tel Aviv: Krugozor, 1998), 30–32; Iurchuk et al., *Sovetskaya*, vol. 1, 452.

In this and other documents describing her heroism, no mention is made of the fact that Tanya Marcus was Jewish.

Olga Svetlichnaya was also an underground activist in Kiev, and underground members held meetings in her apartment and hid there when the Germans were looking for them. It also served as a hiding place for Soviet soldiers who had escaped captivity and who wanted to join partisan units. She supported herself by baking cookies and selling them in the market. The week before the liberation of Kiev she was arrested and tortured but did not betray her comrades. On November 6, 1943, she was saved from certain death when Soviet tanks entered the city before the Germans could execute her. Hiding behind the name Olga Svetlichnaia was a Jewish woman named Golda Izrailovich, wife of Soviet pilot Vasily Svetlichnyi. She and her young children had not managed to evacuate from Kiev, and with the help of friends she acquired forged documents and moved to an apartment where she was unknown.[101]

Soviet sources also mention a Jew named Boris Sondak, an underground member in Dnepropetrovsk, who participated in blowing up the bridge over the Dnieper River. Sondak and his comrades were arrested in October 1942 and executed.[102]

According to the *Einsatzgruppe* report dated November 11, 1941, an underground group was exposed in Mogilev in Byelorussia. Of the 55 members who were arrested, 22 were Jews, who according to the report "worked with fanatical zeal to further strengthen the organization." The report also stated that they had been liquidated and that "collective measures were carried out against the Jews" in Mogilev.[103]

One of the most active underground groups in Odessa was led by V. Molodotsov. They attacked Romanian soldiers, carried out acts of sabotage and relayed information to Moscow. The group, which was 25 strong, was betrayed by one of its members. On September 10, 1942, the *Odesska Gazzetta* published an article about the Romanian military tribunal of the members who had been captured. The list of accused included eight clearly Jewish names. It is reasonable to assume that some of the remaining 17 were Jews, even though their names did not indicate it. Twelve of the accused, including the eight Jews,

---

101. Sheinker, *Geroism Evreev*, 191–92.
102. Iurchuk et al., *Sovetskaya*, vol. 1, 435–37; Berenshtein and Elisavetskii, *Evrei Geroi*, 36–37.
103. Arad et al., *Einsatzgruppen Reports*, Report no. 133, p. 232.

were sentenced to death and executed on October 24, 1942, and the remainder were sentenced to lengthy prison terms.[104]

According to the *Einsatzgruppe* report dated September 15, 1942, "fifteen members of an illegal Communist organization under the leadership of a Jew were arrested in Berdichev [Ukraine].... They intended to set the grain harvest on fire and to derail trains."[105]

In Zaporozhye in the Ukraine an underground was organized in April 1942, under the name of the Gonchar Group. It was composed of workers from the Zaporozhstal factory and sailors who had participated in the defense of Odessa and managed to slip out and reach Zaporozhye. One of its leaders was a Jew named Leonid Wiener, a sailor. On July 23, 1943, the Germans discovered the underground, arrested 40 of its members (Wiener among them) and executed them on September 14, 1943. After he died, a letter to his wife and children was found among his clothing. The letter stated: "We are dying. Whoever finds this, send it to Voznesenka, 26 Baranova St., apt. 4." At the end of the letter he wrote: "Liuba, when the children grow up tell them [about what happened to me] and keep them safe. Kiss them for me as a loving mother. I send you kisses as well. Goodbye, goodbye forever. Leonid."[106]

Extensive research on the role of Jews and their activity in the non-Jewish underground in the occupied Soviet territories has yet to be conducted, and will certainly reveal many names of Jews who held key positions and carried out extraordinary missions.

10. UNDERGROUND AND ESCAPE FROM THE SITES OF AKTION 1005

The German authorities did not content themselves with merely killing Jews, but also worked to obliterate the traces of their crimes. By the spring-summer of 1942, news of mass murders began to emerge in Soviet and Allied media. It also seems that SS *Reichsführer* Himmler, after the German defeats at the Moscow front in the winter of 1941–42, realized that Germany might lose the war, and for historical and practical reasons (the Nazi leaders might be called to account for

---

104. YVA, M-33/315. The Jews were David Karsnoshtein, Ilya Zussovsky, Shaya Feldman, Abraham Buchhalter, Zhenia Forman, Frieda Khayat, Hariton Levinson and Dionisii Shemberg.

105. Arad et al., *Einsatzgruppen Reports*, 362.

106. Leonid Weiner, "Zapiska," *Voice of the Disabled* 16 (2002): 39.

their crimes), the traces of their crimes had to be erased. He ordered that special SS units called *Sonderkommando 1005* be set up, headed by *Standartenführer* Paul Blobel. Their duty was to open the mass graves and cremate the bodies. To train *Sonderkommando* 1005's commanders and the concentration camp staffs to erase the traces of the murders, special courses were organized at the Janovksi camp at Lvov. From 1943 to 1944, before the Germans retreated from the occupied territories of the Soviet Union, hundreds of mass graves were opened, the bodies removed and cremated, the ashes tossed to the winds and tilled into the earth. Jewish camp inmates and Soviet prisoners of war carried out the actual work. The prisoners employed in *Aktion* 1005 knew that the Germans would not let them live once their work was completed. Their underground activity, therefore, had a single objective: escape. Similar activities took place at many *Aktion* 1005 sites, but the better known ones, which had partial success, took place at Babi Yar in Kiev, Ponary near Vilnius and the Ninth Fort in Kaunas.

About 100 Jews, mostly prisoners of war, and a further 200 non-Jews, mostly captured underground members and partisans, were employed in cremating corpses at Babi Yar. Work was carried out during the day, and at night the workers were penned in an underground structure, their legs chained. Zachar Trubakov, a Jew who managed to escape from Babi Yar, testified:

> Throughout our time in Babi Yar there was not a moment we did not think about escape.... The underground group consisted of Volodya Kuklia, Yaakov Kapper, Leonia Duliner [and another 13 names, mostly of Jews] and myself.... [The escape] took place on the night of September 29, 1943. It was symbolic: two years ago on September 29, the Fascist occupiers murdered tens of thousands of people [in Babi Yar].[107]

The escape took place after midnight. At the designated time, the door opened and people broke out, shouting "Hurrah." There was a guard tower opposite and the Germans opened fire on the escapees, most of whom were killed on the spot; others were chased and caught in Kiev and its surroundings. Only 15 of the escapees, mostly Jews, were alive when Kiev was liberated.[108]

At the Ninth Fort in Kaunas, 64 prisoners, four of them not Jewish, were employed in cremating corpses. The prisoners were held in underground cells

---

107. *Sovietish Heimland* (a Yiddish newspaper published in the Soviet Union), 6 (1977): 110–11.

108. Ibid., 162–69; YVA, TR-10/761.

with barred doors and windows. The escape from the fort in late November 1943 was initiated by members of the ghetto underground who had been caught by the Germans on their way to the Augustova forests, along with some Jewish prisoners of war. They were joined by "Brigadier Sasha," a prisoner of war who had directed a group of workers at the fort and who could move around freely. The underground leadership worked out an escape plan whereby they would tunnel out of one of the cells under the fortress walls and all the prisoners would escape. After a few days of silent, secret digging, they hit rock and had to stop. Brigadier Sasha had an alternative plan. He pointed to a dark cell with a steel door. Examination revealed a tunnel leading to the fort's courtyard, and from there another tunnel led to a slope in the field that contained no guard posts.

The escape was set for Christmas, December 25, 1943, at the end of the day when the guards would be celebrating and some of them would be drunk. Since not all the prisoners knew about the plan, the underground leadership decided to inform them on the day of the escape. Three groups formed: one of Jews from Kaunas who planned to return to the ghetto, one of prisoners of war whose main objective was reaching the forests, and one of men who had decided to search for asylum with Lithuanian friends. The four non-Jews decided to return home.

The escape went according to plan, and on the night of December 25, all 64 prisoners managed to escape. As dawn broke on December 26, the Germans discovered they were gone and began a manhunt. Of the 25 escapees who planned to reach the ghetto, 19 managed to enter and go into hiding, six were captured near the ghetto and shot. Footprints in the snow helped the Germans to capture the prisoners of war who wanted to reach the forests. Some of those who had reached the ghetto were helped by the underground to get out and join the partisans in the Rudniki forests.[109] According to the report prepared by the Sipo in Lithuania on January 13, 1944: "On the night of December 25, 1943, there was an escape from the fort of prisoners from Enterprise 1005b. The escape was not noticed at first, and when it was, an immediate manhunt for the fugitives began. So far, we have managed to catch 37 of them, five of whom were shot trying to escape."[110]

---

109. Tsvi Baron and Dov Levin, *History of an Underground* [Hebrew] (Jerusalem: Yad Vashem, 1962), 162–69; Feitelson, *Truth*, 202–39; 333–39.
110. TsGA LitSSR (Tsentralnyi Gosudarstvennyi Arkhiv Litovskoi SSR), Fond 44, Opis 1, Delo 61.

In Ponary near Vilnius, 80 Jews were employed in cremating corpses; ten of them were prisoners of war. They were kept penned in an underground bunker situated in a pit six-to-eight meters deep with their legs chained; to enter it they climbed down a ladder which was then raised. After the escape of the prisoners from the Ninth Fort, the bunker was fenced in with barbed wire and mines were planted around it.

At the beginning of October 1943, some of them planned an escape. One of the planners was a prisoner of war named Yuri Ferber, who was an engineer. The plan was to dig a tunnel 30–35 meters long from the bunker under the barbed wire fence. In January 1944, they began work under Ferber's direction, digging with soup spoons at night. They hid the earth they removed under their pallets and between the double boards separating the cells, and constructed supports to keep the tunnel from collapsing. One of the most difficult problems was keeping the tunnel on an exact course and keeping it away from guard stations.

It took them three months to finish the tunnel. The breakout took place on the night of April 16, 1944. The shackles were sawed off the prisoners' legs with a metal file found while exhuming the bodies. About 40 prisoners managed to escape through the tunnel before the guards noticed them and opened fire; the remaining prisoners stayed in the bunker. About 25 of the escapees were shot or captured, 15 managed to escape and 11 of them reached the Rudniki forests and joined the partisans.[111]

The conditions under which the undergrounds operated at the *Aktion* 1005 sites were harsher than those in the ghettos: the prisoners were held in cells and bunkers, in most instances they were shackled and carefully guarded, and therefore organizing and carrying out escapes were daring undertakings that had almost no chance of success. Most of those who escaped were killed, but the few who succeeded were saved, since without a doubt they would have been murdered once their work was completed. At the many dozens of *Aktion* 1005 sites where escape was not organized or where escape attempts were unsuccessful, there were no survivors. Members of the Jewish undergrounds at the *Aktion* 1005 sites proved that resourcefulness, initiative and not abandoning hope could make it possible for at least some of them to survive.

---

111. Arad, *Ghetto in Flames*, 444–45; Abraham Sutzkever, *Vilnius Ghetto* [Hebrew] (Tel Aviv: Shakui, 1947), 198–99.

11. JEWISH PRISONERS OF WAR IN THE UNDERGROUNDS AND UPRISINGS

The Fate of Jewish Prisoners of War

The fate of Soviet Jewish soldiers who were captured by the Germans was harder and crueler than that of their non-Jewish comrades. Their struggle to survive had almost no chance of succeeding, and in fact most of them perished. Before the Germans discovered their nationality, the Jewish prisoners suffered from the same cruelty with which the Germans treated all their Soviet prisoners of war. They died of starvation, sickness and cold in the camps or on forced marches over hundreds of kilometers to the camps in the rear areas.

Soviet and German sources that relate to Red Army prisoners of war do not give any numbers of Jewish prisoners at all, so the estimates are general. Within the pre-1939 borders, the Jews made up 1.78 percent of the population. If it is assumed that they made up the same percentage in the Red Army, then of the 5,750,000 Soviet prisoners of war, about 102,000 should have been Jews. In reality, the number was smaller. There were Soviet prisoners of war who deserted to the enemy, especially during the first half year of the war. Jewish soldiers, on the other hand, who knew that the Germans would treat them brutally and murder them, were not among those who willingly went into captivity. Thus the number of Jewish prisoners of war can be estimated at between 80,000 and 85,000.

Near the front there were prisoner collection points (*Armee-Gefangenensammelstellen*). Prisoners were brought to them as soon as they were captured, and after a stay of a few days were transferred to transit camps (*Durchgangslager*, *Dulags* for short). Most of the camps were set up in open areas, surrounded by barbed-wire fences interspersed with guard towers. From the *Dulags* the prisoners were transferred to permanent camps called *Kriegsgefangenen-Mannschaftsstammlager* (*Stalags* for short), which were established in the more rear areas of the occupied territories of the Soviet Union, or in the *Generalgouvernement* and in Germany. Officers were separated from the other prisoners at the collection points and held in different camps. Conditions in the *Stalags* were marginally better than those at the collection points and *Dulags*.

The first order dealing directly with the deliberate murder of some Soviet prisoners of war issued prior to the invasion was known as the Commissars Order, and gave the German army power to execute all prisoners who were commissars or Communist activists. To implement the order, an agreement was reached between the army and the SS about placing Security Police (Sipo) teams in prisoner-of-war camps. The agreement also stated that Jewish prisoners of war were to be murdered. It was the army's task to select the groups destined for extermination and to hand them over to the camp Sipo teams, which usually were in charge of the actual executions. On July 17, 1941, Heydrich issued his *Einsatzbefel* No. 8, which stated: "The following must be singled out: all the important state and party functionaries...the political commissars in the Red Army...members of the Soviet-Russian intelligentsia, all the Jews.... Executions should not take place inside the camps but nearby."[112] An extensive web of informants (*Vertrauensmanner*) operated among the prisoners, and it was their job was to supply information to the camp authorities about the presence of commissars and Jews and about activity among the prisoners.[113]

The only way for a Jewish prisoner of war to survive was to hide his identity. Many Jewish soldiers tried to do so but only a few succeeded. There were three main obstacles: physical appearance, circumcision and non-Jewish prisoners who would inform the Germans. From the first days in captivity, the Germans scrutinized the prisoners to discover who was Jewish. Lieutenant Alexander Abugov, a Jew who was taken prisoner during the first weeks of the war, told the following story:

> On July 28 [1941] we were surrounded.... Many soldiers managed to change their uniforms for civilian clothing and tried to convince others to get rid of their weapons, to change their clothing and stop fighting the useless war, for the Germans had surrounded us and there was no place to run to. I decided to sneak away alone.... I went eastward and on the way entered a village.... I decided to take off my officer's uniform and dress myself like a peasant.... I stayed in the village until August 5. At dawn I heard the Germans surrounding the village and searching for men of draft age.... I was taken prisoner.... They led us toward Uman. We covered 40–50 kilometers a day without food or water.... On the 12th day of captivity the Germans announced a role call according to nationality. Every nationality had a sign with

112. Trial of the Major War Criminals (Nuremberg, 1947), 111–13, Nuremberg Documents, PS-502.
113. Nuremberg Documents, PS-1519; Christian Streit, *Keine Kameraden: Die Wehrmacht und die sowietischen Kriegsgefangenen 1941–1945* (Stuttgart, 1978), 181–82.

a heading. The first column was for Jews, and as a Jew I stood in it, in the first group of five. After us, in the same order, were the Russians. An SS officer came, walked around.... I was wearing a hat with a wide brim and I looked like a peasant. The SS officer came close to me and said, "Are you a Jew (*Jude*)?" I had never heard the word in Russian so I didn't understand him. He called for an interpreter who asked me which nationality I belonged to. Only then did I understand what was going on and I answered that I was Russian. The SS officer struck me on the back with his stick, yelled at me, yanked me out of the column of Jews and shoved me in with the Russians.

On the 13th day of captivity they marched us, some 8,000 prisoners, to the camp in Vinitsa.... The Vinitsa camp was the first in which I saw what it meant to be a Jewish prisoner.... A 50-square-meter building was allocated for 600 Jewish prisoners of war. The building was separated from the rest of the camp by a barbed wire fence.... After midday the persecution of Jewish prisoners began.... During my ten-day stay at the camp, almost none of the Jews survived....[114]

Jewish Prisoners of War in Underground Activities

In the prisoner-of-war camps, especially in the *Stalags*, where prisoners were held for longer periods of time, undergrounds were organized for purposes of escape and/or sabotaging the goods produced by the factories they worked in. Prisoners of war incarcerated in the death camps were among the organizers and activists of undergrounds and uprisings.

One of the best known uprisings was in the Sobibor death camp, led by Lieutenant Alexander Pechersky. He was captured at the front at Vyazma in the fall of 1941. For more than six months he managed to hide the fact that he was Jewish, and only in May 1942, during an attempted escape, did they discover he was a Jew. His luck held when he was brought before the SS, because instead of shooting him they transferred him to their slave-labor camp on Shiroka Street in Minsk. The camp employed hundreds of Jewish prisoners of war and Jews from the Minsk ghetto in various physical tasks. At the end of September 1943, the Germans liquidated the Minsk ghetto, and 2,000 Jews, some of them prisoners of war, were transferred from it and from the camp on Shiroka Street

---

114. YVA, 03/2375.

to Sobibor. When they arrived at the camp they were sent directly to the gas chambers, with the exception of 80 men who were identified by the Germans as builders; they were left alive to work in the camp. Most of them were Jewish prisoners of war, Pechersky among them.

At that time there were about 700 Jewish inmates at Sobibor, and an underground existed there whose objective was uprising and mass flight. When the leaders of the underground learned that there was an officer among the latest arrivals, they offered him the command. Pechersky agreed and planned the uprising, which took place on October 14, 1943. The Jewish prisoners of war who had military experience played a central role. The rebels killed 11 SS men and wounded some of the Ukrainian unit who guarded the camp. The overwhelming majority of the Jews were killed during the uprising and in the ensuing hunt for escapees. About 100 camp inmates, among them some dozen prisoners of war, escaped. Part of them, including Pechersky, joined the Soviet partisans and fought in their ranks until the end of the war.[115]

A different kind of underground activity initiated and led by Jewish prisoners of war took place on German soil. In March 1943, an underground organized in the Soviet officers' prisoner-of-war camp in Schwanseestrasse, Munich. The camp was called General Camp No. 9, and its inmates worked at one of the factories of the Farbenindustrie chemical company, which developed and manufactured synthetic fibers for the military industry. Branches of the underground were established in other camps in south Germany. The underground was called the Joint Brotherhood of Prisoners of War (Bratskoe Sotrudnichestvo Voennoplennykh), and its objective was to sabotage manufactured goods and equipment in the factories, to keep prisoners from volunteering to serve in the German army, to kill informers and traitors among the prisoners and to organize an escape. At that time the Germans were engaged in a propaganda campaign to enlist prisoners as volunteers in anti-aircraft units because of increased Allied bombings, and to find recruits for General Vlasov's "Russian Liberation Army" (Russkaya Osvoboditelnaya Armia). The objective of the escape was either to reach Switzerland or to mingle with the millions of workers from the occupied territories of the Soviet Union who were brought to work in Germany, and turn them into anti-German saboteurs as well. The

---

115. For the underground and uprising at Sobibor, see Yitzhak Arad, *Belzec, Sobibor, Treblinka: The Operation Reinhard Death Camps* (Bloomington and Indianapolis: Indiana University Press, 1987), 306–41.

officers' underground also planned to incite rebellions among the prisoners of war and the millions of foreign slave laborers from the various countries of occupied Europe, in collaboration with anti-Fascist elements in Germany. That was planned to take place when the Third Reich was on the verge of collapse and the Allied armies approached Germany's borders. To that end the underground stockpiled weapons found by prisoners engaged in clearing out buildings damaged by Allied bombings.

The underground was composed of hundreds of prisoners of war, and it had cells in labor camps of workers brought from the Soviet Union. One of the underground organizers and leaders was an officer named Georgi Fesenko. He was a Jew who passed himself off as a Ukrainian and whose real name was Josef Feldman, a physician who had been born in the Zhitomir region. In October 1941, he was captured near Uman in the Ukraine. He escaped, acquired Ukrainian documents in the name of Fesenko and was sent to work in Germany. He spoke German well and was sent to the Schwanseestrasse camp in Munich as an interpreter. Because of his job he could move freely around the camp. He began organizing an underground and found a partner in a Latvian major named Karl Ozolin, commander of a Soviet bomber squadron, who had been captured when his plane was shot down in August 1941. Feldman and Ozolin set up an underground committee that included a Jewish lieutenant named Vladimir Moiseyev, an Odessan whose real name was Boris Groisman, and a Jewish captain named Mikhail Singer, a native of Stalingrad, who as a prisoner also used an assumed non-Jewish name, and other Russian officers. One of the underground leaders in the Mosburg camp near Munich, which was in contact with the Schwanseestrasse underground, was a Jewish captain named Boris Klassov, whose real name was Abraham Yazhemsky, who had been captured in Sevastopol. There were other Jewish officers in the underground who had managed to hide their identities, but no details are known about them. The underground was in contact with a group of anti-Fascist Germans. According to one of the sources, this group was made up of University of Munich students headed by Hans Sholl, who was arrested by the Gestapo in April 1943. The trial of the students lasted from December 1944 to January 1945, when they were executed.[116]

---

116. Efim Brodskii, *Oni Ne Propali Bez Vesti* (Moscow: Mysl, 1987), 72, 89–91, 95, 97, 114, 130–31.

The head of the Gestapo in Munich, *Standartenführer* SS Shefer, sent a report to his superiors in Berlin stating that Feldman had worked for the NKVD before the war, that during the war he had been a battalion commissar and had been captured and after his escape he had been sent by the Central Committee of the Communist Party to Germany to organize resistance groups among the Soviet prisoners of war and slave laborers. None of the details was correct. Feldman had not belonged to the NKVD, nor had he been a commissar nor sent to Germany. He went on his own initiative because he apparently thought that it would be easier for him to survive there as a Jew pretending to be a Ukrainian. However, Shefer's report did contain some truthful information:

> Feldman had forged documents under the name of Giorgi Fesenko.… He arrived in Munich on June 1, 1942, working as an interpreter in the transit camp of the workers from the east, on Schwanseestrasse. Russian prisoners of war were held at the camp from the beginning of November 1942. They were mostly high-ranking officers who were sent from there to various tasks. Feldman stayed in the camp as an interpreter. He immediately began spreading hostile anti-German propaganda among the prisoners, claiming that the Germans were going to shoot them and advising them to organize an escape. Apparently he had the possibility of listening to radio broadcasts from Moscow [in the lodgings of] a Russian immigrant [i.e., an anti-Soviet Russian who had come to Germany after the Civil War] and spread what he heard to the Russian prisoners.…
>
> Feldman exploited his job as an interpreter to learn about the political opinions of the camp prisoners, and it was easy for him to get transfers to other camps for prisoners who did not support his activities. Within a short time he found a most talented partner in the figure of an air force major named Ozolin (who had been born in Riga in 1902) for the purpose of forming a secret organization.… At the end of March or the beginning of April 1943, Feldman told Ozolin that very shortly there would be signs of unrest among the civilian population of Munich because many of them were not content with the food supply and with the terrorist [i.e., Allied] bombings. They both reached the conclusion that the population's discontent should be supported by the activity of their secret organization. To that end Ozolin prepared a plan for the prisoners in the camp, according to

which Lieutenant Mikhail Shikhert (the man responsible for Hut No. 10) and his men would surround the anti-aircraft battery near the camp, gain control of the guns and other weapons and kill the gunners. The mission of Captain Singer, responsible for Hut No. 9, would be to attack and disarm the camp guards. At the same time, Lieutenant Vladimir Moiseyev (Boris Groisman) would open huts 6, 7 and 8 [and release the men inside].... Russian prisoners of war who worked cleaning up the aftermath of the terrorist bombings of Munich had procured at least 10 handguns, brought them to the camp and distributed them to reliable men.[117]

The Gestapo found out about the Joint Brotherhood of Prisoners of War and arrested 314 of its leaders and operatives. Josef Feldman was tortured to death during interrogation on March 10, 1944, and 92 members of the organization, including Groisman, Singer and Yazhemsky, were shot on September 4, 1944.

12. CONCLUSION

Of all the European countries conquered by the Nazis, the first Jewish underground groups organized to wage an armed battle with the Germans were in the occupied territories of the Soviet Union. This was because the Jews there were the first to face total physical annihilation. The underground organizers realized that it was Nazi German policy to murder all the Jews and understood that their response could only be resistance, which might even save some of the Jewish population. This was manifested by ghetto uprisings and partisan fighting in the forests, or both: first the uprising, followed by breaking out of the ghetto for the forest. The first underground nuclei were formed from the Zionist youth movements, the young Bund members and members of the Communist Party who remained under German occupation.

However, even in the occupied territories of the Soviet Union it took the Jews months before they understood they were facing total annihilation. Not in every place where there were mass murders of Jews did they learn the truth. Where the murders were committed during the first weeks and months of the occupation, the Jews did not have the time to understand what was awaiting them or to organize and acquire the weapons necessary for armed resistance. That was the fate of most of the Jews living in the Baltic states and in the pre-

---

117. Ibid., 108–9, 129.

1939 areas of the Soviet Union, among them the large Jewish communities of Kiev and Odessa. Only in places where some of the Jews were left in ghettos at the end of the waves of *Aktionen* did the nuclei of fighting undergrounds emerge. The realization that German policy was aimed at the total annihilation of the Jews, and that it was going to take place in "our" ghetto, was a necessary condition for organizing a fighting underground in the ghetto and/or leaving to fight with the partisans.

Another condition for effective organization was the ability to acquire arms, which were essential for resistance actions within the ghetto, surviving in the forest and waging war as partisans. Sources were limited, and the best places were the German depots of captured arms where ghetto Jews and members of the underground worked. The organizations also manufactured their own weapons: hand grenades, Molotov cocktails, knives and axes. Another source was the local population, which had collected and hidden weapons when the Polish army collapsed in September 1939 and when the Red Army retreated in June and July 1941. To acquire weapons, one had to locate them, make certain their owners would not inform the German authorities and then pay an exorbitant price. Quite often the money was paid but either the weapons were not delivered or they were unusable; if cheated, the Jews could do nothing, while the vendor could always turn them over to the Germans. The Jewish undergrounds in the ghettos did not receive weapons either from the non-Jewish undergrounds or from the partisans operating in the forests.

The weapons they did manage to acquire were smuggled into the ghetto through the gates and breaks in the fences, through sewer pipes and tunnels which served as passageways from the ghetto to the outside world; they were smuggled in coffins and garbage wagons. Some members of the Jewish police force who guarded the ghetto gates helped in smuggling the arms. To that end the underground enlisted members of the Jewish police and even sent its own members to serve in the force.

Another factor influencing the organization of an armed underground was demography. In the annexed territories and in the areas around Minsk, which were occupied by the Germans during the first days or weeks of the war, there was no organized evacuation and no mass draft for the army. As a result, the overwhelming majority of the Jews remained in the occupied territories, including the youngsters, the natural reservoir for a fighting underground. The more eastern regions, on the other hand – the pre-1939 areas – were occupied later, after the evacuation of institutions and factories had been organized and after most of the men had been drafted into the army. Most of the Jews who remained there were either children, women, the elderly or the disabled, and thus there was no human foundation on which to build a fighting underground.

In most towns where the ghettos continued to exist even after the *Aktionen*, undergrounds of between a few dozen to hundreds of members organized. In some of the ghettos they hoped to leave for the forests and fight in the ranks of the partisans, and in others to organize an uprising. The differences in objective were often ideological: in the Minsk ghetto, for example, where the organization was Communist and generally Soviet, the underground wanted to send its members into the forests to fight as partisans, as the authorities in Moscow had demanded. The Jewish-national aspect, including rescuing Jews, was secondary and came later. In the Vilnius ghetto, on the other hand, where the FPO was the main underground organization and most of its members belonged to Zionist youth movements, the Jewish-national aspect was foremost. When the organization was established, it was decided that "self-defense [was] a national act, the fight of the people for its honor." The FPO's battle regulations stated that it viewed itself "as part of the Jewish population in the ghetto," and did not want to alienate itself by leaving for the forests as long as the ghetto was still standing. One of its fundamental elements was the rescue of Jews via a mass escape from the ghetto, during the uprising which would break out when the Germans decided to liquidate the ghetto.

Nevertheless, there were factors that influenced the underground's objectives more than ideology. The presence of nearby forests where partisans were active and their readiness to accept Jews into their ranks was no less important.[118] Those were the conditions prevailing in the Minsk region during the first months of the occupation, which were compatible with the underground's Communist-Jewish ideology. In the Kaunas ghetto, the Communist group that organized at the end of 1941 did not plan to send their members into the forests because there were no large forests in the region and no Soviet partisan activity. Only when conditions changed in the fall of 1943 and Soviet partisans were active in the forests, even if they were somewhat distant, was a way found to leave the ghetto. In Vilnius the FPO planned a ghetto uprising, but once contact was made with partisans in the forests in the spring and summer of 1943, and the

---

118. For the attitude of the Soviet partisan movement toward the Jews in the forests, see chapter 5.

ghetto inhabitants did not respond to the call for an uprising in the beginning of September 1943, the option of the forest prevailed.

In the smaller ghettos, especially in western Byelorussia, the undergrounds' first choice was to leave for the nearby forests, and when Soviet partisans organized in them and did not reject the Jews, the ghetto inmates began leaving. Even the undergrounds that planned uprisings wanted to join the partisans eventually.

The relations between the undergrounds, the *Judenrat* and the ghetto population were complex. They were principally influenced by the underground's limited ability to rescue Jews and by the palpable danger caused to the entire ghetto population by bringing weapons into the ghetto or by some inmates escaping to the partisans. An uprising in the ghetto could not save the overwhelming majority of its inmates. It could help a few escape, but then there was the question, to where? Only in the rarest instances was it possible to find a haven among the local population,[119] and the forest was no place for children, women and the elderly; only young people with weapons could operate and survive there.

Therefore, in confrontations between the underground and the *Judenrat*, the ghetto population usually sided with the *Judenrat*, and one very prominent example was the Wittenberg affair in the Vilnius ghetto. There were also confrontations in the ghettos of Pinsk, Baranovichi, Novogrudok and others. In all such cases, the *Judenrat* could not bend the underground to its will. Quite the opposite was true: the stronger side was usually the underground, which had weapons, while the only weapon the *Judenrat* or the general ghetto population could muster was moral pressure. It should be noted that in every case in which moral pressure was exerted, the underground folded and put only itself in danger, not the Jews of the ghetto.

In some of the ghettos, the *Judenrat* and ghetto police collaborated with the underground, as was the case in Minsk, Kaunas and many small ghettos. In many ghettos members of the Jewish police belonged to the underground, and in the ghettos in Kaunas, Riga and Minsk scores of police were executed. Cases in which the Jewish police openly aided the Germans were few, and such conduct was not characteristic of the Jewish police in the occupied territories of the Soviet Union.

---

119. For the attitude of the local population to the Jews, see chapter 5.

In the ghettos where the underground planned an armed uprising, it was always planned for the eve of the certain, complete destruction of the ghetto, when an uprising was the only alternative to going to the pits to be shot. In Vilnius, Baranovichi and other places where it was uncertain whether the *Aktion* taking place or about to take place was in fact the one that would put an end to the ghetto, the uprising was postponed and in the end was not carried out. In the small ghettos of Lakhva, Tuchin, Glubokoe and some others, uprisings did take place because both the underground and ghetto inmates realized that the end had come and that it was the only way to save at least a few Jews.

The fighting Jewish undergrounds tried to make contact with anti-German undergrounds outside the ghetto because they needed their help to acquire weapons and leave for the forests, and on occasion to find shelter with them. Having an ally outside the ghetto was an important morale booster and made the underground members feel that they were not isolated. In certain cases, as in the Wittenberg affair or the collapse of the Minsk ghetto underground, the relations with the non-Jewish undergrounds ended in the worst fashion possible: the exposure, arrest and execution of scores of underground members. With the exception of marginal aid provided in Minsk and Kaunas and the exodus of the last group of FPO members from the Vilnius ghetto, the Jewish undergrounds received no help at all from their non-Jewish counterparts.

Many of the underground leaders and activists in various places were refugees, individuals who wound up in various places because of the vagaries of war and the Holocaust. Some of them had fled from the German occupation in Poland only to find themselves once again in occupied territory when the Germans invaded the Soviet Union. Among the many refugees who headed and were active in the underground movements mentioned above, the following should be especially noted: Hersh Smolar from the underground in the Minsk ghetto, Alter Dworzecki in Dyatlovo and Shmuel Rufeisen in Mir.

The important part refugees played in organizing and operating the underground was based on certain common characteristics of individual refugees. Escape from home, sometimes alone, before the occupation or from an *Aktion* can only be carried out by an active individual with personal initiative who does not accept the given situation and tries to fight against it. Under the conditions of ghetto life, with annihilation a constant threat, those qualities were manifested in the search for a way out, the refusal to accept the situation as it was and the decision to fight. Another factor was that most of the refugees were alone; they were not responsible for families – neither wives, children nor parents. By leaving the ghetto and fleeing to the partisans in the forests, they did not abandon their families, whose existence, even if temporary, depended on them. In fact, worry for the family's future and the desire to care for their fate was what prevented many of the ghetto inmates from joining underground activity.

The fighting Jewish underground movements operated under difficult conditions, different from those experienced by all the other anti-German undergrounds in occupied Europe. They operated in closed ghettos surrounded by the enemy, under the continual threat of *Aktionen*; a good percentage of the local populations were hostile; they had few weapons, which were acquired through great personal danger; and they received no help from any external group or body. Nevertheless, in some of the ghettos they succeeded in staging uprisings during the final *Aktion,* and in almost all places where an underground existed, it enabled thousands of Jews to escape to the forests and fight as partisans.

CHAPTER FIVE:
JEWS IN THE FORESTS AND IN PARTISAN WARFARE

1. INTRODUCTION

The thousands of square kilometers of forests, broad reaches of swampland and the undeveloped road system in the occupied territories of the Soviet Union created the ideal conditions for partisan warfare. The forests served as bases for the thousands of Jews who joined the Soviet partisan movement or who sought rescue from the German annihilation machine. With the onset of the second stage of the German mass murder campaign in the spring of 1942, larger numbers of Jews began making their way to the forests. They were usually young and mostly members of ghetto undergrounds who wanted to join the partisans and fight the murderers of their people. In addition, escape into the forests could mean survival. Among the escapees were also families that included women and children, who usually organized themselves in family camps around a nucleus of armed men whose duty was to guard the camp and provide food. Many of the Jews arrived in the forests even before the organized Soviet partisan groups. They wandered in small groups, seeking food and shelter, dependent to a large degree on the kindness of the non-Jewish population, many of whom were anti-Semitic and readily betrayed Jews to the Germans.

The local population living close to the forests frequently entered them for economic reasons (to cut wood, collect mushrooms and pasture their animals) and usually knew the location of partisan bases and Jewish family camps. Such information was essential to the Germans in their anti-partisan campaign and when hunting Jews in the forests. Conversely, information about the presence and operations of the German forces in the vicinity or within the forests was essential to partisan survival and warfare. Although the local population suffered severely from German reprisals against anyone who assisted the partisans, there were still regions where, whether out of national loyalty or in response to German terrorism and exploitation, substantial segments of the population identified with and helped the partisans.

Even in these regions, the attitude toward the Jews remained unchanged. The local populations were unwilling to suffer the punishment inflicted on those who did not inform the Germans of Jews and partisans in their vicinity. Under such circumstances, it was almost impossible for the Jews to maintain a continued independent existence in the forests. However, the local population had to accept the presence of Jews among the ranks of the Soviet partisans or in family camps under partisan protection, either out of loyalty to Soviet partisans or fear of their reaction.[1]

The continuing existence of Jewish partisans and family camps depended on three factors: the forests had to be large enough to hide in, the Jews had to be armed and there had to be Soviet partisans ready to have Jews in their ranks. Large forests that Jews from the ghetto could reach on foot in only a few nights' travel were found in western Byelorussia (including the Pripet marshes), around Minsk and northern Volhynia. It was there that most of the Jewish partisans and family camps organized between 1942 and the summer of 1944, when the region was liberated by the Red Army. The partisan activity in the regions, where there were still Jews closed in ghettos began to make itself felt in the summer of 1942. At that time the Central Staff of the Soviet Partisan Movement had not yet taken control of most of the groups of partisans in these regions, and some of these groups were hostile to the very existence of Jews in the forests.

Rescuing the civilian population was not one of the Soviet partisan movement's missions. That was especially true for the Jews, the only nation for which total annihilation was a matter of German policy, and both the Soviet authorities and partisans were aware of it. Nevertheless, some orders were given that indirectly influenced the fate of the Jews in the forests. A decision of the Central Committee of the Communist Party of Byelorussia in February 1943 defined the tasks of the partisan units in Byelorussia. Included in these tasks was the directive "to rescue the Byelorussian population from robbery and annihilation at the hands of the enemy.... The deportation of Soviet people to slavery in Fascist Germany must be prevented, and to that end the military activities of the partisans must be increased."[2]

There was no mention of the Jews in the central committee's missive, and the decision was made after most of the Jews in Byelorussia had already been

---

1. For partisan organization and activity in the forests in the occupied territories of the Soviet Union, see chapter 3.
2. Bystrov et al., *Sovetskie Partizany*, 364–65.

murdered. The statement about robbery and annihilation referred mainly to the peasants living in regions where there was partisan activity, many of whom were murdered or deported to slave labor camps in Germany while their villages were burned. Thousands of peasants fled to the forests, seeking refuge in places under partisan control. It should be noted that the operative part of the decision to increase partisan military activities was intended to prevent local inhabitants from being deported to work in Germany. The annihilation of the population behind the German lines did not influence the outcome of the war, but adding to the work force in German industry and agriculture meant that more Germans could be drafted into the army, and that was what the partisans were supposed to prevent. However, the statement about rescuing the "Byelorussian population" enabled partisans of good will to help the Jews in the forests.

Jews were among the first groups of partisans, both those that organized in the forests and those that were sent from behind the Soviet front to organize and operate in the occupied territories. The first ghetto Jews who left to join the partisans came from Minsk. After the large *Aktion* of November 7, 1941, six men left to join the partisans in the forest near Rudensk, 30 kilometers (18 miles) east of Minsk.[3] There is no information about Jews leaving the other ghettos at the end of 1941, most probably because the 1941–42 winter was particularly hard, and survival in the forests would have been virtually impossible. Many Jews did leave in the spring and summer of 1942, when the second wave of mass murders began, and many of them arrived in some of the forests before the partisans. More than once they met groups of armed men who were not yet part of the organized Soviet partisan movement, and many of them were anti-Semitic and made life difficult. The Jews who came to the forests during the second half of 1942 and the beginning of 1943 found units there that were part of the Soviet partisans under the command of the Central Staff of the Partisan Movement.

Even after control of the forests passed into the hands of the partisan units operating under the command of the central staff and most of the independent groups had been integrated into it, the trials of the Jews did not end. Many partisan commanders did not hide their anti-Semitism and refused to accept Jews who reached the forests unarmed, and families were out of the question. Those who were not integrated in partisan units set up family camps varying from dozens to hundreds of people.

---

3.   E.G. Ioffe, *Stranitsy Istorii Evreev Byelarusi* (Minsk, 1996), 140–41, 144–45; YVA, 033/2689, 5.

Summer dwellings in the forests consisted of easily constructed huts of branches and lengths of cloth or tarpaulins. The basic long-term structure built in the forest was called a *zemlanka,* a hole dug in the ground to the depth of a man's height covered with tree trunks and earth and camouflaged with branches.

Life in the forests was difficult and perilous. German army and police units could carry out spot raids at a partisan base or a Jewish family camp at any time when they received information from local population or their intelligence service. Occasionally large German security forces carried out widespread manhunts and combed the forests. They would surround a large area and search it thoroughly, capturing and killing many forest dwellers. Such searches could last from between two to four weeks, and afterwards the German forces would be returned to their previous duties or continue hunting in a different forest. The Germans did not have sufficient forces to permit them to stay in any one place for a long period of time, and one way or another, most of the partisans managed to avoid the manhunts. The main victims were the Jews in family camps. Rivka Dudik-Gabinet, who fled from Kurenets to the forests with her parents on September 9, 1942, when the ghetto was liquidated, wrote as follows:

> When we reached the forest, we found a handful of wretched Jews, hungry and dirty from the smoke of the fires they lit at night. We had come to a cruel world, and we had to trudge along roads and paths in the forests, to go to farmers in the middle of the night to beg for a bit of bread or a few potatoes…. We greatly feared the coming winter…. What would we do when the snow began falling and our tracks betrayed us to the farmers who came into the forest to gather wood? Where would be get food from?… After we finished building the *zemlanka,* which was nine meters square, 18 of us moved into it…. There was a stove at the entrance and the women gathered around it during the day to cook potatoes, and the other half of the *zemlanka* held two tiers of bunks. At the top it was warm but at the bottom it was very cold…. Hunger drove us crazy….
>
> During the winter Jews from Kurenets and the surrounding area were attacked and killed, and they were only a few kilometers from us. We were lucky and the Germans didn't find us during our first winter in the forest. On the morning of the day before Passover

in 1943, someone came to us from the partisans and told us that the neighboring village was full of Germans. There was a swamp not far away and we fled there. Soon we could hear the German guns, and we were like wild animals fleeing from a hunter.… In the evening we did not hear more shouts and barking dogs, and then we understood that the Germans had left the forest.… We went back to our *zemlanka* and found that it had been completely destroyed.[4]

Despite the hardships and danger in the forest, the stream of Jews fleeing from the ghetto grew steadily. At the beginning there were no more than a few thousand, but as the number of *Aktionen* increased in 1942, the number of Jews leaving for the forest rose to the tens of thousands. There were those who arrived before the *Aktionen* and later those who fled during them and during the uprisings that broke out in some of the ghettos. Jews from the ghettos and camps continued escaping to the forests until the summer of 1944, when the Red Army liberated the occupied territories of the Soviet Union (with the exception of western Latvia).

The forests where the Jews sought refuge and conducted partisan warfare had a combined area of hundreds and even thousands of square kilometers. Most of the Jews concentrated in the following forests (from north to south):

- The area around Minsk: the Rudensk and Koidanovo forests

- Western Byelorussia: the Kozyany, Naroch, Nacha, Naliboki, Lipichany and Volche-Nora forests, and the forests and swamps of Polesie

- Southeastern Lithuania: the Rudniki (Rudniku) forests

- Western Ukraine: the Kokhov and northern Volhynia forests

There were also smaller concentrations of dozens to a few hundred Jews in the Vinitsa and eastern Galicia forests.

---

4. Kalcheim, *With Proud Bearing*, 232–34.

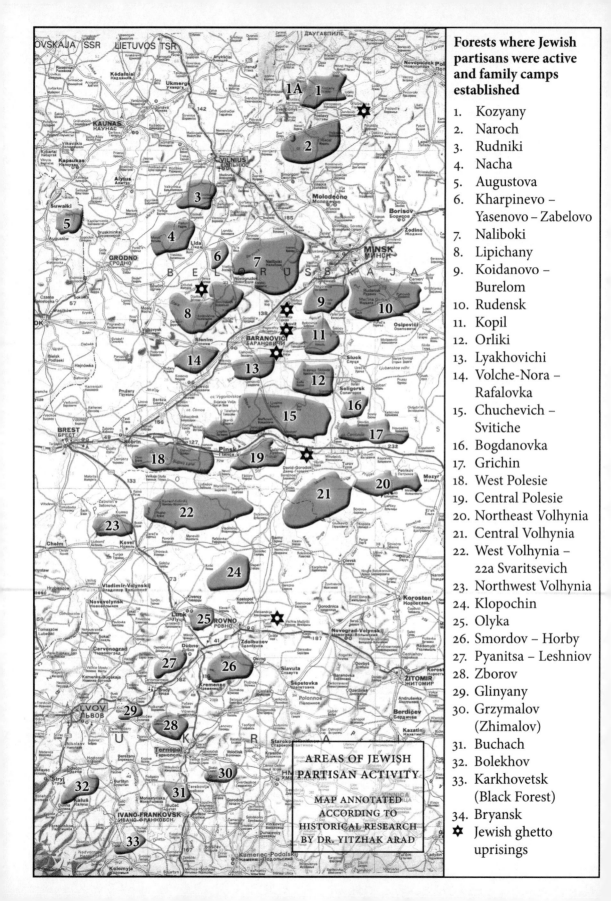

Forests where Jewish partisans were active and family camps established

1. Kozyany
2. Naroch
3. Rudniki
4. Nacha
5. Augustova
6. Kharpinevo – Yasenovo – Zabelovo
7. Naliboki
8. Lipichany
9. Koidanovo – Burelom
10. Rudensk
11. Kopil
12. Orliki
13. Lyakhovichi
14. Volche-Nora – Rafalovka
15. Chuchevich – Svitiche
16. Bogdanovka
17. Grichin
18. West Polesie
19. Central Polesie
20. Northeast Volhynia
21. Central Volhynia
22. West Volhynia – 22a Svaritsevich
23. Northwest Volhynia
24. Klopochin
25. Olyka
26. Smordov – Horby
27. Pyanitsa – Leshniov
28. Zborov
29. Glinyany
30. Grzymalov (Zhimalov)
31. Buchach
32. Bolekhov
33. Karkhovetsk (Black Forest)
34. Bryansk

✡ Jewish ghetto uprisings

AREAS OF JEWISH PARTISAN ACTIVITY

MAP ANNOTATED ACCORDING TO HISTORICAL RESEARCH BY DR. YITZHAK ARAD

2. THE FORESTS IN THE MINSK DISTRICT: RUDENSK AND KOIDANOVO

The first Soviet partisans organized around Minsk in the fall of 1941 in the Rudensk-Cherven forest south and southeast of the city. One of the groups was headed by Alexander Sergeyev, whose nom de guerre was Bistrov. The groups were made up of Communists and Komsomol members who had not managed to evacuate and Red Army soldiers who had remained behind the German lines. Some of the groups joined forces, and in February 1942 one of them was named the 208th Stalin Partisan Battalion. In March 1942 the Communist Party's underground district committee began its operations south of Minsk and organized all the partisan *otryad*s (detachments), which gradually became brigades. In May 1942 wireless communications were established with the Soviet lines, and the partisans began operating as part of an organized movement. In the summer of 1942 they set up an airstrip where Soviet planes could land.[5]

Contact between the ghetto underground and the 208th Battalion was established by Fedya Shedletsky, who was sent to the ghetto by Sergeyev to ask the *Judenrat* for clothing and medicine. Smolar met Shedletsky and promised to send the partisans what they requested and also proposed sending men from the ghetto underground. At the beginning of 1942 Shedletsky returned to the ghetto saying that Sergeyev was willing to accept ghetto men on the condition that they were armed and brought medicine with them. As a result, in February 1942, Shedletsky led three groups out of the ghetto, a total of about 50 men, most of whom had served in the Soviet army[6] and who integrated into the 208th Battalion. After a German manhunt for partisans in March 1942, the battalion moved to the Mogilev district and contact with the ghetto underground was broken off.[7] There is no information about those who joined the 208th from the ghetto.[8]

---

5. A.L. Manaenkov, *Partizanskie Formirovania Belorusii v Gody Velikoi Otechestvennoi Voiny* (Minsk, 1983), 403, 436–38.

6. Smolar, *Soviet Jews*, 84–85, 91–94; Cholawski, *In the Eye*, 148. For more information on Shedletsky in the ghetto, see chapter 4:2, "The Establishment of the Underground."

7. Cholawski (*In the Eye*, 149) wrote that a fourth underground group that left the ghetto in the Rudensk region for the 208th Battalion's base found it deserted after a battle between the partisans and the Germans.

8. Manaenkov, *Partizanskie Formirovania*, 436–37.

During the first half of April 1942 two underground groups left the Minsk ghetto to set up independent bases for those who would follow. One group, in the Rudensk forest, was commanded by Israel Lapidot and had between 20 and 30 men. The other, a group of 20, was commanded by Nahum Feldman and stumbled on Germans as they left the ghetto, suffered losses and returned. Feldman reorganized the group and, at the end of April or the beginning of May 1942, left the ghetto and reached the Staroselsk forest in the Koidanovo district, about 40 kilometers southwest of Minsk.[9] Lapidot sent envoys to the ghetto to get more men, and his unit quickly grew to 100 and was named after Kutuzov. The *otryad* was joined by local residents and gradually lost its Jewish character. At first they operated independently, but at the end of September 1942 they became part of the 2nd Minsk Brigade. Their first operations, while they were still independent and most of their fighters were Jewish, were an attack on the police station in the village of Khotlyani, in which 12 policemen were killed; an attack on the Samoilovo estate in which the police defending it were killed; mining railroad tracks; ambushing German forces; and destroying bridges on the Osipovichi-Minsk road. In July 1943 a Russian commander replaced Lapidot. The *otryad* lost many men but continued its operations until the Red Army arrived in June 1944.[10]

Groups from the Minsk ghetto continued arriving at Feldman's base. In June 1942 the ghetto underground helped Semyon Ganzenko, a Red Army officer, escape from a prisoner-of-war camp in Minsk and transferred him to Feldman's unit. Ganzenko took over the command of the Budiony *otryad* and some non-Jewish fighters joined it. Feldman was appointed *otryad* commissar. They operated independently until December 1942, after which they joined the Stalin Brigade. In December 1943 they reorganized and some of their men formed a new *otryad*. Budiony operated until July 1944, when the Red Army arrived.[11]

Dozens of Jews from the Minsk ghetto joined the Frunze *otryad*, which organized in the forests southwest of Minsk. In September 1942 it was large enough to be turned into the Frunze Brigade, including within its ranks the

9. A. Pismenny, *Partizanskaia Druzhba* (Moscow, 1948), 156–57, 160–63; Smolar, *Soviet Jews*, 115–16; Cholawski, *In the Eye*, 160.

10. Pismenny, *Partizanskaia Druzhba*, 164–65; Manaenkov, *Partizanskie Formirovania*, 409–10.

11. Pismenny, *Partizanskaia Druzhba*, 157–58; Manaenkov, *Partizanskie Formirovania*, 37–38; Smolar, *Soviet Jews*, 131.

Dzerzhinsky *otryad* and the Lazo *otryad*. The Lazo *otryad* was composed largely of Jews from Minsk, including Ziskin, its commander. Soviet sources say very little about the Lazo *otryad*.[12] The Parkhomenko *otryad* was also composed of escapees from the Minsk ghetto. In September 1942 Smolar, who had been one of the heads of the Minsk ghetto underground, arrived at the Frunze Brigade and met with Feldman and Ganzenko, and the three decided to set up a base to receive Jews from the Minsk ghetto, including women and children.[13]

Hundreds of Jews, alone and in groups, escaped to the forests without the help of the ghetto underground, some of them independently and others through connections they had with local residents. According to Saul Rubinchuk, a former Red Army soldier who had fled the ghetto after the March 2, 1942, *Aktion*:

> We left without being involved with any organization, we were just three comrades who talked about it together.... We walked until we came upon a patrol. They were partisans and led us away.... We met Nikitin, the commander of a partisan *otryad*. He had about 100 fighters.... They gave us weapons and we stayed with them.... I knew Nikitin from Minsk, his last name was Steingart and he was Jewish. In the *otryad* they didn't know that.... He commanded a tank brigade and his [army] had been surrounded and everyone dispersed. He and several of the soldiers stayed together.... There were four or five Jews among them.[14]

Smolar, who after leaving the ghetto became a member of the partisan staff in the Ivenetz region, wrote about the anti-Semitism and suspicion Jews faced in the forests:

---

12. Smolar, *Soviet Jews*, 157–58; Cholawski, *In the Eye*, 168; Manaenkov, *Partizanskie Formirovania*, 83–84. According to the sources, the Dzerzhinsky *otryad* was established in September 1942 and made up of residents of the Koidanovo district. The Lazo *otryad* was established in December 1942 and disbanded in February 1943, when the Germans began hunting for them in the forests. No mention is made of commanders or the number of people involved.
13. Smolar, *Soviet Jews*, 158–60, 166. The base was named the 106th Unit. See below for more information regarding the base.
14. Testimony of Saul Rubinchuk, YVA, 03/3955.

The influence of Nazi racism [and] of the anti-Semitic propaganda put out by the collaborators was felt particularly strongly by those who fled from the German prisoner-of-war camps.... There were cases in which Jewish partisans were sentenced to death for crimes of negligence, which certainly did not deserve such punishment....

Tevl Shimonovitch [came] to me and demanded I go with him: "Come see.... They too are spilling our blood!"...Not far from the Neman River there were bodies of several Jewish women who had been shot. They had swum across the river...and been killed by "our forces," by partisans.... I went to the headquarters bunker and asked who had killed the Jewish women who fled from the Nazi murderers. I got my answer from the representative of the Byelorussian partisan movement's headquarters, Vladimir Tsariuk: "We were warned that the Gestapo sent a group of women to poison the partisans' pots of soup, we're at war, nothing can be done about it..." The headquarters of the Frunze Brigade decided to put all the Jews into a separate unit and to name it after Lazo. We regarded that as an expression of their desire to isolate us, and to leave us empty[-handed] and with nothing.[15]

Many instances of anti-Semitism are mentioned in documents and publications about the situation of the Jews in the forests and among the partisans.[16]

The number of Jews in the forests and in the partisan *otryad*s in the Minsk district can only be estimated. Smolar wrote of a census taken of Jewish partisans immediately after the liberation to estimate the number of Jews who had left the ghetto for the forests. He estimated that during the 25 months the ghetto was in existence, close to 10,000 Jews escaped to the forests.[17] That would seem to be an exaggeration, considering how difficult it was to leave the ghetto and what conditions were like in the forests; many of those who escaped died on the way.

---

15. Smolar, *Soviet Jews*, 170–75, 177–79. In November 1942, Ponomarenko, the head of the Central Partisan Movement Headquarters, instructed the partisans in the Minsk region to be suspicious of those who came from underground organizations in Minsk since there were traitors among them. The word "Jews" was never used, but it was clear that his instructions also referred to those who came from the ghetto.

16. Leonid Smilovitsky, "Anti-Semitism among the Partisans in Byelorussia," *Yalkut Moreshet* [Hebrew] 59 (1955): 53–61.

17. Smolar, *Soviet Jews*, 209.

A Soviet book whose data are official and reasonably reliable gives the number of partisans in Byelorussia according to district and brigade as they were in the summer of 1944, when the Red Army liberated the area and before the units were disbanded. The data given refer to the Byelorussians, Russians and Ukrainians in every brigade; the others, among them the Jews, are lumped together as *"drugie natsionalnosti"* (other nationalities). Accordingly, there were 40,000 partisans in the Minsk district when the Red Army arrived in July 1944; 2,500 of them were listed as *drugie natsionalnosti*.[18] Since Jews were the second-largest national group in Byelorussia, and Russians and Ukrainians are not included in the number, it can be assumed that 75–80 percent of the 2,500 were Jewish, i.e., 1,875–2,000, and that the others were Caucasians and Asians, former prisoners of war and a number of Poles. Among the Byelorussians, Russians and Ukrainians there were also Jews who hid their nationality and there is no way of knowing their numbers. Only live partisans were counted when the Red Army came; those who fell were not taken into account.

Because of the conditions prevailing in the forests many wounded partisans died, regardless of the nature of their wounds. In addition, the Germans shot those they captured. Partisans who stayed in the forests for longer periods faced more dangers and more of them fell than those who joined the partisans during the last months before the liberation. Among those who stayed in the forests and fought as partisans for long periods were large numbers of Jews, most of whom had fled to the forests as early as 1942 and were active as partisans for a year and a half to two years. As Soviet sources do not mention the numbers of dead partisans, only an estimate can be given. Regarding the 171 members of the 51st Jewish partisan *otryad,* which was operating in the Baranovichi area, 72 were killed in the forests and on the front, that is, 42 percent.[19] The 51st fought under the same conditions as the other partisan *otryad*s, and assuming that 42 percent is too high to be a general percentage, it can be estimated that in other units 25–35 percent died. To the 1,875–2,000 Jewish partisans who remained alive, therefore, 470–700 who died should be added. Thus it is fair to say that 2,350–2,700 Jewish partisans operated in the Minsk district. This Minsk model will be used to estimate the number of Jewish partisans active in other districts.

---

18.   Manaenkov, *Partizanskie Formirovania*, 403–10, contains detailed lists which include the number of partisans in each brigade in the Minsk district.
19.   Shner-Nishmit, *51st Company*, 303–8.

Many of those who fled from the Minsk ghetto went to the forests near Vitebsk, Mogilev and other districts, and a large number to those in Baranovichi. They are not included in the statistics for Minsk.

3. THE FORESTS OF KOZYANY AND NAROCH

The Kozyany forests lie in the Vileika district in northwestern Byelorussia. Some independent partisan groups were already active there in the summer of 1942, but only by the fall did these groups come under the authority of the Central Staff of the Partisan Movement. In the beginning of September 1942, the Spartak *otryad* came to the Kozyany forests from the Vitebsk region. It consisted of a few dozen fighters commanded by Arkady Ponomarev, and it integrated some of the independent partisan groups into its ranks. In the spring of 1943, the Voroshilov Partisan Brigade commanded by Fiodr Markov established its base in the Kozyany forests.

The Kozyany forests were used as a base by other partisan units as well. Chief among them was the Lithuanian Zalgiris (Green Forest) Brigade commanded by Shumauskas. Its nucleus came to the Naroch forests (south of Kozyany) at the beginning of the summer of 1943. In July 1943, the District Committee of the Communist Party headed by Ivan Klimov organized in the Naroch forests, putting him in control of the partisan movement in the entire Vileika district. The situation of the Jews in those forests was greatly influenced by the attitude of the brigade commanders and Klimov.

Hundreds of Jews fled to the Kozyany forests to escape the *Aktionen* carried out between June and August 1942. Those who escaped the ghetto and were wandering in the forests were at the mercy of local population.[20] When winter came their situation worsened, not only because of the cold but because their footprints in the snow led their pursuers right to them, and hundreds of Jews had no choice but to leave the forest and go to the ghetto at Glubokoe, the only

---

20. According to Gefen et al., *Jewish Partisans*, 163, "The Germans paid 20 kilograms [44 lbs] of salt for turning in Jews.... There were farmers who met Jews wandering in the forests and convinced them to come with them, promising to hide them, and then turned them over to the police.... Yehiel Gutterman, a five-year-old child, was given to a farmer from the village of Volky by his grandfather, and his parents gave them a large amount of property. When the farmer learned they had been killed, he strangled the child. There were two other children hiding with the farmer, the sons of Yehiel-Hersch Lipshin from Kozyany. He informed the Byelorussian police...and a policeman killed them."

one still remaining in the Vileika district. Those who remained in the forest organized into two family camps. One, of about 50 individuals, was composed of residents of Iodi, and the other, about the same size, of Jews from Kozyany and the neighboring towns.

Leib Volyak, who was born in the Jewish village of Stoyachishki, became the leader of a group of Jews who had been moving around in the forests as early as the winter of 1941–42. As they were looking for partisans they met a group of 25 men, most of them former prisoners of war, who disarmed them, stole their clothing and kept guard over them. At night, without weapons and half-naked, they managed to escape.[21] With great difficulty they acquired weapons and were among the first to be accepted into the Spartak *otryad*. That occurred in September 1942, and within a few weeks the number of Jews in Spartak had grown to 30. Volyak distinguished himself in battle, especially in repelling German attacks on the *otryad* base and in Spartak's attack against the town of Kozyany.[22]

During the second half of November 1942, the Germans began a wide-scale manhunt, and to evade them Spartak divided into small groups and moved to the forests in the Vitebsk district. Those who suffered worst were the members of the two Jewish family camps:[23] some were caught and killed and some managed to escape and wandered through the forest looking for food. Volyak, who remained in the Kozyany forests after Spartak left, gathered some dozen members from the family camps and a few Jewish partisans who had been separated from their units during the manhunt, and with his leadership and bravery they survived in the forest until the spring of 1943.[24] At that point Spartak, reinforced by more partisans, returned to the Kozyany forests and became a brigade. Volyak and other Jews rejoined Spartak, whereupon Volyak was appointed a platoon commander.

Information about the number of Jews in the Spartak Brigade is inconsistent. It is estimated that it contained about 100 Jews, more than 10 percent of all the partisans in the brigade.[25] Jews without weapons, those in family groups

---

21. Ibid., 164–67.
22. Cholawski, *Resistance*, 96–97.
23. Gerlach (*Kalkulierte*, 900) notes that between November 23 and 29, 1942, the German forces hunted partisans in the Glubokoe region. The operation was called Nurnberg and during it 1,826 Jews were shot.
24. Gefen et al., *Jewish Partisans*, 171–75; Manaenkov, *Partizanskie Formirovania*, 191.
25. Gefen et al. (*Jewish Partisans*, 177–78) states that there were 150 Jews in Spartak.

who had survived the winter and those who had hidden with farmers preferred the forest, where they organized into family camps of 400–500; Jewish partisans from various units provided them with food.

Beginning in the spring of 1943, Jews who had fled from the Svencionys and Glubokoe ghettos began arriving in the Kozyany forests. A 22-member underground group from Svencionys came in May 1943 and joined the 60-strong Chapaev *otryad* of the Voroshilov Brigade. Two days later it was announced that seven unarmed members of the group had to leave and search for weapons, and only then would they be accepted into the *otryad*. They were given one short-barreled *otrezanka* rifle. The Svencionys Jews were stung by the injustice but had to follow orders. They did not return to Chapaev, but a few weeks later joined the Vilnius *otryad* of the Lithuanian Zalgiris Brigade.[26]

In September 1943 the German forces conducted another wide-scale manhunt, and the partisan commanders decided to split the units into small groups and to infiltrate through the German lines into the more eastern forests of Byelorussia. The Jewish family camps were left to face their fate alone. Following the initiative of camp members from Kozyany who were familiar with the forest, 300 Jews found asylum on a small island hidden in the swamp. Many were killed in the manhunt, which lasted for four weeks. When the partisan units returned to the Kozyany forests, they heard that captured Jews had revealed the locations of partisan camps. The camps were in fact empty, but the accusation only served to increase the anti-Semitic expressions against the Jews.[27]

One of the manifestations of partisan anti-Semitism was the negative attitude toward the family camps, whose inhabitants they regarded as a nuisance. Leib Volyak organized the camps to support the partisans, setting up a flour mill, bakery, sewing workshop and shoemaker's shop, all of which worked for the partisan good. In return for services rendered, relations improved and the partisans provided them with food. However, despite the support they provided, the family camps in the Kozyany forests were never recognized as part of the Soviet partisan movement.[28] Volyak, the most distinguished Jewish partisan

---

26. Shimon Kanc, ed., *Svintzian Region Yizkor Book* [Hebrew] (Tel Aviv, 1956), 1727–28, according to the testimony of Mote-Heshel Bushkanets, who was one of the seven ordered to go looking for weapons.

27. Ibid., 186–87; Smuschkowitz et al., *From Victims to Victors* (Toronto: Canadian Society for Yad Vashem, 1992), 191–92.

28. Smuschkowitz et al., *Victims*, 159; Gefen et al., *Jewish Partisans*, 188–89.

of the Kozyany forests, fell in battle against German forces during the winter of 1943–44.

The Naroch forests were named after the large Naroch lake, which lay north of the main district city of Vileika, about 50 kilometers (31 miles) south of the Kozyany forests. There were many towns in the area, among them Oshmiana, Vileika and Kurenets, each home to between several hundred to several thousand Jews. During the *Aktionen* conducted in the summer of 1942, hundreds fled to the Naroch forests. Young men, some of them armed, looked for ways to contact the partisans, and the families organized into camps. However, until the fall of 1942, the Central Staff of the Partisan Movement did not control the independent partisan groups in the Naroch forests.

On November 17, 1942, V.V. Karpov, deputy commander of an intelligence and communications unit (*razvedivatelno-sviaznaia gruppa*), sent a report to Ivan Klimov that dealt with the state of the local population and partisan activity in the Vileika district. In regard to the situation of Jews in the forests of the Vileika district during that period, he wrote:

> The Jewish population is terrorized. Unarmed, they congregate under the shadow of the forests, begging for food and dressed [in clothes supplied] by the local peasants, sometimes even resorting to force. In [unclear] there are 300 Jews, in Krasnogo, 250, in the Ianshei region, 68, in Zacherna, 87, etc. Sometimes they are joined by escaped prisoners of war and carry out what they call "economic activities," in which they take various kinds of food from the local population. The partisans do not help them and they accept Jewish youngsters into their ranks unwillingly. There were cases of partisans from the Bogatirev unit…disarming Jews who came to them and sending them back. Anti-Semitism among the partisans is quite strongly developed.… Jewish youngsters and men show a desire to join the partisans. A positive initiative regarding support of the Jewish population was taken by Timchuk, the commissar of the Mstitel *otryad*, who organized a tanning workshop in the Malinovski forest where Jews from the ghetto worked. The Jewish youth and men evince a desire to join partisan *otryad*s, but their mood indicates that they would like to cross the front.[29]

29. GARF, Document 69-1-1067, 241–42.

Regarding Karpov's reference to Jews who wanted to cross the front into the Soviet Union, such a limited possibility existed in the summer–early fall of 1942. Between the spring and fall of 1942, there was a breach in the German front near Vitebsk, created as a result of the Soviet winter offensive, which was called the Surazh Gate (*Surazhskie Vorota*). Hundreds of Jews from the Kurenets ghetto and some other ghettos were transferred eastward toward Polotsk by Soviet partisans during their nocturnal passages through the forests. Some of the Jews walked hundreds of kilometers and crossed the front lines through the Surazh Gate, while others were killed in German ambushes along the way. As noted, one of the moving forces behind getting Jews through the front lines was Ivan Timchuk, who had been a Communist activist in Kurenets before the war and knew many of the Jews he met in the forests. Zalman Gurevich supplied the following testimony:

> The Mstitel partisan *otryad* came to the forest…and I immediately saw someone I knew. It was Timchuk, the *otryad* commissar…. He told us that two groups had already crossed the front…. The rumor of leaving the forest had taken wing, and many Jews were preparing to go eastward (toward Vostok)…. The commissar gathered together most of those who were leaving and described the difficulties awaiting them, telling them that they would take side roads and go through fields and forests, and even then only at night….
>
> In the middle of November 1942…about 300 people left the forest, about 200 of them Jews from Kurenets and the rest from neighboring towns. We were accompanied by three partisans…. When the sun set we began walking. At first everything went well, but then parents with small children and older people showed signs of suffering. The distance between the groups gradually increased… [and] 300 people were strung out over a kilometer…. The children cried and their parents quieted them. Suddenly shots were fired at us from rifles and machine guns…. Everyone lay on the ground. There were no more groups and no more partisans…. We discussed a plan for returning to the forest we had left…. The first group [of about 50] managed to cross to the east…but I returned in a terrible frame of mind…. The Mstitel *otryad* had left the forest…[and] the Jews were

in the middle of a forest, torn apart and without a roof over their heads, and winter was on the way.[30]

Nevertheless, there were Jews who did manage to cross the front. On September 12, 1942, 70 Jews, most of them from Dolginovo, left the Naroch forests and at the beginning of November 1942, after having walked for two months, they crossed the front lines. Others did the same.[31] There are no statistics regarding the numbers of Jews who managed to cross the front, but between 1,000 and 1,500 is a fair estimate.[32] To that number should probably be added several hundred who died along the way, whether killed by enemy bullets or physical hardships.

The initiative to rescue Jews by leading them to the Soviets through the Surazh Gate was taken by the Mstitel *otryad* and credit should be given mainly to Commissar Timchuk, whose *otryad* used the gate for their partisan needs. Since such actions were not carried out by other partisan units – even in areas such as Minsk, which was closer to the Surazh Gate – it can be assumed that no order came from Moscow to rescue Jews, but rather that it was a local initiative based on humanitarian or other considerations.[33]

Parallel to these rescue operations, there were many instances in which Jews in the Naroch forests were abused by partisans. One such event occurred in a family camp during the spring or early summer of 1943. A member of this camp testified: "One day a group of partisans who belonged to Major Cherkasov's unit, all of whom had been former prisoners of war, arrived. They fell

30. Kalcheim, *With Proud Bearing*, 155–59.
31. Testimony of Yaakov Segalchik, YVA, S-63/1628; testimony of Abraham Klorin, YVA, K-265/3185; Aharon Meirowicz, ed., *The Book of Kurenets* [Hebrew] (Tel Aviv, 1956), 144, 201, 258–60, 292. Meirowicz brings testimonies of Jews whom the partisans helped to cross the front line through the Surazh Gate.
32. A news item from Moscow printed in the now defunct Tel Aviv daily newspaper *Davar* on January 27, 1943, praising a partisan unit that helped 1,500 Jews cross the front.
33. Shalom Cholawski ("The Underground and Partisan Activity of the Jews from Ghetto Korenetz," *Yalkut Moreshet* 59 [1995]: 70) writes that Florian Sokolov, the commander of the Mstitel *otryad*, "suggested help to the Jews in crossing the lines to the Soviet rear areas on the condition that they give up their gold. He collected their gold and jewelry and assigned two Russian partisans to accompany them." Sokolov's first name was not Florian, but rather Anatoly Feyodorovich, and he commanded Mstitel from September 1942 to September 1943.

upon us and took our guns and clothing. We tried to defend ourselves but could not. There were many of them and they were better armed than we were, and they threatened to kill us."[34]

At the beginning of the summer of 1943, conditions in the Naroch forests gradually improved for the Jews when representatives of the Central Staff of the Partisan Movement gradually began taking control of the independent partisan groups. The Voroshilov Brigade, commanded by Markov, was the first to set up camp in the Naroch forests and began operating at the end of 1942, gradually turning it into their main base. During 1943 other partisan units arrived, including the Dubator and Lithuanian Zalgiris Brigades, and scores of armed Jewish youth joined them.

An important turning point in Jewish activities in the Naroch forests occurred when the FPO underground group arrived from Vilnius. Contact was made between Markov and the FPO through members of the Svencionys ghetto underground who joined the brigade. They told Markov about the FPO and suggested they go to the Vilnius ghetto and bring fighters to the brigade. Markov accepted the suggestion and at the beginning of June 1943, sent some Svencionys youngsters to contact the FPO. The FPO, whose ideology favored uprising within the ghetto, refused to send its members to the forest. Nevertheless, the Svencionys youngsters did manage to get a group of 25 people from the ghetto to join them on their way back to the forests.

During the second half of July 1943, a few days after the Wittenberg affair, Markov again sent the youngsters from Svencionys to the ghetto.[35] This time, as a result of the Wittenberg affair, the FPO decided to send 22 of its members to the forest under the command of Yosef Glazman. On July 23, 1943, they left the ghetto with a guide and passed through the labor camp at New Vileika (Naujoji Vilnia), where they were joined by 14 more Jews. On their way to the forest they were ambushed by Germans and, inexperienced in battle, nine were killed and the rest scattered. Glazman, however, managed to reassemble 13 and lead them to Naroch. After the *Aktion* of September 1–4, 1943, five organized groups totaling 150 FPO members escaped to the forest, along with three other groups

---

34. Korczak, *Flames*, 226–27, quotation from a testimony of Meir Khadash.
35. For information on the Wittenberg affair, see chapter 4:3, "FPO-Judenrat Relations."

whose members did not belong to the underground. Thus there were between 250 and 300 young Jews from the Vilnius ghetto in the Naroch forests.[36]

Contact with Vilnius and the FPO was important for Markov, not only as a source of fighters, but also to liaise with an underground Polish Communist group in Vilnius called the Organization for Active Struggle.[37] On April 25, 1943, after a mass grave of Polish officers killed by the Soviet NKVD was discovered in the region of Katyn near Smolensk, the diplomatic relations between the Polish government-in-exile and the Soviet government were severed. This sharpened the dispute between the two governments about the future borders between the two countries. Moscow ordered the Soviet partisans to fight the Polish underground and the growing Polish partisan movement active in western Byelorussia.[38] The Soviet government wanted to use Polish pro-Communist groups in their struggle against the Polish government-in-exile, and the Polish Association for Active Struggle in Vilnius was one such group. On August 4, 1943, Markov sent a report to Soviet partisan headquarters and Red Army intelligence, which read as follows:

> In Vilnius there is a Polish anti-Soviet center that operates Polish nationalistic organizations…to establish a Polish government in the region when the German army retreats.… Based on your instructions, we are taking all measures [against them]. In addition, I contacted a Communist organization in Vilnius that is based on the principles of the west Byelorussian Communist Party.… Most of its members are Russian, Polish and Jewish, and there are some Lithuanians as well.… I suggest organizing the Poles into an association to fight the occupier, whose members will be reliable and counterbalance the Polish nationalists, and thus we will be able to attract the Polish masses to us and to hamper the activities of the anti-Soviet Polish organizations.[39]

---

36. Kalcheim, *With Proud Bearing*, 177–78, 187–89. Some of the youngsters from Svencionys who were sent to the Vilnius ghetto by Markov were Moshe Shutan, Yeshika Gertman, Alexander Bogen and Moshe-Yudke Rudnicki.

37. For information about this group, see chapter 4:3, "Contacts with Non-Jewish Underground Groups."

38. Boradyn, *Niemen*, 90–92, 100–102. For the relations between the Soviet partisans and the Armia Krajowa, see chapter 3.

39. Ibid., 291.

The FPO was a means of connection with the Polish communist group in Vilnius. Members of the FPO, most of whom had belonged to Jewish national movements in the past, wanted to carry out their fighting in the forests as a separate Jewish unit operating within the Soviet partisan movement. There were also many Jewish youths in the Soviet partisan units who, for national reasons and because of the anti-Semitism they encountered, wanted a separate Jewish unit.[40] When Glazman arrived in the forest, he suggested to Markov that a Jewish *otryad* be established within the Voroshilov Brigade, which would take in the Jews coming to the forests and those who did not yet belong to any partisan *otryad*, as well as the other FPO members who would come from Vilnius.

According to Soviet partisan organizational structure, Vilnius was part of Lithuania and therefore under the general authority of the Lithuanian Soviet partisan movement, as were the underground organizations operating there and in the forests. Markov discussed the issue with Zimanas of the Lithuanian Zalgiris Brigade, which commanded the Vilnius region and whose headquarters were in the Naroch forests, and he was in favor of establishing a Jewish unit. It is reasonable to assume that both Markov and Zimanas were in favor because they expected it to take in all the Jews who were already in the forests and did not belong to other units. They were regarded as a nuisance, and the partisan command, representing as it did the Soviet government, could not completely ignore them.

The Jewish partisan Mest (Revenge) *otryad* was established in the Naroch forests in early August 1943 as part of the Voroshilov Brigade under the command of Fiodor Markov. Zerah Rogovski (Butinas), a Jewish paratrooper from Lithuania, was put in charge of it. It initially consisted of 70 fighters but grew to 250 in September 1943, when underground members arrived from Vilnius and were joined by other Jews who were hiding in the forests. Many members of the unit, which included women, were unarmed. The unit participated in

---

40. Korczak, *Flames*, 229. She wrote, "In conversations with partisans the idea of a Jewish unit was mentioned, and many desired it. When the FPO fighters came from Vilnius, headed by Yosef Glazman, there was already a nucleus willing to take the mission upon itself.... Glazman had had the idea of a Jewish unit while still in the ghetto, and saw himself as an FPO emissary championing Jewish fighting in the ghetto and in the forest, and when he came he began working to put the idea into practice."

several operations carried out by the Voroshilov Brigade, including the attack on the town of Miadel.[41]

The Revenge Unit existed a mere seven weeks. On September 23, 1943, its base was visited by Markov and Ivan Klimov, secretary of the District Committee of the Communist Party. Its members were ordered to line up next to the Komsomolski partisan *otryad*. Markov and Klimov delivered speeches, informing the partisans that the Revenge *otryad* was being disbanded and those with weapons would be integrated into the Komsomolski under the command of Volodya Saulevich. Some of the Revenge *otryad* would not be integrated into Komsomolski but would form a maintenance group (*proizvodstvenniaia gruppa*) to service the partisan units. The latter were left with few weapons; the fate of the remaining majority was not mentioned. Clearly they would be left in the forests, unarmed and with no organization.[42] According to Moshe Kalchheim, who was there at the time:

> Markov (or Klimov, I don't remember exactly) informed [us] that the headquarters of the partisan movement had decided to disband the Jewish Revenge Unit because there was no place among the Soviet partisans for a separate Jewish unit, and Jews had to be integrated in partisan units in accordance with nationality accepted in the Soviet Union, such as Byelorussians, Lithuanians, Ukrainians, etc. We were shocked. It was incomprehensible that the Jewish unit was about to be disbanded on orders from above. But the worst was yet to come, when Volodka Saulevich separated the Jewish from the non-Jewish partisans and he and his comrades disarmed the Jews and handed over their weapons to the non-Jews, who, like us, had just arrived in the forests from the nearby towns....[43]

The Soviet partisan movement's organization was based on the various Soviet republics – Byelorussia, the Ukraine, Lithuania, etc. – occupied by the Germans, and this was the basis for the claim that there was no place for a separate Jewish unit. In addition, the "economic activities" carried out in the villages by entirely Jewish partisan groups gave the local population the impression that most of the partisans, commanders included, were Jewish, exactly what

---

41.   Kalcheim, *With Proud Bearing*, 18–19; Korczak, *Flames*, 229–30.
42.   Kalcheim, *With Proud Bearing*, 19–20, Shutan, *Ghetto and Forest*, 188–89.
43.   Kalcheim, *With Proud Bearing*, 70–71.

German propaganda claimed. That, combined with the fact that most of the Revenge partisans had had no previous military training (as opposed to groups of former prisoners of war), might have been viewed as a justification for the unit's disbandment. However, the way in which the partisan command chose to disband and disarm the Revenge was offensive, and the outcome was worse: most of the units' members were left unarmed in the forests, sentenced to starvation and easy prey for German manhunts. That, in fact, was the fate of most of them in the manhunt that began in late September 1943 in the Naroch forests and continued in the direction of Kozyany.[44]

The partisan command in the Naroch forests discovered the Germans were planning the manhunt and ordered the *otryads* to move northward to the Kozyany forests, and eastward to those in the Lepel region. Some of the partisan forces that had not managed to leave the forests before the Germans closed them off split their units into small groups, which were ordered to infiltrate through the Germans encircling them or simply to break through. About 200 members of the disbanded Revenge, including the maintenance unit, appealed to Saulevich, the commander of the Komsomolski *otryad*, to let them join, but he refused and even ordered warning shots to be fired at those who tried to follow. The Komsomolski also split into small groups, at which time the Jews who belonged to the *otryad* were separated from the others and left to their own devices. Some of the Jews who were left in the forest found shelter in the swamps, and some of them did manage to survive, but the others, an estimated 100–200, were killed by the Germans. Zimanas ordered Glazman and 35 Jewish partisans with him to move to the Kozyany forests where some members of the Lithuanian Brigade still remained. On October 8, 1943, a German force surrounded Glazman's unit as they were on their way and, with the exception of one young girl, killed them all in battle.[45]

During the second half of October 1943, once the manhunt had ended, the Voroshilov Brigade returned to the Naroch forests and those Jews who had survived organized into family camps. Their situation improved during the winter of 1943–44, when partisan headquarter supervision of the various units increased and discipline tightened. Markov reestablished his brigade's

---

44. The manhunt the Germans called Fritz took place between September 24 and October 10, 1943.

45. Korczak, *Flames*, 239–43; Kalcheim, *With Proud Bearing*, 72–73, 194.

entirely Jewish maintenance unit.[46] Following the parachute drops of Soviet weapons, the young Jews who had stayed in the family camps were accepted into the partisan *otryad*s and many of them distinguished themselves in battle. One of the best-known partisans in the Naroch forests was Yitzhak Blatt from Glubokoe, the reconnaissance commander of the Chapaev *otryad*, who fell in an attack on a German stronghold at the beginning of 1944. The young Jews of the Vilnius *otryad* of the Zalgiris Brigade mined railroad track along the Vilnius-Daugavpils line, derailing trains.[47]

The overall number of partisans who were active in the Kozyany and Naroch forests was 12,600, among them 600 in NKVD and army intelligence units. About 950 of the overall number were included in the category of "other nationalities."[48] Following the Minsk model, it can be determined that 700–760 of them were Jewish. If the fallen are added, the number of Jewish partisans in the Vileika region was between 950 and 1,100. It can be estimated that 900–1,300 Jews found asylum in the family camps in the forests in the Vileika region. That number does not include the Jews who crossed the front lines to the Soviet rear areas. Many members of the family camps died in German raids and manhunts, some fell in battle with the unorganized groups marauding through the forests and hundreds of others survived.

4. THE RUDNIKI AND NACHA FORESTS

The Rudniki forests, located about 50 kilometers (31 miles) southwest of Vilnius, have an area of about 2,500 square kilometers (1553 square miles), and the main Vilnius-Grodno road runs through it. About 40 kilometers (25 miles) southwest of the Rudniki forests and northwest of Lida, on the Byelorussia-Lithuania border, are the Nacha forests, which are about the same size. The

---

46. Kalcheim, *Flames*, 80, 196, 200. For a short time Markov also set up a Jewish unit commanded by Alexander Bogen, whose mission was to secure the forest clearings where weapons were parachuted in from the Soviet front.

47. Gefen et al., *Jewish Partisans*, 79–80; Shmerke Kaczerginski, *The Partisans Are Marching* [Yiddish] (Bamberg: Otto-Verlag, 1948), 16–21, 136–42. Kaczerginski wrote about two young Jews from Svencionys who belonged to the Vilnius *otryad*: Boris Yochai, who participated in mining German trains 15 times, and Yitzhak Rudnicki, who participated 14 times. Kaczerginski himself belonged to the Vilnius *otryad* and recorded its history and the actions of individual partisans in the forests.

48. Manaenkov, *Partizanskie Formirovania*, 163–219.

local population was mostly Lithuanian and Polish. The activities of the Soviet partisans in the Rudniki forests began in the summer of 1943 when a group of paratroopers for "special operations" (*spets gruppa*) arrived. The vanguard of the Soviet-Lithuanian partisans, commanded by Marians Mitseika, whose nom de guerre was Gavris, came to the Rudniki forests from the Naroch forests in September 1943 to prepare a base to which to move the southern headquarters of the Soviet-Lithuanian partisans under the command of Zimanas.

The first Jews in the Rudniki forests were about 70 members of Yehiel's Struggle Group, who came from Vilnius during the first half of September 1943 after the September 1–4 *Aktionen* in the ghetto. The group, only a third of which was armed, was headed by Nathan Ring, who had been a police officer in the ghetto. They set up their base near that of a group of paratroopers, but their request to join them was rejected on the grounds that most of them, both men and women, were unarmed.

At the end of September 1943, 70–80 FPO members arrived, having fled the ghetto on September 23 when it was liquidated. The group, headed by Abba Kovner and Communist activist Chyena Borowska, settled into the base set up by Yehiel's Struggle Group, and together the two organizations had about 150 members. Kovner and Borowska appealed to Gavris to establish a Jewish unit under the aegis of the Soviet-Lithuanian partisan movement. He accepted command of the unit but postponed the decision about a Jewish unit until Zimanas arrived in Rudniki. He appointed Kovner as commander of the Jewish camp and Borowska as commissar, ousting Nathan Ring. The exchange increased tensions in the Jewish camp, which had already been felt in the ghetto between the FPO and Yehiel's Struggle Group.[49] Gavris's decision was influenced by the fact that in the past, Nathan Ring had belonged to Beitar, which was considered a right-wing Zionist youth organization, and had been a police officer in the ghetto. The new commanders moved the camp deeper into the forest onto an island in the middle of the swamps. In October there were new arrivals from labor camps in Vilnius, accompanied by guides who were sent from the forest, and the Jewish camp reached 350 people.

To make command and control more efficient, the Jewish camp was divided into four *otryad*s: Mest (Revenge, as noted above), commanded by Abba Kovner; Za Pobedu (For Victory), commanded by Shmuel Kaplinski; Smert Fashismu (Death to Fascism), commanded by Yaakov Praver; and Borba (Struggle), com-

---

49.   Korczak, *Flames*, 208–9.

manded by Aharon Aharonowich. As their numbers grew, difficulties arose concerning food supplies and the necessity for "economic actions," which were harder and more dangerous to carry out in the Rudniki forests than in other areas of partisan activity. The Germans were in full control of the region around the forest; there were good roads cutting through the forests that enabled the Germans to move quickly; and the local Lithuanians and Poles were hostile to the Soviets and for the most part anti-Semitic. As partisan activity increased, some of the villages organized for "self-defense" with arms provided by the Germans, and the first casualties of the Jewish *otryad*s occurred during "economic actions." The Jewish *otryad*s began to acquire military experience and sabotaged roads, bridges and electric and telephone lines; they also seized weapons in the villages and took revenge on local collaborators who had participated in murdering Jews.[50]

When Zimanas came to Rudniki in October 1943, he took charge of all the units belonging to the Soviet-Lithuanian partisan movement in southern Lithuania. One of his first orders was to put an end to unarmed groups coming into the forest from Vilnius. That was a hard blow for those who wanted to save Jews and enlarge the Jewish force in Rudniki. Officially, the reason for Zimanas's order was that he did not want a large number of unarmed people in the forest, particularly given the difficulties of procuring food. But, in addition, the Soviet-Lithuanian partisans in the Rudniki forests might well have asked that the Jews in their ranks remain a minority. The number of Lithuanians who joined the partisan ranks at that time was extremely small, and a large number of Jews would have identified the movement as Jewish and reinforced the animosity of the local population to the Soviet partisan movement.[51]

At the beginning of November 1943, after the failure of the Kaunas ghetto underground to reach the Augustova forests, Zimanas permitted the underground leadership to send its members to Rudniki.[52] As a result there were more Jews in Rudniki, which compromised the national composition of the Soviet-Lithuanian partisan movement. With that in mind, and planning to enlarge the scope of partisan activities in southern Lithuania, Zimanas decided to send some of the Jewish *otryad*s from Rudniki to the Nacha forests.

---

50.   Ibid., 253, 256–58.
51.   Levin, *They Fought Back*, 187–88; Arad, *Ghetto in Flames*, 454–56.
52.   For more information on the failure to reach the Augustova forests, see chapter 4:2, "The Establishment of the Underground."

Individual Jews and Jewish families had reached the Nacha forests by the spring and summer of 1942. Most of them had arrived from the Radun ghetto, which was liquidated in May 1942, while others had come from the ghettos of Lida, Eisiskes, Voronovo and the neighboring towns. There were 300–350 in all, most of them organized into family camps. In March 1943, Soviet partisans headed by Anton Stankevich came to the Nacha forests and took command of several groups of armed Jews and of former prisoners of war who were in the forest, and established the Leninsky Komsomol *otryad*. In the summer of 1943, Yehiel's Struggle Group in the Vilnius ghetto made contact with the Leninsky Komsomol, and on June 24, 1943, 28 Jews left the ghetto to join them. They were ambushed by Germans on their way to the forest and most of them were killed. In October 1943, the Germans conducted a large-scale manhunt in the forest, inflicting losses on the Leninsky Komsomol, although some of them managed to escape to other forests. Most of the Jews in the family camps were murdered in that manhunt and in the ones carried out during the preceding summer.[53]

Zimanas ordered the Smert Fashismu and Borba *otryad*s to move to Nacha and establish a base there, where, they were told, Soviet partisans were already operating. On November 3, 1943, a group of 111 Jews left; about a third of the group were women, and only 13 had guns. Berl Shereshnevsky, a Communist and former FPO member, was placed in command. After a few days they reached their destination. Without food, without radio communication with the brigade and with very few weapons, the Jews found themselves amongst the hostile Polish population around Nacha. They did not find the Soviet partisans, who had left during the October manhunt, and in the middle of December were forced to return to the Rudniki forests. The Nacha plan had failed. It was not the group's failure, but rather, like the march to the Augustova forests by the Kaunas ghetto underground, that of those who sent them there. The mission had been given to a force that was neither trained nor properly armed. Even veteran, well-trained partisan units like the Leninsky Komsomol could not hold out in the Nacha forests, and surrounded by a hostile population and threatened by German manhunts, the group of Jews were forced to leave.

The failure of the Nacha expedition was exploited to disband the Jewish *otryad*s. At the beginning of 1944, dozens of non-Jewish partisans joined the two *otryad*s that had returned from Nacha and their commanders were replaced

---

53.   Levin, *They Fought Back*, 188; Manaenkov, *Partizanskie Formirovania*, 4; Arad, *Ghetto in Flames*, 383–84, 458.

with Lithuanians. Jews were made deputy commanders. In the early spring, non-Jewish commanders were appointed to Mest and Za Pobedu, replacing Kovner and Kaplinski, and they had several dozen non-Jewish partisans added to their ranks.[54]

The partisan command opposed purely Jewish units, and as a result they were disbanded in Rudniki, as they had been in Naroch. Zimanas did not disperse them in the sense of abandoning them in the forest, as had been the case of the Revenge unit in Naroch, but rather integrated them into multinational *otryad*s and replaced their commanders with Russians and Lithuanians. The new commanders had superior military training and experience, which they used to introduce firmer discipline and improve the fighting ability of the *otryad*s, most of whose members were still Jewish. They received more and better weapons, and carried out more missions. However, the changes also lowered the morale of some of the Jewish fighters: married couples were placed in separate units, and strict military discipline was very difficult for many of then to adapt to.[55]

The existence of Jewish partisan units in the Rudniki forests was a matter of interest for the Central Staff of the Partisan Movement in Moscow, which received reports about hundreds of Jewish partisans who were coming to the forest. On October 16, 1943, a top-secret letter was sent from the central staff headquarters to Antanas Snechkus, the commander of the Soviet-Lithuanian partisan movement, whose headquarters were behind Soviet lines. The letter was signed by the deputy commander of the Central Staff of the Partisan Movement, Commissar KGB (*gosbezopasnosti*) Belchenko, and Colonel Anisimov, head of the intelligence division, and read as follows: "According to the information we have, there are about 300 Jews in the Rudniki forests (60 kilometers northwest of Lida) who escaped from the Vilnius ghetto. They are armed and regard themselves as a Jewish partisan *otryad*. They bought their weapons from the police. I request you verify the truth of this information through your partisans and report back to us."[56] The Soviet-Lithuanian partisan headquarters regarded the matter as urgent, and the following day, October 17, 1943, sent their answer, signed by Snechkus and the head of the intelligence department, Lieutenant-Colonel Baranauskas:

---

54. Arad, *Ghetto in Flames*, 459; Levin, *They Fought Back*, 188.
55. Korczak, *Flames*, 275–77.
56. GARF, Fond 69, Opis 1, Delo 757, p. 146.

> In answer to your letter.… According to our information, which we sent you in our intelligence reports no. 8 on September 24, 1943, and no. 11 on October 8, 1943, approximately 200 Jews who escaped from the Vilnius ghetto with their leaders contacted our partisan *otryad*s in the Rudniki forests. The Jewish partisan *otryad* is under the command of one of our operational groups. We have been informed that the Jewish partisan *otryad* has only a few weapons, but we have no information how they acquired their weapons.[57]

The answer did not satisfy the Central Staff of the Partisan Movement and more information was requested. They sent a letter to Snechkus on November 3, 1943, demanding he "instruct the operational group active in the Rudniki forests to procure and transmit detailed information about the Jewish partisan *otryad*." On November 15, as soon as such information had been obtained from Zimanas's headquarters in Rudniki, another report was sent to the central staff with the following information:

> In September 100 Jews came to Gavris's group from the Vilnius ghetto, 20 of them women. They were armed with short-range weapons. After them came 97 more. On September 24 the Germans liquidated the ghetto. The Jews were organized into four *otryad*s of 65 partisans. These are the names of their commanders: Aharonowich, Brand, Kovner and Kaplinski. Their commissars were Yudeitis and Borowska. On October 4 a group from the Jewish *otryad* destroyed the telephone-telegraph [poles] for a distance of four kilometers [2.5 miles].[58]

The above correspondence clearly shows that on September 24 and October 8, 1943, Gavris's operational unit in the Rudniki forests sent reports about the arrival of armed Jews. The information was transmitted to the Central Staff of the Partisan Movement headed by Ponomarenko. Additional information about the Jews in the Rudniki forests was apparently received from the paratroopers to whom the members of Yehiel's Struggle Group, who came from Vilnius during the first half of September 1943, first appealed. Following receipt of the information, a letter was sent on October 16 showing the underlying suspicion of the Jews who fled from Vilnius: "They bought their weapons from the police," i.e., the Jews had dealings with the German police. The headquarters of the

---

57. Ibid., Delo 742, p. 30.
58. Ibid., 31–32.

Lithuanian partisans wrote in answer, "We have no information as to how they acquired their weapons." The correspondence must have continued and there must have been wireless transmissions as well, but documentation is unavailable. It is reasonable to assume that the order to disband the purely Jewish *otryad*s in the Rudniki forests was given after an exchange of letters with the Central Staff of the Partisan Movement, according to their policy regarding all Jewish partisan *otryad*s in the forests. In the Rudniki forests this general policy was accompanied by the above-mentioned suspicions.

Zimanas organized the partisans under his command into three brigades: the Vilnius, Kaunas and Trakai brigades. At the end of November 1943, members of the Kaunas ghetto underground began arriving in the Rudniki forests and by May 1944 there were 200 of them. They were attached primarily to two *otryad*s, Vperod (Forward) and Smert Okupantam (Death to the Occupiers) of the Kaunas Brigade. The underground members from Kaunas were not cordially welcomed. Nehemia Endlin wrote of his arrival at Smert Okupantam:

> We were met by the commander, Kostia Radionov, and Commissar Dima Davidov, who said, "Why have you come here – to fight the enemy or to hide from him? And if to fight, then with what? With your bare hands? The weapons you brought are good for committing suicide, not for shooting the enemy!" We hadn't expected such a welcome and were very offended. In addition, our belongings were searched and certain items were confiscated.[59]

As the Kaunas Jews grew experienced in partisan warfare and began participating in joint military operations, sharing the fate of the other soldiers, the attitude toward the Jews gradually changed for the better.

An incident that particularly clouded the relations among the Jewish partisans occurred in November 1943. Six Jewish partisans who had previously been ghetto policemen in Vilnius were executed. The decision was made by the commanders of the *otryad*s and the "special department" (*spets-otdel*) at the brigade headquarters, and the sentence was handed down in a very arbitrary fashion.

The head of the special department in the Vilnius Brigade was a Lithuanian named Stankevich. The first policemen to be executed were Vovek Zaltzstein and Lotek Zalwasser, who arrived in Rudniki in the middle of October 1943. Two Jewish partisans accused them of having revealed Jews hiding in *malinas*

---

59. Levin, *They Fought Back*, 193; Endlin, *Memoirs*, 129.

during the *Aktion* of December 1941. No investigation was carried out and Stankevich sentenced the two to death. Their execution was exceptional: they were ordered to leave on a partisan mission with others, and were then shot along the way by their fellow partisans. The fate of the four other ex-policemen, among them Nathan Ring, was the same. They had belonged to Yehiel's Struggle Group, and informants claimed that they had collaborated with the Sipo during *Aktionen* and were Gestapo agents. Such a revelation did not need much corroboration in the forest, for according to partisan policy, if someone was accused of something, even if there was doubt, it was better to execute him than to leave the issue in doubt. In addition, Nathan Ring and his comrades had belonged to the anti-Communist Beitar movement and were ghetto policemen. They were executed in the same fashion: sent on a partisan mission outside the camp and shot.

The leaders of the Jewish partisans, Abba Kovner and Chyena Borowska, knew the four had been arrested and were aware of the sentence before it was carried out. The executions, especially that of Nathan Ring, who had distinguished himself in partisan actions and was held in high esteem, sent shock waves through the Jewish partisans, and many of them were convinced they were unjustified. Abba Kovner justified the executions, and Alexander Rindziunski, one of the Jewish partisans, wrote: "Abba Kovner stated that anyone who collaborated with the enemy in crimes against the Jewish people should not be forgiven."[60]

Following the reactions of the Jewish partisans, and after Kovner and Borowska appealed to Zimanas, there were no further trials of *otryad* fighters who had formerly been ghetto policemen. The execution of the six, who had not been interrogated and against whom there was no real proof, was exceptional among Jewish partisans in the forests. It should be viewed in light of the extenuating circumstances, in which the loss of close family members was still an open wound and people were looking for someone to blame, and in addition, the lives of individuals did not have much value at a time of mass murders and the brutality of the war.

There were no family camps in the Rudniki forests, so that children, entire families and older people, who generally composed family camps, were almost completely absent. The overwhelming majority of the Jews had come

---

60.   Alexander Rindziunski, *The Destruction of Vilnius* [Hebrew] (Lohamei Hagetaot and Hakibbutz Hameuhad, 1987), 156–57 ; Gefen et al., *Jewish Partisans*, 112–14.

in organized groups from the Vilnius and Kaunas ghettos and from their undergrounds, and were young – the right age to serve in partisan units – and were absorbed into the various *otryad*s. The Jewish *otryad*s accepted them all, including those who came unarmed.

From fall 1943 until summer 1944, the Soviet partisans in the Rudniki forests had another enemy to cope with, the Polish Armia Krajowa. By the second half of 1942, small AK groups were operating in the area, but their activities intensified substantially between fall 1943 and summer 1944, especially Operation Buzha.[61] During the operation Soviet partisans and the AK fought one another, and neither avoided murdering civilians suspected of supporting the other side. As part of the Soviet partisans, the Jewish partisans participated in clashes with the AK and also sustained losses in the battles.[62]

The AK regarded the Jews as a pro-Soviet element and generally were anti-Semitic. A non-known number of Jews, who sought refuge in the villages and forests in west Byelorussia where the AK was active, were killed by them.[63] Adolf Pilch, known as Gura, was the commander of an 850-man AK unit in the Stolbtsy district (east of Novogrudok and close to the Naliboki forests). Pilch wrote that between December 1943 and June 1944, they killed 6,000 "Bolsheviks."[64] The number was an exaggeration, but it is reasonable to assume that part of them were Jews, whom the AK considered Bolsheviks. German Security Police reports refer to the murder of Jews at the hands of "Polish gangs." According to a report written on December 18, 1943, "On December 14, 1943, at 1400 hours, a Polish gang [*polnische Bande*] from the village of Mickonai belonging to the Kannyava rural council, stopped a gang of Jews [*Judenbande*] in the house of one of the peasants. The Poles shot the Jews." According to a report written on April 1, 1944, "On the night of March 24, 1944, a Polish gang shot 12 Jews in the village of Borunai in the Kuceviciai regional council. One of the Jews was found hanged."[65]

---

61. Boradyn, *Niemen*, 37–41. For AK activity, see chapter 3.
62. Korczak, *Flames*, 278–79, 284–86, 292.
63. Ibid., 263; the testimony of M. Bazilyan, YVA, 178/1977, 28–30.
64. Turonek, *Bialorus*, 207–8. Turonek relied on an article Pilch wrote for *Spotkanie* 21-22 (a Polish periodical published in Paris) in 1984. Boradyn (*Niemen*, 209) wrote that 6,000 was an exaggeration and unverified by Soviet sources. In footnote 181 on the same page, he wrote that Pilch's men had killed "600" men.
65. Osobii Arkhiv, Fond 504, Opis 1, Delo 14. The archive, whose existence was kept secret until the end of the 1980s, holds documents the Soviet occupation forces seized in Germany.

In the mini-war waged by the Soviet partisans and the AK in west Byelo-russia, the regional German authorities and the AK had a mutual enemy and a mutual objective of fighting against the Soviet partisans. The common interests between the two led to meetings held in early 1944. Members of the local German authorities, the SS and the Abwehr represented the Germans in the negotiations, and the AK was represented by unit commanders who operated in the forests of the Vilnius and Novogrudok districts.

An agreement was reached and went into effect on February 16, 1944, which in effect was an armistice. According to its general terms, it determined the areas from which the AK could operate without interfering with the German forces; weapons, ammunition and medicine would be supplied to AK units to support them against the Soviet partisans; and wounded AK members would be treated at German military hospitals. According to German documents referring to the agreement, the AK would fight against "Bolshevik-Jewish gangs" (*Bolschewistischen-Judischen Banden*).[66] The bloody clashes between the AK units and the Soviet partisans took place in various regions, including the Rudniki forests where the Poles were trying to gain a foothold, and they continued until the Soviet army arrived in July 1944. Occasionally there was contact between Soviet partisans and AK units, leading to local, temporary cease-fire agreements between the two sides.

There were 600–700 Jewish partisans in the Rudniki forests, most of them from the Vilnius and Kaunas ghettos. The exact numbers of Soviet partisans are unobtainable, but there were probably 1,700–2,000 partisans, 30–40 percent of whom were Jewish.[67] The Jewish partisans from the Rudniki forests were with the forward Red Army units that entered the liberated Vilnius.

---

66. Ibid.; the report of the Kaunas Sipo, written on February 2, 1944, was transmitted from Riga to the RSHA in Berlin. The report was also transmitted to the Sipo in Minsk and Warsaw. It is entitled "Gangs of White Poles" (*Weisspolnische Banden*) and is four pages long. It gives the details of the agreement and is signed by the head of the Sipo in the *Generalkommissariat* of Lithuania, SS-Oberführer Dr. Fuchs. Sdzislaw Siemaszko, "*Wilenska AK a Niemcy*," in *Zeszyty Historyczne* (Paris, 1994), 198–222. The AK representatives at the meetings were Major Zigsmund Szendzielasz and Major Alexander Krzyzanowski, both AK commanders in the Vilnius district. Turonek, *Bialorus*, 203–8; Boradyn, *Niemen*, 173–74, 178–79, 181, 206.

67. See Kaplanas, *Gitlerovskaia*, 274. Kaplanas wrote that the number of Soviet-Lithuanian partisans was 9,187, taken from a list of names in the Lithuanian Communist Party archives. The number is an exaggeration, and probably includes many Lithuanians who joined the partisans during the last days or weeks before

JEWISH PARTISANS IN LIBERATED VILNIUS (JULY 1944);
FRONT: RACHEL RUDNICKI

5. THE FORESTS OF NALIBOKI,
LIPICHANY AND VOLCHE-NORA

The Naliboki and Lipichany forests lie in the center of western Byelorussia and cover thousands of square miles, extending to the forests in the Koidanovo region south of Minsk, a few dozen kilometers from Novogrudok, Lida and dozens of other towns and cities that were home to tens of thousands of Jews. The forests were part of the Baranovichi-Novogrudok district and the Neman and Szczara rivers run through them.

the German army was repulsed. It even includes the names of policemen who until then worked for the Germans. It does not refer to the number of partisans who were in the Rudniki forests. Because of their limited area and the fact that the Soviet partisans arrived at a relatively late date, and based on documents in the author's hands, it is reasonable to assume that, as noted above, there were no more than 2,000 of them. Levin (*They Fought Back*, 181) writes that in the Rudniki forests there were about 2,000 partisans, including some *otryad*s that were not part of the Soviet-Lithuanian partisan movement.

Independent partisan units were active in the forests by the spring of 1942, but as the year progressed they organized into *otryad*s and even brigades, although they had no contact with the Central Staff of the Partisan Movement behind Soviet lines. The turning point came in March 1943, when General Vasili Chernishev, the secretary of the District Committee of the Communist Party, came from the Soviet rear to the Naliboki forests. He and his staff were the supreme Soviet authority in Naliboki, and gradually took command of all the partisan units active there.[68]

TUVIA BIELSKI

Beginning in the spring of 1942 with the massive *Aktionen* in western Byelorussia, hundreds of Jews came into the forests. They came to the Naliboki forests from Novogrudok, Lida, Yivya, Mir, Koldichevo, Naliboki and other towns and villages. They also came from the Minsk ghetto after wandering through other forests. Some of them, especially the younger ones who were armed and organized, joined partisan units and took part in the fighting. Families with women, children and the elderly, and young unarmed Jews who had not been accepted by the partisans, organized into family camps. The lives of the Jews in the Naliboki and Lipichany forests were not much different from those in Kozyany and Naroch. Unique, however, were the large family camps of Tuvia Bielski and Shalom Zorin.

Bielski's camp began as the family's search for asylum; they had come from the village of Stankewiche near Novogrudok. Tuvia, his brother Asa'el and several other families had not entered the ghettos in Novogrudok and Lida, but at the end of 1941 began wandering through villages and forests, looking for shelter with peasant acquaintances. Their parents and some of their family members were murdered in the *Aktion* in the Novogrudok ghetto on December 7, 1941. The 30-odd survivors, some of whom were armed, gathered in the forest in May 1942. They decided to call their group the Zhukov *otryad*, and Tuvia, the eldest brother, was chosen to command it.

---

68. Manaenkov, *Partizanskie Formirovania*, 24–25.

Tuvia was a natural leader, brave and impressive. He organized the unit in the Bochkowichi forest in the Novogrudok district, and periodically moved it from place to place to make finding it difficult. He strove to increase its numbers, both for the sake of security and to rescue as many Jews as possible, despite the fact that acquiring food for large numbers of people was very difficult. Members of the *otryad* were sent to the Novogrudok ghetto to bring out more Jews. Rumors about the Bielski camp reached the ghettos in Lida and elsewhere, and people kept coming; by the end of 1942 its population was between 200 and 250. Asaël commanded the armed nucleus, whose role was to secure the camp, carry out the "economic actions" and procure more arms. Chief of staff was Lazer Malbin, who was a good organizer and had military experience from his service in the Polish army. The armed nucleus carried out attacks on German transportation and retaliatory raids against collaborators with the Germans and peasants who had murdered Jews.[69]

Providing food for an increasingly large camp was, as noted, a difficult mission. The villages in western Byelorussia were for the most part poor, and not only did the Germans require the peasants to provide quotas from their crops, but the Soviet partisans also confiscated their agricultural produce. The peasants had no choice but to give up their food to the Germans and partisans, but opposed giving it to Jews. Many of them informed the German authorities and complained to the Soviet partisans that Jews from the forests were robbing them of their small amounts of remaining food, and that soon there would be nothing left. In the summer of 1942, Bielski learned that the *otryad* commanded by Victor Panchenko, to whom peasants had complained of Jewish "robbers," had decided to destroy his camp. He arranged a meeting with Panchenko and convinced him that his unit was nothing more than an ordinary partisan unit fighting the Germans, and eventually the two decided to cooperate.[70] Regarding their collaboration and other actions, Bielski wrote:

---

69. Partiinyi Arkhiv TsK KP Belorusii, Fond 3599, Opis 4, Delo 272, pp. 33–49 (henceforth "Bielski Report"). The report is handwritten and is entitled "The history of the Kalinin partisan *otryad*." That was the official name given to Bielski's camp after the large-scale manhunt in the Naliboki forests. It is signed by Tuvia Bielski, *otryad* commander; Malbin, chief of staff; and Shelyatovich, the *otryad*'s commissar. It describes the *otryad*'s history and was presented to the headquarters of the Byelorussian partisan movement on September 16, 1944, after the liberation of Byelorussia by the Red Army.

70. Nechama Tec, *Defiance: The Bielski Partisans* (New York and Oxford: Oxford

On October 16, 1942, together we ambushed German gendarmes on the Novogrudok–Novoelnya road, destroying a vehicle and acquiring arms: two light machine guns and three rifles.... Even before that, on September 20, we joined forces with Panchenko's *otryad* and attacked the train junction at Jatsuki on the Baranovichi-Lida line, killing four Germans and wounding seven.... On December 8, 1942, we waited in ambush near the train junction between Jatsuki and Novoelnya, killing two Germans and stripping them of their arms.... In the fall of 1942 we set fire to the Novoelnya sawmill where there was a lot of timber. In addition, eight government estates in the area were set on fire, where there was a large stock of seeds and agricultural equipment.[71]

Bielski perceived his mission as rescuing Jews from the ghettos and providing them with a haven. As far as he was concerned, the participation of his men in military actions against the Germans was important but secondary, and served mainly to justify to the Soviet partisans the camp's existence in the forest and its "economic actions." There were many Jewish partisans in the forests who disagreed, and thought that fighting the Germans was preferable to saving Jews. In a discussion with Baruch Levin, one of the most distinguished Jewish partisans, who claimed that the mission of the Jews in the forests had to be fighting, and that "their lives have no value, only revenge has value," Bielski answered that "since there are so few of us remaining, for me the most important thing is that Jews survive."[72]

During the winter of 1942–43, Bielski's camp of 200–250 settled in the Zabelovo forest in the Novogrudok region. The Jews were terrified of the first winter in the forest and of leaving footprints in the snow after "economic actions," and it was only Bielski's leadership that kept the camp together. In November 1942, 40 fugitives from the Novogrudok ghetto, among them women and children, came to the camp. Since there was no room in the *zemlanka*s and it was unlikely that enough food could be found, they were sent to the Lipichany forests; unfortunately, upon arrival they fell victim to a German manhunt.[73]

University Press, 1993), 74–76.
71.   Bielski Report, 3–4.
72.   Levin, *In the Forests*, 113; the quote is from there. For giving priority to saving Jews, see Tec, *Defiance*, 61–80.
73.   Tec, *Defiance*, 62, 89–90.

Fearing that the manhunt would reach them as well, in December 1942 Bielski moved his camp to the Khrapinevo forest near the towns of Lyubcha and Iwie. On January 5, 1943, some of Bielski's men were at a farm near the forest and were surprised by German forces. In the ensuing battle nine of them were killed, including Bielski's wife. During the winter they were twice attacked by German and Lithuanian police but managed to get away.[74] In an "economic action" undertaken in March 1943, nine of Bielski's fighters were killed when a local peasant informed the Germans of their presence. Asael Bielski led a retaliatory action, killing the peasant and setting the farm on fire.[75]

In the spring of 1943, Jews arrived from the Lida ghetto, and during six weeks the camp grew from 250 to 750, more than 70 percent of them unarmed. Because of the increase in numbers, at the beginning of the summer the camp moved to the Yasenovo forest. On June 8 they were attacked by German forces and local police, but they had been warned by the camp scouts, and those who were armed managed to cover the escape of the rest of the camp; five of Bielski's fighters were killed. According to the Bielski Report, eight Germans and local policemen were also killed.[76]

Because of the camp's growth, they decided to move to the Naliboki forests, which were much larger and under partisan control. The move was authorized by General Chernishev. The passage was difficult and dangerous and lasted several weeks, but during the second half of June 1943, they reached the Naliboki forests. A short time after their arrival, the Germans carried out a manhunt, code-named Operation Hermann, which lasted from July 13 to August 11, 1943. The partisans called it "the great manhunt," and employed their customary tactics: they either infiltrated or broke through the German forces searching the forest. The Bielski camp managed to find shelter in a large swamp and were saved.[77]

During that manhunt, the partisans suffered many losses, units fell apart and discipline collapsed, and the partisans began turning on the Jews. After the manhunt the partisans in the Naliboki forests were reorganized. Bielski's unit was divided in half and about 100 men were transferred to the Ordzonokidze *otryad* of the Kirov Brigade. The rest, commanded by Bielski himself, were

---

74. Ibid., 91–92; Bielski Report, 4–5.
75. Tec, *Defiance*, 102–3.
76. Bielski Report, 6–7.
77. Ibid.

recognized as a family *otryad* whose official name was Kalinin and which was directly subordinated to General Chernishev, who appointed Ivan Shlyatovich as *otryad* commissar. The *otryad* became a service and supply unit for the other partisan units in the area. Bielski wrote about the new role and activities of his family *otryad*:

> At the base [we] established workshops and employed more than 200 skilled [but] unarmed workers, including cobblers and tailors. A sausage factory was established, as were a soap-manufacturing plant, a bakery, a blacksmith's shop, a clinic and a hospital. The factories and workshops served the partisan groups in the Naliboki forests. Their services were important to the partisans, who in return supplied food, equipment and raw materials....[78]

The camp also had a school for its 60 children, and continued to take in not only Jews who had escaped to the forests but Jewish partisans whose commanders, for anti-Semitic and other reasons, had decided to get rid of them and sent them to Bielski. Between January and June 1944, when the Red Army arrived, the *otryad* grew from 750 to 1,000–1,200. It became a Jewish town within the forest, and even had a cemetery for those who died or fell in battle.[79]

Given the conditions prevailing in the forests, strict discipline was necessary, and for serious infractions men were tried and even executed. A Jew from Lida named Byalobroda was accused of informing the German police about Jews who smuggled food into the ghetto and continued his criminal behavior in the forest. When he participated in "economic actions" he used to steal valuable objects, which was considered a serious crime. He was sentenced by Bielski and executed. Another Jew executed by Bielski was Israel Kessler. He organized a group of people who tried to leave Bielski and form their own unit. He complained to General Chernishev that Bielski was holding gold and jewelry – items that had to be turned over to partisan headquarters. Chernishev investigated the charge and cleared Bielski. In his efforts to undermine Bielski, Kessler organized a petition against Bielski, which some of the members of the *otryad* signed. Bielski viewed the matter as attempted rebellion, tried Kessler

---

78. Partiinyi Arkhiv TsK KP Belorusii, Fond 3599, Opis 4, Delo 272, pp. 10–11.
79. Bielski Report, 8, 10–11.

and sentenced him to death. The incident infuriated some of the partisans but others justified the execution.[80]

During the German retreat large numbers of their forces crossed the Naliboki forests, and the partisans, among them Bielski's men, attacked them. On July 9, 1944, while the armed core of the *otryad* had distanced itself from the camp in a search for Germans, a retreating German unit came upon the camp and killed 11 of its members. When the area was liberated there were 1,200 Jews in Bielski's *otryad*, a quarter of them women.[81] The partisan command disbanded Belski's *otryad* in July 1944, a few days after it arrived in Novogrudok.

SHALOM ZORIN

Another family camp in the Naliboki forests, which contained hundreds of Jews from the Minsk ghetto, was that of Shalom Zorin. Zorin, who had been a partisan during the October revolution, had fled from Minsk and joined the Parkhomenko *otryad*, where he was put in charge of a reconnaissance unit. The flight from the Minsk ghetto increased after the large-scale *Aktion* of July 1942, mainly to the Burelom forest, which lay about 40 kilometers (25 miles) southwest of Minsk near the city of Koidanovo. Jews from Minsk, especially women, children and the aged, wandered through the forests looking for asylum, and the only solution was to establish a family camp.

There is more than one version of the history of Zorin's camp. According to Smolar, he and Nahum Feldman, who

---

80. Bielski Report, 11; Tec, *Defiance*, 177–83; Yehoshua Yoffe, *Partisans* [Hebrew] (Tel Aviv, 1951), 161–62. Yoffe belonged to Bielski's unit and is critical of his sentencing Kessler to death. He wrote: "There were a lot of people who were dissatisfied because of the bias and favoritism in the camp.... There were men who stood guard for entire days or nights and others who were completely excused from guard duty. The commanders did not even let anyone complain. 'That's the way I want it' was the answer to complaints."

81. Tec, *Defiance*, 199–201; Bielski Report, 12–13.

was a commissar in the Budioni *otryad*, appealed to Semyon Ganzenko, the *otryad*'s commander, and described the severe problems of the Jews in the forests who had not been accepted into partisan units and the distress of those who were still living in the ghetto. Ganzenko decided to establish a special base in the Burelom forest which would take them in.[82] In the report sent to the Central Committee of the Byelorussian Communist Party, Smolar wrote the following about the establishment of Zorin's camp:

> The partisans in the Koidanovo district who had left the ghetto were well aware of what conditions inside were like. Comrade Ganzenko, the commander of the Budioni *otryad*, sent envoys to the ghetto to get people out. They started streaming out, men, women, children and the elderly. In a short time about 500 came to the area of the partisan village of Skrimatova. The District Committee of the Communist Party in the Baranovichi region agreed, and those who were fit to fight were put into the Parkhomenko *otryad*. The rest went into Family *Otryad* 106, whose commander was Shalom Zorin, from Minsk. There was a special group of child guides…and they, and also guides from the Kutuzov *otryad* (from the Frunze Brigade), got more than 1,000 Jews out of the Minsk ghetto. About 680 went into Family *Otryad* 106 and about 200 went into the Parkhomenko *otryad*. The others went to the Kutuzov, Kalinin and other *otryad*s in the Naliboki forests.[83]

According to a different version, Zorin himself initiated the establishment of the camp. Anatoly Wertheim, chief of staff of the Zorin camp, testified as follows:

> At the beginning of 1942, when the Communist Party did not yet have much influence on what was going on in the forest, Soviet partisan camps sprang up. The first Jews came into the forest and that was when the problems began. First [the partisans] did not want old people and then they did not want children. There was also a lot of popular anti-Semitism, and they did not even want to accept armed young people, but took their weapons away.…
>
> And then it was like a story from the Bible. Once Zorin went to a certain village and saw three or four children, and knew that they

---

82. Smolar, *Soviet Jews*, 158–60.
83. YVA, 033/2689, p. 17. The report was written during August–September 1944, a few weeks after the liberation.

were Jewish. When he approached them they became deathly afraid. He spoke to them in Yiddish, "*Kinderlach*," he said.... And then they told him they had run away from the ghetto and had nowhere to go, and that there were more Jews in the cowshed.... Zorin went to those Jews and again saw the tragedy.... They said that someone had told them that the partisans killed Jews who escaped from the ghetto and that they were living in fear. Zorin said to his commander, "There are 30–40 Jews, and they have to be brought to the camp." The commander refused but Zorin wouldn't back down and said they couldn't go on like that. He had an idea: "If you can't [take them in], we'll organize a Jewish camp and begin a rescue operation." For that he could get authorization.[84]

Zorin's *otryad* was established in April 1943. By that time the partisans in the Minsk area were already under the command of the Central Staff of the Partisan Movement and needed their permission for the creation of such an *otryad*. According to a document written on October 3, 1943, relating to Zorin's *otryad*, "Five months ago the Party and the government instructed *otryad* commander Zorin to set up a family camp to protect the lives of the Jewish women, children and aged whose husbands, fathers and sons were fighting for the liberty of the people on the fronts of the Patriotic War."[85]

Zorin's *otryad* organized in the forest near the village of Skrimatova. Since it was too small for hundreds of people, the Stalin Partisan Brigade's commander, who was responsible for the region, decided that the *otryad* would move to the Naliboki forests, and the move was made in June 1943. They went to the forests' northern region, in the Yvenets district, and in the middle of July, even before they could settle into the area, a large-scale manhunt was carried out. Zorin's *otryad* found refuge on the Krasna Gorka island in the large swamps. After the manhunt they returned to their former base.

During the manhunt the Germans burned the villages near the forests and drove away their inhabitants, leaving no one to reap the crops. Partisan headquarters ordered Zorin's *otryad* to do the reaping, and when they had finished

---

84. Testimony of Anatoly Wertheim, YVA, W-158/2809, pp. 2–4.
85. *Partiinyi Arkhiv TsK KP Belorusii, Minsk*, Fond M, Opis 41, Delo 83, 22. The document, which gives the history of the Zorin *otryad*, was presented by its commanders to the headquarters of the Byelorussian Partisan Movement.

the crops were put at headquarters' disposal.[86] Commanders of partisan units who did not want Jews transferred the Jews in their units to Zorin's camp. A document signed by Kliuchko, the commander of the Frunze Brigade, reads, "To the commander of the Jewish national *otryad*, Comrade Zorin. Based on the order from the [partisan] command of the Yvenets district, 28 Jews are being transferred to you, 12 of them armed with rifles."[87]

The *otryad* continued growing. A report of its manpower sent to the partisan command on January 1, 1944, stated that there were 556 members, 280 of them women. The partisan command allotted them four villages in which to carry out "economic actions."[88] There was a company of 50–70 armed men who dealt with camp security, "economic actions" and military operations. Occasionally the *otryad* had to send 30–40 men on large-scale operations in which several partisan units participated. Zorin also turned the camp into a maintenance unit for the other units in the area. According to Wertheim:

> That simple Jew [Zorin] understood that it was impossible to keep people idle and he had the following idea: anyone who was not a fighter had to be productive in some way. He also understood that such productivity would help them maintain their self-respect. He organized a large hospital where nurses and 13 doctors worked, and it became the Nalikobi forest's medical center.... He established a cooperative of tailors who sewed [clothing] for the partisans...from parachutes brought from all over the forest. There were shoemakers, a workshop for weapons, a flour mill, a sausage factory and a school for the children.... Zorin's men were mostly Soviet Jews and they had always worked.... Anti-Semitism was very strong among the partisans.... When [Zorin and Bielski's] units were set up the relations were no better. But the fact they were organized and under the command of the partisan headquarters and had the same rights as any other partisan camp...helped a little to fight anti-Semitism and gave us someone to turn to if clearly anti-Semitic measures were

---

86. Ibid., Fond 3500, Opis 4, Delo 277.
87. Ibid.
88. Ibid. The report also gave the professions of the *otryad* members, the number of Communist Party and Komsomol members, the numbers of commanders and deputy commanders, etc.

taken against us. That was shown in 1943, when the Poles – the Polish Legion – murdered ten of Zorin's partisans.[89]

On November 17, 1943, 12 of Zorin's partisans set out on an "economic action" near the village of Dubniki in the Yvenets district, taking horses and wagons with them. There was a Polish partisan unit in the village at the time, commanded by Sergeant-Major Zdislav Narkewicz. One of the peasants told the Polish unit that the "Jews were stealing their property," and the Poles came and opened fire on Zorin's men, who thought Germans were attacking them. They retreated, leaving behind the horses, wagons and the small amount of food they had gathered. When they realized they were being attacked by Poles, they returned and demanded the horses and loaded wagons. The Poles, who greatly outnumbered them, attacked, took their weapons and arrested them, only one managing to escape. The next day the Poles murdered them. One who was only wounded pretended to be dead and when the Poles left he returned to Zorin's camp; he and the Jew who had managed to escape reported what had happened.

When the incident was investigated, it was discovered that the perpetrators of the attack were not Soviet partisans, but rather Polish nationalists. An Armia Krajowa force of hundreds, called the "Polish Legion," was active in the Naliboki forests and the surrounding villages. Many members of the unit, including their commander, Lieutenant Kaspar Milaszewski, had served in the local police at Yvenets, and had afterwards organized as an underground AK unit and escaped together into the forest in the beginning of the summer of 1943. They joined the Soviet partisan movement in the area and their *otryad* was named after Thadeush Kosciuszko, an 18th-century Polish popular hero. Milaszewski adroitly concealed from Soviet command the fact that they were part of the AK.

On June 22, 1943, General Chernishev received orders from the Central Committee of the Byelorussian Communist Party regarding "military-political missions in the western districts of Byelorussia." He was instructed to use every measure possible against "the bourgeois-nationalist Polish units and groups." At the end of October 1943 it finally became clear to the partisan command in the area that the Kosciuszko *otryad* belonged to the AK and that they were engaged in anti-Soviet activities.

---

89. Testimony of Anatoly Wertheim, YVA, W-158/2809, 5–7. For anti-Semitism in the Naliboki forests, also see Smolar, *Soviet Jews*, 171–84.

On November 4 Chernishev sent a telegram to Ponomarenko, head of the Central Staff of the Partisan Movement, and requested authorization to disarm the Kosciuszko *otryad*. Authorization was granted on November 14,[90] and the murder of Jewish partisans by Kosciuszko members provided him with a concrete reason: General Chernishev had long since planned to disarm the Polish *otryad*, and with the murder of Zorin's men he saw his chance. On the night of November 30, 1943, a large partisan force surrounded the Polish base, and on the following morning the Poles' weapons were confiscated. Some of the local residents who belonged to the Polish *otryad* were scattered among other partisan units and some were sent home. The investigation of the Polish commanders lasted more than three weeks, and in the end they were tried by the partisans and accused of establishing an anti-revolutionary Polish national organization and of anti-Soviet activity. The murder of Zorin's men was mentioned only briefly in the trial. Five senior commanders, including Milaszewski, were arrested and flown from a partisan airstrip to Moscow for interrogation, and five others were executed. Narkewicz and his men, who had committed the murders, escaped, entered German service and fought against Soviet partisans.[91]

The official name of Zorin's camp was "the Jewish family *otryad*" (*Yevreiski semeinnyi otryad*), but on March 25, 1944, General Chernishev's headquarters changed it to "Partisan *otryad* 106."[92] The reason for the change is unclear, possibly the desire to equate it with regular partisan *otryad*s, and possibly the word "Jewish" was inconvenient for the partisan commanders in the area. Separate Jewish units were against Soviet partisan movement policy, and they were disbanded in the Naroch and Rudniki forests. However, disbanding Zorin's *otryad* would have presented the problem of what to do with his noncombatants, and the solution was to change the name.

Bielski's and Zorin's men often met in the forest. Wertheim wrote of the relations between them that "they were like good neighbors. Sometimes the camps

---

90. Boradyn, *Niemen*, 152, 295–96. The source records the exchange of telegrams between Chernishev and Ponomarenko.

91. Smolar, *Soviet Jews*, 172; testimony of Yosef Markevinsky, YVA, M-174/3126; testimony of Wertheim, pp. 7, 22–24; Turonek, *Bialorus*, 121–22, concerning the decisions of the Byelorussian Communist Party regarding the Poles; Boradyn, *Niemen*, 158, 165–67.

92. Institut Istorii Partii pri TskKPB, Fond 3500, Opis 4, Delo 277 (M41).

were fairly close.… The commanders visited one another and the men did as well.… Relations were friendly. Even today Zorin and Bielski are friends."[93]

At the beginning of July 1944, when the German army was retreating through the Naliboki forests, they came upon fighters from Zorin's *otryad*. In the ensuing battle seven of Zorin's men were killed, and he himself was wounded and his leg amputated. On July 9, 1944, when the Red Army reached the Naliboki forests and before it was disbanded, Zorin's *otryad* numbered 558 men, 137 of them armed.[94]

The success stories of Bielski's and Zorin's family camps were exceptional in those times of hardship and cruelty. The Jews survived, first and foremost, because of their leaders, both of them simple, common-sense people. Neither had previously led an organized body. Tuvia Bielski was a humble cloth merchant and Zorin was a carpenter. They fled to the forests to rescue themselves and their families and to fight the Germans, the murderers of their people. They knew that remaining in the ghettos was a death sentence and were aware of the fate of the Jews in the forests who wandered, hungry and unarmed, at the mercy of the local peasants and the organized and unorganized partisans. Bielski and Zorin understood that they had to collect those Jews into an independent camp with an armed nucleus that could protect them. They also knew that to ensure that the partisan command in the forests would countenance them and not brand them as parasites, their armed members would have to participate with the partisans in battles against the Germans – which the Jews wanted to do in any case – and their noncombatants would have to be productive in a way that would serve the partisan *otryad*s operating in the area. Thus General Chernishev and the local command recognized the family camps as partisan units and allowed them to carry out "economic activities," without which they would not have been able to survive; as a result of Bielski's and Zorin's foresight, most of the Jews in their camps did survive.

The situation of the Jewish partisans and members of family camps in the Lipichany forests southwest of the Naliboki forests was particularly difficult because of their location. The Lipichany forests were one of the largest and most-western forested expanses in which organized Soviet partisans operated. Through them ran roads and railroads linking Bialystok and Minsk, and Bara-

---

93. Testimony of Wertheim, 12. Shalom Zorin died in 1974 and Tuvia Bielski died in 1987; both of them were buried in Israel.
94. Ibid., 15–16; Smolar, *Soviet Jews*, 196–97.

novichi, Lida and Vilnius. They were also the main routes for German Army Group Center, and therefore, partisan activity in the region endangered those vital arteries for the Germans. For that reason the Germans carried out more manhunts in the Lipichany forests than in the Naliboki and other forests. During the second half of 1942, partisan *otryad*s were active there, and in December 1942 they were organized into the Lenin Brigade which, like other units operating in the Lipichany forests, was under the command of General Chernishev.

The first Jewish partisans had tried to get a foothold in the Lipichany forests as early as the spring of 1942. During the second half of April 1942, Dr. Dworzecki came to the forest with an underground group from the Dyatlovo (Zhetl) ghetto, but after a few weeks he and some of his men were murdered by a band of partisans.[95] Jews from Slonim and the towns of Dyatlovo, Belitsa, Kozlowshchina, Novoelnya, Molchad, Derechin and the slave-labor camp at Dworets arrived at the Lipichany forests. From among the Jews of Dyatlovo, who had arrived there after the massacre of August 1942, a Jewish partisan unit was organized under the command of Hirsch Kaplinski, one of the ghetto's underground activists. It consisted of about 120 members, some of them armed. During the two months of their independent existence they obtained weapons and retaliated against local collaborators who had persecuted and betrayed Jews escaping from the ghetto. In late September the unit joined the Orlyani partisan unit, commanded by Nikolai Vakhonin, and became its 3rd Company. Kaplinski's men participated in attacks on German garrisons and police stations, including the garrison in the town of Ruda-Yaworskaia in October 1942.[96]

A Jewish partisan unit commanded by Dr. Yehezkel Atlas was also active in the Lipichany forests.[97] When the Derechin ghetto was liquidated in July 1942, he organized the escape to the forests. He attached some dozens of Jews who had escaped from Kozlowshchina and Dyatlovo to his partisan group. They joined Boris Bulat's *otryad*, which was part of the Lenin Brigade.

On August 10, 1942, the Bulat and other units attacked the town of Derechin. Atlas and his men participated in the battle, as did dozens of Jews from other units and from family camps who had been recruited to assist in evacuat-

95. See chapter 4:8, "Underground Activity and Armed Resistance in the Small Ghettos."

96. Gefen et al., *Jewish Partisans*, 386–87.

97. Atlas had arrived in the town of Kozlowshchina, north of Slonim, in 1939 as a refugee from Poland. He was a physician and worked in the region's rural areas, becoming acquainted with many of the local inhabitants.

ing the wounded partisans and to arm themselves with weapons taken during the attack. Scores of local and German police were killed. The partisans also suffered losses, some of them Jews. About two weeks after the attack, a large German force conducted a manhunt, named Operation Hamburg, in the forest. Bulat's people joined the battle and both sides suffered heavy losses, and about ten of Atlas's partisans fell.[98] Atlas and his men participated in many battles, including the attack on Kozlowshchina and the sabotage of the bridge over the Neman River. He was highly respected among the Jews in the forest as well as by the partisan commanders.

During Operation Hamburg, which began on December 10, 1942, and lasted for two weeks, the partisan units joined battle with German soldiers. The opposing forces were unequal, and the partisans of the Lenin Brigade split into small units to infiltrate through the Germans and move to other forests. Scores of Jewish partisans, among them two Jewish unit commanders – Atlas and Kaplinski – fell during the battles that took place during the manhunt.[99]

The fate of thousands of Jews who fled from the surrounding towns and gathered in the family camps in the Lipichany forests was tragic, since they were the main victims of the December 10 manhunt. The presence of women, children and the elderly in the family camps restricted mobility, and in the absence of advance information the family camps had no way of knowing that the Germans were coming. A female partisan wrote as follows:

> The groups in the family camps passed terrible days, defenseless and without shelter as they were. Many fell at the hands of the murderers and the rest wandered through the forest hungry, [with] torn [clothing] and exhausted, carrying small children in their arms. The children's hands froze and the adults' legs were paralyzed with cold. That was the situation until the end of December.... Scores of Jewish families were abandoned to their bitter fate. They fell ill with typhus, scabies, their frozen hands and feet became infected, people simply fell in the forest and there was nothing we could do to help them because the partisan commanders forbid us to visit the sick lest infectious diseases spread among the partisans. On January 28...I got a wagon full of bread and brought it for the hungry and sick. I came upon

---

98. Gefen et al., *Jewish Partisans*, 343–56; Shmuel Bornshtein, *Dr. Atlas's Company* [Hebrew] (Tel Aviv: Hakibbutz Hameuhad, 1965), 61–67.

99. Bornshtein, *Dr. Atlas's Company*, 111–12; Cholawski, *Resistance*, 173–76, 192.

an awful sight: not far from the bunkers a cemetery had sprung up, full of the children and their parents who had died from hunger and disease.... The filth, scabies, lice and disease had reaped their toll.[100]

After the German operation in January 1943, Russians and Ukrainians were appointed to command Kaplinski's unit and it lost its Jewish character. Many Jews distinguished themselves as fighters in the Borba (former Orlyani) unit and participated in attacks on German garrisons in the towns of Nakrishki, Dyatlovo and others in the region. They also took part in battles against the AK units operating to the west of the Lipichany forests. The AK attacked a family camp of Jews from Belitsa, north of the Neman River, several times, killing many.[101] Hundreds of Jewish partisans continued to fight in the Lipichany forests in active units until the Red Army arrived in July 1944.

German reports stressed that they killed 6,172 (or 6,874) of the enemy in Operation Hamburg, of whom 2,988 (or 3,658) were Jews.[102] There were also many who died of hunger and disease. Very few Jews survived in family camps in the Lipichany forests after Operation Hamburg.

Among the partisan units deployed in the forested regions south of Slonim, especially in the Volche-Nora forests, there were Jews who, in the course of the massacre in the summer of 1942, had arrived from Slonim and the towns of Biten, Kosovo and others. Jewish partisan activity began in those forests in June 1942, when several dozen members of the Slonim underground arrived. They had contacted the Shchors Unit commanded by Pavel Pronyagin in the Rafalovka forest while they were still in the ghetto.[103] The subunits of Shchors were known as the 51st, 52nd, 53rd and 54th Companies. The Slonim underground members were admitted to the 51st Company, but when growing numbers of Jews joined it, a large number of non-Jews and its commander left to join other units because they did not wish to belong to a unit that was mainly Jewish.

Pronyagin, the commander of Shchors, appointed Captain Yefim Fyodorovich to command the 51st Company. He was a Jew from Gomel and an escaped POW, and the 51st Company, which had quickly grown to 150 members, became a Jewish company. At that time Shchors had no contact with the Soviet rear or with the Central Staff of the Partisan Movement, so that it may be assumed

---

100. Gefen et al., *Jewish Partisans*, 390.
101. Ibid., 396–400.
102. Gerlach, *Kalkulierte*, 900, 907; Turonek, *Bialorus*, 152.
103. Manaenkov, *Partizanskie Formirovania*, 149.

that Pronyagin was unaware of the policy against establishing Jewish partisan units. Once Fyodorovich was appointed commander, the 51st Company moved to the Volche-Nora forests, which were much larger than the Rafalovka forest. A professional soldier, Fyodorovich put his people through a course of rigorous military training. The company consisted of four platoons, three of whose commanders were Jewish. The company managed to construct a 45-mm anti-tank gun out of spare parts they found in the forests.[104]

The 51st Company first saw battle in a Shchors attack on Kosovo on August 2, 1942. It was the largest attack in the region at that time and involved about 500 partisans. Kosovo still had a small ghetto. Yaakov Sheptinsky, who took part in the battle, described it as follows:

> Our company was ordered to arrive at the town center and to occupy the police station.... We took up positions exactly opposite the ghetto.... The ghetto inhabitants watched us from behind the barbed wire fence with fear and amazement.... We entered the police station... and opposition ceased.... Fyodorovich got us up [and sent us] to occupy the church, but heavy machine-gun fire from the church made us drop to the ground again.... We brought the 45-mm anti-tank gun in and directed it on the church. They were shooting at us from the windows and steeple. The partisans broke in and opposition ceased.... The battalion retreated from the town. Our 51st Company took up the rear guard and the ghetto prisoners left with us. The youngsters who had managed to obtain weapons will join us and the rest will live in family camps.[105]

The liberation of the Kosovo ghetto was one of the few events in which Soviet partisans rescued Jews and enabled them to leave for the forests in the midst of an operation with other objectives. The operation was unique in that Jewish partisans constituted one of the main forces liberating the ghetto Jews. Most of the Kosovo Jews who reached the forests settled in a family camp. Jews in Bitan, which still had a small ghetto of a few hundred, heard about Kosovo and in August and September 1942, most of them escaped to the forests and organized themselves into a family camp.[106]

---

104. Shner-Nishmit, *51st Company*, 80, 108–10, 113.
105. Ibid., 124–25.
106. Ibid., 125, 139.

The battle route of the 51st Company was long and bloody. The company participated in an attack on the training camp used by local Byelorussian police volunteers in the village and estate of Gvinovich, close to Bitan. After the attack the Germans concentrated forces in the Volche-Nora region in preparation for a manhunt. The Shchors command decided to evacuate the area and to move southeast toward the Polesie swamps, leaving the family camps behind to face their fate. On its way eastward, the 51st participated in an attack on a police station in the village of Chemili and in the fierce battle to cross the Oginski channel on September 13, 1942. The Shchors and the 51st Company suffered heavy losses, with many killed and wounded. Fyodorovich, the 51st Company commander, was badly wounded in the course of battle. Knowing medical care was impossible, he asked to be shot by his men, who complied with his request. After his burial Lieutenant Viktor Guzevski took command of the 51st. A field hospital established in the Polesie swamps under the management of Dr. Abraham Blumovich saved many of the Shchors wounded.[107]

The Shchors arrived at the Polesie swamps toward the end of September, and in October the 51st took part in the attack on the town of Khotynichi. Local Byelorussians had gradually joined the 51st, and as their numbers increased the Jewish partisans were exposed to much anti-Semitism, especially on the part of the Shchors chief of staff, Karp Merzliakov. On October 20, 1942, Merzliakov informed the company that due to disciplinary misdemeanors, more than thirty Jewish partisans were being removed from the company. The people whose names were called were all experienced partisans. The disciplinary misdemeanors of which some of the Jews were accused had indeed taken place, but the Shchors command took advantage of the situation to get rid of a large number of Jews and change the company's Jewish character. The expelled partisans, some of whom were armed, wandered through the forests for many weeks and eventually came upon the partisan unit commanded by Vasili Vassiliev, who accepted them.[108]

In early fall 1942, Alexei Kleshchev came to the Polesie region from behind Soviet lines, having been sent to represent the Central Committee of the Byelorussian Communist Party and the Byelorussian partisan staff. He exercised his authority over the partisans, who until then had been operating independently,

---

107. Ibid., 159–63; Gefen et al., *Jewish Partisans*, 318–19.
108. Shner-Nishmit, *51st Company*, 192–97; Manaenkov, *Partizanskie Formirovania*, 608–9.

including Shchors. Kleshchev implemented Soviet partisan policy, according to which there were to be no Jewish partisan units, and ordered the 63 Jewish partisans still in the 51st Company to be dispersed among other Shchors units.[109] With that, the battle history of the Jewish 51st Company came to a close. It was organized in June 1942 in the Volche-Nora forests and disbanded in January 1943 in the swamps of Polesie. The company members continued as Shchors partisans in other *otryads* until the region was liberated in the summer of 1944. When it was organized, the 51st had 171 Jewish partisans, 65 of whom fell in the forests. After the Red Army arrived, those who remained were drafted and 13 died on the front. About 46 percent of the 51st Company did not live to see the victory over the Germans.[110]

The family camps of Jews from Bitan and Kosovo that remained in the Volche-Nora forests after the Shchors partisans left were sorely tried by the frequent Germans manhunts, the first of which took place on September 18, 1942. The trials of the Bitan family camp were described by one of its members as follows:

> September 20, Yom Kippur eve, the group moved to a nearby grove… and we came under rifle fire. We broke into a frenzied run.… They called after us, "Halt!" The children were crying all the time and we had no strength left to run.… Enemy planes continued following us. People were running like hunted animals, with no food and no water. Of the more than 300 before the manhunt only 100 were left alive, the rest perished. Dead bodies were strewn all over the paths and people envied their dead comrades.[111]

The Jews of Kosovo shared a similar fate. Some tried to escape the siege and make their way to the swamps of Polesie, many fell and others were captured by the Germans. After the manhunt only about 135 Jews remained alive in the Volche-Nora forests. The partisans returned and forced them to leave for the Rafalovka forest, a distance of about 8 kilometers (5 miles). It was smaller than Volche-Nora, less dense and closer to Bitan, and it was dangerous to stay

---

109. Shner-Nishmit, *51st Company*, 203–7.
110. Ibid., 174–75, lists the names of all 171 members of the 51st Company and notes the names of the fallen.
111. Ibid. During August and September 1942, German forces carried out a large operation, known as Operation Sumpfieber, against the partisans in extensive areas of *Generalkommissariat* Byelorussia.

there. After the Germans conducted a manhunt in the Rafalovka forest in late December 1942, local peasants (who had received weapons from the Germans to protect themselves from partisans) attacked the family camp on January 20, 1943, and only 70 of the camp's Jews survived. Another manhunt in March 1943 claimed the lives of a further 20, after which the partisans allowed the survivors to return to the Volche-Nora forests. Before the manhunts and attack, between 800 and 1,000 Jews from Bitan, Kosovo and the other local towns had found shelter in family camps in the Volche-Nora forests; only about 50 survived.[112]

The Soviet sources relating to the nationalities and numbers of the partisans in the 22 brigades and five independent *otryads* operating in the Baranovichi-Novogrudok forests, which united with the Red Army in the summer of 1944, give a total of 17,500. About 2,100, or 12 percent, were of "other nationalities." There were also about 4,500 partisans who did not belong to the district partisan formation, making a grand total of 22,000 partisans, of whom 2,600 belonged to "other nationalities."[113] According to the Minsk model, Jews made up about 1,950–2,100 of that number, to which should be added 500–735 Jews who fell in partisan activities. Based on that estimate, there were 2,500–2,700 Jewish partisans in the Naliboki, Lipichany and other forests in the Baranovichi-Novogrudok district. A different source quotes data provided by Yefim Gapiev, commander of a partisan unit in the Lida region (part of the Baranovichi-Novogrudok district), who gave a general breakdown of the nationalities of the 4,852 partisans he commanded. He noted that on July 1, 1944, when the report was written, there were 1,196 "from the ghettos," i.e., Jews, or 25 percent of the total number that joined forces with the Red Army.[114] Based on that figure, the number of Jewish partisans in the Baranovichi-Novogrudok family camps was between 3,500 and 4,200.[115]

---

112. Ibid., 175–76, 181.
113. Manaenkov, *Partizanskie Formirovania*, 25–28.
114. Boradyn, *Niemen*, 70–71.
115. Yitzhak Arad, "Jewish Family Camps – An Original Means of Rescue," in *Rescue Attempts During the Holocaust* , ed. Yisrael Gutman and Efraim Zuroff (Jerusalem: Yad Vashem, 1977), 337 (a series of lectures and discussions that took place at Yad Vashem's second international conference in April 1974). The numbers do not include the armed corps in Bielski's and Zorin's camps. The 3,500–4,200 statistic quoted is higher than the one in the article, and is based on a higher estimate of the number of Jews in the family camps in the Volche-Nora forests.

6. THE FORESTS AND SWAMPS IN POLESIE AND SOUTHWESTERN BYELORUSSIA

The Polesie region has thousands of square kilometers of forests and the largest swamps in Byelorussia. The Prypyat River, the largest branch of the Dnieper, runs through the center and divides the area into northern and southern Polesie. A road and railroad of great strategic importance to the German army were also located there, passing though Brest-Litovsk to Minsk and Gomel, and from there to Moscow. Most of the local population was Byelorussian, although there were Polish and Ukrainian minorities. The region's topography made it ideal for partisan warfare, and their activities began there earlier than in other locations. Many Soviet troops remained stranded in the forests in the second half of 1941 and were the first to organize as partisans.

By the end of July 1941, a partisan *otryad* commanded by Vasili Korzh (nicknamed Komarov) began limited activity near Pinsk. Korzh had fought in the ranks of the International Brigade during the Spanish Civil War. The *otryad* started with some dozens of partisans but continually grew. In 1942 it became the Pinsk Brigade and in 1943 it changed to the Pinsk Formation, acting mainly in northern Polesie. The testimonies of Jewish partisans often mention the names of other commanders of the brigades operating in Polesie, such as Filip Kapusta; Grigory Linkov ("Batia"), who was parachuted in from behind Soviet lines at the end of 1941 to head a special intelligence and sabotage unit, which grew until it became a brigade; and Anton Brinsky, who was the commissar of Linkov's brigade, and who in 1942 established a partisan brigade in southern Polesie, which was primarily active in northern Volhynia. After the arrival of Alexei Kleshchev, secretary of the Pinsk District Committee of the Communist Party, in September 1942, and Sergei Sikorski, secretary of the Brest-Litovsk District Committee of the Communist Party, in April 1943, the partisan units operating in the Polesie forests came under the full control and command of the Central Staff of the Partisan Movement.[116]

The forests and swamps of Polesie attracted thousands of Jews who had escaped from the ghettos and camps in southern Byelorussia, as well as those from the northern regions of Volhynia. The latter came from Baranovichi, Pinsk and dozens of local towns and cities. Some of them organized into partisan units,

---

116. Manaenkov, *Partizanskie Formirovania*, 95, 122–3, 212, 367, 407–8; Spector, *Holocaust*, 279–83.

others joined Soviet units, and others, for the most part unarmed or families, organized into family camps.

The Orliki and Kopil forests, which were further south, lay to the east of the pre-September 1939 international Polish-Soviet border, northwest and southwest of Slutsk. A few partisan units operated there, and in May 1942 they organized as the Voroshilov Brigade under the command of Filip Kapusta. There had been Jews in partisan units from the beginning, but when the Germans carried out massive *Aktionen* in the spring and summer of 1942, hundreds more arrived. They came from Kletsk, Nesvizh, Lyakhovichi, Kopil and Timkovichi in Byelorussia.[117]

The Jews who came to the Kopil forests organized into an independent unit, though only some of them were armed. At first there were 40 or 50 of them, but they were soon joined by others who had been wandering in the forests. There were Soviet and Polish Jews in the camp, and relations between them were friendly. Kapusta's camp was nearby and the inmates of the camp made contact with his partisans but were not accepted into the brigade, primarily because they had very few weapons. Only after the Jewish unit armed itself with the weapons it found in a burial site of Soviet soldiers did Kapusta let them join his brigade. They became the Zhukov *otryad*, and Gilchik was appointed as commander. Gilchik was a Soviet Jew from Kopil who had been in the forests with Kapusta before the other Jews arrived. The partisan command trusted the Soviet Jews, preferring them to the Polish Jews. Gilchik knew how to defend the honor of his men from partisan anti-Semitism. At first there were 50–60 Jews in the *otryad*, but they were soon joined by 15–20 Byelorussians and Russians, a few of them former prisoners of war. Within a short time the *otryad* contained 100 fighters, and they were later joined by 20 Jews who had escaped from Stolbtsy in September 1942.[118]

The Zhukov *otryad* took part in various partisan operations, including storming and destroying the police station in the town of Doktorovichi (southeast of Kopil), which was wedged into the area the partisans controlled. In November and December 1942, the Germans carried out two manhunts in

---

117. For the underground and revolt in Kleck and Nesvizh, see chapter 4:8, "Underground Activity and Armed Resistance in the Small Ghettos."

118. The history of the Zhukov *otryad* is based on Cholawski's *Resistance* (470–502), and on Moshe Kahanovich, *The Fighting of the Jewish Partisans in Eastern Europe* [Hebrew] (Tel Aviv: Ayanot, 1954), 32, 124, 141, 286, 288, 330–31, 348, 357.

the Kopil forests in which the partisans suffered losses but in general escaped unscathed.

At the beginning of the winter the entire brigade moved south to the Orliki forests, in the northern region of the Polesie forests, which were larger than the Kopil forests. Kapusta's partisans reorganized there, and the Zhukov *otryad* was included in the 27th Chapayev Brigade, commanded by Nikolai Shestopalov. At the end of January and the beginning of February 1943, 120 Jews who had fled from the Sverezhna labor camp near Stolbtsy came to the Zhukov *otryad*, increasing its numbers to 250. Shestopalov demanded they hand over all their money and possessions for the purchase of weapons, and they did so. It can be assumed that some of the money remained in the hands of the brigade commanders and their close associates, as had happened in other partisan units, since it was well known that weapons were not bought by partisans but taken by force during the battles with German security forces and from the local residents.

The *otryad* took part in the attack of the police station in Loktishi and mined railroad tracks in the Hantsevichi region. On February 10, 1943, the Germans began a manhunt in the Orliki forests,[119] and Shestopalov's brigade evaded them by passing though the frozen swamps. At the beginning of April, after an arduous trek of six weeks, the brigade reached the Chuchevich forest, north of the town of Luninets. They moved from one location to another in the forests of northern Polesie, continually clashing with German forces. In the summer of 1943, the Zhukov *otryad* returned to the Kopil forests to continue its partisan activity there.

At the end of 1943, brigade headquarters replaced Gilchik as commander with a Russian named Baranov, a Red Army officer, and the Jewish character of the Zhukov *otryad* began to change. At that time there were 150 Jewish partisans in the *otryad*, and dismissing Gilchik for no reason other than his nationality embittered many of them. Gilchik left the *otryad*, as did some of other Jewish fighters, and non-Jewish partisans replaced them. Following an order issued by brigade headquarters and Zhukov's new commander, more than 50 women, children and elderly were taken out of the *otryad*, and joined by a few armed Jewish fighters, they organized into a family camp and moved to the Svitiche forests in northern Polesie. Another family camp of about 50 Jews sheltered in

---

119. The code name for the manhunt was Operation Hornung, and it was carried out in the Lenin-Hantsevichi forest between February 8 and 22, 1943.

the Kopil forests. The two camps gradually grew, their ranks swelled by Jews who had been in hiding and a few who had escaped from labor camps, like the one at Koldichevo near Baranovichi, which still existed during the second half of 1943. At the end of 1943 and the beginning of 1944, families of Byelorussian partisans began arriving into the forests, as did ordinary peasants whose villages had been burned by the Germans during manhunts and whose physically fit inhabitants had been deported to work in Germany. Some of them joined the Jewish family camps, and partisan brigades provided them with food. There were 300 people in the camp near Svitiche, most of them Jewish, commanded by Eliezer Segal from Hantsevichi. Despite the manhunts, 200 of them were still alive when the Red Army liberated the area.

In February 1944, the Zhukov *otryad*, which still had a Jewish majority, was transferred to the Molotov Brigade in the Lyakhovichi forests. There the *otryad* attacked and sabotaged the German army's main transport routes between Brest-Litovsk and Minsk. On July 12, 1944, the *otryad* joined the Red Army and most of its Jewish fighters were drafted into service, many of them dying on the front.

The most active partisan units in the forests between Hantsevichi and Luninets (the central region of northern Polesie) was the Korzh (Komarov) Pinsk Brigade, later the Pinsk Formation. Hundreds of Jews who had fled during the Lakhva uprising or escaped from the Pohost-Zahorodski and Luninets ghettos and other towns gathered in the Grichin forests northwest of Lakhva and in the Bogdanovka forest northwest of Pohost and organized family camps. A few of them, mostly the young, were accepted by the partisan units. Others participated in the partisan attack on the town of Lenin in September 1942 and released the 28 Jews who were still there.[120]

In May 1943, Korzh proposed to the 200-member family camp in the Bogdanovka forest that they organize an independent partisan *otryad* that would belong to his formation. His proposition was enthusiastically accepted, and the *otryad* was named the Kaganovich *otryad*. It is unclear why the name was chosen, whether for national reasons – that is, as a recognition for the Jewish politburo member Lazar Kaganovich – or whether the partisan command wanted to hint at the *otryad*'s Jewish composition. Its first commander was Shlomo Zandvais, who was replaced in July 1943 by David Bobrov, and from November 1943 until its disbandment in February 1944, it was commanded by

---

120. Gefen et al., *Jewish Partisans*, 639; Kahanovich, *Fighting*, 208.

David Rogozin. The Kaganovich *otryad* blew up the Pohost-Zahorodski sawmill and mined the Liakhovichi-Luninets railroad. However, the existence of a Jewish *otryad* was against Soviet partisan policy, and it was disbanded after nine months. According to a Soviet source dealing with the partisan units operating in Byelorussia, "The Kaganovich *otryad* was established in May 1943 and was active in the Logishin district. During July and August 1943 it operated as part of the Kirov Brigade and until November acted independently. In February 1944 it was disbanded and its members dispersed among other *otryad*s in the brigade."[121]

The activity of the Soviet partisans in the Bialystok district as part of and under the command of the Central Staff of the Partisan Movement began only at the end of 1943. The forests there were smaller than those in Polesie and the roads were better, thus facilitating the operations of the German forces. In addition, most of the population was Polish and anti-Soviet. The main bases of the Soviet partisan units that belonged to the Bialystok District Formation were in the forests of western Polesie in the Brest-Litovsk district, and from there they left to operate in the Bialystok district. South of Bialystok, in the forests near the town of Bryansk, a Jewish partisan unit of a few dozen fighters from the towns in the region organized under the command of Yosef Broide. It operated in collaboration with a local partisan *otryad*, participated in attacks on German transport routes and took revenge on murderers of Jews. Near Broide's base there was a Jewish family camp with some dozens of individuals who had come from the local ghettos and escaped from the trains taking Jews to Treblinka. Broide's unit and the Jews in the family camp suffered from attacks by the AK, which was active in the area, and suffered losses during German raids.[122] In July 1944 the Red Army liberated the region and most of Broide's people and those in the family camp survived.

On the day the partisans joined forces with the Red Army, the total number of partisans operating in the regions of Polesie and southern Byelorussia – including the districts of Brest-Litovsk, Pinsk, Polesie and Bialystok – was 35,500, of whom 2,500 belonged to "other nationalities."[123] According to the Minsk model, and taking into consideration the number of Jews among the "other

121. Gefen et al., *Jewish Partisans*, 644–46; Manaenkov, *Partizanskie Formirovania*, 618 (source of the quotation).

122. Jose Broide, *Memoirs of a Jewish Partisan in the Forest of Bryansk* [Hebrew] (Tel Aviv, 1974), 81–107, 113–18; Manaenkov, *Partizanskie Formirovania*, 97–101.

123. Manaenkov, *Partizanskie Formirovania*, 100, 123, 601, 628.

nationalities" who fell in the forests or had hidden their identity, the overall number of Jewish partisans in the forests of Polesie and southwestern Byelorussia was between 3,200 and 3,750. It can be estimated that in the same areas there were between 1,500 and 2,500 Jews who had found shelter in family camps or who had hidden in the forests and neighboring villages.

7. The Volhynia Forests

The topography of the Volhynia region in the western Ukraine is varied. In the north there are forests and swamps stretching to Polesie, but further south the forests become smaller and the swamps disappear. Most of the population was Ukrainian, although there were large Polish and (in northern Volhynia) Byelorussian minorities. Three partisan movements operated in Volhynia: Soviet, Polish AK and Ukrainian UPA.

In 1943 and until the summer of 1944, the nationalistic Ukrainian armed groups, especially the UPA, controlled the forests in central and southern Volhynia. According to German sources, the strength of the UPA in Volhynia was 30,000–35,000, organized in three divisions.[124] They regarded Jews as enemies and usually killed them when they could.[125]

The AK's activities in Volhynia, in accordance with the organization's policy, were fairly limited. The Poles in Volhynia were faced with a unique problem: the UPA and other extreme Ukrainian nationalistic groups carried out murderous attacks against the Polish population in an attempt to force them to leave the area. Thousands of Polish peasants left their villages for larger settlements, which were better equipped for self-defense, while many fled to the *Generalgouvernement*. With AK support, the Polish villages organized to defend themselves. There were several instances in which the Polish forces and Soviet partisans joined forces against Ukrainian nationalists. Some tens of thousands of Poles and Ukrainians, mainly civilians, were victims in these binational clashes.[126]

---

124. For the UPA, see chapter 3:3, "The Ukrainian Insurgent Army (Ukrainska Povstanska Armia – UPA)"; Torzecki, *Polacy I Ukraincy*, 239–40.

125. Spector, *Holocaust*, 271; Diukov, *Vtorostepennyi Vrag*, 94–98.

126. Prus, *Atamania*, 166–86: Torzecki, *Polacy I Ukraincy*, 257–63, 267. According to Torzecki (267), about 80,000–100,000 Poles were killed in the areas of Volhynia, East Galicia and the Lublin district.

Jews who had fled from the ghettos and found asylum in some Polish villages in central Volhynia joined the local defense forces.[127]

Independent Soviet partisan groups had become active in the Volhynia forests, especially in the north and northeast, as far back as the fall of 1941. As in other areas, the first partisan groups were soldiers who had been trapped behind the German lines or escaped prisoners of war, and some of them were Communist activists who had not been able to evacuate before the occupation. In addition, there were small groups of a few dozen Red Army or NKVD members who had been parachuted in at the end of 1941 and the beginning of 1942. In the summer of 1942, a Soviet *otryad* "for special duties" of about 100 fighters came to the forests east of the Sluch River in eastern Volhynia. They were commanded by Colonel Dmitri Medvedev, who hid the fact that he had a Jewish father. His unit grew to 150, about a quarter of whom were Jewish – including his deputy, Captain Alexander Lukin. The *otryad* was supposed to operate in the districts of Rovno and Lvov, primarily gathering intelligence. Medvedev's men and the local residents whom he enlisted infiltrated German government institutions and transmitted important information to Moscow, including the first notice that Hitler had set up his headquarters near Vinitsa in the summer of 1942. For his operations behind German lines, Medvedev was awarded the title of Hero of the Soviet Union.[128]

Independent groups of Soviet partisans continued to operate in the Volhynia forests until the end of November 1942, when Colonel Anton Brinsky came to northeastern Volhynia from southern Polesie. Brinsky's arrival was prompted by the large-scale raids carried out by the partisan brigades of Sydor Kovpak and Alexander Saburov, who came to southern Polesie from the eastern Ukraine in December 1942.[129] Brinsky set up his base between the Styr and

---

127. Spector (*Holocaust*, 258–61, 266–67) writes about the Huta-Stepanska villages in the Panska-Dolina district near the town of Mlynov, Kurdyban near Dubno, and Przebraze near the town of Sofievka – all of whose Jews joined the local Polish self-defense forces.

128. Berenshtein and Elisavetskii, *Evrei Geroi*, 125–31. Medvedev fought in the Red Army during the Civil War and served in the NKVD, and before serving in the Volhynia forests he commanded a partisan unit in the forests of central Russia near Bryansk. See also Mark Shteinberg, *"Partizanskie Komandiry–Evrei,"* *Evreiskii Kamerton–Novosti Nedeli* (a Russian-language weekly published in Israel), August 16, 2001.

129. During the summer of 1942 the Kovpak and Saburov partisan brigades operated

Gorin rivers and organized the partisan groups in the area into one brigade under his command. At the end of January 1943 Vasil Begma, who had been secretary of the District Committee of the Communist Party in Rovno, was parachuted in and took command of the partisans in northeast Volhynia, who had organized into the Rovno Partisan Formation. The partisan movement obtained a foothold in northwest Volhynia only in the middle of 1943, when the Volhynian Formation commanded by Alexei Fiodorov began its activity there.

Jews who had escaped from the ghettos during the mass *Aktionen* carried out in the spring and fall of 1942 wandered through the forests looking for Soviet partisans to join. On September 3, 1942, a telegram was sent from an NKVD group operating in the Volhynia forests to the Central Staff of the Partisan Movement in Moscow, which read as follows: "On September 1, 1942, we received the following information from the region of Rovno in the Ukraine: 'Groups of between 15 and 20 Jews who escaped from the killing sites are hiding in the forests around us. Their wives and children were shot. The desire for vengeance burns within them. They can be organized into a fighting *otryad*. They need weapons.'" A handwritten notation in the margin adds: "Prepare instructions for contacting those men and organizing them into an independent *otryad*. [Signature illegible], September 7, 1942."[130]

One of the first groups of partisans in Volhynia was organized in the Sarnik area, north of Manevichi, at the end of 1942. It was commanded by Lieutenant Alexander Abugov, a Jewish prisoner of war who had escaped from the Germans, and Maxim Misiura, a local Communist activist. The Jews in the *otryad*, who came from Sarnik, Dubrovitsa and other towns, made up the majority of its 50 fighters. In February 1943 they joined Brinsky's brigade as the Voroshilov *otryad*; Misiura was appointed commander while Abugov was appointed commander of the reconnaissance squad. Another partisan unit operating in the same area

---

in the Bryansk-Somi forests on the border between the eastern Ukraine and the Russian Republic. Following the German attack on Stalingrad and the Caucasus mountains, on September 15, 1942, the central staff ordered the two brigades to move to the Ukraine west of the Dnieper, deep behind German lines, to interfere with their supply routes to the front, where the German army had made their main effort at that time. The Kovpak and Saburov brigades left for a march of 700 kilometers (435 miles) behind German lines, which lasted from the end of October to the beginning of December. Saburov and his unit remained in the Zhitomir area and eastern Volhynia, and Kovpak continued westward and southward.

130. GARF, Fond 69, Opis 1, Delo 746, p. 220.

was commanded by Yosef Sobesiak (nicknamed Max). Like Misiura, Sobesiak was a local Communist who had remained behind enemy lines. In the summer of 1942, he and a Ukrainian named Mikola Konishchuk (nicknamed Kruk) collected a group of Jews, Poles and local pro-Soviet Ukrainians and began a series of revenge operations against Nazi collaborators. The unit grew to 40–50 fighters, most of whom were Jewish. In the beginning of the spring of 1943 the unit was attached to the Voroshilov *otryad* and the number of Jewish fighters in the *otryad* reached 80.[131]

In the spring of 1943 there were close to 200 Jews in Brinsky's brigade. With the establishment of Begma's Rovno Formation, the Voroshilov *otryad* left Brinsky's brigade and was made a part of the Rovno Formation. A family camp commanded by Yefrem Bakalchuk was located near the *otryad*. Some of the sources mention Boris Bazykin, a Jew who commanded an *otryad* in northern Volhynia. His *otryad* distinguished itself by attacking the railroad station at Strelsk, north of Sarny, sabotaging an armored train and derailing eight German trains. In the fall of 1943 the *otryad* was ambushed by Germans in the Vladimir-Vilenski area, and Bazykin and most of his men were killed.[132]

Many unarmed Jews – women, children and the elderly – found a haven in the forests of northern Volhynia. Most of them came during the *Aktionen* of the spring and fall of 1942. Before they escaped to the forests, some had tried to find shelter in local villages, but the hostility, apathy and fear of the local peasants drove most of them to the forests. Before the representative of the Central Staff of the Partisan Movement took over command, the commanders of the local partisans, Sobesiak, Konishchuk and Misiura, had to solve the problems of the noncombatants in their camps, who hampered the units' mobility and hindered partisan operations. To solve the problems, they set up a few family camps for the 500–600 Jews from Manevichi, Rafalovka and neighboring towns. The camps were moved to the region of Krasnyi Bor, which was closer to the forests and swamps of Polesie and thus more secure. Konishchuk, who was put in charge of protection of the camp, alloted a few armed partisans at the disposal of its commanders, Mikhail Bart and Abram Plotnik, and made sure the camp's members had food. Misiura, who operated further to the east, beyond the Styr River, set up a family camp in the Svaritsevich forests with about

131. Spector, *Holocaust*, 277–79; Berenshtein and Elisavetskii, *Evrei Geroi*, 67–69.
132. Bernshtein and Elisavetskii, *Evrei Geroi*, 68; Anton Brinsky, *Partizanskaya Druzhba: Vospominania o Boevykh Delakh Partisan-Evreev* (Moscow, 1948), 72.

350 Jews from Sarnik, Vysotsk and the surrounding area. In northern Volhynia there were family camps of Jews who organized on their own initiative, took care of their own security and provided their own food.[133]

Despite the efforts made by Konishchuk, Sobesiak and Misiura, conditions in the family camps were hard and providing food, medical care and security was always problematic. Colonel Brinsky, who arrived in the area in November 1942, officially authorized the initiative taken by the partisan commanders and listed their obligations to the family camps. On December 17, 1942, he issued the following order:

> Considering the fact that in the areas in which our *otryad*s operate in the forests and farms there are many civilians – women, children and the aged – hiding from the German terror, and that they have neither roof nor food, to rescue them I hereby order that three civilian camps be established and that all the women, children and aged be brought to them. My deputy, Comrade Anishchenko, will determine the camps' locations. I place the responsibility for providing them with food and clothing on *otryad* commanders Konishchuk and Sobesiak. One such camp is to be established in the area of operations of the *otryad* commanded by Korchev. The *otryad* commanders will provide every civilian camp with millstones for grinding grain. I forbid all partisans to visit the camps unnecessarily. Only a limited number of people may know the camps' locations. Tracks should not be left that might lead to their discovery. *Otryad* commanders Konishchuk, Sobesiak and Korchev are to equip the camps with heating stoves and provide them with the necessary number of milk cows. A person capable of dealing with medical issues should be assigned to each camp. Five armed fighters are to guard each civilian camp. Comrade Anishchenko will verify that this order is carried out and report to me by January 1, 1943.[134]

Brinsky tried to use the order to completely separate the partisan units from the noncombatants. The word "Jew" does not appear in his order, but at that time, at the end of 1942, almost all the women, children and aged in the forests were Jews. Afterwards, when the Germans burned villages, murdered local

---

133. Spector, *Holocaust*, 327–41.
134. YVA, M-37/1332.

inhabitants and expelled many of them to labor camps, many of the villagers and partisan fighters' families fled to the forests, and family camps were erected for them as well. There were camps populated by Jews and non-Jews alike. In the middle of 1943, after Fiodorov's Volhynian Formation took control of the forests northwest of Volhynia, its men faced the same problem as did Brinsky: the presence of a population, Jewish and non-Jewish, that was not fit to fight. Fiodorov established a family camp for them in which 300 people lived, more than half of them Jews.

The most famous Jewish partisan unit in the eastern Volhynia forests was headed by the engineer Moshe Gildenman, whose nickname was Uncle Misha. They were organized in the small ghetto in the town of Kuritz after the *Aktion* in May 1942. On September 23, 1942, 12 of them escaped to the forests, among them Gildenman and his son. With the exception of Gildenman, who was 40 years old, they were all young men in their late teens, and their only weapons were two pistols. The crossed the Sluch River and went northward, eventually coming across Medvedev's partisans, who refused to accept them and suggested they keep going to the forests and swamps on the far side of the Sarny–Olevsk railroad. Gildenman and his men carried out a few operations, including attacking the house of a woodsman and ambushing police, thereby obtaining more weapons. The group grew to 20, four of whom were women. At the end of October or the beginning of November 1942, they attacked the police station in the village of Vezhitsy, taking 12 rifles and four submachine guns, sufficient to arm the entire group. They attacked a large farm, killing six police and wounding several more. At the end of January 1943, they met partisans from the Saburov Formation. Gildenman's partisans were accepted into the formation and Gildenman was appointed platoon commander. As time passed, more men joined and the platoon became a company with a Jewish minority. Gildenman and his unit operated in the northern Zhitomir district and participated in many missions. When the Red Army attacked in October 1943, a unit from the 13th Army crossed the Prypyat River near Chernobyl and was surrounded by Germans. Gildenman, who was operating in the area, contacted the unit and led it through the forests and swamps to evade the encirclement. After his unit joined with the army, he continued fighting as a captain in the engineering corps until the end of the war.[135]

---

135. Berenshtein and Elisavetskii, *Evrei Geroi*, 69–73.

The situation of the Jews who escaped to the forests of northwestern Volhynia was more difficult than that of those in the northeast. Only after Alexei Fiodorov's Volhynia Formation arrived in the summer of 1943 did the situation of the survivors improve. One of the groups was composed of ten Jewish families who had fled from the village of Datin (about 35 kilometers north of Kovel) at the end of August and beginning of September 1942. They had arms, some of which they had acquired in a battle with police. They repelled attacks of Ukrainian bands and UPA units and retaliated against those who had killed Jews, and even managed to evade a manhunt carried out at the end of December 1942. There were other groups of Jews in the same area who had fled from Shatsk and Luboml, each with a few dozen members, and their lives in the forests were similar to that of those who had fled from Datin. After Fiodorov's men arrived, some of the Jews were accepted in the *otryad*s and the others organized into family camps. A group of armed young Jews escaped to the forests from Kovel, came upon a partisan unit from the Linkov Formation commanded by Nasyekin and asked to join. Their weapons were confiscated and they were ordered to return to Kovel to acquire more arms. When they refused, Nasyekin's men shot them. One of them survived, returned to Kovel and recounted what had happened. The incident convinced others to give up the idea of escaping into the forests.[136]

Soviet partisan activity was more limited in the center of Volhynia, south of the Kovel–Sarny railroad. Those who operated there came from the partisan bases located in northern Volhynia, and returned to their bases after completing their missions. In 1943 the UPA and other nationalistic Ukrainian groups became active there with the aid and support of the local population. Nevertheless, and despite the hostile atmosphere, a few groups of Jews from towns in the area attempted to gain a foothold in the forests and to fight the enemy. One, with its few dozen members commanded by Haim Votchin and Gad Rosenblat, arrived at the beginning of September 1942 from the town of Sofyevka, northeast of Lutsk, and began operating in the Klopochin forest. They sabotaged shipments of grain sent to the Germans and attacked collaborators and killers of Jews. After young Jews from the town of Kolki joined Sofyevka's men, there were 40 in the unit. In December 1942, after four months of independent activity, the Kolki-Sofyevka group met Kovpak's partisans and joined them. Kovpak's

---

136. Ibid., 303, 306.

commanders allowed the Jews to decide if they wanted to continue as a Jewish group or to join the other *otryad*s. Gad Rosenblat wrote:

> All the men preferred to join other *otryad*s. After they had finally met an organized partisan brigade they had no desire to be separate from it. Our men were not sufficiently well-trained to operate independently and fight in unknown regions. We wanted to learn from the experienced partisans…and dispersed among them.[137]

Their decision was different from that of other Jewish groups operating in Byelorussia, where they fought to preserve an independent Jewish unit. It is reasonable to assume that beyond the reasons given by Rosenblat, which were correct, the decision to disperse as a Jewish unit was also influenced by the hostile UPA activity, which made it difficult for partisans to operate in the Volhynia region.

One hundred Jews from the village of Osova, south of the town of Stepan, came to the forest. They were led by Yitzhak Zakusta, who had been born in Osova, served in the Red Army, was captured by the Germans, escaped and returned to his village. His men attacked the local police station and took weapons. About half of the group (most of the women and children) died in the manhunt carried out by the Germans in December 1942. In April 1943 there were 63 men in the Osova unit, and 27 of them fell in a battle with the Germans. In May 1943 they met partisans from the Rovno Formation and joined them.[138]

Smaller family camps, where 50–100 Jews lived, organized in the forests around Olyka, Ratno and the surrounding areas. Some of them were set up under partisan aegis and provided services for the partisan units, such as those of Bielski and Zorin in Byelorussia. During German manhunts, especially in January 1943, the partisans helped evacuate some of the camps northward to the swamps, thereby saving their inhabitants.

The area south of the Vladimir Volynski–Lutsk–Rovno line had relatively few forests, was densely populated and had better roads than other areas of Volhynia. In addition, the region was controlled by UPA units, with the result that Soviet partisan activity was limited there. Under such conditions, the situation of the Jewish partisans who had fled from the ghettos was more difficult.

---

137. Gad Rosenblat, *Fire Engulfed the Forest* [Hebrew] (Lohamei Hagetaot: Hakibbutz Hameuhad, 1957), 100.

138. Ibid., 237–40.

Twenty-three men from Olyka came to the forest at the end of 1942, joined 30 Jews who were already there and together established a partisan unit. They attacked collaborators, sabotaged the Kibertsy–Rovno railroad line several times and defended themselves against attacking UPA forces. On January 9, 1943, the Germans carried out a manhunt in the forest, and most of the members of the unit were killed. Those who survived reorganized, joined forces with other Jews who were hiding in the area and wandered from forest to forest, continually fighting off the UPA and losing most of their men. A similar fate befell some of the 28 poorly armed Jews from in and around Mizoch, who had situated themselves in the Horby forests south of the village. In the middle of April 1943, they were attacked by the UPA and half of them were killed. A group of Jews from Dubno and some Poles organized in the nearby Smordov forests. They were joined by some prisoners of war. They were commanded by Yitzhak Wasserman and two Polish brothers named Jurgelewicz. In the spring of 1943 all 30 of them died in a battle with the Germans.[139]

Another group from Dubno with more than 40 members constructed a bunker in the forest for the winter. Local residents informed the Germans, whereupon large forces surrounded the bunker and killed most of the men. Forty men from Radzivilov, northeast of Brody, commanded by Meir Viner, operated in the area and met Kovpak's men in the summer of 1943, as the latter were on their way to the Carpathians. Kovpak's men refused to accept them into their ranks and the group continued its activities independently. In August 1943 the Germans carried out a manhunt and most of the group was killed, Viner among them; when the Red Army reached the area in March 1944, only 16 of them were still alive.[140]

A group from Radzivilov operated in the most southern region of Volhynia. In the winter they settled in the Leshniov forests, about 20 kilometers (12 miles) north of Brody, where they united with a few dozen former prisoners of war. During a short period more men came from Radzivilov and Brody and the group grew to 100, most of them Jewish. The most prominent Jewish figure in the *otryad* was platoon commander Yehiel Prokhovnik. The independent *otryad* attacked small groups of Germans and Ukrainian police stations and had no contact with the organized Soviet partisan organization, which never reached the area. In September 1943 the Germans conducted a manhunt in the

---

139. Spector, *Holocaust*, 311–15.
140. Ibid., 315–18.

forest and most of the *otryad* was killed; the few who survived died fighting the UPA. Other groups of Jews were active in the forests of southern Volhynia, among them one from Vladimir-Volhynsk, but they were all killed either by the Germans or the UPA, and no one was left to testify to their activities.[141]

The Jews who came to the forests of southern Volhynia were isolated, and the great distance from the partisan bases in the north made it impossible to reach them. Their main focus was on survival and their offensive initiative was not great, but in the situation in which they found themselves they could not survive for long, and most of them were either killed by Germans or the UPA.

According to estimates, about 2,500 Jews lived in the family camps, most of which were located in the forests of northern Volhynia. Of these, more than half survived the war. Most of those who survived were in camps protected by partisan *otryad*s. An estimated 1,700–1,900 Jewish partisans operated in the Volhynia forests.[142] According to the lists of names of the Volhynian Partisan Formation, there were 314 Jewish partisans in that formation alone.[143]

8. THE FORESTS OF EASTERN GALICIA

As opposed to the other areas discussed above, eastern Galicia had relatively few forests and a well-developed road system. Most of the local population were Ukrainians and there was a large Polish minority, mainly living in the cities. Eastern Galicia was the center of the Ukrainian nationalist movement and most of the Ukrainians there were anti-Soviet, anti-Polish and anti-Semitic. From the spring and summer of 1943, the UPA controlled the forests, fighting against the Soviet partisans and attacking Polish villages as they did in Volhynia. Between a paucity of forests, UPA control and a hostile population, the Soviet partisan movement did not succeed in gaining a foothold in the area. Kovpak crossed eastern Galicia on his way to the Carpathians between July and August 1943, but his units did not manage to hold ground there.

Groups of Jews who organized in the ghettos acquired a few weapons and escaped to the forests, and in the absence of Soviet partisans, wandered in small groups and built bunkers in which to live and hide. They used their weapons to get food or bought it from local villages. Most of them did not survive, as

---

141. Ibid., 318–20.
142. Ibid., 323, 332.
143. Berenshtein and Elisavetskii, *Evrei Geroi*, 167. The number is based on the lists of names of partisans in the possession of Berenshtein and Elisavetskii.

they were either murdered by the Germans, the Ukrainian police or the UPA, or by local peasants who robbed and killed them. It was almost impossible to conceal the whereabouts of the Jews in the forests, and hostile elements in the local population informed the Germans and UPA as to their location, making it relatively easy to find and kill them.

Information about those Jews and their fate is limited because often all the members of the group were killed. There were isolated instances of Jews who survived: some in the forests, others in hiding with local peasants, and a few who managed to join Kovpak's men as they traversed the region; some found small groups of Soviets partisans who lived in the forests without contact with the organized partisan movement. There were also a few who found a haven in Polish villages that wanted to defend themselves from UPA attacks, and they accepted armed Jews who would fight at their side. Those few Jews are the source of much of the information about the Jews in the forests of eastern Galicia.

A few groups of armed young Jews escaped to the forests during the *Aktionen* carried out in Stanislavov (Ivano-Frankovsk) at the end of 1942 and beginning of 1943, and with Jews from local towns they organized into three distinct partisan groups. One was commanded by Anda Luft, a woman who had formerly been a chemical engineer. On November 5, 1943, police surrounded them, and in the ensuing battle most of them were killed, Luft among them. Another group of several dozen fighters from Stanislavov commanded by Oskar Friedlander operated in the forests around Buchach, and his men attacked a local Ukrainian police station. A third group gained a foothold in the Karkhovetsk forest, nicknamed the Black Forest (*Chernyi Les*) in the Delyatin region, about 30 kilometers (19 miles) south of Stanislavov. Some of its fighters were accepted into Kovpak's brigade when it passed through.[144]

During the second half of 1943, 300 Jews escaped from the town of Bolekhov, northwest of Stanislavov, to the local forests, some of them seeking asylum with peasants in the area. About 100 of them were murdered by the Germans in the manhunts of the 1943–44 winter, and 40 were killed in the flour mill where they were hiding. Dozens were killed by the UPA during the first half of 1944. A few survived and contacted a small Soviet partisan unit operating in the Dolina forests south of Bolekhov and were accepted by them. A small group from Bolekhov commanded by Mikhail Gershovski joined Kovpak's men. Thirty Jewish

---

144. Yones, *Smoke*, 353; Weiss et al., *Encyclopedia of Jewish Communities: Poland*, vol. 2, *East Galicia* [Hebrew] (Jerusalem: Yad Vashem, 1980), 376.

partisans commanded by Hershel Birenbaum, some of them from Buchach, operated in the Grzymalov forests southeast of Skalat. They united with a group of Soviet paratroopers and fought with them until the arrival of the Red Army.[145]

Several dozen young Jews from Borshchev, south of Ternopol, escaped to the local forests at the end of May and beginning of June 1943, just before the ghetto was liquidated, and were joined by others from Skala, a town close to Borshchev. They fought and sometimes initiated battles with Ukrainian police and UPA fighters. On December 6, 1943, the Germans surrounded them and most of them died in the ensuing firefight, but they managed to inflict losses on the Germans. Some of the Jews committed suicide rather than be taken prisoner. The few who survived joined Kovpak's men as they passed through.[146]

In December 1942, when the ghetto in the town of Glinyany, east of Lvov, was liquidated, dozens of young Jews escaped to the forests. A group of about 40, some of them armed, situated itself close to the nearby village of Bogdanovka. Local Ukrainians discovered their bunker and attacked, and all the Jews were killed. Another group was hiding in the forests near Zeniuv, and most of them were killed by local Ukrainian peasants. Others from Glinyany found refuge in the Krushenko forest and later united with a Soviet partisan unit, fighting in its ranks until the area was liberated.[147]

Groups of young Jews fled to the forests from many of the neighboring towns, including Zborov, Zolochev and Peremyshlyany southwest of Ternopol; Chortkov and Buchach to its south; Skalat to its southeast; Javorov to the west of Lvov; and Stryi and Rogatin to the south and southeast of Lvov. Only a few survived; the others were killed in German manhunts or by the UPA.[148]

During the winter of 1942–43, Jews escaped from Gorodenka, southeast of Stanislavov, to the local forests. From the last months of 1943 until March 1944, they suffered greatly at the hands of the UPA, but nevertheless, some of them managed to cross the border into Romania, which was not far away. The Polish village of Hanachov, near Peremyshlyany, was a target of UPA attacks. The Jews in the surrounding forests, among them families, were accepted into the village and defended it, helping to repel hundreds of UPA fighters who attacked on the night of February 3, 1944. On April 10, 1944, however, the UPA

---

145. Yones, *Smoke*, 349; Kahanovich, *Fighting*, 245.
146. Yones, *Smoke*, 350–51; Weiss et al., *Jewish Communities*, 106, 339–400.
147. Yones, *Smoke*, 351; Weiss et al., *Jewish Communities*, 144.
148. Yones, *Smoke*, 350–59; Weiss et al., *Jewish Communities*, 205, 223, 227, 391, 404, 413–14, 442, 448.

attacked with a force of about 1,000, took over the village and shot many of the Poles and all the Jews.[149]

A rare event in partisan history occurred in the town of Skalat at the end of July and beginning of August 1943, when Kovpak, on his way to the Carpathians, occupied it and liberated the labor camp, where there were still about 100 Jewish craftsmen and their families. A Jewish witness of the events in Skalat wrote:

> When the partisans began making preparations to leave the city, the Jews asked them to take them along. The partisans, however, refused, saying they needed soldiers, healthy men, and not Jews from the camps who could barely walk. Nevertheless, about 30 of the healthier Jews escaped with the partisans, under no circumstances wanting to stay in a place of certain death.... Most of them were killed in a large-scale battle in the Carpathian Mountains.[150]

From the Jews from Skalat and other Jews in the Kovpak brigade, a Jewish unit, the 7th Company, was established. With its 75 members, commanded by Joel Shcherbata, it was part of the brigade's 1st Battalion. The other commanders in the company were appointed from among the Jewish partisans. On their way to the Carpathians they were strafed by German planes, reducing the company to 45 fighters. Kovpak's men suffered heavy losses in the battles in the Carpathians, and on their way back to Polesie the brigade split into small units. Most of the Jews in the 7th Company were killed. The survivors of Kovpak's raid to and from the Carpathians gathered in the Glushkevichi forests, northeast of Sarny. Only 18 survivors of the 7th Company reached the gathering place.[151]

There were only a few family camps in the forests of eastern Galicia for the same reasons that prevented the development of the Soviet partisan movement. In the Karkhovetsk forest there was a family camp of 100 Jews who had escaped from Stanislavov. During August or September 1943, the UPA surrounded the camp and killed 15 Jews, captured and tortured 33 more, forced them to dig their own graves and then killed them. Only 15 of the Jews who were in the camp at

---

149. Yones, *Smoke*, 351; Prus, *Atamania*, 170.

150. Kahanovich, *Fighting*, 207–8. Kahanovich quoted Abraham Weissbard, *A Township Is Dying: The Story of Skalat* [Hebrew] (Munich: The Historical Society, 1948), 133–35; Rosenblat, *Fire*, 202.

151. Rosenblat, *Fire*, 206–7, 210–11, 239–41, 245, 269; Gefen et al., *Jewish Partisans*, 285–88.

the time managed to escape.[152] About 200 Jews lived in various family camps in the Pyanitsa forests near Brody. A Jewish Red Army soldier, who came upon one of the camps during the liberation of the area in July 1944, wrote:

> By chance I came upon two huts where 80 Jews were living. I also saw old women about 75 years old, young boys and girls, even children, the youngest of whom was 3. They had lived in those huts in the forest for 16 months and there had been more of them, but of the four thousand Jews in the Brody, Zolochev and surrounding localities, only 200 were still alive, and those 80 I found were some of them.... They also had weapons, a few rifles and pistols, with which they took revenge on the Fascist beasts.[153]

In the forests of eastern Galicia there must have been other family camps but none of their members survived. A few thousand Jews escaped from the ghetto and labor camps in eastern Galicia, but the conditions in which they lived were terrible and only a few hundred survived. The Jewish partisan units that organized there, whose total number of members can be estimated at 300–400, for the most part defended themselves, the result of conditions and relative forces, and their objective was survival. They initiated only few partisan actions in comparison with Jewish partisans in other regions.

9. THE FORESTS IN THE EASTERN TERRITORIES (WITH THE EXCEPTION OF MINSK)

The Jews in the pre-1939 territories of the Soviet Union were almost completely annihilated during the first weeks and months of the war, before they realized what was happening and before the partisans had organized in the forests as a force to be reckoned with. In addition, men who could have fought as partisans were enlisted in the Red Army, and many Jews worked in factories and institutions that were evacuated to the east before the German occupation. Therefore, most of the Jews who remained in territories occupied by the Germans were women, children and the elderly, who were not suited for partisan life and warfare.

---

152. Gefen et al., *Jewish Partisans*, 243–44; Kahanovich, *Fighting*, 152–53.
153. Kahanovich, *Fighting*, 153. The quote is from Ehrenburg and Grossman, *The Black Book*, 114–15.

Nevertheless, Jews fought as partisans in all the pre-1939 territories of the Soviet Union occupied by the Germans where the partisans operated, and their numbers can be estimated at several thousand. They were mostly Red Army soldiers who had either been stranded behind German lines and knew what their fate would be as prisoners of war, or who out of loyalty to their homeland remained in the forests and organized into multinational partisan units. Some of those Jewish partisans were prisoners of war who had managed to escape from the camps before the Germans discovered their identity and murdered them.[154] In the more eastern territories, which were occupied several months after the outbreak of the war, the Soviet authorities (the Communist Party, the Red Army and the NKVD) established core groups for partisan warfare and intelligence purposes and left them behind in the occupied territories, and there were many Jews among them. There were also partisan *otryad*s that organized during the first stages of the occupation to cross the front lines and join the Red Army.

In the Brovari region near Kiev, a partisan *otryad* of 70 fighters, 11 of them Jewish, organized in September 1941, and fought their way eastward, crossing the front. The following was written about their battles and the fate of the Jewish fighters:

> In the battle near Berezan the company commander, Moise Lachmanovich, fell in a clash near the village of Lipnyaki in the Barishevka region. Sophia Polskaya was killed. Abraham Beitler fell near Yagotin. His daughter Tania, who had been taken prisoner, was hanged in Yagotin's town square. In November 1941…Major Abraham Zimmerman died a hero's death in the battle of Krasnokutsk in the Kharkov district…. Only two of the 11 Jewish partisans survived: Solomon Dubkin from Berdichev and the nurse, Riva. On March 15, 1943, the 15 partisans remaining from all the *otryad*s managed to cross the front lines and unite with the Red Army.[155]

Jews and non-Jews from the village of Lyady, west of Smolensk, organized as partisans in the late fall of 1941, at the beginning of the occupation when the Jews were enclosed in the ghetto. The unit called itself the Nikolai *otryad*, after

154. For the German treatment of Jewish prisoners of war, see chapter 4:10, "Underground and Escape from the Sites of *Aktion* 1005."
155. Berenshtein and Elisavetskii, *Evrei Geroi*, 212.

its commander. It was the first partisan unit in the Lyady region, but it did not last: some of its Jewish members were killed and the others dispersed.[156] At the end of 1941, a partisan *otryad* of about 20 Jews commanded by Sergei Grishin organized near the town of Dorogobuzh east of Smolensk and moved to the forests. In March 1942, the Germans conducted a manhunt but the *otryad* managed to evade it before the forest was surrounded.[157] No other information is available about them.

A partisan *otryad* that had been left behind by the Soviet authorities before the retreat was active in the district of Chernigov, in the northeast Ukraine. It was commanded by Semen (Shimon) Khanovich, the chairman of the Gremyach region Communist party council. The *otryad* numbered 125 partisans, all poorly equipped. During September–November 1941, they carried out attacks on German posts and objectives. In January 1942 German forces discovered the partisan base and surrounded it; in the ensuing battle most of its members, including Khanovich, were killed. In the Dnepropetrovsk district, among some dozens of hastily formed partisan *otryad*s that had been left behind the German front was a small *otryad* of 19 fighters, among them 9 Jews, commanded by Benyamin Shakhovich, the head of the Dnepropetrovsk city finance department. The *otryad* set up its base in the forests around Novomoskovsk. In September–November 1941, Shakhovich's *otryad* mined roads and railways, and in cooperation with another *otryad*, attacked a German unit in the village of Volnoe, killing 30 German soldiers. Another action that the *otryad* participated in was the liberation of 300 Red Army soldiers from a POW camp. On January 5, 1942, Shakhovich's base in the Novomoskovsk forests was surrounded by an SS unit, the battle lasted for hours and all its members fell. The *otryad* ceased to exist.[158]

Among the partisans in the pre-1939 Soviet Union were Jews who hid their identity and wandered from one village to another, looking for partisans. The story of Reuven Fleksa, a 15-year-old boy from the village of Sliva east of Minsk, is an odyssey of wandering and searching for partisans. Sliva's Jews were deported to a small ghetto of 400 in the town of Bogushevichi, and every day some were executed. One of those murdered was Reuven's father:

---

156. Slava Tomarkin, "The Nikolai Partisan Brigade," *Voice of the Disabled* (September 2002): 5–7.

157. Slava Tomarkin, "Grishin Led Us," *Voice of the Disabled* (April 2003): 5–6.

158. Berenshtein and Elisavetskii, *Evrei Geroi*, 212–14.

My mother was determined that my older brother and I should run away.... That was at the beginning of November [1941]. We hid in the forest.... In 1941 we didn't meet partisans in Byelorussia. We decided to go toward the front...and change our names. We didn't look particularly Jewish.... On December 5, 1941, we marched along the Osipovichi–Mogilev railway...all the way to Mogilev. We told everyone that we had been in prison for delinquency and that the Germans had come and opened the prison and let us out, and that we were going home.... We arrived in Mogilev. People told us that to cross the bridge over the Dnieper we needed documents from the Germans and we didn't have anything like that. We were afraid they would make us get undressed and see we were Jews.... Since we couldn't cross the Dnieper we walked along the bank.... On January 1, 1942, the Dnieper had frozen over and we crossed the ice, finding ourselves in the Chernigov district. Then we turned east and reached the Sumy district near the city of Putivl. On the same day, May 20, 1942, Kovpak's partisans took over the city. But to reach them we had to cross the Seim River and access to it was well guarded. Only at the beginning of June 1942 could we cross the river in the Kursk district....

We met the partisans on June 13, 1942.... When we did, some of them asked us all kinds of questions because they thought we were spies. We told them immediately that we were Jewish. They asked us how we had reached them and were very surprised that two boys without documents could have come so far.... We had walked more than a thousand kilometers [620 miles]. They took us into the partisan company. Naturally, it was a happy day for me when I received a rifle.... There were other Jews in my platoon, one of them was named David Tsirlin.... I don't remember any serious anti-Semitic incidents.[159]

Hundreds of Jews wandered, looking for partisans. Most of them died; others reached their destination. They joined and fought in the partisan *otryad*s as individuals. According to existing documentation, including memoirs, no mention is made of Jewish partisan units, with the exception of one *otryad* in

---

159. Pinchas Agmon, ed., *Later Testimony: Holocaust Survivors from the Ukraine Tell Their Stories* [Hebrew] (Lohamei Hagetaot: Hakibbutz Hameuhad, 1997), 214–17.

the area of Vinitsa in the eastern Ukraine. In many of the sources dealing with partisan fighting, individual Jews can be identified by their names. Jewish names are mentioned in the lists of names of various *otryad*s, proving that in certain areas there were many Jews in the ranks of the partisans. A list of names gathered on November 13, 1942, includes 16 partisans from the Leningrad district who were decorated by the Supreme Soviet of the Soviet Union for bravery in fighting the enemy, and three of them have Jewish names: Naum Iskovich Golod, Lazer Shmuelevich Izaakson and Mikhail Abramovich Fishman, all of whom received the Order of the Red Star.[160] It can be assumed that some of those with Russian names were also Jewish.

Almost all of the Jews in the Mogilev, Vitebsk and Gomel districts east of Byelorussia were killed at the end of 1941. Nevertheless, during 1942 and 1943, partisan units organized and their numbers grew as the war dragged on, until there were several thousand Jews in the partisans' ranks. There were also Jews who had escaped from the Minsk ghetto and wandered eastward until they joined the partisans, especially in the nearby Mogilev district. According to the Minsk model, the number of Jewish partisans in the Mogilev district can be estimated at between 1,500 and 1,650; in the Vitebsk district, between 700 and 800; and in the Gomel district, between 600 and 700.[161]

There are statistics for the Soviet partisans operating in the occupied territories of the Soviet Union, but not even partial numbers of national composition, with the exception of the statistics for the partisans in Byelorussia. Thus the following data are based on documents in the possession of the author. A report sent on March 17, 1942, to Kommissar Ryazanov, the deputy political head of the 5th Army, concerning the partisans in the Smolensk region, noted the following:

> In accordance with your instructions I examined the District Committee of the Smolensk Communist Party, and I can state with certainty that in the various regions [of the Smolensk district] the following partisan *otryad*s are active: in Temkino there are 65 men; in Yartsevo, 650; in Semlevo, as many as 1,500; in Dorogobuzh, about 2,200. In the last two [regions] there were about 40 Jewish fighters, formerly residents of Smolensk.[162]

---

160. GARF, Fond 69, Opis 1, Delo 458, p. 106.
161. Manaenkov, *Partizanskie Formirovania*, 220–368.
162. Tsentralnyi Arkhiv RF, Fond Armia 5, Opis 5064, Delo 18, p. 303. There was a

After a wave of mass murders during the second half of 1941 in the area of Vinitsa in the *Generalbezirk* of Zhitomir, small ghettos remained in some of the cities, most of which were liquidated in the spring and summer of 1942. Jews fled from the ghettos of Vinitsa and Yilintsy to the forests and joined the partisans. A few *otryad*s were active in the forests around Yilintsy-Gaisin, which lie to the southeast of Vinitsa, and in 1943 they were united and became the 2nd Stalin Partisan Brigade commanded by A. Kondratiuk, whose headquarters were in the Shabelyansk forest. There were Jews in the brigade's various *otryad*s, among them those who hid their identity.[163] A family camp was set up within the brigade under the command of David Modrik, a Jew who had fought in the Red Army, been taken prisoner, posed as a Ukrainian, escaped and returned to Yilintsy. The family camp began with Jews who had fled from Yilintsy, which in the summer of 1942 still had dozens of Jewish craftsmen and their families who had been moved to a collective farm near the city. Zinaida Modrik, the wife of the camp commander, told the following story:

> It happened in August 1942.... My husband decided that we had to leave for the forests, for the partisans.... He decided to get the elderly, the sick, the women and the children out of the ghetto, no matter how, and to hide them in the neighboring villages for the time being. Everyone had friends and acquaintances here and there. One dark night we, the young people, 15 men and three women, left for the forests....
>
> We wandered around looking for partisans. We finally found a partisan patrol in the Shabelyansk forest, where there were *otryad*s belonging to the 2nd Stalin Partisan Brigade.... The partisans showed us where to settle down and we began setting up the Jewish partisan camp.... The next day they brought us food and told us that they could not provide us with weapons. The person in charge said, "If you want to be partisans, find weapons, no matter how." ... Every night we went out on missions, we lay in ambush, disarmed

---

small ghetto in Smolensk until the summer of 1942.

163. Pinkhas Agmon and Anatolya Stepanenko, *Vinitskaia Oblast: Katastrofa I Soprotivlenie* (Tel Aviv and Kiev, 1994), 116–18. Agmon and Stepanenko list the names of 60 Jewish partisans in the brigade. They present the testimony of Zakhar Sapozhnikov, a Jew, who as a prisoner of war, managed to hide his identity. He escaped on November 2, 1943, and reached the 2nd Stalin Partisan Brigade, where he continued to hide the fact that he was Jewish.

Germans and policemen who guarded the local sugar factories, mined railroads…and thus we gradually acquired weapons.…

We went to get the old people, women and children from the Ukrainian families we had hidden them with after we left the ghetto.… By the end of 1942 there were 250 Jews in our *otryad*.… Everyone had something to do: the old people guarded the camp, the children took care of the animals, the women cooked, washed, baked bread.… The worst battles took place at the end of the winter of 1943–44. The Germans combed the forest. I remember the last battle with the Fascists, just before our meeting with the Red Army. Many of our fighters fell, many were wounded. In February 1944, we joined forces with the Red Army.[164]

There were Jews in the ranks of other partisan units operating in the Vinitsa district. At the end of 1943 and beginning of 1944, the Lenin Cavalry Partisan Brigade was organized, commanded by Mikhail Vladimirov. According to an official document of partisan headquarters in the Ukraine, when the Red Army reached the region and the brigade was disbanded on April 1, 1944, 31 of the 1,186 partisans were Jewish. The number did not include those who had died or hidden their identity. The Jews were the third largest national group in the brigade, after Ukrainians and Russians.[165] Of the 359 fighters serving in the partisan unit commanded by Vladimir Slesarenko, which operated in the Vinitsa district between June 1943 and March 1944, 15 were Jewish. In that unit as well, the Jews were the third-largest national group, after the Ukrainians and Russians.[166] The names of 242 Jewish partisans are mentioned in the list of partisans in the Vinitsa district,[167] but it is reasonable to assume that not all the Jewish partisans were on it, and that the names of many of the fallen do not appear. There were 64 Jews in the Shchors Zhitomir Formation, which

---

164. Ibid., 128–131.
165. Ibid., 132–54: the testimony of Sophia Zaitseva, a Jewish woman who fled from Vinitsa and became a partisan in the Shchors *otryad* in the Lenin Cavalry Brigade. The document is from the headquarters of the partisan movement in the Ukraine, YVA, M-37/268.
166. YVA, ibid.
167. Agmon and Stepanenko, *Vinitskaia Oblast*, 156–73; the lists were prepared from documents found in the national archives of the Vinitsa district.

operated in the Zhitomir district under the command of Malikov, and in the partisan formation in the Kiev district there were 63 Jews.[168]

Jews distinguished themselves in battle and attained commanding ranks in many of the partisan units operating in the pre-1939 Soviet Union territories. A comprehensive study of the subject would reveal many Jews and much information about them. From the little that is known, two names should be noted: Yefem Korentsvit, a native of Odessa, who changed his name to Yevgeny Volyanski, and Leonid Bernstein, a native of the town of Shpikov in the district of Podolya. When the war broke out the two were lieutenants in the Red Army, and when they were surrounded, did not become prisoners but turned to partisan activity. Volyanski operated in the Smolensk area, and Bernstein around the city of Cherkassy in the Ukraine. Volyanski commanded a partisan reconnaissance unit, distinguished himself in battle, was wounded at the end of 1942 and evacuated by plane from a partisan airfield strip to Moscow for medical treatment. After he recovered he was parachuted behind German lines in the Ukraine, where he commanded the intelligence unit in the partisan formation of Yakob Melnik until April 1944. After the arrival of the Red Army, he was parachuted into Slovakia, where he fought with the local partisans until the end of the war. Bernstein was chief of staff of the Pozharski *otryad* and directed many partisan missions in the Smelya region, south of Cherkassy. At the end of 1943 his *otryad* joined the Red Army. Heading a unit, in May 1944 he was parachuted behind German lines into the Pshemysl region in southeast Poland. In September 1944, his unit crossed the border into Slovakia and participated in the Slovakian uprising (August–October 1944) against the Germans. The uprising failed, and at the end of November 1944 Bernstein and his unit managed to break through the front and rejoin the Red Army.[169]

Partisan units were organized in besieged Leningrad and sent to fight behind German lines on the Leningrad front. The 17th Partisan *Otryad* was composed of young Komsomol members, students and trainers from the institute for outstanding athletes. Its commander was a Jew named Boris Erenprais and the *otryad* head of staff was Ilya Shuster. They had 150 volunteer members. After a short period of basic training in the besieged city, they infiltrated behind enemy lines and on their first day in the German rear they

---

168. Berenshtein and Elisavetskii, *Evrei Geroi*, 188.
169. Ibid., 79–111.

fought against a German force, inflicting losses on them. Another partisan unit that operated in the Leningrad district and distinguished itself in battle was the Boevoi *otryad* commanded by Mordoch Novakovksi. In one of the actions near the village of Tiurikovo, they captured some German soldiers and police along with the six winter wagons they were riding on. From the prisoners they learned the password that would enable them to enter the village. Novakovski hid partisans under the straw in the wagons and used the password to enter the village at night. They quietly overcame the guards and with hand grenades attacked a building in which there were soldiers from the Death Heads SS Division, killed dozens of them, took their weapons and left the village. The attack is referred to in the partisan history of the Leningrad region as the "Tiurikovo Operation."[170]

Evrei Geroi Soprotivlenia, a book documenting the Jews in the Ukrainian resistance movement, gives the names of 2,945 Jewish partisans and their units.[171] The list is based on documentary material from archives in the Ukraine. Another source, which examined lists of names of Ukrainian partisans, found the names of 3,640 Jews who were active in partisan *otryad*s in the Ukraine.[172] These lists do not include Jewish partisans who belonged to *otryad*s that were not part of the organized Soviet partisan movement. They also do not include the names of Jewish partisans who operated in the occupied territories of the Russian Federate Republic, such as the regions around Leningrad, Smolensk, Kursk and Bryansk. The number of Jewish partisans who were active in all the areas of the Ukraine (including Volhynia and eastern Galicia) and in the occupied territories of the Russian Republic can be estimated at between 5,000 and 6,000. That estimate does not include the Jews in family camps in Volhynia and eastern Galicia, which was between 4,750 and 5,750 people. The estimates do, however, include those who fell in the forests.

---

170. Mark Friedson, "Leningradskie Partizany," *Voice of the Disabled* (1988): 54–55. Friedson was a partisan in the Boris Erenprais unit.
171. Berenshtein and Elisavetskii, *Evrei Geroi*, 246–332.
172. Shmuel Spector, *Evrei v Partizanskom Dvizheni I Podpole v Ukraine: Ten Holokosta* (Moscow, 1998), 82–84. Spector found 560 names of Jews who were active in underground groups in various cities in the Ukraine.

10. CONCLUSION

Organized groups and individual Jews left for the forests in all the occupied territories, from the end of the first stage of the Holocaust (the beginning of the spring of 1942) until the end of the German occupation. By the spring of 1942, the Jews who had survived and were closed in the ghettos were already aware that the German policy of annihilation, which at that point was being implemented, would sooner or later reach them. As mentioned above, three main factors were necessary for the existence of thousands of Jewish partisans and members of family camps: large wooded areas, weapons, and the presence of Soviet partisans.

The large forests that could be reached on foot within a night or two – in areas in which there were still Jews – were in western Byelorussia, around Minsk and in northern Volhynia. That was where most of the Jewish partisans and family camps organized and operated from 1942 until the summer of 1944, when the Red Army arrived. To fight and survive in the forest, it was necessary to be armed upon leaving the ghetto or to acquire a weapon upon arrival. The limited sources of weapons dictated the number of Jews who could gain a foothold in the forests.

The survival of the Jews in the forests for an extended period of time, whether in the ranks of the partisans or in family camps, also depended on the presence of Soviet partisans and their willingness to accept the Jews. The activity of the Soviet partisans in areas in which there were still Jews began to make itself felt in the spring and summer of 1942. Some of the men in those groups were anti-Semitic and attacked the Jews in the forests. In 1943, when the representatives of the Central Staff of the Partisan Movement took control of the partisan units that until that time had acted independently, their attitude toward the Jews improved somewhat. But in many cases Jews were still discriminated against, ousted from the partisan *otryad*s, disarmed and left to their fate when the Germans conducted manhunts.

The Jewish partisan *otryad*s were disbanded as a matter of principle, since the Soviet partisan movement was not organized along national lines but according the Soviet republics, and there was no Jewish republic in the Soviet Union. But the way in which the Jewish *otryad*s were disbanded was clearly anti-Semitic. They had all been established on the annexed territory in 1939–40, especially in western Byelorussia and the Vilnius district, and their organizers had ideological reasons for emphasizing their national uniqueness and the fact that they were fighting against the murderers of their people, against Nazi Germany. The desire to preserve a Jewish framework in the forest was also the result of a feeling of comradeship and of sharing a common fate – feelings that were strengthened upon witnessing the anti-Semitism among the partisans.

The Jews in the pre-1939 Soviet territories, on the other hand, had ideological reasons for not wanting to organize their own national partisan units. According to their worldview when they organized in the Minsk ghetto, the members of the Jewish underground who went into the forests regarded themselves as part of the Communist camp and as part of the nations of the Soviet Union who were fighting against the German occupier. Therefore, when they went into the forests, their objective was not to establish independent Jewish partisan units, but rather to fight as ordinary partisans. However, despite the differences in attitude between the Jews from the post-1939 territories and those from the pre-1939 territories, it was not left to them to decide the existence or nonexistence of separate Jewish *otryad*s, but rather to the Central Staff of the Partisan Movement.

For the Jewish family camps the situation, as described above, was grave. In addition to the German manhunts, whose main victims they were, the attitude of many of the Soviet partisans, who saw the Jewish family camps as a nuisance, worsened their already sorry plight. Things changed, however, toward the second half of 1943, when the Central Staff of the Partisan Movement had taken control of the forests in which family camps were located. They could no longer ignore the thousands of Jewish women, children and elderly, all Soviet citizens, who were fighting for survival. At the same time, the family camps, on their own initiative, found ways to become useful to the partisans. Tuvia Bielski and Shalom Zorin turned the family camps of several thousand Jews in the huge Naliboki forests into a productive force, and there were similar developments in other forests.

In addition to the Soviet partisans, the local population was a factor in the possibility of the Jews' existing in the forests, both as partisans and in family camps. The peasant population in areas where the partisans operated suffered greatly from German reprisals against anyone who aided the partisans or even failed to provide information about them. Nevertheless, because of both national reasons and as a reaction to German terrorism and exploitation, there were areas in which much of the local population identified with the partisans and provided them with aid and support. After the German defeat at Stalingrad, the return of the Red Army was a real possibility, and that too influenced the local population positively toward the partisans, since they were afraid of Soviet reprisals. Young local residents joined the partisans and formed the majority in many of the *otryad*s. However, the ingrained anti-Semitism of the local population remained. They did not change their attitude toward the Jews in the forests, and they were unwilling to expose themselves to German retaliation because of Jewish partisans. That said, it can be stated that in western Byelorussia, where most of the Jews were concentrated in the forests, the local population had a more positive attitude toward the Jews than in the western Ukraine. The situation was particularly difficult in Lithuania and Latvia, where even the Soviet partisans did not manage to establish bases in the forests, to say nothing of the Jews.

In 1943, armed anti-Soviet groups belonging to the UPA and the Polish AK began operating in the forests of western Byelorussia and the western Ukraine. They were diehard anti-Semites, identifying the Jews with the hated Soviet rule. They prevented Jews from finding refuge or establishing partisan bases in the areas that they controlled and murdered many of them.

The Jews in the occupied territories of the Soviet Union exploited the forests for fighting and for survival. Nowhere else in occupied Europe did tens of thousands of Jews fight in the forests behind German lines or find a safe haven. The Jewish partisans, together with their non-Jewish comrades, contributed to the victory over Nazi Germany.

Accurate statistics for the numbers of Jewish partisans and family camps in the forests are not available. The conditions under which the Jews lived and fought made it impossible to keep records, and their number can only be estimated. The following table shows the number of Jews operating in the forests in the various districts of the occupied territories of the Soviet Union.

No.	Region/District	Partisans	Family camps	Forests[1]
1	Minsk	3,000–4,000	\	Koidanov, Rudensk, Kopil
2	Vileika	950–1,100	900–1,300	Kozyany, Naroch
3	Vilnius	600–700	\	Rudniki
4	Novogrudok-Baranovichi	2,500–2,700	3,500–4,200	Naliboki, Lipichany, Volche-Nora, Nacha
5	Brest-Litovsk, Pinsk	3,200–3,750	1,500–2,500	Polesie and southwest Byelorussia, Bryansk
6	Mogilev	1,500–1,650[2]	\	\
7	Vitebsk	700–800	\	\
8	Gomel	600–700	\	\
9	Volhynia	1,700–1,900	2,500	Svaritsevich, Kokhov, Chuman
10	East Galicia	300–400	2,000–3,000	Black Forest, Zhimalov, Pyanitsa
11	East Ukraine, Russia	3,000–3,700	250	\

Total number of partisans: 19,050–22,400
Total number of members of family camps: 10,650–13,500

1. The most important forests in every region are listed here; there were others with Jewish partisans and family camps.
2. Some of the partisans in the Mogilev group were actually from the Minsk ghetto.

The arrival of the Jews in the forests, whether to participate in partisan fighting or to find shelter and survive, was solely the initiative of the Jews themselves. The Soviet partisan movement took no direct action on behalf of the Jews. Nevertheless, the presence of the Soviet partisans provided the conditions that made it possible for thousands of Jews to fight the Nazi enemy and for thousands more to seek refuge in the forests. According to estimates, about two-thirds of the Jews in partisan units and about half of those in family groups lived to see the end of the war and the liberation.

AFTERWORD

Nazi Germany was defeated by the joint efforts of the Allied forces headed by Britain, the Soviet Union and the United States. However, the decisive frontline and the battles where Nazi Germany was defeated were fought by the Soviet Union in the Great Patriotic War. The fate of the war was decided in the battle at the gates of Moscow (from the end of 1941 until March 1942), the battle of Stalingrad (through the autumn and winter of 1942 and early 1943), and in the battles in the Kursk-Oriel salient (July and August 1943), making the defeat of Germany only a matter of time. The Allied landing in Normandy in June 1944 and the strategic bombings of German cities hastened the defeat and the fall of the Third Reich and contributed a great deal to the final victory. However, the die was cast before then in the battlefields of the Great Patriotic War, through the superhuman efforts made by the people of the Soviet Union and the enormous price they paid: millions of soldiers who fell on the front or were killed in captivity and millions of civilian victims sacrificed on the Soviet home front – many times more than those of Britain, the United States or any other Allied country. The Soviet Jews played a meaningful role in the war effort – on the battlefield, in the military industry and in the struggle in the German rear – and they paid a high price in human life to achieve victory.

The Jews of the Soviet Union fought on every front of the war, from Murmansk in the far north to the Caucasus mountains in the south, from Brest-Litovsk and the Soviet-German border to the gates of Moscow and the streets of Stalingrad, and to the battles within the heart of Berlin and the victorious end of the war. They served in every branch of the army, in the ground forces, the air force and the navy. Most of them were ordinary soldiers, privates and sergeants, but among them were officers in every rank, up to division, corps and army commanders, air-force squadron leaders, captains of ships and admirals of fleets. There were 305 Jewish generals on the various fronts of the Great Patriotic War and dozens more who were half-Jewish. They were rewarded with combat medals and decorations, and about 150 of them were awarded the title of Hero of the Soviet Union. In no other Allied army were there so many high-ranking Jewish officers or a parallel number of the highest decorations for heroism as in the Red Army – and this despite the policy set down by the senior Soviet leadership in Moscow of restricting the advance of Jews through the command ranks and of limiting the number of high decorations they could receive.

The Soviet military industry provided the army with the weapons without which victory would have been impossible. During the first days of the war, the Soviet Union lost thousands of planes, a few in air fights but almost all of them on the ground in German surprise attacks. The Soviets suffered losses of thousands of tanks, artillery and other equipment during their retreat in the first half year of the war. Close to 80 percent of the Soviet military industry was located in the territories occupied by the Germans before the end of 1941 or in the areas around Moscow and Leningrad, which turned into front lines. As the factories were evacuated to the east and rapidly put back into production under the most difficult conditions imaginable, the Jewish factory directors, engineers and developers of new weapons played an extremely important role. Men like Boris Vannikov, who laid the foundations for the evacuation and subsequent continued operation of the defense industry; Isaak Zaltzman, a central figure in tank production; and Semyon Lavochkin and Mikhail Gurevich, who developed planes, filled key posts in the weapons industry.

By the beginning of 1942, the Soviet military industry had started supplying tanks, planes and other vital equipment in ever-increasing quantities to cover the extensive losses suffered by the Red Army during the first half year and to arm the new divisions of enlisted men sent to the front. The number and quality of planes, tanks, guns and other weapons grew, outstripping the German military industry – despite the fact that the Germans had at their disposal all the military capabilities of the countries of occupied Europe.

In dozens of ghettos and camps behind the German front, underground Jewish organizations sprang up with the objective of fighting the Nazi enemy. The undergrounds were formed in large ghettos, such as those in Minsk and Vilnius, and in the smaller ones, such as Lakhva and Svencionys. Their organizers and activists came from the entire political spectrum: Zionists, Bundists, Communists, and many of no particular political affiliation. The underground was organized and operated under conditions and with problems far more difficult than those faced by the non-Jewish undergrounds in the European countries: the Jews were penned up in closed ghettos, fenced in and guarded, and yet they managed to arm themselves with no help from the "outside." A complex relationship existed between the underground, the *Judenräte* and the ghetto inmates based on the danger to the ghetto's existence posed by smuggling in weapons and leaving for the forests. However, with the exception of a few conflicts, such as the Wittenberg affair in the Vilnius ghetto, the underground and the *Judenrat* coexisted peacefully, and in several ghettos the underground was aided by the *Judenrat* in its activities and in getting people into the forests. There were certain ghettos in which members of the *Judenrat* belonged to the underground and were among its leaders.

In addition to the idea of fighting the enemy, the objective of the ghetto underground was to try to rescue its members and other ghetto inhabitants from certain death. Hundreds left the ghettos for the forests before liquidation and fought as partisans. In the ghettos where the undergrounds planned uprisings, the uprisings were set for the eve of the ghetto's liquidation. That was because in an uprising most of the population would be killed and the chances of survival were small. Thus the uprisings in the ghettos of Tuchin, Glubokoe and others were planned for the last minute, when it was clear that there was nothing to lose. Most of the inhabitants were in fact killed during the uprisings, but hundreds managed to escape and reach the forests.

Because of the widespread hostility of the local population, the Jews could only gain a foothold and remain in the forests for extended periods of time if there were Soviet partisans there as well. Before the Central Staff of the Partisan Movement took over the control and command of the independent partisan units or of the armed gangs in the forests, many of them carried out atrocities and were hostile to the Jews in the forests. However, even later on, when the Central Staff of the Partisan Movement took control and Jews were accepted into the ranks of the Soviet partisans, Jews were discriminated against. While local non-Jewish residents and prisoners of war who reached the forests were accepted into the partisan ranks without being required to bring weapons, the Jews were generally accepted only if they were armed. Despite the difficulties, about 20,000 Jews fought within the ranks of the Soviet partisans and thousands more organized into family camps. Many Jewish partisans distinguished themselves in fighting the enemy, and as noted, about two-thirds of them lived until the liberation; the others fell in the forests.

No official data exist about the overall number of Soviet partisans or about who could be called a partisan. According to one of the quasi-official Soviet publications, "During the war there were about 6,200 partisan *otryads* operating behind German lines and underground groups with a membership of more than a million...."[1] That number is too high by hundreds of percent-

---

1.   Kirian et al., *Slovar-Spravochnik*, 351.

age points. The term "underground groups" was never defined, nor was what constituted underground activity. Reports were exaggerated and their sources were interested in showing massive activity, while the upper echelons receiving the reports wanted to show that the people in the occupied territories were acting against the Germans. The same was true for the numbers of partisans cited. In our assessment, and based on the vast amounts of material studied, there were no more than 250,000–300,000 Soviet partisans, about 6.7–8 percent of them Jewish.

Like the Jews in the ghettos, the 80,000–85,000 Jewish prisoners of war struggled to survive. Underground activity was prominent among Jewish prisoners of war who worked at the *Aktion* 1005 sites, in the death camp at Sobibor and in the prisoner-of-war camps in south Germany.

The contribution of thousands of Jewish women to the Great Patriotic War against Nazi Germany is not to be forgotten. Many of them were decorated for their actions and their names are recorded in the war's historiography: Paulina Gelman, the pilot who went on many missions and was awarded the title of Hero of the Soviet Union; the scout and radio operator Masha Sinelnikova, who crossed the front lines many times and transmitted information from the German rear; Tanya Marcus, the underground member from Kiev who pretended to be a Georgian princess and fraternized with German officers, obtained important information from them and even shot some of them; and Masha Bruskina from Minsk, who helped Soviet prisoners of war to escape from German captivity and join the partisans. The last three were captured and executed for their activities. There was also the nurse, Riva Orman, who treated hundreds of wounded soldiers on the front. Hundreds of women were active in the ghetto undergrounds and contributed greatly to its achievements, and many young Jewish women fought in the partisan ranks in the forests.

* * *

Between 490,000 and 520,000 Jews served in the Soviet army. In addition there were at least 20,000 Jewish partisans, so that the total number of Jews fighting under the Soviet banner was about 510,000 to 540,000. The estimated number of Jewish soldiers who fell on the battlefield is based on the general estimate of Soviet losses, without taking into consideration the number of Soviet prisoners of war who died in German captivity. The number of soldiers killed in the Great Patriotic War (dying on the front, from wounds sustained in battle, killed in accidents, etc.) was 6,885,000. About 1.78 percent of them, or more than 122,000, were Jewish, in accordance with the percentage of Jews in the army and the Soviet population. To that number should be added 75,000–80,000 who died in captivity and 7,000 partisans who fell in the forests. Thus the number of Jewish soldiers who died in the Great Patriotic War was between 204,000 and 209,000 – about 40 percent of all the Jewish soldiers who served in the Red Army and with the partisans. It is the highest percentage of all the nations of the Soviet Union and among all the other nations that fought in the Second World War. The numbers of the fallen bear witness to the immense contribution of Soviet Jewry in the battle against Nazi Germany.

BIBLIOGRAPHY

Abramov, Vadim. *Smersh* [Russian]. Moscow: Yauza and Eksmo, 2005.

Abramovich, Aron. *Leningradskaia Bitva*. Tel Aviv, 1990.

___. *V Reshaiushchei Voine*. Tel Aviv, 1981.

Afanasev, Yuri N., ed. *Drugaia Voina 1939–1945*. Moscow: Rossiiskii Gosudarstvennyi Gumanitarnyi Universitet, 1996.

Agmon, Pinkhas, ed. *Later Testimony: Holocaust Survivors from the Ukraine Tell Their Stories* [Hebrew]. Lohamei Hagetaot: Hakibbutz Hameuhad, 1997.

___, and Anatolya Stepanenko. *Vinitskaia Oblast: Katastrofa I Soprotivlenie*. Tel Aviv and Kiev, 1994.

Ailsby, Christopher. *Images of Barbarossa: The German Invasion of Russia, 1941*. Dallas: Potomac, 2002.

Altshuler, Mordechai. *Soviet Jewry on the Eve of the Holocaust*. Jerusalem: Ahava, 1998.

___, et al., ed. *Sovetskie Evrei Pishut Ile Erenburgu 1943–1966*. Jerusalem: Yad Vashem and Hebrew University, 1993.

Arad, Yitzhak. *Belzec, Sobibor, Treblinka: The Operation Reinhard Death Camps*. Bloomington and Indianapolis: Indiana University Press, 1987.

___. *Ghetto in Flames*. Jerusalem: Yad Vashem, and New York: Anti-Defamation League, 1980.

___. *The Holocaust in the Soviet Union*. Lincoln: University of Nebraska Press; Jerusalem: Yad Vashem, 2009.

___. "Jewish Family Camps – An Original Means of Rescue." In *Rescue Attempts During the Holocaust*, edited by Yisrael Gutman and Efraim Zuroff. Jerusalem: Yad Vashem, 1977.

___. *The Partisan*. New York: Holocaust Library, 1979.

___, et al., eds. *Einsatzgruppen Reports*. New York: Holocaust Library, 1989.

Artyomov, Bratskii Boyevoi Soyuz Narodov S.S.S.R. v. Vielikoi Otechestvennoi Voyne. Moscow, 1975.

Baron, Tsvi, and Dov Levin. *History of an Underground* [Hebrew]. Jerusalem: Yad Vashem, 1962.

Berenshtein, Leonid, and Ster Elisavetskii. *Evrei Geroi Soprotivlenia*. Tel Aviv: Krugozor, 1998.

Birman, Zipora. "Bialystok Ghetto." In a document entitled "To My Dear Friends, Wherever They Are, There." Yad Vashem Studies 2: 289–90.

Bor-Komorowski, Tadeusz. *Armia Podziemna*. London: Studium Polski Podziemnej, 1989.

Boradyn, Zygmunt. *Niemen Rzeka Niezgody*. Warsaw: Oficyna Wydawnicza Rytm, 1999.

Bornshtein, Shmuel. *Dr. Atlas's Company* [Hebrew]. Tel Aviv: Hakibbutz Hameuhad, 1965.

Brinsky, Anton. *Partizanskaya Druzhba: Vospominania o Boevykh Delakh Partisan–Evreev*. Moscow, 1948.

Brodskii, Efim. *Oni Ne Propali Bez Vesti*. Moscow: Mysl, 1987.

Broide, Jose. *Memoirs of a Jewish Partisan in the Forest of Bryansk* [Hebrew]. Tel Aviv, 1974.

Bullock, Allan. *Hitler and Stalin: Parallel Lives*. New York: Vintage, 1993.

Bystrov et al., eds. *Voina v tylu Vraga*. Moscow: Izdatelstvo Politicheskoi Literatury–Politizdat, 1974.

____, eds. *Sovetskie Partizany*. Moscow: Izdatelstvo Politicheskoi Literatury–Politizdat, 1961.

Chirlin, A., and P. Biryukov, eds. *Inzhinernye voiska v boyakh za Sovietskuyu Rodinu*. Moscow: Voenizdat, 1970.

Cholawski, Shalom. *In the Eye of the Hurricane* [Hebrew]. Tel Aviv: Hebrew University of Jerusalem and Moreshet, 1988.

____. *The Jews of Belorussia during World War Two* [Hebrew]. Tel Aviv: Moreshet and Sifriat Hapoalim, 1982.

____. *Resistance and Partisan Struggle* [Hebrew]. Jerusalem: Yad Vashem, and Tel Aviv: Moreshet, 2001.

____. "The Underground and Partisan Activity of the Jews from Ghetto Korenetz." *Yalkut Moreshet* 59 (1995): 70.

Chuykov, Vasily. *The War for Stalingrad* [Hebrew]. Tel Aviv: Maarakhot, 1970.

Dallin, Alexander. *German Rule in Russia, 1941–1945: A Study of Occupation Policies*. London: Macmillan, 1957.

Diukov, Alexander. *Vtorostepennyi Vrag, OUN, UPA I Reshenie Evreiskogo Voprosa*. Moscow: Istoricheskaya Pamyat, 2009.

Diupiui, Ernst, and Trevor Diupiui, eds. *Vsemirnaia Istoria Voiny*. Vol. 4. Saint Petersburg-Moscow: Kniga, 1999.

Ehrenburg, Ilya, and Vasily Grossman. *The Black Book*. New York: Holocaust Library, 1980.

Elishkavich, Moshe. "As Our Fathers Commanded Us: Four Years in the Red Army." *Voice of the Disabled* (2003).

Encyklopedia Drugiey Wojny Swiatowej. Warsaw, 1975.

Endlin, Nehemia. *Memoirs of a Jewish Guerilla Fighter* [Hebrew]. Tel Aviv, 1980.

Fatal-Knaani, Tikva. *Grodno Is Not the Same* [Hebrew]. Jerusalem: Yad Vashem, 2001.

Feitelson, Alex. *The Truth and Nothing but the Truth.* Jerusalem: Gefen Publishing House, 2006.

Friedson, Mark. "Leningradskie Partizany." *Voice of the Disabled* (1988).

Gefen et al., eds. *The Jewish Partisans* [Hebrew]. Merhavya: Sifriat Hapoalim, 1958.

Gelman, Boris. *Prichina Smerti-Rasstrel.* Sevastopol, 2004.

Gerlach, Christian. *Kalkulierte Morde.* Hamburg, 1999.

Gogun, Alexander C. "*Partizany protiv Naroda.*" In *Pod Okkupatsiei v 1941–1944,* edited by A. Gogun et al. Moscow, 2004.

Guderian, Heinz. *Panzer Leader.* New York: De Capo, 2001.

Guri-Podryatchik, Joseph. *Soviet Jews in the War against Nazi Germany* [Hebrew]. Masua and Sifriat Poalim, 1971.

Herbert, Ulrich. "*Zwangarbeit in Deutschland.*" In *Erobern und Vernichten,* edited by Peter Jahn and Reinhard Rürup. Berlin: Argon, 1991.

Hitler, Adolf. *Mein Kampf.* Translated by Ralph Manheim. Sentry Edition. Boston: Houghton Mifflin, 1943.

———. *Reden und Proklamationen, 1932–1945.* Edited by Max Domarus. Neustadt a.d. Aisch: Verlagsdruckerei Schmidt, 1962–63.

Ioffe, E.G. *Stranitsy Istorii Evreev Byelarusi.* Minsk, 1996.

Kaczerginski, Shmerke. *The Partisans Are Marching* [Yiddish]. Bamberg: Otto-Verlag, 1948.

Kadikis, A., ed. *My Obviniaem.* Riga, 1967.

Kahanovich, Moshe. *The Fighting of the Jewish Partisans in Eastern Europe* [Hebrew]. Tel Aviv: Ayanot, 1954.

Kalcheim, Moshe, ed. *With Proud Bearing: Chapters in the History of Partisan Fighting in the Naroch Forests* [Hebrew]. Tel Aviv: Irgun Hapartisanim, 1991.

Kanc, Shimon, ed. *Svintzian Region Yizkor Book* [Hebrew]. Tel Aviv, 1956.

Kaufmann, Max. *Die Vernichtung Der Juden Lettlands.* Munich, 1947.

Kershaw, Ian. *Hitler, 1936–1945: Nemesis.* New York: W.W. Norton, 2001.

Kirian, M.M. et al, eds. *Velikaya Otechestvennaya Voina 1941–1945, Slovar-Spravochnik.* Moscow: Politizdat, 1988.

Klimenko, I., ed. *Voina Narodnaya*. Smolensk: Moskovskii Rabochyi, 1985.

Korczak, Ruzka. *Flames in Ashes* [Hebrew]. Merhavya: Moreshet, 1956.

Korngrun, P., ed. *Encyclopedia of the Jewish Diaspora: Memorial Book for the Countries of the Diaspora and Their Communities* [Hebrew]. Ternopol. Jerusalem: Society for Encyclopedias of the Diaspora, 1955.

Kostyrchenko, Gennadi. *Out of the Red Shadows: Anti-Semitism in Stalin's Russia*. New York: Prometheus, 1995.

___. *Tainaya Politika Stalina*. Moscow: Mezhdunarodnye Otnosheniya, 2001.

___, ed. *Rossia XX Vek, Gosudarstvennyi Antisemitism v SSSR: Ot nachala do kul'minatsii, 1938–1953*. Moscow: Materik, 2005.

Kozlov, M.M., ed. *Velikaia Otechestvennaia Voina 1941–1945 Godov, Encyklopedia*. Moscow, 1985.

Krivosheyev, G.F., et al. *Grif Secretnosti Sniat*. Moscow: Voennoye Izdatelstvo, 1993.

Kumanev, G.A. *Voina I Zheleznodorozhnyi Transport SSSR 1941–1945*. Moscow, 1988.

Landman, Dan. "Fighting in the Crimean Peninsula." *Voice of the Disabled* (2003).

Lerner, Mikhail. "Jewish Submarine Officers in the Soviet Union Fleet during the War against the Nazis." *Voice of the Disabled* (November 2005).

Leshch, Yosef. "In the Trenches and Strong Points." *Voice of the Disabled* (November 2003).

Leshchinsky, Yaakov. *Soviet Russia: From the October Revolution to the Second World War* [Hebrew]. Tel Aviv: Am Oved, 1943.

Levin, Baruch. *In the Forests of Vengeance* [Hebrew]. Tel Aviv: Hakibbutz Hameuhad, 1968.

Levin, Dov. "Facts and Estimates of the Jews in the Red Army during the Second World War" [Hebrew]. In *Masua* 19.

___. *They Fought Back: Lithuanian Jewry's Armed Resistance to Nazis, 1941–1945* [Hebrew]. Jerusalem: Institute of Contemporary Jewry, Hebrew University, 1974.

___. *With Their Backs to the Wall: The Armed Struggle of Latvian Jews against the Nazis, 1941–1945* [Hebrew]. Jerusalem: Institute of Contemporary Jewry, Hebrew University, 1978.

Lichtenstein, P., and Y. Rabinowicz, eds. *The Slonim Notebook* [Hebrew]. Tel Aviv, 1962.

Lidovski, Eliezer. "*Viderstand Organizatzieh*." In *The Book of Baranovichi* [Hebrew], edited by Stein. Tel Aviv, 1953.

Lobanok, V.E., ed. *Partiinoe Podpole v Belarusii*. Minsk, 1984.

Manaenkov, A.L. *Partizanskie Formirovania Belorusii v Gody Velikoi Otechestvennoi Voiny*. Minsk, 1983.

Meirowicz, Aharon, ed. *The Book of Kurenets* [Hebrew]. Tel Aviv, 1956.

Merridale, Catherine. *Ivan's War: Life and Death in the Red Army*. New York: Metropolitan Books, 2006.

Mininberg, Leonid. *Sovetskie Evrei v Nauke I Promishlennosti SSSR v Period Vtoroi Mirovoi: Voiny, 1941–1945*. Moscow: Its-Garant, 1995.

Müller, Norbert. *Deutsche Besatzungspolitik in der UdSSR*. Köln: Pahl-Rugenstein, 1980.

____. *Die fasistische Okkupationspolitik in den zeitweilig besetzten Gebieten der Sowjetunion, 1941–1944*. Berlin: Deutscher Verlag der Wissenschaften, 1991.

____. *Wehrmacht und Okkupation, 1941–1944*. Berlin: Deutscher Militarverlag, 1971.

Oliesky, Y., et al. *Haim Yellin: Ghetto Fighter and Writer* [Hebrew]. Tel Aviv: Igud Yotzei Lita, 1980.

Ortenberg, David. *Takaia Vypala Mne Sudba*. Jerusalem: Nevo Art, 1997.

Overy, Richard. *Russia's War: A History of the Soviet Effort, 1941–1945*. New York: Penguin, 1998.

Parchuk, Abram. "From Stalingrad to Koenigsberg." In *Facing the Nazi Enemy: The Fighters Speak, 1939–1945* [Hebrew]. Vol. 1. Edited by Shmuel Burshtein et al. Tel Aviv, 1961.

Pinkus, Benjamin. *The Jews of Russia and the Soviet Union* [Hebrew]. Sdei Boker: Ben-Gurion University of the Negev, 1986.

Pismenny, A. *Partizanskaia Druzhba*. Moscow, 1948.

Platonov, R.P., et al., eds. *V Nepokorennom Minske*. Minsk: Belarus, 1987.

Ponomarenko, P. *Vsenarodnaya Borba v Tylu Nemetsko-Fashistskikh Zakhvatchikov, 1941–1944*. Moscow: Nauka, 1986.

Popov, Alexei. *Diversanty Stalina*. Moscow: Yauza Eksmo, 2004.

____. *NKVD I Partizanskoie Dvizhenie*. Moscow: Olma, 2003.

Pospelov, P.N., et al. *Istoria Velikoi Otechestvennoi Voiny Sovetskogo Soiuza 1941–1945*.

Proniagin, Pavel. *U Samoi Granitsi*. Minsk, 1976.

Prus, Edward. *Atamania UPA*. Warsaw: Instytut Wydawniczny Zwiazkow Zawodowych, 1988.

Rado, Shandor. *Pod Psevdonimom Dora*. Moscow: Voenizdat, 1978.

Rapoport, Louis. *Stalin's War against the Jews: The Doctor's Plot and the Soviet Solution*. New York: Simon and Schuster, 1990.

Read, Anthony, and David Fisher. *The Deadly Embrace: Hitler, Stalin and the Nazi-Soviet Pact, 1939–1941*. New York and London: W.W. Norton, 1988.

Redlich, Shimon. *War, Holocaust and Stalinism: A Documented History of the Jewish Anti-Fascist Committee in the USSR*. Luxemburg: Routledge, 1995.

Register of Jewish Survivors. Vol. 2, *List of Jews in Poland*. Jerusalem: Jewish Agency, 1945.

Reznik, Nissan. *Budding from the Ashes: The Story of Hanoar Hatzioni Youth in the Vilnius Ghetto* [Hebrew]. Jerusalem: Yad Vashem, 2003.

Rindziunski, Alexander. *The Destruction of Vilnius* [Hebrew]. Lohamei Hagetaot and Hakibbutz Hameuhad, 1987.

Rockman, Alan. *Jewish Participation in the International Brigade in the Spanish Civil War, 1936–1939*. Michigan, 1984.

Rosenberg, Yevgenii, and Irina Elenskaya. *Pinskie Evrei*. Brest, 1997.

Rosenblat, Gad. *Fire Engulfed the Forest* [Hebrew]. Lohamei Hagetaot: Hakibbutz Hameuhad, 1957.

Rozauskas, E., ed. *Documents Accuse*. Vilnius: Gintaras, 1970.

Rzheshevski, O.A., et al. *Velikaia Otechestvenna Voina, Sobytia, Liudi, Dokumenty*. Moscow: Politizdat, 1990.

Sadovskaya, Sofia. "Sparks in the Night." In *Minsk, Jewish Metropolis: A Memorial Anthology* [Hebrew]. Vol. 2. Edited by Shlomo Even-Shoshan. Jerusalem, 1985.

Schleunes, Karl. "The Making of War and the Final Solution." In *The Shoah and the War*, edited by Asher Cohen et al. New York: Peter Lang, 1992.

Schoenberner, Mira, and Gerhard Schoenberner. *Zeugen zagen aus: Berichte und Dokumente uber Judenverfolgung in Dritten Reich*. Berlin, 1988.

Schulte, Theo J. *The German Army and Nazi Policies in Occupied Russia*. New York: Berg, 1989.

Sergiichuk, Vladimir. "*Tankovii korol* [King of the tanks]." *Raduga* [Rainbow] 5 (1991).

Shapiro, Gershon. *Under Fire: The Stories of Jewish Heroes of the Soviet Union*. Jerusalem: Yad Vashem, 1988.

___, and C. Averbukh, eds. *Ocherki Evreiskovo Geroizma*. Tel Aviv and Kiev, 1994.

Sheinker, Leonid. *Geroism Evreev na Voine*. Tel Aviv: Krugozor, 2003.

Shner, Aron. *Plen* [Russian]. Jerusalem, 2003.

Shner-Nishmit, Sara. *The 51st Company: The Story of the Jewish Partisan Group from the Slonim Ghetto* [Hebrew]. Tel Aviv: Lohamei Hagetaot and Misrad Habitahon, 1990.

Shpitkovsky, Abram. "In the Red Army." In *Facing the Nazi Enemy: The Fighters Speak, 1939–1945* [Hebrew]. Vol. 1. Edited by Shmuel Burshtein et al. Tel Aviv, 1961.

Shpitsburg, Moshe. "*Trizhdy Slava Synu Gruzinskogo Evreistva*." *Golos Invalidov Voiny* 170 (2002).

Shtaras, P. "*Rol KP Litvy v Organizatsii i Razvitsii Partizanskoi Borby*." In *Gitlerovskaia Okkupatsia v Litve*, edited by O. Kaplanas. Vilnius: Mintis, 1966.

Shutan, Moshe. *Ghetto and Woods* [Yiddish]. Tel Aviv: Vaad Lehantzahat Halehima Hayehudit, 1971.

Siemaszko, Zdzislaw A. *Wilenska AK a Niemcy: Zeszyty Historyczne*. Paris, 1994.

Smilovitsky, Leonid. "Anti-Semitism among the Partisans in Byelorussia." *Yalkut Moreshet* [Hebrew] 59 (1955): 53–61.

Smolar, Hersh. *Soviet Jews behind the Ghetto Barrier* [Hebrew]. Tel Aviv: Tel Aviv University, 1984.

Smuschkowitz et al. *From Victims to Victors*. Toronto: Canadian Society for Yad Vashem, 1992.

Sovetskaya Ukraina v Gody Otechestvennoii Voiny. Kiev: Naukova Dumka, 1985.

Sovetskii Encyklopedicheskii Slovar. Moscow, 1986.

Sovetskii Tyl v Pervyi Period Velikoi Otechestvennoi Voiny, Sbornik Dokumentov. Moscow, 1988.

Spector, Shmuel, ed. *Encyclopedia of Jewish Communities: Poland* [Hebrew]. Vol. 5, *Volhynia and Polesie*. Jerusalem: Yad Vashem, 1990.

____. *Evrei v Partizanskom Dvizheni I Podpole v Ukraine: Ten Holokosta*. Moscow, 1998.

____. *The Holocaust of Volhynian Jews, 1941–1944*. Translated by Jerzy Michalowicz. Jerusalem: Yad Vashem, 1990.

Stalin, Joseph. *O Velikoi Otechestvennoi Voine Sovetskovo Soyuza*. Moscow, 1950.

The State Archive of the Russian Federation (GARF). Moscow.

Stepashin, S.V., ed. *Organy Gosudarstvennoi Bezopasnosti SSSR v Velikoi Otechestvennoi Voine*. Moscow: Kniga, 1995.

Stockfisch, David, ed. *The Book of Nesvizh* [Hebrew]. Tel Aviv, 1976.

Streit, Christian. *Keine Kameraden: Die Wehrmacht und die sovietischen Kriegsgefangenen 1941–1945*. Stuttgart, 1978.

Sutzkever, Abraham. *Vilnius Ghetto* [Hebrew]. Tel Aviv: Shakui, 1947.

Sverdlov, F.D. *Encyclopedia Evreiskogo Geroizma*. Moscow: Dograf, 2002.

___. *Evrei Generaly*. Moscow, 1993.

___. *Soldatskaia Doblest, Ocherki o Voinakh-Evreiakh-Polnykh Kavalerakh Ordena Slavy*. Moscow: Kniga, 1992.

___. *V Stroiu Otvazhnykh, Ocherki o Evreyakh-Geroyakh Sovetskogo Soiuza*. Moscow: Kniga, 1992.

___, and A. Ya. Vainer. *Voiny Evrei na Frontakh Velikoi Otechestvennoi*. Moscow: Izdatelstvo Fonda Holocaust, 1999.

Tamir, Nahman, ed. *The Book of Pinsk* [Hebrew]. Tel Aviv, 1966.

Tec, Nechama. *Defiance: The Bielski Partisans*. New York and Oxford: Oxford University Press, 1993.

Tenenbaum-Tamaroff, Mordechai. *Pages from the Fire* [Hebrew]. Tel Aviv: Hakibbutz Hameuhad, 1947.

Timor, Arkady. *Comrades in Arms: Jews Fighting in the Soviet Army, 1941–1945* [Hebrew]. Tel Aviv: Maarakhot, 1971.

___. "Jews in the Red Army." In *Jewish Soldiers in the Armies of Europe* [Hebrew], edited by Yehuda Slutzky and Mordechai Kaplan. Tel Aviv: Maarakhot, 1977.

___, ed. *Journal of the Soldiers and Partisans Disabled in the War against the Nazis* 16 [Hebrew] (2002): 94.

___, ed. *Journal of the Soldiers and Partisans Disabled in the War against the Nazis* 20 [Hebrew] (2006).

___, ed. *Journal of the Soldiers and Partisans Disabled in the War against the Nazis* 16 [Hebrew] (2002).

___, ed. *Journal of the Soldiers and Partisans Disabled in the War against the Nazis* 13–14 [Hebrew] (1998).

Tomarkin, Slava. "Grishin Led Us." *Voice of the Disabled* (April 2003).

___. "The Nikolai Partisan Brigade." *Voice of the Disabled* (September 2002).

Torzecki, Ryszard. *Polacy I Ukraincy*. Warsaw: Wydawnictwo Naukowe PWN, 1993.

Toynbee, Arnold J, ed. *Documents on International Affairs 1939–1946*. Vol. 1, *March–September 1939*. London: Oxford University Press, 1951.

Trepper, Leopold. *My Red Orchestra* [Hebrew]. Jerusalem: Idanim, 1975.

Tucker, Robert C. *Stalin in Power: The Revolution from Above, 1928–1941*. New York: W.W. Norton, 1992.

Turonek, Jerzy. *Bialorus pod Okupacja Niemiecka*. Warsaw: Ksiazka I Wiedza, 1993.

Ushpolis, Grigori. *Trevozhnoe Vremia*. Tel Aviv, 1997.

Vaksberg, Arkady. *Stalin Against the Jews*. New York: Knopf, 1994.

Volkogonov, Dimitrii. *Stalin: Politicheskii Portret*. Moscow: Novosti, 1992.

Voyenny' Historicheski Zhurnal 1, no. 6 (1940): 69.

Warlimont, Walter. *Inside Hitler's Headquarters, 1939–45*. Translated by R.H. Barry. London: Weidenfeld and Nicolson, 1964.

Weiner, Leonid. "Zapiska." *Voice of the Disabled* 16 (2002).

Weiss, Aharon, et al. *Encyclopedia of Jewish Communities: Poland* [Hebrew]. Vol. 2, *East Galicia*. Jerusalem: Yad Vashem, 1980.

Weissbard, Abraham. *A Township Is Dying: The Story of Skalat* [Hebrew]. Munich: The Historical Society, 1948.

Werth, Alexander. *Russia at War: 1941–1945* [Hebrew]. Tel Aviv: Maarakhot, 1968.

Wilhelm, Hans-Heinrich. *Rassenpolitik und Kriegfuhrung*. Passau, 1991.

Yad Vashem Archives. Yad Vashem, Jerusalem.

Yones, Eliyahu. *Smoke in the Sand: The Jews of Lvov in the War, 1939–1944* [Hebrew]. Jerusalem: Yad Vashem, 2001.

Zaderecki, Tadeusz. *When the Swastika Ruled Lvov* [Hebrew]. Jerusalem: Yad Vashem, 1982.

Zhits, Dan. "The History of the Minsk Ghetto in Light of the New Documentation" [Hebrew]. Master's thesis, Bar Ilan University, 1999.

Zhukov, Georgii Konstantinovich. *The Memoirs of Marshal Zhukov*. New York: Delacorte, 1971.

Zuckerman, Yitzhak, and Moshe Bassok, eds. *The Book of the Ghetto Wars* [Hebrew]. Lohamei Hagetaot, 1954.

Index

M